Simon Gray

PLAYS ONE

Simon Gray was born in 1936. He began his writing career with *Colmain* (1963), the first of five novels, all published by Faber. He was the author of many plays for TV and radio, also films, including the 1987 adaptation of J. L. Carr's *A Month in the Country*, and TV films including *Running Late*, *After Pilkington* (winner of the Prix Italia) and the Emmy Award-winning *Unnatural Pursuits*. He wrote more than thirty stage plays, among them *Butley* and *Otherwise Engaged* (which both received *Evening Standard* Awards for Best Play), *Close of Play*, *The Rear Column*, *Quartermaine's Terms*, *The Common Pursuit*, *Hidden Laughter*, *The Late Middle Classes* (winner of the Barclay's Best Play Award), *Japes*, *The Old Masters* (his ninth play to be directed by Harold Pinter) and *Little Nell*, which premiered at the Theatre Royal Bath in 2007, directed by Peter Hall. *Little Nell* was first broadcast on BBC Radio 4 in 2006, and *Missing Dates* in 2008. In 1991 he was made BAFTA Writer of the Year. His acclaimed works of non-fiction are *An Unnatural Pursuit*, *How's That for Telling 'Em, Fat Lady?*, *Fat Chance*, *Enter a Fox*, *The Smoking Diaries*, *The Year of the Jouncer*, *The Last Cigarette* and *Coda*. With Hugh Whitemore he adapted his *Smoking Diaries* for the stage: *The Last Cigarette* was directed by Richard Eyre in 2009. Simon Gray was appointed CBE in the 2005 New Year's Honours for his services to Drama and Literature. He died in August 2008.

For more information please visit
www.simongray.org.uk

also by Simon Gray

collected editions
PLAYS TWO
(*Otherwise Engaged, Dog Days, Molly, Pig in a Poke, Man in a Sidecar,
Plaintiffs and Defendants, Two Sundays, Simply Disconnected*)

PLAYS THREE
(*Quartermaine's Terms, The Rear Column, Close of Play,
Stage Struck, Tartuffe, A Month in the Country, The Idiot*)

PLAYS FOUR
(*Hidden Laughter, The Common Pursuit, The Holy Terror,
They Never Slept, After Pilkington, Old Flames*)

PLAYS FIVE
(*Cell Mates, Life Support, Just the Three of Us, Japes,
Little Nell, The Old Masters, The Late Middle Classes*)

stage plays
MELON, MICHAEL, SEPARATELY AND TOGETHER, JAPES TOO, THE PIG TRADE,
HULLABALOO, THE LAST CIGARETTE (with Hugh Whitemore)

television plays
DEATH OF A TEDDY BEAR, THE PRINCESS, A WAY WITH THE LADIES,
SPOILED, THE DIRT ON LUCY LANE, THE STYLE OF THE COUNTESS

radio plays
THE HOLY TERROR, THE RECTOR'S DAUGHTER, WITH A NOD AND A BOW,
SUFFER THE LITTLE CHILDREN, LITTLE NELL, MISSING DATES

television films
THE REAR COLUMN, QUARTERMAINE'S TERMS, THE COMMON PURSUIT,
RUNNING LATE, FEMME FATALE, UNNATURAL PURSUITS

non-fiction
THE EARLY DIARIES
(*An Unnatural Pursuit, How's That for Telling 'Em, Fat Lady?*)
FAT CHANCE, ENTER A FOX, THE SMOKING DIARIES,
THE YEAR OF THE JOUNCER, THE LAST CIGARETTE, CODA

fiction
SIMPLE PEOPLE, COLMAIN, A COMEBACK FOR STARK,
LITTLE PORTIA, BREAKING HEARTS

films
BUTLEY, A MONTH IN THE COUNTRY

audio books
THE SMOKING DIARIES, THE YEAR OF THE JOUNCER,
THE LAST CIGARETTE, CODA

SIMON GRAY

Plays One

Butley

Wise Child

Dutch Uncle

Spoiled

The Caramel Crisis

Sleeping Dog

faber and faber

This collection first published in 2010
by Faber and Faber Limited
74–77 Great Russell Street, London WC1B 3DA

Typeset by Country Setting, Kingsdown, Kent CT14 8ES
Printed in England by CPI Bookmarque, Croydon, Surrey

Butley was first published in 1971 by Methuen and Co. Ltd,
and included in Simon Gray, *Key Plays*, published by
Faber and Faber Ltd, 2002

Wise Child first published by Faber and Faber Ltd, 1968

Dutch Uncle first published by Faber and Faber Ltd, 1969

Spoiled first published by Faber and Faber Ltd, 1971

The Caramel Crisis first published by Faber and Faber Ltd
in *The Definitive Simon Gray 1*, 1992

Sleeping Dog first published by Faber and Faber Ltd, 1968

All the plays in this volume were also included in
The Definitive Simon Gray 1, published by Faber and Faber Ltd, 1992

A CIP record for this book is available from the British Library

978-0-571-25472-9

2 4 6 8 10 9 7 5 3 1

Contents

Directing Simon Gray's Plays

HAROLD PINTER

Simon Gray asked me to direct *Butley* in 1970. I found its savage, lacerating wit hard to beat and accepted the invitation. I then went on to direct another seven of his plays, finishing with *The Late Middle Classes* in 2000. Apart from the fact that, during the course of these thirty years, Simon and I formed an indissoluble friendship, my involvement in his plays represents a uniquely rich and vivid part of my professional life. It's something I remain truly thankful for.

The extraordinary thing about *Butley*, it still seems to me, is that the play gives us a character who hurls himself towards destruction while living, in the fever of his intellectual hell, with a vitality and brilliance known to few of us. He courts death by remaining ruthlessly – even dementedly – alive. It's a remarkable creation and Alan Bates as Butley gave the performance of a lifetime.

In *Otherwise Engaged* Alan Bates inhabited the other side of the coin. Simon Hench sees his obligation as one of self-protection. He will not allow himself to be known. His defensive mechanisms are almost perfect (almost but not quite). His lethal wit is of another kind to Butley's. He trips people up and lays them bare with a consummate delicacy, out of apparent compassion for them, as it were. The play is quite beautifully shaped. Alan Bates was again brilliant and Nigel Hawthorne uproarious as his brother Stephen.

Close of Play is, I suppose, the darkest of Simon's plays. It was never appreciated by the critical fraternity, which failed to understand it for what it was – a radical exploration of poetic drama. Its range of operation, its sleight of hand, its command of varying modes of language, its use of monologue and chorus – all this moved far away from its ostensible naturalism. The character of Daisy was a wonderful one. Peggy Ashcroft rehearsed the part for about a week, but then, in great pain, had to leave the company for a cartilage operation. We were left with a splendid cast and a highly professional understudy, but Peggy Ashcroft was much missed.

St John Quartermaine in *Quartermaine's Terms* is a masterly portrayal of an innocent. It is tender and unerring, never sentimental. Edward Fox's performance was memorable, a figure moving among elusive shadows, lost in alien territory – in fact the action around him might as well be taking place on Mars. But this shadow world finally proves to be only too concrete and Quartermaine finds himself up against the real, the harsh, the indifferent dark. Directing the play was both joyful and heartbreaking.

The Late Middle Classes I found a rich and beautifully wrought piece of work. Directing it was extremely satisfying but the production ran into deeply unsettling waters. The enterprise began with a miracle of casting. The central role (a thirteen-year-old boy) we found very difficult to cast. Suddenly we stumbled upon a fifteen-year-old girl (Sarah Bedi) who passed as a good-looking thirteen-year-old boy. She was wonderful; precise, contained, mysterious. Her sister (Anne Bedi) became her understudy and was almost as good. So we had two girls masquerading (very successfully) as boys. In the programme we called Sarah Sam and Anne Alex.

We opened the production at Watford, where it broke all box-office records, but theatrical politics blocked the play's presentation in London. The play, graceful, tough and poignant, deserved to be seen by many more people.

Life in the theatre hasn't brought me anything more rewarding than directing Simon Gray's plays.

First published as an Introduction to *Key Plays* (2002), after which Harold Pinter directed his ninth Gray play, *The Old Masters* (2004). All are included in *Simon Gray Plays 1–5*.

BUTLEY

For Roger Gard
1936–2000

Butley was first presented by Michael Codron on 14 July 1971 at the Criterion Theatre, London. The cast was as follows:

Ben Butley Alan Bates
Joseph Keyston Richard O'Callaghan
Miss Heasman Brenda Cavendish
Edna Shaft Mary Wimbush
Anne Butley Colette O'Neil
Reg Nuttall Michael Byrne
Mr Gardner George Fenton

Director Harold Pinter
Designer Eileen Diss

Characters

Ben Butley

Joseph (Joey) Keyston

Miss Heasman

Edna Shaft

Anne Butley

Reg Nuttall

Mr Gardner

Act One

An office in a college of London University. About ten in the morning. The office is badly decorated (white walls, greying, plasterboard) with strip lighting. There are two desks opposite each other, each with a swivel chair. Ben's desk, left, is a chaos of papers, books, detritus. Joey's desk, right, is almost bare. Behind each desk is a bookcase. Again, Ben's is chaotic with old essays and mimeographed sheets scattered among the books, while Joey's is neat, not many books on the shelves. On each desk there is a table lamp and in front of each desk a hard chair. There is one telephone, on Ben's desk, the flex of which is long enough to reach Joey's desk. There are a few hard-backed chairs around the walls, and one armchair, in Ben's corner of the room. On the wall is a blown-up picture (photograph) of T. S. Eliot, with a smear across it and one of its corners curled. The panels to the office door are frosted glass, behind which people, when they approach, are dimly seen.

Ben is a heavy smoker, and should smoke more frequently than the text indicates. Joey does not smoke.

As the curtain rises, Ben enters, in a plastic raincoat, which he takes off and throws into his chair. He has a lump of cotton wool on his chin, from a particularly nasty shaving cut. He goes to his chair, sits down, looks around as if searching for something, shifts uncomfortably, pulls the plastic mac out from under him, searches through its pockets, takes out half a banana, a bit squashed, then throws the raincoat over to Joey's desk. He takes a bite from the banana, removes it from the peel and drops the last piece onto his desk. Then he throws the peel onto Joey's desk. He slumps into his chair – a long pause – the telephone rings.

Ben Butley, English. Hello, James, have a nice break? (*A pause – he mouths a curse.*) Sorry, James, I can't talk now – I'm right in the middle of a tutorial – bye. (*Then he touches the cotton wool and tries to pull it off. He lets out an exclamation. Touches his chin, looks at his finger. In an undertone:*) Bugger! (*He gets up, looks under his desk, drags out a bulging briefcase from which he pulls an opened bag of cotton wool. He delves into his briefcase again and takes out a tin of Nescafé. He shines the base on his sleeve, then holds it to his chin as if it were a mirror. He tries to put the cotton wool on, then switches on the light. It doesn't come on. He sticks the cotton wool on. He shoves the Nescafé tin back into his briefcase and stuffs the cotton wool into his jacket pocket. He goes across to the main switch and flicks it on. The strip lighting flickers into brilliance. He checks the cotton wool using the glass door of his bookcase as a mirror, then, unable to bear the strip light, flicks it off again. He goes across to Joey's desk and tries the lamp. It comes on. He wipes stray wisps of cotton wool from his fingers with the banana skin, then drops it into the clean ashtray on Joey's desk. He switches off Joey's lamp and carries it across to his desk. There is a shape at the door, then a knock.*) Bugger! Just a minute! (*He carries his lamp across to Joey's. The door opens cautiously.*) A minute, I said. (*He goes to the door and checks it with his hand.*) Hello.

Student (*off*) Hello.

Ben (*after a pause*) Can I help you?

Student (*off*) Well, it's my tutorial. On Wordsworth. 'The Prelude'.

Ben Oh. No, I can't give tutorials during the first week after the break, I'm afraid. Too much administration.

Student (*off*) Oh? When should I come, then?

Ben Come at the same hour of the same day of next week.

Student (*off*) Next week?

Ben Next week. If we keep to our timetable we'll know where we are, won't we? All right?

> *He closes the door. He goes back to his desk, sits down and takes out of his pocket a copy of* Cecily Parsley's Nursery Rhymes.

'The Prelude'.

> *He shudders, then turns a page, reaches for the light, clicks it. Nothing happens. He gets up and goes over to Joey's desk, tries the light, it comes on. He sighs. He sits down in Joey's chair, opens one of his drawers, props his feet in it, and settles down to read. Joey comes in with a briefcase. He puts it down on his desk, clears the banana peel into the waste-paper basket, picks Ben's raincoat up, carries it over to the peg, puts the desk lamps back on their respective desks. He turns on his table light – it comes on.*

Good morning.

Joey Good morning.

Ben Nice to see you.

Joey Nice to be seen. What's the matter with your chin?

Ben I'm trying to cultivate cotton wool on it. Your own is shining pleasantly, what did you have to work with, a razor?

Joey What did *you* use?

Ben Anne left one behind. Behind the fridge, to be exact. So either mice have taken up shaving, or that stubble was sheared from her calves. I thought of mounting a tuft in a locket. You needn't have taken the only one we have.

Joey It also happens to be the only one I have.

Ben Couldn't you have shared Ted's? It's no pleasure slicing open my chin with my estranged wife's razor blade. The symbolism may be deft, but the memory still smarts.

Joey I didn't mean to take it, in point of fact. I put it in the bag without thinking.

Ben Lust is no excuse for thoughtlessness. And where is your bag? (*He stands up and peers round for it.*)

Joey What? Oh, I left it with Reg.

Ben Reg? Who's Reg?

He perches on the front of his own desk with his feet up on a chair and lights a cigarette. Joey hastily occupies the vacated desk chair.

Joey Reg is his name.

Ben Whose name?

Joey Ted's.

Ben Reg is Ted's name?

Joey The one you call Ted is the one I call Reg. He calls himself Reg too.

Ben How sweet.

Joey In fact, everybody calls him Reg except you. You call him Ted.

Ben Why do I do that, I wonder?

Joey To embarrass me.

Ben Oh yes, that must be it. (*Pause.*) Did you have a good weekend?

Joey It was all right. (*Pause.*) Have you seen James this morning?

Ben Ah! Our professor! He's just been hounding me on the telephone. He and Hazel spent most of the break in bed recovering from one of Hazel's gastric goulashes.

Joey Did he say anything? I mean, are there any details yet?

Ben You want details of James's diarrhoea?

Joey You know what I mean. About my board.

Ben Ah. About your board. Now when is that, exactly?

Joey A fortnight tomorrow.

Ben Indeed? A fortnight tomorrow? Mmmm. Where the hell is it?

He begins to search in his desk drawers – Joey comes over to him.

Joey What?

Ben It's no real advance. (*Sits.*) But it's got some interesting things in it. Damn! Anyway –

'How do you do, Mistress Pussy?
Mistress Pussy, how do you do?'
'I thank you kindly, little dog,
I fare as well as you!'

Joey Did he say anything?

Ben You're genuinely interested in this promotion of yours, aren't you? Why? (*Little pause.*) No, he didn't say anything. Your name didn't come up, and there's no reason that it should until, in the normal course of events and strictly according to the rules, the board is rigged, the strings are pulled, and it's passed over for that of someone more closely related to the Principal, or with more distinguished qualifications. I should warn you that there are almost as many of the latter as of the former.

> Cecily Parsley lived in a pen,
> And brewed good ale for gentlemen;
> Gentlemen came every day.

Joey goes to his shelves and takes down a book.

> Till Cecily Parsley ran away.

Why? (*Ben crosses to Joey.*) Why has he got your bag?

Joey He happened to pick it up for me when we got off the train.

Ben Not many young men are as gallant these days. You haven't been home yet, then?

Joey To the flat? No. (*He sits at his desk.*)

Ben Ah. Why not?

Joey Because I didn't have time, obviously. (*He begins to correct a set of essays from his briefcase.*)

Ben I waited for you.

Joey Did you? Sorry.

Ben (*watches him*) You had a nice little mid-term break then, did you?

Joey It was all right.

Ben Well, are you going to tell me about it, or shall I probe and pry?

Joey I'd rather let it slip out naturally, if I may?

Ben But you're much more charming under interrogation. My natural force plays excitingly with your natural submissiveness. Or has your holiday changed you, as we say in the trade, radically? (*He opens Joey's briefcase.*) Ah-hah! I thought so! (*As Joey looks up.*) Blake! Why is your briefcase bulging with Blake! (*He opens one of the books and takes out a piece of paper.*) What's this?

Joey I happen to be lecturing on him this half. (*He tries to take the book and notes from him.*) Kindly don't mess my notes up. Can I have it back, please?

Ben Notes to whom? Reg?

What immortal hand or eye
Could frame thy fearful symmetry?

Ted is certainly quite symmetrical – in a burly sort of way.

Did he who made the lamb make thee? (*Laughs.*)

Joey All right, all right, let's *be* infantile. (*He goes across to Ben's desk and picks up his briefcase.*)

Ben (*drops Joey's book and notes, lunges across and grabs his own briefcase*) No, bags first go. I haven't unpacked it for weeks.

He opens it, as Joey returns to his marking. He pulls out an empty Scotch bottle, then a red-covered manuscript.

It's laid out like a film script. It must be an American MA thesis – Ah – 'Henry James and the Crucified Consciousness' – aaah. (*Ben wanders over to Joey's desk,*

13

*pulls out a blue sock, puts the thesis down on Joey's
desk, along with a few more papers, files, crumpled
newspaper, the Nescafé tin and the briefcase itself.)* Now
where's the other? – There must be a pair –

Joey *(picks up the thesis)* You mean you forgot to give
his thesis back?

Ben Not yet. So far I've forgotten to read it. Forgetting
to give it back will come later. Failing Americans is a
slow and intricate ritual and that's what they come here
for – the ritual – Aaah, here it is. *(He takes out another
sock. It is red. He picks up the blue. Looks at them.)*

Joey Those are mine. Naturally.

Ben Naturally you're very welcome. *(He tosses the socks
at Joey.)* Personally I wouldn't be caught dead wearing a
pair like that. *(He lifts up his trousers, studies his socks.)*

Joey Those happen to be mine, too.

Ben You really must give up buying cheap socks. I can
feel a hole growing around the toe.

Joey *(savagely)* Perhaps if you bothered to cut your
toenails – *(He picks up the thesis and essays Ben has
dropped.)*

Ben Are we going to have a tantrum?

Joey The thing is to stop your rubbish creeping across
to my side of the room. *(He makes as if to stack them
neatly, then crams them savagely into Ben's shelves.)*
Here, anyway. *(He goes back to his desk and continues
marking.)*

Ben *Are* we? I'd quite enjoy one.

Joey Would you?

Ben Then I'll know you're back, you see. You've been a little thin on presence so far.

Joey There's not enough room.

Ben sits down cross-legged on the top of Joey's desk and watches Joey. He clears his throat delicately. He smiles genteelly.

Ben (*genteel*) I was just wondering if I might inquire as to how your friend is, may I?

Joey smiles.

Hoh, h'I'm so glad.

Joey continues transcribing marks.

May h'I hask, done all those, 'ave we?

He takes the essay Joey is holding.

Ho, but you 'adn't done them last week, 'ad you? Did you do them on the train, going h'up with your friend?

Shape at the door, Ben doesn't notice.

H'I h'always say that h'if h'a job's worth doing h'it's worth h'ignoring.

Knock on the door. Ben turns, starts to move rapidly to it. When it opens, Miss Heasman, a pretty, competent-looking girl, steps in.

Miss Heasman Oh, sorry, I was just wondering when my tutorials are.

Ben Same as last term, except of course for this week.

Miss Heasman You didn't take me last term. My name is Heasman, Carol Heasman. I'm replacing Mrs Grainger.

Ben Mrs Grainger?

Miss Heasman Yes. She said she didn't get to see you often, owing to administrative tangles.

Ben Mrs Grainger got into administrative tangles?

Miss Heasman No, you were busy with them.

Ben If only they'd let us get on with it and teach. (*Laughs.*) Anyway, you'd better come at the same hours as Mrs Grainger, all right?

Miss Heasman I expect so. What were they?

Ben Could you find out from Mrs Grainger, please?

Miss Heasman I'll try.

Ben Thank you.

> *He holds the door wider. Miss Heasman goes out. Ben returns to his desk.*

I didn't care for that one at all, there was an air of mad devotion about her that reminds me of my wife's mother, the mad monk.

> *Looking at Joey, who is still transcribing marks. Joey tries to go on working. In a normal tone, after a pause:*

You're in trouble, Joey.

Joey What? (*He looks up.*)

Ben I'm sorry. I've been wondering how to tell you. But as you've still got a fortnight before the board. (*Sits. Pause.*) A member of the department has his knife out.

Joey Who?

Ben That pre-break meeting we had – the one you had to leave early – to meet Reg?

Joey Yes. Well?

Ben The contemporary books list?

Joey Yes. Well, go on.

Ben On the face of it, you were very adroit. You didn't actually support me, but you indicated a certain, attitude shall we say? By coughing into my speeches with dialectical authority. You wouldn't have thought that so genteel a rhetorical device could give offence. On the face of it. Eh?

Joey But who – who did I offend?

Ben (*gets up and perches on the front of his desk again*) First of all, who proposed that a contemporary novels list – Burroughs, Genet, Roth, etc. – be added to our syllabus?

Joey You did.

Ben And who opposed it?

Joey Everybody else. Except – me.

Ben Who won?

Joey We – you did. They gave way in the end – didn't they?

Ben (*sinisterly*) Oh yes, it was passed unanimously – but I happen to know that one person – one powerful person there – resented *our* victory and blamed you – yes, you – for it.

Joey But this is ridiculous! It's absolutely – I scarcely said anything anyway.

Ben Exactly. But this person was hoping – was *relying* – on you to oppose that book list with every cell in your body.

Joey Ben, please – eh?

Ben Think, child, think! Who had most to lose by that list being passed? Who is *most* affected?

Joey Nobody. Nobody at all. You're the one who's going to teach it, they'll be *your* lectures, *your* seminars, *your* tutorials . . .

Ben (*after a long pause, as Joey, realising, looks at him*) Exactly. Precisely. Absolutely. Fool! Imbecile! Traitor! Lackey! – I wouldn't be caught dead reading those books. And you know how it exhausts me to teach books I haven't read. Why didn't you oppose me?

Joey It's your fault. Your instructions were quite clear.

Ben Haven't you heard of a sub-text? It's very fashionable now. In fact, I remember advising you to use the word twice in every paper when I was guiding you through your finals. (*He goes to examine him.*) But what's the matter, dear? You're looking a little peaky around the gills, wherever they are? Were you frightened, a trifle? You needn't be – you played the toad to perfection. (*He returns to his desk.*)

Joey Is there a sub-text to that? Or can I take it as straight abuse?

Ben It's straight abuse. Can you take it?

Joey (*trembling slightly*) No, not any longer. (*He gets up, and begins to pack his briefcase.*)

Ben Where are you going?

Joey To the library.

Ben Why?

Joey I've got a lecture at twelve.

Ben But you're not running away from me so soon?

Joey And there are a few things on my Herrick I've got to dig up.

He goes to the door – Ben cuts him off.

Ben Dig up! (*Laughs.*)

Diggory, diggory Delvet
Little old man in black velvet
He digs and he delves
You can see for yourselves
The holes dug by Diggory Delvet.

(*Fingering it.*) It is velvet, isn't it, this jacket?

Joey tugs his sleeve away.

No, don't flounce.

They stand staring at each other.

You were due back last night, remember?

Joey Did it make any difference?

Ben In that I spent the evening expecting you.

Joey In point of fact, I said I'd be back either last night or this morning.

Ben Also you didn't phone.

Joey I was only in Leeds for four days. Of course I didn't phone.

Ben Why not? Language difficulties? I reserved a table at Bianchi's. I was going to take us out.

Joey (*after a pause*) I'm sorry.

Ben shrugs. They each return to their desks.

It just didn't occur to me –

Ben It doesn't matter.

Joey I'm sure I said –

Ben Yes, yes, I expect you did. I assumed you were coming back, that's all. And as I spent four days on the phone to people who weren't there – bugger! (*He sits down at his desk.*) I'm sorry. All right? And if that doesn't satisfy you, Edna thinks well of you, and James is more than happy.

Joey How do you know?

Ben These things slip out. Under my persistent questionings.

Joey Edna's actually very important, isn't she? (*He goes across to Ben and sits on the hard chair in front of Ben's desk.*)

Ben It depends rather on the context.

Joey I mean in terms of influence –

Ben You mean in terms of promotion?

Joey Well – (*Grins.*)

Ben She'll certainly sit on your board, yes. Don't worry. You'll get your lectureship. Then you'll be safe for ever.

Joey I like Edna, in point of fact. No, really. We came in on the Tube together this morning. She was telling me about her Byron –

Ben Can we actually – do you mind? – not discuss either Edna or Byron but most of all Edna on Byron, for purely private reasons just at the moment. The thought of them weighs on my spirit. (*Pause.*) Tell me, while you were amusing yourselves in Leeds, I saw a film on television about a publisher who hates himself. I've been meaning to ask you – does Ted hate himself?

Joey He quite likes himself, actually.

Ben I don't blame him. He seemed an amiable sort of chap the one time I met him, even though his mouth was full of symbolic sausage and his fist around a tankard of something foaming symbolically. I had the impression that most people would like him. And as he seemed exactly like most people, only from the North, ergo, he'd be favourably disposed towards himself only more so, or not?

He smiles. Joey also smiles.

Tell me, does he ever discuss his work with you? Or does he leave it behind him at the office? When you go around for one of those little dinners, does he put his feet up, perhaps, while you slave away over a hot stove, or does he do the cooking? No, I don't mean to probe – or am I prying? For instance, in our professor's ménage Hazel rips the meat apart with saw-edged knives while James brews up sauces from *Guardian* headlines. In my ménage, when I had one – remember? – Anne under-grilled the chops and over-boiled the peas while I drank the wine and charted my dropping sugar-count. Now that you and I are sharing my life again I open the tins and you stir the Nescafé again, just as we always used to do, those evenings, at least, when you're not cooking for Reg or Reg isn't cooking for you – which, arriving where we began, does it happen to be? And if it's the former, why, now I think of it, have you never cooked for me, do you think?

Joey He does the cooking, in point of fact.

Ben Christ, I feel awful. (*Pause.*) Do you know, all the time you were away, I didn't have one telephone call. I consider that very frightening. Not even from Tom.

Joey Oh. (*Pause.*) I thought you found his company intolerable.

Ben But one likes, as they say, to be asked. Also one likes people to be consistent, otherwise one will start coming adrift. At least this one will. (*Stands up.*) Also how does one know whether Tom is still the most boring man in London unless he phones in regularly to confirm it? This is the fourth week running he's kept me in suspense. He and Reg have a lot in common, haven't they? (*Pause. He sits on the desk.*)

Joey (*drily*) Really?

Ben Didn't Ted do his National Service with the Gurkhas?

Joey I really can't remember. I've never been very interested in Ted's – Reg's – military career, which was anyway about a decade ago.

He goes back to his own desk. Ben follows him.

Ben Oh, but the experience lives on for us through our born raconteurs – and Ted is something of a raconteur, isn't he? That magnificent anecdote of his – surely you remember?

Joey No. (*He picks up his briefcase and moves towards the door.*) I really must get to the library –

Ben No, wait. (*Blocks his way.*) You repeated it to me. About the Gurkha and the bowl of soup. (*He holds up two fists.*) I don't know if I can do your imitation of his accent – woon day Chef was in ta kitchen – is that close? – stirring ta soup wi' his elbows – wan in coom a little tyke –

Joey I remember.

Ben I was sure you would. Your imitation of Reg made me laugh so much that I was prepared to overlook its cruelty. Anyway, my point was simply that Tom's a great

National Service bore, too. There's that six-volume novel he's writing about it – that's something else. Yes. He's stopped showing me his drafts. (*He goes back to his desk.*)

Joey The last time he brought one around you dropped it in the bath.

Ben It! He brought around seventeen exercise books, of which I dropped a mere three into the bath. No, I don't like his silence. It's sinister.

Joey Well, you could always phone him up. (*He starts for the door again.*)

Ben I haven't finished. (*He comes over, takes Joey's briefcase from him and sits in Joey's desk chair.*)

Joey I must do something on this bloody lecture.

Ben Why? You're looking furtive. Why are you looking furtive?

Joey I'm not looking at all furtive.

Ben Have you seen Tom recently?

Joey No. No, I haven't.

Ben When did you last hear from him?

Joey (*shrugs*) Perhaps he's busy.

Ben Of course he's busy. He's too dull to be anything else. The question is, why has he stopped being busy with me? (*He returns to his own desk and sits on the hard chair.*) Do you think he's dropped me? His attentions have been slackening since my marriage broke up, now I come to think of it.

Joey (*carefully*) He's very fond of Anne, isn't he?

Ben (*laughs*) That's an idea. I must find out whether he's been hounding her.

Joey But Anne – (*Stops.*) She likes him, doesn't she?
I mean, I always thought – had the impression that she
was fond of him?

Ben Oh, I expect she became addicted. She took up all
my vices except drinking, smoking and you. She never
cared for you. Did you know that?

Joey I had my suspicions. Thank you for confirming
them.

Ben She said that Tom became a schoolteacher because
he had to prove, after three years of being taught by me
at Cambridge, that education was still a serious affair.
Whereas you wanted to get back to your old college here
and with me because you were incapable of outgrowing
your early influences. Nursery dependence. This analysis
was based crudely on the fact that you are homosexual.
She also said you were sly and pushing, and that she
didn't trust you an inch.

Joey You never told me this before.

Ben You never asked me before.

Joey I didn't ask you now, either.

Ben I know. But I got tired of waiting. (*Pause.*) Do *you*
like *her*?

Joey I thought we were friends.

Ben I'm sure you still are. (*He sits in the armchair, Joey's
briefcase tucked under his arm.*) She just can't stand you,
that's all. Something about you gives her the creeps,
was her word. Creeps. (*Laughs.*) What's the matter? Are
you upset? (*Joey shakes his head.*) You shouldn't be.
It was just her way of getting at me. Don't you see how
I emerge? As someone whose protégé is a creep? But
I didn't take offence. I don't see why you should.

Pause. Joey tries to take his case – Ben clutches it to him.

Tell me, what does he do, Reg's dad?

Joey looks at him.

(*Smiles.*) But we're not ashamed, are we?

Joey (*pause*) He owns a shop.

Ben What sort of shop?

Joey Just a shop. (*He walks away from him.*)

Ben Just a shop? Just a shop like Harrods, for example. What does he sell?

Joey (*after a pause*) Meat, I think.

Ben You think. Did you ever see the shop?

Joey Of course. Why?

Ben Was there meat on display?

Joey Yes.

Ben In that case he either owns a meat museum or if it was for sale you're quite right, he owns a shop that sells meat. He's what's called a butcher.

Joey (*sits on the hard chair in front of Ben's desk*) That's right, he's a butcher.

Ben Mmm-huh. And do they live over their shop?

Joey (*hesitates*) No. They live in, um, in a place just outside Leeds, in point of fact.

Ben In Point of Fact? And what sort of place is it – a Georgian terraced house, a Chippendale-style flat, a dug-out, a rural cottage; a bungalow?

Joey Yes. A bungalow.

Ben A bungalow, eh? Now let's see, starting with the garden, do they have, say, plaster gnomes in the garden?

Joey And also much to your satisfaction, say, an electric fire with coals in it, and a sofa decorated with doilies and a revolving bookcase with the collected works of Mazo de la Roche –

Ben In the garden? How witty!

Joey And their front doorbell plays a tune, can you believe that?

   Pause.

They happen to be very nice people, nevertheless.

Ben Nevertheless what?

Joey (*emphatically*) Nevertheless they happen to be very nice people.

Ben (*sits on the edge of his desk, leaving Joey's briefcase in the armchair*) What tune? (*Pause.*) Does Reg's mother work in the shop too?

Joey No.

Ben Oh. Where is she then, in the daytime?

Joey Out.

Ben Out where?

Joey Just out.

Ben She has a job, then?

Joey Yes.

Ben And where does she do this job? On the streets?

Joey You could put it like that, yes.

Ben What does she do? Sweep them?

Joey No.

Ben She walks them?

Joey Yes, in point of fact.

Ben The precise suburb is irrelevant. (*Pause.*) So Reg's mother is a prostitute.

Joey giggles, checks himself.

Joey No, she's a – traffic warden.

Ben She isn't! But what on earth did you do?

Joey Nothing in particular.

Ben You went to a football match?

Joey Football match?

Ben Hasn't it caught on there? Here in the South we place it slightly below music and well above theatre, in the cultural scale. Did you?

Joey What?

Ben Go to any football matches?

Joey Well done. Yes, we did. We went to a football match – and furthermore we wore rosettes, coloured scarves and special hats and carried rattles.

Ben You didn't! (*Laughs.*) Rattles and rosettes? You didn't! You poor old sod. Why in Christ did you stay? (*Pause.*) All right then, why did he take you there? Is it like bringing one's latest girl back to the folks –?

Joey His friends back. He doesn't like people to know he's queer. A lot of the time he doesn't like me to know. But I suppose he probably took me there as a kind of compliment – and perhaps as a test.

27

Ben To see if you could take him *au naturel*?

Joey That sounds reasonable, yes.

Ben And could you?

Joey He's much more natural as a London publisher who knows all about food, and cooks marvellously. Much more natural and much more convincing.

Ben But tell me – the butcher and the traffic warden – do they *know* –

Joey Know what?

A shape appears at the door. Ben charges out as Miss Heasman knocks.

Ben Oops! Sorry!

Miss Heasman Sorry!

Ben (*off*) Just dashing up to the Registrar's – some administrative tangle. Mrs Grainger, isn't it?

Miss Heasman (*off*) Miss Heasman! I can't find Mrs Grainger but I'm very anxious for a session on *The Winter's Tale*.

Ben Good God! Are you really? Well, keep trying and perhaps by next week . . . I go up here. Goodbye.

Ben dodges back and surprises Joey as he tries to leave.

– that you and Reg have it off together?

Joey Of course not. (*Shuts the door.*) And now I think I'd like to stop talking about it if you don't mind. I'm beginning to feel queasy.

Ben Recollections of tripe and stout?

Guilt, Lord, I pray
Answer thy servant's question!
Is it guilt I feel
Or is it indigestion?

Don't worry, *rognons au vin* at Bianchi's will calm the unsettled soul. (*He sits on his desk – lights a cigarette.*)

Joey Tonight you mean? For dinner?

Ben I hardly fancy them for tea.

Joey Um, the thing is, I'm, um, going around to Reg's tonight. (*Pause.*) I – I didn't – I'm sorry, it just seemed impossible not to go, under the circumstances.

Ben Mmm-huh. (*Little pause.*) I'm willing to treat Reg if necessary.

Joey Well, you see Reg has already got our dinner.

Ben Oh? And what's he got for your dinner?

Joey (*laughs*) Well, kidneys, as a matter of fact. His father gave him some special – English kidneys. As a treat. Lamb's kidneys.

Ben Mmm-huh.

  Little pause.

Joey Sorry.

Ben There's no problem. I'll get some more and Ted can cook them for me.

  Joey goes back to his desk. Pause.

What's the matter?

Joey I'd rather you didn't.

Ben Mmm-huh. May one ask why?

Joey It might be awkward.

Ben Oh? May one wonder why?

Joey Perhaps he doesn't like you very much.

Ben You surprise me. I thought he'd taken rather a fancy, on our one meeting.

Joey (*sits*) On your one meeting you pretended you thought he was an Australian and addressed him as 'Cobber'. You also pretended you thought he was an interior decorator, in order to remind him of Ted, whom he knew to be his predecessor. You were also sick over his shoes. It was a terrible evening. He hated you.

Ben You never told me this before.

Joey You never asked me before.

Ben *That* was creepy. (*Pause.*) Anyway, you exaggerate. The confusion over his national identity and profession lasted a mere twenty minutes at the beginning of the evening. It took me some twenty seconds to be sick over his shoes at the evening's end. The intervening hour was an unqualified success, in spite of the odd misunderstanding that developed into the occasional quarrel. Also you know very well that I'd taken up drinking again because I was still brooding over Anne's departure. I had what is called a drinking problem. I no longer have it.

Joey Let's face it, Ben, you drink every night. Very heavily.

Ben Exactly. There's no problem. I'm used to it again.

Pause.

Well, Joey?

Joey shrugs awkwardly.

I might also be glad of a chance to make it up. I enjoy being on terms with your chaps. (*Pause.*) Also I don't fancy a fifth night of eating alone. (*Pause.*) Well?

Joey He won't want you to come.

Ben Have you asked him?

Joey No.

Ben Then why don't you? Come on. Let's find out. (*He picks up the telephone, and hands it to him.*) Well?

Joey He's not there.

Ben How do you know, unless you try?

Joey He said he wouldn't be there until after lunch.

Ben stares at him.

He told me he had some things to do.

There is a shape at the door, not noticed by Ben and Joey, followed by a knock, and simultaneously Edna comes in. She is in her late forties and carries a small pile of folders.

Edna Hello, Ben. Joey.

Ben Hello, Edna.

Joey Hello.

Edna Am I barging in on something?

Joey No, not at all, in fact I was just on my way to the library. (*He picks up his briefcase and stands up.*)

Edna Oh, it's no good going there. It's closed while they instal a new security device. It won't be opened until this evening.

Joey Oh.

He sits down again. Ben goes to his desk.

Edna Isn't that a comment on our times? Do you know, I found a couple of students in the canteen. They actually pretended to have heard from some source or another that there were no tutorials during the first week of the half. What do you think of that?

Ben (*sits at his desk*) *Folie de grandeur.* They must learn to leave such decisions to us.

Edna Exactly. I wonder what they'd have to say if we started putting them off for any nonsensical reason that came into our heads.

Ben Yes, I often wonder that. There's so much about them one never finds out. I mean they come, they go away –

Edna (*sits opposite Ben*) Do you know anything about my particular black sheep, by the way? His name's Gardner.

Ben Gardner? Gardner, Gardner.

Joey Yes, he comes to the odd lecture, aloof in feathers.

Ben Feathers?

Joey He wears a kind of hat with feathers in it.

Edna Yes, that dreadful hat. I wish there was some action we could take about that, too. You don't remember him, Ben?

Ben I certainly can't place the hat.

Joey Isn't Gardner the one you had a conversation with just before the break? In a pub? You mentioned –

Ben A feathered youth? In a public house? Certainly not.

Edna Actually, the reason I asked whether you remember him, Ben, is that you interviewed him for his place here.

I've just looked him up in the files. (*She hands Ben Gardner's open file.*)

Ben Possibly. I only remember the ones we manage to reject, like Father O'Couligan.

Edna I must say, Ben, his headmaster's report was very unfavourable.

Ben I'm not surprised. Father O'Couligan was in his forties. The headmaster must have had him in the sixth form for a couple of decades at least. And frankly five minutes of O'Couligan was as much as I –

Edna No, I was talking about Gardner. I simply can't help wondering what made you take him.

Ben Well, Edna, I suppose I must have decided he wasn't fit for anything else.

Edna A university isn't a charity, you know.

There is a silence.

Ben Do you mean for me, Edna? Or for the students?

Edna I'm not in the mood to be flippant about the more loutish of our students today. Not with the committee's report on the Senate House fresh in my mind.

Ben Sorry, what report?

Edna It was in *The Times* this morning.

Joey I read it. In *The Guardian*. It was very disturbing.

Ben looks at him.

Edna Disturbing! They completely destroyed the Velium Aristotle. Completely destroyed it. *That* was their way of protesting about South Africa.

Joey I thought it was about Rhodesia. The University maintaining relationships –

SIMON GRAY

Edna Well, one excuse is as good as another, of course.

Ben James said it was the Greek Colonels. But perhaps we're underestimating their capacity for direct logical connections. Perhaps they were protesting about the Velium Aristotle.

Edna It wouldn't surprise me. I had one or two last term who were mutinous about *The Faerie Queene*.

Ben You mean the Principal? He really should learn discretion.

Edna (*after a short pause, releases a burst of ghastly laughter*) No, Ben, you mustn't say things like that. (*Laughs again.*) Besides, the Velium Aristotle is no laughing matter. But I intend to nip Gardner in the bud before he gets completely out of hand. I'm not having any bomb-throwing hooligan skipping *my* seminars!

Ben Any bomb-throwing hooligan has permission to skip mine. (*He gets up and moves towards the door.*)

Edna (*retrieves Gardner's file from Ben's desk*) Well, there's no point in my haranguing you. I suppose I'd better take it to James.

Ben To James?

Edna Certainly. Gardner is ripe for a Dean's Report. Oh, I meant to say, you and Anne must come around soon, if you could bear an evening in my poky little flat. And Joey, of course.

Ben Thanks.

Joey (*enthusiastically*) I'd love to.

Edna How's the baby?

Ben Oh, very well. As far as one can tell. With babies, I mean.

Edna Yes, they are indecipherable, aren't they? How old is he now?

Ben He's (*thinks*) six or seven months, about.

Edna It's wretched of me, but I've forgotten his name. Though I do remember him as a bonny little thing.

Ben Miranda.

Joey Marina.

Ben Yes. (*Laughs.*) Marina. He's called Marina.

Edna Oh dear, oh Ben, I'm sorry. I always think of babies as 'hims' or 'its'.

Ben Well, it's probably safer these days. Our ends never know our beginnings.

Edna Any teeth yet?

Ben Just the – uh – (*wags his finger around his mouth*) *gums*, you know, and a few wisdom . . . or whatever they're . . .

Edna That sounds most satisfactory. Are you all right for baby-sitters?

Ben Baby-sitters. (*Laughs.*) Oh, no problem. Marina's mother is a marvellous baby-sitter. Anne has simply added a contemporary skill to Goethe's ideal woman. (*After a pause.*) I'm afraid we are going through what we professionals know as a sticky patch.

Edna Oh dear. Ben, I'm sorry. I don't know what to say. You must both be desperately unhappy. (*Pause.*) I do hope she's not in that flat all by herself.

Ben Oh, we sorted that out. She told me that if I was half a man I'd leave. But on discovering that *she* was, she left herself. She's with her mother. Together they make up two pairs. I imagine Marina is the odd man out.

Edna I see. Oh dear. (*Pause.*) It's always so sad for the children.

Ben Yes, we do suffer the most.

Edna Where are *you* now, Joey, are you still in that bedsitter?

Joey (*little pause*) No. (*Another pause.*) I've moved back in with Ben again, in point of fact.

Edna Oh, so you're both back where you were then.

Ben Exactly.

Edna By the way, did I mention that the little office next to mine's going begging at last? So if either of you wants a place of your own . . .

Ben Thanks, Edna, but we're used to roughing it down here.

Edna It's up to you, of course . . . Well, I must leave you two to get on with it. (*She goes to the door.*) If you should clap eyes on young Gardner, please send him straight up to me on pain of a Dean's Report.

She goes out. There is a silence.

Ben I enjoyed that. It was so graceful. In a little office next door to Edna. Christ. What does she want him for? (*He returns to his desk.*) She's got her own coterie – all those boys and girls that look as if they've got the curse permanently. (*Little pause.*) Her obsession with Byron is one of the more *triste* perversions. But she shouldn't be allowed to practise it with students. She's got her bloody book for therapy.

Joey She's finished her book. That's what she was telling me on the Tube this morning.

Ben Well done, Edna. I suppose it means another two decades while she finds a publisher.

Joey She's found one.

Ben She never did understand her role. Which is not to finish an unpublishable book on Byron. Now the centre cannot hold. Mere Edna is loosed upon the world. (*Pause. Sits in the armchair.*) Bloody woman! (*Pause.*) Bugger! (*Pause.*) Bugger! The Dean's Report!

Joey It *was* Gardner you told me about, then? The boy who complained about Edna's seminars in a pub.

Ben Edna holds her seminars in a pub? I shall have to report this.

Joey The one you said was interesting.

Ben I don't find anything interesting about a student who complains of Edna's seminars. You did it yourself years ago, and you're as dull as they come.

Joey Did you encourage him?

Ben As far as I remember, which is frankly nothing, we had a perfectly respectable conversation about Edna's vagina, its length and width.

Joey Oh God!

Ben You mustn't be jealous, Joseph. The young are entitled to the importunities that you once enjoyed.

Joey (*gets up and walks towards Ben*) I can't afford to quarrel with Edna. Besides, I've got to like her.

Ben Because you've got to, doesn't mean I've got to.

Joey She thinks of us as allies. If you upset her, she'll blame me too.

Ben What the hell are you doing here anyway? You're not lecturing until later. You could have gone straight home and tidied up your room. It's in a disgusting state.

Joey The only room in the flat that isn't in a disgusting state is mine.

Ben Really? Then can you explain why it looks as if a large, dignified and intelligent man has been going to seed in it?

Joey (*after a pause*) Did you have to use my room?

Ben Do you think I could put up with the mess everywhere else? You're out most evenings, it's easy for you to keep your room clean. I don't see why you shouldn't learn what it's like to stay at home and fret your way into a drunken coma.

Joey, after a moment, goes back to his desk and sits down.

Is *that* your tantrum? How piffling.

Joey Look, Ben, I've got this lecture. Can I do some work, please? As I can't go to the library – please?

Ben (*goes to him*) When will you phone Reg up, then?

Joey I told you. After lunch.

Ben Why are you lying about his being out? (*He points Joey's desk lamp directly into his face in interrogation.*)

Joey I don't make a habit of lying.

Ben Which is why you go on being so bad at it.

There is a shape at the door. Ben looks towards it, hurries to his feet, as there is a knock. He goes over to the door, opens it a fraction.

(*jovially*) Good morning, good morning, good morning.

Student (*off*) I just wanted to find out about my tutorials.

Ben Good. Good. Have you got an essay, please!

Student (*off*) Well no, I mean you haven't set one.

Ben Well, do me one for next week, all right?

Student (*off*) Well, what on?

Ben You must decide for yourself, can't expect spoon-feeding. Righto. (*He shuts the door, comes back rubbing his hands.*) I think that's the lot –

As a shape comes to the door, there is a knock. The door opens as Ben spins around.

Miss Heasman I found Mrs Grainger, she says she would have come to you on Tuesdays at two if you'd been able to see her.

Ben So be it. Tuesdays at two with our fingers crossed. (*He crosses them.*)

Miss Heasman Today is Tuesday.

Ben Ah well, I wouldn't have been able to see her again today, I'm afraid, as she would have needed a week in which to do me an essay.

Miss Heasman Poor Mrs Grainger. But I'm all right, as I've done one.

She takes one out of her file, and hands it to Ben, who takes it reluctantly.

I haven't put a title on, but I thought: 'Hate and Redemption in *The Winter's Tale*'.

Ben Needs work. (*He hands the essay back.*) That title.

Miss Heasman Don't you want to read it before the tutorial?

Ben No, you'll have to read it aloud to me. Unless, I tell you what, give it to me now and I'll do my damnedest to get it read before next week.

Miss Heasman (*her eyes go to Ben's desk*) No, I'll read it aloud. Two o'clock, then. (*She turns and goes out.*)

Ben (*imitates her walk and slams the door*) Bugger! (*He comes back to his desk.*) 'Hate and Redemption' – I told you she was mad. She must be a secret agent, in Edna's employ . . . (*He picks up a handful of essays from the desk then drops them one by one on the floor.*) Hate and Redemption, Pity and Terror, Sin and Salvation. (*dropping more essays onto the floor*) Faith and Despair in *Pride and Prejudice*, *The Mill on the Floss*, Appley and Dappley, Cecily Parsley. (*liturgically, as he is dropping essays. He looks at his desk.*) Why don't those cleaning women do their job properly? Standards are declining everywhere. Ruskin's char threw Carlyle's *History of the French Revolution* out with the other rubbish. But then they took a pride in their work in those days. (*He picks up another essay, looks at it, laughs and sits down.*) I should think Reg would enjoy cooking my kidneys. It sounds worse than settling my hash. Anne's mother, the mad monk, settles the hash of bus-conductors, milkmen, postmen, anyone stupid enough to waste their time insulting her. 'Oh, I settled his hash all right.' She probably got the taste for it after she killed off her husband. I wonder if there was any reference in the coroner's report to the state of his hash. This hash, my life . . . this long disease my . . . (*He begins to read, then lets it slip from his fingers, leans back, picks reflectively at the cotton wool.*) Why the hell did we call her Marina?

> I made this, I have forgotten
> And remember.
> The rigging weak and the canvas rotten
> Between one June and another September.

Born in June, May . . . April . . . February . . . November . . . Conceived in September . . . So sometime in early

September there was what you might call a seminal
fuck . . . Where? In the park once we . . . let me think,
beneath the trees.

> Beneath the trees there is no ease.
> For the dull brain, the sharp desires
> And the quick eyes of Woolly Bear.

It must have been our last, we were already fallen into the
sere, the yellow leaf, a flash of thigh in the yellow leaf.

> What seas what shores what granite islands towards
>   my timbers
> And woodthrush calling through the fog
> My daughter.

Joey You do miss her then?

Ben (*goes over to Joey*) You know, what marks you out
as a repressed as well as a practising pervert is your
sentimentality over children. Marina doesn't need a
mother or father, she needs a pair of hands, to pick her
up, change her, put things to her mouth, put her down
again.

Joey But later on she might need a father.

Ben You generally have the taste to let *me* raise the
subject of my ruined marriage.

Joey I can't help wondering whether you miss it.

Ben Only the sex and violence. And these days one can
get those anywhere.

Joey So there's absolutely no chance . . .

Ben Chance of what?

Joey Of your marriage reviving. You don't want it to?

Ben Reviving? It's never died. I consider it inviolate. I'm
a one-woman man and I've had mine, thank God.

41

Joey But things can't just go on as they are.

Ben Can't they? Why not? (*He takes the telephone directory from his desk and begins to look up a number.*)

Joey But supposing she wants to marry again.

Ben Good God! Who would want to marry *her*?

Joey You did.

Ben That was before she'd been through the mill . . . (*He begins to run his finger down the column.*)

Joey (*standing up*) Listen, Ben, you could be making a mistake about Anne. If you really don't want to lose her –

Ben (*goes to the telephone on Joey's desk*) Your conversation is beginning to sound as if it's been stitched together from song titles of the fifties. (*He begins to sing.*) Making a mistake about Anne . . . If you really don't want to lose her . . .

Joey Look, Ben, I'm trying to tell you something.

Ben Haylife and Forling's . . .

Joey looks at Ben. Ben sings as he dials.

Three-four-eight – owe-seven-two-owe.

Joey What are you doing?

Ben (*sits down and speaks into the telephone*) Ah, hello – can I speak to Mr Nuttall, Reg Nuttall, please?

Joey (*hurrying over to the telephone*) He's not there.

Ben Thank you.

He waits, humming and smiling at Joey. Joey seizes the telephone, they wrestle over it, Ben hangs on to it.

(*into the phone, crouched away from Joey*) No, I'm waiting for Mr Nuttall, please.

Joey All right. All right. I'll do it.

Ben hands him the receiver. Joey puts the receiver down and holds on to the telephone. There is a pause.

Ben Well?

Joey Do you intend to stay in the room while I find out if he'll have you to dinner?

Ben Certainly. But you needn't stay while I find out. (*He goes to pick up the telephone.*)

Joey (*shouts*) I said I'd do it!

Ben (*a long pause*) But what *are* you afraid of? He can only say no, in which case I'll only make your life a living hell.

Joey Perhaps I'm afraid he'll say yes.

Ben Well, you do worry for him, don't you, dear?

Joey Why do you think it's him I'm worried for?

Ben Oh, we all know how you worry for yourself. (*He reaches for the telephone.*)

Joey holds it tight, and looks at Ben. Ben laughs and reaches for it.

Joey (*runs away with it followed by Ben*) You're a fool, Ben. A bloody fool!

Ben stops. The telephone rings. Ben takes the telephone and puts the base down on his desk. Joey sits down at his desk.

Ben Butley, Nursery. (*Laughs.*) Oh hello, James, what? Ah, well, I was just pondering those lines –

His rhythm was present in the nursery bedroom,
In the rank ailanthus of the April dooryard –

(*Pause.*) No, no, I'm quite free. (*Little pause. He mouths a curse.*) Gardner? Gardner, Gardner, Gardner. No I don't recall a student called Gardner – What year is she? Ah! *He!*

He grimaces at Joey. A shape appears at the door.

Oh God, poor Edna.

There is a knock on the door. He claps his hand over the mouthpiece.

(*to Joey*) Block that student! (*Into the receiver.*) He says I *what*? No he must have misunderstood me. I don't recall telling a student . . .

Joey has gone to the door, opens it, then steps back. Anne comes in. Ben sees Anne, gapes at her and turns back to the telephone.

Look, I appear to have miscalculated, I've got a student after all, speak to you later, eh? Bye. (*He hangs up. There is a silence.*) How are you?

Anne Thank you. And you?

Ben Coping with Edna. Do you remember Edna? The one you called a human contraceptive? Do you remember?

Anne Actually, I called her a pill.

Ben Well, I updated you.

He laughs. Another silence.

Anne How are *you*, Joey?

Joey Oh. Um, very well thanks. Um, how's Miranda?

Anne Marina. She fills her belly and her nappy. She grows the odd tooth. She cries.

Ben How adult. Except for the odd tooth, one loses that. (*Pause.*) Actually, I've been thinking of finding a new dentist. I know you dote on Tonks, darling, but he's terribly camp. One sits in that chair with one's whole body at his mercy. (*To Joey.*) Who do you go to?

Joey A man in Pimlico.

Anne Joey's teeth are always in marvellous condition.

Ben Are they? Let's see.

Joey What?

Ben Let's see your teeth.

Joey grimaces. Ben goes close, inspects them.

You're quite right. (*To Anne.*) They sparkle. Although from time to time I've noticed – (*He hums 'Christ the Lord is risen today'.*)

Anne (*laughs, to Joey*) One of Ben's marriage jokes. I'm surprised you haven't heard it.

Joey Well, I haven't.

Anne How flattering for me.

Joey (*after a pause*) Well, I think it'd be better if I – I'd better get along. (*He picks up his briefcase.*)

Ben Why?

Anne Because he's embarrassed.

Ben Are you?

Joey I've got a lecture.

Ben He has. On Blake.

Anne Ah. Then he'd better go.

Joey goes out.

Ben He's very sensitive. You frighten him.

Anne Because he's creepy, and he knows I know it.

Ben Yes. I've told him. He took it surprisingly badly.

Anne (*pause*) You've settled down nicely together again, then, have you?

Ben We have our ups and downs.

Anne That's all right then. May I sit? (*She sits on the hard chair in front of Ben's desk.*)

Ben I went to see you over the weekend, as arranged, but you were out.

Anne Yes, I'm sorry.

Ben Grounds for a scene, though, don't you think?

Anne Oh, I should wait. (*Little pause.*) I had to see Tom's headmaster about a job.

Ben And did you get one?

Anne Yes.

Ben Good. (*He stares at her.*) But you look a trifle peaky around the gills – wherever they are. I can never locate them on Joey. Are you all right?

Anne I'm fine.

Ben Good. I saw Marina instead. I expect your mother the mad monk told you.

Anne She said it was very quick. Like a visit from the postman.

Ben I was there for twenty minutes. You'd better check on the postman. Ah! (*He sits at Joey's desk.*) Well, this is almost as delightful as it's unexpected, to what is it owed?

Anne I came to find out whether you wanted us back.

Ben (*after a pause*) Is that an offer?

Anne No. It's a question. I'd like the truth, please. Do you want us back?

Ben Frequently. (*Little pause.*) But not permanently. Do you want to come back?

Anne No.

Ben We've cleared that up, then. I think we're going to get on very well from this time forth, don't you?

Anne (*pause*) Joey hasn't told you, then?

Ben Told me what?

Anne He's known for weeks. His – what's his name – friend Reg must have told him.

Ben Reg?

Anne Tom told him. At least, he told me he had.

Ben Tom? Tom and Reg? What on earth have Tom and Reg got to do with us?

Anne He's asked me to marry him.

Ben (*after a pause*) Which one? (*Pause.*) You're not. (*Laughs.*) You can't be.

Anne Yes I am. Do you mind?

Ben Yes, yes, I mind very much. (*Pause, he pulls himself together.*) After all, a man's bound to be judged by his wife's husband. The most boring man in London – you said yourself he was the dullest man you'd ever spent an evening with.

Anne That was before I got to know him properly.

Ben And what do you call him now?

Anne The dullest man I've ever spent the night with. But I don't mind. Why should you?

Ben Because – because I shall miss old Tom, that's why. I'm too old to make mature new friendships with bores, far too impatient. (*He walks round to his own desk.*) They have to grow on you steadily, hours by hours through years on years, until they're actually doing their bit towards holding you together. Like ivy around crumbling walls. (*Little pause.*) Is that why you want him?

Anne Are you going to make difficulties?

Ben What?

Anne About the divorce?

Ben Divorce?

Anne You see, I'm not allowed to marry him until I'm divorced from you. It's the law of the land. Are you going to make difficulties?

Ben This is humiliating.

Anne But deserved. By both of us.

Ben (*laughs*) I'll bloody make difficulties all right. After all, this is liable to be the only phase of our marriage that I shall enjoy. At least since the moment in the registry office when the clerk who handled our contract was under the impression that he was supposed to bind me for a year or two to the mad monk your mother. (*He gets up and faces her across his desk.*) I'll have to have my fun somewhere, won't I? Because, after all, one moment of pleasure isn't much out of a whole year, is it?

Anne It's a moment more than I had.

Ben And how many moments do you expect from your next?

Anne I shan't count them. I'm not in it for fun, you see. I never was. And nor were you.

Ben Oh. What *was* I in it for?

Anne Perhaps you wanted a break.

Ben Well, I'm certainly getting one, aren't I?

Anne Or perhaps you were frightened. But it doesn't matter any more because you're not any more. And I suppose you needn't ever try again, now that you've found out whatever it is you were determined to learn. (*Pause.*) I don't care. Not at all.

Ben Then you're halfway there. And Tom will certainly teach you to sit still. (*He walks round behind her and comes to face her.*) If you must get married again, surely we can do better for you than that. After six weeks you'll be the two most boring men in London. There are signs already. You're developing a new tone – a combination of the didactic and the enigmatically stoic – that's more than halfway towards Tom's prose style. By the way, does he know that you greet spring and its signs of life with wheezing and sneezes from your hay fever? Tom endorses spring. He admires it for its moral exuberance. (*Pause.*) Do you still make little popping sounds when you drink your coffee? No, it's your nose – your nose I've always taken exception to, or is it your mouth? You can't marry Tom.

Anne I can.

Ben All right, you probably can. You can probably do a lot of hideous things. You're tough, versatile and brutal. What I mean is, don't.

Anne Why not?

A shape appears at the door.

Well?

A pause.

Edna (*knocks, steps in*) Can I have a word? (*She is obviously distraught.*)

Ben By all means. (*He gestures to Anne.*)

Edna Oh, I'm sorry, I didn't realise – I'll look back later, if I may. (*She goes out.*)

Anne He's asked me to live with him until we get married. Are you going to make trouble?

Ben Tell me, when did we last have it off? Was it that time in the park, beneath the trees, or did we have a quick go subsequently, in bed or under the kitchen table, Joey and I were trying to work it out –

Anne rises. He jumps away, as if expecting a blow, shields his face, then laughs, shakily.

You're going to live with him *until* you get married, did you say? At least that's a realistic prospectus. (*He calls out, as Anne leaves.*) Bye, darling. Bye-bye, sweet princess, goodbye . . . (*He closes the door behind her and stands pulling at the cotton wool on his chin. He pulls it off.*) Ahh, Butley is himself again. (*Hums 'Christ the Lord', then sings.*) Christ your breath is bad today haa-aa-al-it-osis. Haa-aa – (*He breaks off, trembling. He sits down at his desk, puts his hand to his face, takes it away, looks at it, touches his chin, inspects his fingers.*) Bloody woman! Bloody woman! (*He feels in his pocket and takes out more cotton wool.*)

Curtain.

Act Two

The office as before. It is shortly after lunch. When the curtain rises Miss Heasman is sitting on the hard chair by Ben's desk, reading from her essay. Ben is apparently asleep in the armchair, a cigarette in his hand.

Miss Heasman (*a pause – she looks at Ben*) 'Hermione's reawakening – the statue restored to life after a winter of sixteen years' duration – is in reality Leontes's reawakening, spiritually, and of course the most moving exemplification of both the revitalisation theme and thus of forgiveness on the theological as well as the human level.'

Ben Level?

Miss Heasman Yes.

Ben The human *level*?

Miss Heasman Yes. Um, shall I go on?

Ben Mmm.

Miss Heasman 'The central image is drawn from nature, to counterpoint the imagery of the first half of the play, with its stress on sickness and deformity. Paradoxically, *The Winter's Tale* of a frozen soul –'

Ben Bit fishmongery, that.

Miss Heasman (*laughs mirthlessly*) '– is therefore thematically and symbolically about revitalisation.'

Ben Sorry. Re-whatalisation?

Miss Heasman Re-*vi*talisation.

Ben (*gets up and goes to Miss Heasman*) Thematically and symbolically so, eh?

Miss Heasman Yes. (*She looks towards him challengingly.*) 'The central image is drawn from –' no, we've had that – um. 'In this context –'

Ben Can you see?

Miss Heasman What?

Ben (*aims his desk light at Miss Heasman's essay, forgets to turn it on, goes to a hard chair in the corner of the room and sits down out of view*) There.

> *Miss Heasman, after a moment, leans over, turns on the light.*

Sorry. No irony intended. (*Pause.*) 'Context.'

Miss Heasman Um, yes. 'In this context it might be said that Leontes represents the affliction that is a universal, and so contingently human evil, and in this sense, the sense of a shared blight . . .'

Ben (*lets out a noise like a laugh, pretends to be coughing*) Sorry. Yes, a shared blight – yes, look, how much longer is it exactly?

> *Miss Heasman fumbles through the pages – Ben goes over to his desk.*

I'll tell you what, as our time together's drawing to a close, read the last two or three sentences, so we can get the feel of your conclusion.

> *Miss Heasman looks pointedly at her watch, riffles through her pages. Ben picks at the cotton wool on his chin, drums his fingers, checks these movements, smiles attentively when Miss Heasman looks at him.*

Miss Heasman Ready?

Ben Please, please.

Miss Heasman 'So just as the seasonal winter was the winter of the soul, so is the seasonal spring the spring of the soul. The imagery changes from disease to floral, the tone from mad bitterness to joyfulness. As we reach the play's climax we feel our own – spiritual – sap rising.'

Ben (*after a long pause*) Sap?

Miss Heasman Sap.

Ben Sap. Sap. Yes, I think sap's a better word than some others that spring rhymingly to mind. Good. Well, thank you very much. (*Pause.*) He had a ghastly time of it, didn't he?

Miss Heasman Who?

Ben Leontes. I mean, Shakespeare doesn't leave him alone for a minute – as you point out. He gets hold of the poor old bugger and gives it to him thematically and symbolically, he afflicts him with imagery – floral and diseasal, didn't you say?

Miss Heasman Floral was Perdita.

Ben She's an affliction, too, though, isn't she? And all those levels – as you note – so exhausting for him.

Miss Heasman I'm sorry, I don't understand.

Ben No, I'm just agreeing with you.

Miss Heasman Um, with what exactly?

Ben That he doesn't give Leontes much chance. First he sends him mad with jealousy, then he teaches him a moral lesson. And talk about free speech – (*Laughs.*) Every observation illuminating a theme or developing a symbol – we see eye to eye on all that.

Miss Heasman Actually I found it very moving.

Ben (*after a pause*) You *liked* it?

Miss Heasman Very much. Very, very much.

Ben I'm so sorry. A slight misunderstanding. (*Pause.*)
What do you want to do – I mean, after your exams?

Miss Heasman Teach.

Ben English?

Miss Heasman Yes.

Ben Well, I suppose that's more radical than being
a teacher of exams, for which I think you're already
qualified, by the way. I hope you'll take that as a
compliment.

Miss Heasman It isn't meant to be one, is it? But whatever you think of my essay, if I don't do well in the exams,
I might not be able to be a teacher.

Ben Teacher of whom?

Miss Heasman Sixth forms, I hope.

Ben Isn't it more exhilarating to get them earlier?
Sixth-form teachers are something like firemen called in
to quench flames that are already out. Although you can
never tell – recently I've enjoyed reading almost as much
as I did when I was twelve. I do hope I didn't slip through
their net – it makes one lose confidence. But I'm sure
you'll be all right. Perhaps books are just my *madeleines*,
eh?

> Gravy and potatoes
> In a big brown pot
> Put them in the oven
> And cook them very hot.

Miss Heasman I'm sorry?

Ben And so am I. I'm not really myself this afternoon, what do you want to do next week?

Miss Heasman We have to cover at least six Shakespeares.

Ben From what I've heard already, Shakespeare's as good as covered. (*He opens the door.*)

Miss Heasman (*holds out her essay*) Could you please write some comments on this?

Ben It's a good time to be merciless. (*Taking the essay.*) It comes in useful when dealing with the young.

Miss Heasman Believe it or not, you can be as rude as you like. I don't take it personally.

Ben That's another good way of taking the fun out of teaching. Good afternoon, Miss Heasman.

Miss Heasman Thank you.

She goes out. Ben stands at the open door, gestures obscenely after her. Then, aware that he is holding her essay, pinches his nostrils, holds the essay at a distance, makes gagging sounds, pantomimes gas-poisoning as he goes back to his desk. Miss Heasman has come back to the door, stands watching him. Ben drops the essay onto his desk, stiffens, turns slowly. He and Miss Heasman stare at each other. Miss Heasman turns and goes quickly from the room.

Ben (*makes as if to hurry after her, stops*) Oh Christ! Bloody girl! (*He stands for a moment, then takes out an address book, looks up a name, goes over to his desk and dials the number.*) Hello, Kent Vale Comprehensive? Headmaster, please. (*Little pause.*) Ben Butley. (*Aside.*) Friend to Education. (*Into the telephone.*) Thank you. (*He puts the telephone on the desk, runs over to a* *carrier bag, extracts a quarter of Scotch, runs back, clamps it under his chin, unscrews the cap as he talks in a Scottish accent.*) Ahh, hello, Headmaster, sorry to trouble you on a trifling matter, but I've been trying to make contact with one of your staff, Tom Weatherley, and it's proving to be a tricky business. (*Pause.*) Ben Butley, Friend to Tom Weatherley, a member of your staff. Do you ken him? (*Little pause.*) Oh, naturally I don't want to disturb him if he's teaching, but I've got a rather delicate message for him – I'd rather entrust it to someone of authority like yourself, if I may? (*Listens.*) Thank you. It's just that could he and I have a little chin-wag – (*little pause*) chin-wag some time about the proceedings – solicitors, alimony, maintenance, custody, visiting rights – always so sad when there are wee bairns to consider – we always say – property, so on, so forth. (*Pause.*) Oh, I'm Tom's fiancée's husband. I've only just heard the news. By the way, HM, quite a coincidence, my wife that was, Tom's wife to be, Anne Butley that is, might be coming to teach in your school, I believe – do keep an eye out for her, I'd be most obliged. (*He takes the telephone away from his chin, feels his chin, makes a face.*) Oh, and there is one other thing, could you tell Tom that he'll have to foot the bill for any ops this time unless he can get it on the National Health, I've got enough blood on my hands – (*Looks at his fingers.*) at the moment, and it's all my own, ha ha ha, if you see what I mean. (*Little pause.*) Oh you don't, well never mind, HM, I don't really think we educationalists should be expected to see anything but the clouds into which we thrust our heads, eh?

There is a shape at the door. Ben looks towards it.

Love to Tom and Anne when you see them, eh? Goodbye. (*He puts down the telephone, stares towards the door, then takes a swig of Scotch, goes to the door, peers*

through the frosted glass. He drops the Scotch into his
pocket and knocks gently against the glass.)

Tap tappit, tap tappit, he's heard it before.
But when he peeps out there is nobody there

Opens the door.

But packets and whimsey put down on the stair.

(*He walks over to his desk.*) Or is something frightening
him again? Is that why he's peeping through the frosted
glass with his whiskers twitching and his paws to his
nose, eh?

Joey, after a pause, enters – goes to his desk, puts
down his briefcase and turns on the desk lamp.

If it's Anne you were hiding from, she's gone. If it's Edna,
she hasn't arrived.

Joey I heard voices. I thought perhaps you and Anne
were still –

Ben What? Thrashing it out? Having it off? What would
Anne and I still be doing, together in a small room, after
two hours? She was always succinct, even with her
knickers down.

Joey I saw Edna in the common room. She was just
leaving when I went in.

Ben And how did she seem? Jovial?

Joey No, very upset.

Ben Ah.

Joey Was that Miss Heasman I passed in the corridor?

Ben How did she look? Jovial?

Joey She had her face averted. As if she were in tears.

57

Ben Then that was certainly Miss Heasman, yes. Everything seems to be running smoothly, doesn't it? (*He stares at Joey.*) Tell me, what did you make of old Anne turning up in that enterprising fashion?

Joey I don't know.

Ben You don't?

Joey looks at him.

She was under the impression that you've known for some time.

Joey (*a pause*) I did try to warn you.

Ben Yes, and thank you. But tell me, how come that you've known for some time?

Joey Well, actually I got it from Reg.

Ben From Reg? Yes? (*Pause.*) You know I think we're building up a case here for a conspiracy theory of personal relationships. Go on.

Joey (*sits*) Tom's meeting Reg had nothing to do with me. It was something professional, I don't know what, but they got on very well and Tom told Reg and Reg told me, and then Tom phoned Reg and told Reg not to tell me or if he *had* told me to ask me not to tell you until he or Anne had told you.

Ben Yes, I recognise Tom's delicate touch there in your sentence structure. It must have been amusing to hear me chatter mindlessly on about my marriage, eh?

Joey I tried to warn you.

Ben But was it amusing? Was it fun? (*Pause.*) Are you going to answer me?

Joey Sorry. I took the question to be rhetorical.

Ben (*going over to him*) All right. Let me ask you, then, *why* you promised not to mention to your best friend – is that presuming? – that his wife was being screwed by, while contemplating marriage to, the most boring man in London? Is that question sufficiently unrhetorical?

Joey Because I didn't think it was my business.

Ben Not your business? And how many personalities and dramas over which we've gossiped and whinnied in the past years have been our business? There have been some pretty sticky silences between us recently, and here you were, my dear, in possession of a piece of information that was guaranteed to raise at the very least an amused eyebrow.

Joey All right, because I'm a coward, that's why. I'm sorry. (*Pause.*) I *am* sorry, in point of fact.

Ben Matters of fact and points of fact have been cluttering your syntax since you started going steady with that butcher's boy.

Joey I'm sorry because I hoped it wouldn't happen. Now it's a fact and I wish it weren't.

Ben laughs, tugs at the cotton wool on his chin and pulls it off. His hand is trembling.

I'm – I'm sure you could get her back.

Ben How far back?

Joey To live with you. She and Marina.

Ben That's too far back. Far too far back.

Joey Then what will you do?

Ben Grab my quota of fun, that's all. (*He returns to the telephone.*) I'm working to a very tight schedule. I've given myself a mere week to get the most boring – and

tenacious – man in London out of his job and home.
I'm moving on to his landlady now.

Joey Fun?

Ben Or trouble. I can't remember which I've promised
myself.

Joey But what's the point of making trouble?

Ben Fun. (*He dials again.*) Because hounding them from
job and home is no trouble. Local councils, the police,
whole governments do it. Why shouldn't a private citizen
be allowed to join in?

*He waits, then slams down the phone. Joey goes to
the door.*

Where are you going? (*He dials another number.*)

Joey The library's open now. I thought I'd go up –

Ben And hide again? Who from this time?

Joey shrugs.

From Edna. Yes, it must be Edna.

Joey Well, I'm not going to be here when she comes to
have it out with you.

Ben laughs.

I can't help it. *I'm* not going to antagonise her.

Ben OK, I'll do it for you. You run along.

Joey looks at him, hesitates, then makes for the door.

(*Into the telephone.*) Ah, Haylife and Forling, I must say
you do drag out your lunch, some of which, by the way,
appears still to be in your mouth, from the sound of you.

As Joey hurries to him from the door:

This is Joseph Keyston, friend to Reg Nuttall, if you take my meaning – may I speak to him, please?

He hands the telephone to Joey. Joey takes the telephone and puts it down. There is a pause.

You see how life repeats itself, with diminishing climaxes. (*Little pause.*) Well? Is he still out, have you some more moralising to do, or are you simply welching on a promise?

Joey All right. If you want, I'll cancel Reg. We can go to Bianchi's. Just the two of us.

Ben (*in an American accent*) Cancel Reg? Cancel him? (*Laughs.*) This is a human bean you're talking about here, kid, not a cheque, or an order of groceries, but a human *bean*! And frankly, dear, he's more of an attraction than your shy self, at the moment. All our games together are going a trifle stale, Reg and I may be able to find some new ones.

Joey Reg won't be very playful.

Ben Don't worry. I shall get my fun. Besides, in this bag here, kidneys! Yes, kid, kidneys! (*He waves the carrier bag at Joey.*)

Joey (*after a pause*) I'm sorry, Ben. Not tonight.

Ben Mmm, huh. So *you're* not inviting me.

Joey I'm not going. We can either eat at the flat or at Bianchi's. It's up to you.

Ben Well, if you're really not coming then there'll be all the more kidneys for Reginald and myself. What do you think he'll say to that, for an offer? (*A pause.*) Don't you care then?

Joey No. Not any more.

Ben You're not breaking off with him, you competitive child you? Is that what you're trying to tell me?

Joey No. I'm trying to tell you that it'll be much better if you leave that side of my life alone. (*His voice shaking.*) I can't stop you from phoning him up, you can do it any time, Ben, I'm just advising you, because I don't think you'll get much fun from him, I really don't. I know you've had a bad day already, with Tom and Anne, but you're making it worse.

Ben (*makes as if to dial, hesitates, dials*) You're passing up a chance for a Lawrentian-type wrestle. Can't I interest you?

Joey Just remember that I warned you. (*He sits quite still at his desk.*)

Ben Two warnings in one day.

   Joey watches tensely.

Haylife and Forling's? This is Ben Butley, friend to Joseph Keyston, friend to Reg Nuttall, with whom I'd like to speak, please. (*Little pause.*) Thank you. (*He looks at Joey, grinning, is suddenly stopped by his expression.*) What is it? (*Little pause.*) Joey? (*He starts to put the telephone down, checks himself.*) Hello, is that Reg – (*Little pause.*) Ah, his secretary. (*He hesitates, then makes up his mind.*) May I speak to him, please?

   Pause, Ben watches Joey, then offers Joey the telephone. He shakes his head. Ben listens again.

I see. Thank you very much. (*He puts the telephone down, looks at Joey.*) He's out. (*Smiles.*) Is that a relief?

Joey In a sense.

Ben You'd better tell me about it.

Joey What?

Ben Whatever it is you're warning me about.

Joey No. It's nothing.

Ben Come on, Joey.

Joey It doesn't matter. Let it go.

There's a knock on the door. Ben drops the Scotch bottle into his pocket. Edna puts her head in.

Edna Are you free now, please?

She comes in. Ben sits down. Very calmly, smiling.

Now, would you kindly tell me what transpired between yourself and this Gardner?

Joey (*earnestly*) I don't know anything about it, Edna.

Edna (*still calm*) My teaching, it appears, isn't up to his standard.

Ben Indeed. Well, I can assure you, Edna, that it's more than up to mine. I know our society has become insolently egalitarian, but I refuse to believe that the gardener's verdict on your teaching will be given too much weight. I didn't know we had a garden – let alone –

Edna This is the first time in twenty years' teaching that I've been complained about.

Joey It's preposterous. You're a very good teacher, Edna.

Ben All right. Well, let's get this sorted out. To whom did he complain?

Edna To James.

Ben And what did James say?

Edna He said you'd promised Gardner he could have tutorials with you. This conversation apparently took place in a pub.

Ben What? I've had no – well, there was a student, now I come to think of it, but, my God, I'd completely forgotten – I suppose it might have been Gardner, I scarcely took him in. He wasn't wearing feathers in his cap. (*Little pause.*) Previously you talked of a plumed youth, wasn't it? (*Laughs.*)

Edna And you said nothing to him about coming to you for Eliot?

Ben I have an idea he told me he'd become keen on Eliot. That's all.

Edna Keen on Eliot.

Ben Something of the sort. I suppose I assumed he was after a few tutorials – but really I haven't given him a thought.

Edna And did you discuss whether these tutorials are to replace his seminars with me?

Ben Certainly not.

Edna And did you tell him to go to James and explain the circumstances – that he wasn't getting anything out of my seminars?

Ben Is that what James said?

Edna He tried so hard not to tell me what Gardner had said that it was perfectly obvious. He had his diplomatic smile on – the one that makes him look exactly like a rabbit. But I suppose I should be grateful that he didn't encourage that lout to throw my furniture out of the window, or burn my notes. I work very hard for those seminars.

Joey We know you do, Edna.

Edna I don't expect gratitude, far from it. But I do expect a minimum of civilised behaviour. And I expect to be

64

backed up by the Head of the Department and the other members of the staff when I'm unlucky enough to have a bolshy troublemaker in my group.

Joey But of course we'll back you up.

Edna What happened at the Senate House – it's beginning here. The Aristotle is just the beginning. (*She sits down, fumbles in her handbag, closes it.*) But why did they pick on me?

Ben I don't think anybody would want to pick on you, Edna.

Edna Because I'm a woman, that's why. It's always easier to get at a woman. They think we're more vulnerable. Well, in my case, they've got another think coming. I haven't finished with Gardner and like ilk. Not by a long shot. (*Pause.*) How dare he! How dare he complain!

Ben (*stands up*) Look, perhaps the best thing *is* to let me take him on.

Edna There's not the slightest question of that, Ben. Not the slightest. He stays in my seminars. That's all there is to it.

Ben Of course. If that's the way you want it. The only trouble is, you may not see much of him.

Edna In that case, it will be my pleasure to get him suspended. I've already started a Dean's Report.

Ben As you wish. It's certainly your privilege. I just don't see what'll be gained.

Edna The satisfaction of causing him trouble.

Ben Yes, I can see that might be fun.

Edna I don't care. (*She opens her handbag, takes out a handkerchief.*) So you two *are* on his side then?

Ben looks at Joey – they both go over to her.

Joey Certainly not. I think Edna's got every right –

Ben puts his hand on her shoulder.

Edna Leave me alone. (*She pulls her arm away.*)

Ben Edna. (*Gently.*) I'm sorry, Edna. It's my fault for not taking young Gardner seriously.

Edna Nobody takes anything seriously any more. But universities were serious once, yes they were. But now they despise them, yes they do, just as they despise me. Just as you two despise me.

Joey Despise you!

Ben I just didn't want you to be hurt – or worry too much.

Edna That's precisely what I mean.

The telephone rings.

Ben Sorry – (*He answers the telephone.*) Butley, English. Oh, um, hello, actually no, this isn't too good a time. I'm in the middle of something –

Edna (*stands up*) If that's James, please tell him that I'm going home. As education has become optional in this college, I've chosen to cancel my classes for the rest of the day. (*She goes out.*)

Ben Sorry, James. Could we talk later? (*He puts the telephone down, sits on the edge of the desk, has a swig of Scotch, stares at Joey.*) Bloody woman!

Joey So you did agree to take Gardner in, then.

Ben One of us took the other in, all right. I shall find out later which way around it is.

Joey You'll enjoy that, I'm sure.

Ben I deserve it, after all this.

Joey And what about Edna?

Ben Bloody woman, that's all about Edna. She's lucky to be rid of him. It's not my fault she's too vain to admit it.

Joey And all you had to do just now was to keep quiet, and then tell Gardner it couldn't be managed.

Ben But I *am* managing it.

Joey Oh Christ! But what for? What the hell for?

Ben Perhaps I had a sense of vacancies opening up in my life. I needed to fill them, perhaps.

Joey Then why don't you do it from your legitimate students, instead of fobbing them off and refusing to teach them?

Ben (*sitting in armchair*) I haven't got any legitimate students. They're all bastards. Which is my term of endearment for bores. Gardner's interesting. He actually interests me. At least, I think he does, I can't remember him clearly and I'll have to see the hat. You interested me once, dear, and look where it's got you. An assistant lectureship. Of course I don't know if my interest can carry you through your board –

Joey You mean he'll have a relationship with you, don't you? While all poor Edna can offer him is a relationship with Byron, in a properly conducted seminar.

Ben (*hums 'Christ the Lord has risen today'*) Well, Joseph, what chance your lectureship now? Edna says you despise her. And she's quite right. Toadying is the sincerest form of contempt.

Pause. They stare at each other.

I remember when you stood in this room, darkly dressed to colour up your melancholy, and I had you read a little Eliot to me. Do you remember? (*Little pause.*) Little did we know that a long time away, far into the future, we would be worrying and fretting together about your promotion. Our beginnings never know our ends. They're always so sad, so sad.

Joey turns to go.

Don't flounce, Dappley. It doesn't suit your mousey hindquarters.

Joey It's not my fault you buggered everything up with Anne. You don't have to bugger everything up for me, too.

Ben No, I don't. I'm doing it as a favour and for fun.

Joey I'm sick to death of your fun! (*He goes to the door.*)

Ben Bum-twitch, bum-twitch, bum-twitch, bum-twitch!

He laughs and Joey slams the door. He runs after him and shouts down the corridor:

Teacher's pet!

He comes back – has a swig of Scotch, takes the telephone over to Joey's desk, starts to dial, changes his mind, takes another drink. Little pause.

Appley Dappley, little brown mouse
Goes to the cupboard in somebody's house
In somebody's cupboard there's everything nice
Pot, Scotch, french letters
For middle-aged mice.

The telephone rings. Ben answers it.

Woolly Bear, English. (*Pause.*) What? (*Little pause.*) *Who* would like to see Mr Keyston? (*Little pause.*) Indeed? Yes, yes he's here, just a minute. (*He puts his hand over*

68

the receiver, then speaks into it.) Mr Keyston says kindly
send him along to the office. Thank you.

*He puts the telephone down, puts the Scotch into a
drawer, goes to the desk, sits down, takes out a pen.
Feels the cotton wool on his chin. There is a knock.
He pores over an essay as there is another knock.*

Come.

*The door opens. Reg enters. Ben goes on working at
his essay.*

Minute, please. (*Then looks up.*)

Reg Is Joey here?

Ben Good God, it's Reg, isn't it? Of course it is.

*He gets up, goes over, holds out his hand. As they
shake hands:*

I'm terribly sorry, do come in.

Reg Your porter said he was here.

Ben And so he will be. He just went off to have a brief
word with a colleague in distress. How are you?

Reg Very well, thanks. And you?

Ben (*gestures towards his desk*) As you see. (*Laughs.*)

Reg Yes. (*He glances at the desk, appalled.*) Look,
you're obviously very busy. If you just tell Joey I'm at the
porter's desk –

Ben Don't be silly. You sit yourself down over there –
(*offers him a chair*) and I'll just finish this off, I won't be
a minute.

*Reg hesitates, glances at Joey's desk and bookshelves
and lights a cigarette. Ben pretends to go on marking,
makes a few exclamations under his breath.*

69

(*Not looking up.*) What brings you down here, anyway?

Reg I just thought I'd look in.

Ben (*writes furiously*) Have to make my script illegible so that they don't find out about my spelling. There. (*He pushes the essay away.*) To check up, eh?

Reg Check up?

Ben Joey's always saying that if you got your hands on our little room, which is an everywhere, or rather on me, eh? As I'm responsible for the mess we're in – (*Laughs.*) But you should see our flat. Even Joey's room is like a pigsty – naturally, I'm the pig that made it that way. You really must come around and help us out. He says you've done wonders with your little kitchen.

Reg I'm in publishing.

Ben (*puzzled*) Yes?

Reg Not in interior decorating. (*He sits on the hard chair by Joey's desk.*)

Ben Oh God yes. (*Laughs.*) I'm sorry about that. No, I don't get your job wrong any more. It would be inexcusable. I'm always making Joey tell me about it, in fact.

Reg I know. He's always telling me about having to tell you about it.

Ben He says you're a marvellous cook.

Reg I'm glad he eats well.

Ben And keeps his figure, lucky sod. (*Little pause. Gets up and sits on hard chair opposite Reg.*) You know, Reg, I'm very glad to have the chance to speak to you privately – I behaved abominably the last time we met.

I do hope – well, you've forgiven me for your shoes.
I never apologised properly.

Reg It's all right. These things happen.

Ben But your shoes survived, did they?

Reg They were suede.

Ben Oh dear. Suede. (*Pause.*)

Reg Look, you must want to get on. I'll go back to the
porter – (*He gets up.*)

Ben No, you mustn't do that. (*He gets up.*)

Reg I don't mind. In point of fact we were doing a little
business together. He's an Arsenal supporter.

Ben Good God. Is he really? In point of fact?

There is a pause.

Reg So I can let you get on with –

Ben Have a drink? (*He goes to his desk, opens the
drawer.*)

Reg I don't think I ought to.

Ben (*coming back with the Scotch and two soiled
glasses*) You are lucky. Then you'll really enjoy it.

*He pushes one of the glasses into Reg's hand. Reg
peers down into the glass, winces at its condition. Ben
dashes Scotch into it, then into his own.*

I understand you've met my friend Tom. Tom Weatherley,
by the way.

Reg I know Tom, yes.

Ben You know all my domestic news, too, I gather. I only
heard it myself today.

Reg Yes, I heard something about it. I'm sorry.

Ben Do you detest warm Scotch? I don't know how you drink it in your part of the world?

Reg This is fine.

Ben Good. Cheers.

Reg Cheers.

Ben Thanks.

 He drinks. Reg goes to Joey's bookshelves.

It's nice to have some company. These last few hours I've felt quite like Antony at his close – the air is full of the gods' departing musics. So do forgive any tendency to babble, eh?

Reg No, that's all right. I understand.

Ben Cheers. (*He sits on the hard chair by his desk.*) Actually what this whole business has brought home to me is how dependent I am on my past.

Reg (*turning to him*) But it was – excuse me – but it was quite a short marriage, wasn't it?

Ben No, I was talking about Joey.

Reg Oh.

Ben It's as if my marriage were an intermission, if you see. Now I'm catching up with my past again, which is where I suppose my future is also.

Reg Really?

Ben Sorry. I'm being literary. But I always think of *you* as a born romantic. From Joey's descriptions of *your* past. A touch of the butterfly, eh?

Reg Really? And what does Joey say to make you think that?

72

Ben Oh, I don't know – the way you've pulled up your roots in the North, what I imagine to be your emotional pattern, your love of the bizarre.

Reg (*pause*) And how does that express itself?

Ben Joey's always recounting your experiences – for example with the Gurkhas. You were with them, weren't you?

Reg I was stationed with them, yes. About ten years ago, during my National Service.

Ben Exactly. And I scarcely knew what a Gurkha was – I still tend to think he's something you get with a cocktail.

Reg Do you?

Ben They must be tough little towsers.

Reg They are. (*He sits at Joey's desk.*) You didn't do your National Service I take it.

Ben Oh Christ! Sorry, I mean no.

Reg How come?

Ben I got took queer.

There is a pause. Reg puts his glass down.

Oh! You're ready for another one.

Reg No, I – in point of fact, I'd rather not.

Ben This is an altogether different suburb. (*He refills Reg's glass.*)

Reg Sorry? What suburb?

Ben Oh, it's a little joke of Joey's. Almost impossible to explain out of context. (*He pours himself a drink and leans on the front of his desk.*) But how is the world of fiction?

Reg Can't complain.

Ben Cheers. What have you got coming out at the moment?

Reg At the moment I'm doing two cookery books, an authoritative guide to bird-watching in Lincolnshire, the only intelligent account of the farce of El Alamein – by an NCO, needless to say – and a New Testament commentary.

Ben That's your fiction list?

Reg No, that's our list for next month.

Ben No novels at all then?

Reg Well, just one of those historical romances where the hero shoves his sword into assorted villains and his cock into assorted ladies. It won't get the reviews but it'll make us money.

Ben If he did it the other way around you might get both.

Reg (*laughs briefly*) But the point is, you see, by putting that one through we can afford to do something worthwhile later. For instance, I've just made a decision about a novel on National Service life.

Ben Oh, one of those. I thought that vogue was eight years dead.

Reg No, not one of those. This is something special, in my opinion. Of course, it mightn't interest you as you didn't do National Service, but personally I found it moving, witty, gracefully organised – genuinely poetic.

Ben The National Service? Good God! Those qualities are hard enough to come by in art. It's never occurred to me to look for them in life, especially as run by the armed forces. Cheers.

Reg Nevertheless I expect you *will* be curious in this case. Theoretically I can't tell you our author's name as the board doesn't meet until tomorrow, but if I just mention that he's a comprehensive school teacher – (*He raises his glass slowly.*) Cheers.

Ben (*after a pause*) Well, well. (*He sits in the armchair.*) The most boring man in London strikes again.

Reg I'm sorry.

Ben Why?

Reg It must be painful for you.

Ben Why?

Reg Because of his relationship with you. It was wrong of me to have mentioned it.

Ben On the contrary. It was the correct move. Has Joey read it?

Reg Not yet. It was offered to me in strict secrecy – at least until I'd made up my mind. But I can tell him about it now. I think he'll like it.

Ben That's because you don't know him very well, perhaps. He may be something of a dilettante in personal relationships, but he holds fast to standards on important matters. We once drew up a list of the five most tedious literary subjects in the world. National Service came fifth, just behind the Latin poems of Milton.

Reg Really? And what occupied the other three places?

Ben The English poems of Milton.

Reg When I was at Hull I chose Milton for my special subject.

Ben That sounds an excellent arrangement. The thing is to confine him to the North. Down here we can dally with Suckling and Lovelace.

Reg And Beatrix Potter? Joey says you've got great admiration for the middle-class nursery poets.

Ben With reservations. I find some of the novellae a trifle heavy going. (*A pause.*) I call Joey Appley Dappley, did you know?

Reg Do you?

Ben And he calls me Old Mr Prickle-pin. After

Old Mr Prickle-pin, with never a coat to
Put his pins in.

Sometimes I call him Diggory Diggory Delvet, when he's burrowing away at his book.

There is a pause.

Reg What did you mean by being took queer?

Ben (*coyly*) Oh, you know, I'm sure. (*Laughing.*) You do look shocked, Reg.

Reg That's surprising, because I'm not surprised even.

Ben You don't think there's anything shameful in it, then?

Reg In what?

Ben Dodging the draft.

Reg There are thousands of blokes from working-class homes who couldn't. They didn't know the tricks. Besides they'd rather have done ten years in uniform than get out of it that way.

Ben Then you think there's something shameful in being taken queer?

Reg I'm talking about people pretending to be what they're not.

Ben Not what?

Reg Not what they are.

Ben But if people do get taken queer, it's nature we must blame or their bodies, mustn't we? Medicine's still got a long way to go, Reg.

Reg Why do you use that word?

Ben What word?

Reg 'Queer'.

Ben Does it offend you?

Reg It's beginning to.

Ben Sorry. It's an old nursery habit. One of our chars used to say it. Whenever I came down with anything it would be, 'Our Ben's took queer again, poor little mite.' (*There is a silence.*) Although I can see it's a trifle inappropriate for a touch of TB –

Reg TB?

Ben They found it just in time. At my board medical, in fact. Why *do* you object to the phrase, though?

Reg No, no, it doesn't matter. A misunderstanding. I'm sorry.

Ben Oh, I *see. Queer!* – of course. Good God, you didn't think I'd sink quite so low, did you? (*Laughs.*)

Reg I'm sorry.

Ben It's all right. (*There is a pause.*) Cheers. (*He raises his glass.*)

77

Reg Cheers.

Another pause.

Ben Homosexual.

Another pause.

Reg What?

Ben Homosexual. I was just wondering – should one say that instead of 'queer' – in your sense of the word. Homosexual.

Reg It doesn't really matter at all. I don't really care –

Ben Do you feel the same about 'fairies' as you do about 'queers'?

Reg Yes, in point of fact. Since you ask.

Ben Right, I've got that. (*He gets up and moves towards Reg.*) Of course they've almost vanished anyway, the old-style queens and queers, the poofs, the fairies. The very words seem to conjure up a magical world of naughty thrills, forbidden fruits – sorry – you know, I always used to enjoy them enjoying themselves. Their varied performances contributed to my life's varieties. But now the law, in making them safe, has made them drab. Just like the heterosexual rest of us. Poor sods. (*Little pause.*) Don't you think?

Reg (*stands up and puts his glass on the desk*) Oh, there's enough affectation and bitchiness in heterosexuals to be getting on with. (*He glances at his watch.*) Don't you think?

Ben Oh, don't worry. He'll be here in a minute. (*Pause.*) How are things between you two, by the way?

Reg What things?

Ben No complications?

Reg What kind of complications would there be?

Ben In that our routine doesn't interfere with your – plural meaning – routine.

Reg Plural meaning? Meaning what?

Ben Yours and his. Your routines together.

Reg Ah. Well, it has done, frankly, yes. Now you ask. But I don't think it will from now on.

Ben (*sits on the hard chair opposite Reg*) Then you're beginning to get the hang of it? Good. Because sometimes I've suspected that our friendship – going back so far and including so much – so much of his history and so much of my history which has really become *our* history – singular meaning this time – must make it difficult for any new people we pick up on the side.

Reg Like your wife, do you mean?

Ben Well done. Yes, like poor old Anne. She must have felt her share amounted to a minor infidelity, really. I speak metaphorically, of course, but then I suppose marriage is the best metaphor for all our intense relationships. Except those we have with our husbands and wives. (*Laughs.*) Naturally.

Reg So you think of yourself as married to Joey, do you?

Ben Metaphorically.

A pause. The telephone rings. Ben picks it up.

Butley, English. Oh, hello, James – no, I'm afraid I still can't talk properly. I'm in the middle of a tutorial. (*He winks at Reg.*) OK. Yes. Goodbye.

Reg What metaphor would you use when you learned that Joey was going to move in with someone else? Would that be divorce, metaphorically?

Ben (*after a long pause*) What?

Reg (*laughs*) Sorry. I shouldn't do that. But I was thinking that it must be odd getting news of two divorces in the same day.

Ben (*pause*) Joey hasn't said anything.

Reg No. I'm giving the news. You might say that when he comes to me our Joey will be moving out of figures of speech into matters of fact. Ours will be too much like a marriage to be a metaphor.

Ben (*little pause*) I thought you didn't admit to being – what? – different?

Reg There are moments when frankness is necessary. No, our Joey's just been waiting for the right queen, fruit, fairy, poof or homosexual to come along. He's come.

Ben (*after a pause*) Well, isn't he lucky?

Reg Time will tell. I hope so. But I'm tired of waiting to make a proper start with him. I'm tired of waiting for him to tell you. You know our Joey – a bit gutless. No, the truth of the matter is, I've been trying to get Joey to bring you around to dinner one evening and tell you straight, so we could get it over with. I knew he'd never find the nerve to do it on his lonesome. But he's kept dodging about, pretending you were busy, one excuse after another. It's worked out quite well, though, hasn't it?

The door opens. Joey comes in. Sees Reg.

Hello. We've just been sorting things out. Ben and I.

Ben (*to Joey*) Cheers.

Joey stands staring from one to the other.

Yes, our Reg has just been giving me the second instalment of the day's news. But then traditionally, because metaphorically, I should be the last to hear.

Joey (*after a pause*) I wanted to tell you myself.

Ben Wanted to, did you? And were you looking forward to a subsequent scene?

Joey No.

Ben How unlike each other we are. I would have enjoyed it.

Reg (*after a pause*) How did your lecture go?

Joey All right.

Reg Grand. Any more teaching today?

Joey No.

Reg Come on then. (*He moves over to Joey.*) Let's go move your things.

Joey No, I can't, until later.

Reg Why not?

Joey Because there's something I've got to do. (*He glances at Ben.*)

Ben Oh, don't stay on my account.

Joey No. It's something I promised Edna I'd –

Reg Oh. Well, have you got time for a cup of tea?

Joey Yes.

They move towards the door.

Ben Reg.

Reg turns.

Are you coming back after tea?

Reg (*looks at Joey*) I don't see any reason to. Why?

Ben I think you're pretty bloody good, Reg. In your way. It's not my way, but it seems to get you what you want.

Reg So far. But thanks.

Ben goes across to the carrier bag, scrambles in it, comes back with a package, hands it to Reg. Reg takes it.

What's this? (*opening the package*)

Ben My kidneys. Best English lamb.

Reg You've been done. They're New Zealand, thawed.

Ben The small, dapper irony is that I've been trying to join you for supper all day – not to say for the last month. May I anyway?

Joey Of course.

Reg I'm sorry. We can't.

Joey Why not?

Reg Because I've just bought two tickets for the match tonight. From one of your porters. (*To Ben.*) I'm sorry. Perhaps some other time.

He passes the bag of kidneys to Joey, who passes them to Ben.

Ben Thank you. (*He drops the kidneys on his desk.*)

Joey Do we have to go to the match?

Reg Yes. It's an important one. (*To Ben.*) But some other time. Now I'd like that tea, please.

Joey looks at him and leads the way to the door.

Ben (*watches them*) Reg!

Reg turns.

I didn't know you supported a London club too, Reg? (*He picks up the whisky bottle.*)

Reg Leeds are away to Arsenal.

Ben Ah. Well, enjoy it.

Reg Thanks. (*He turns to the door.*)

Ben Reg. (*Reg turns again.*) Will you wear it all, then?

Reg Sorry? What? Wear what?

Ben Your gear and tackle and trim. Have you got it with you?

Reg What? (*Puzzled, he looks at Joey.*)

Ben Your scarf and cloth cap and rattle. Your rosettes and hobnail boots. Isn't that your road, any road, up your road?

Reg I'm parched. Can we compare customs some other time? (*He turns.*)

Ben Reg!

As Reg seems to go on.

Reg!

Reg steps back in.

No, it's not customs, Reg, it's you, old cheese. Personally I don't give a fuck that moom and dud live oop Leeds and all, or that the whole tribe of you go to football matches looking like the back page of the *Daily Mirror* and bellow 'Ooop ta Rovers' and 'Clobber busturds' or own a butcher's shop with cush on ta side from parking tickets.

Joey laughs – Reg sees him.

I really don't, old cheese. No, what's culturally entertaining is yourself. I'm talking about your hypocrisy, old darling.

Reg Is that what you're talking about?

Ben (*making a circle round Joey's desk through the speech*) Because you're only good at getting what you want because you're a fraction of a fake, old potato, you really are. You don't show yourself north except twice a year with your latest boy or sommat in tow, do you? And I bet you get all your football out of ta *Guardian* and television except when you flash a couple of tickets at some soft southern bugger – do you object to that word, old fruit? – like me, to show some softer southern bugger like him – (*gestures at Joey*) how tough you are. Did you cling consciously on to funny vowels, or did you learn them all afresh? I ask, because you're not Yorkshire, you're not working class, you're just a lucky parvenu fairy, old fig, and to tell you the truth you make me want to throw up. Pardon, ooop! All over your characteristically suede shoes.

Joey (*shuts the door*) Shut up, Ben!

Ben (*walking round Reg*) Why, have I upset him? What's the matter, Reg? I thought you liked plain talk and straightforward blokes, brass tacks, hard dos and no bloody metaphors. *I* don't blame you for being ashamed of ta folks, except when you want to come the simple sod – sorry, homo – sorry, bloke. I'd feel ta same in thy clogs.

Joey Ben!

Reg Anything else?

Ben Yes, tell me. (*Comes back to confront him.*) Have you had plain talk and brass tacks about thyself with

moom, when she's back from pasting tickets on cars,
lud, eh, or with dud while he's flogging offal, lud?
Thou'd get fair dos all right then, wouldn't thee? From
our dud with his strup? Or would he take thee down to
local and introduce thee round to all t'oother cloth caps?
'This is our Reg. He's punsy. Ooop, pardon, Reg lud.
Omosexual. Noo, coom as right surprise to moother und
me, thut it did, moother joost frying oop best tripe and
garbuge and me settling down with gnomes to a good
read of Mazo de la Roche.'

*He laughs in Reg's face. There is a pause. Then Joey
makes a spluttering sound, as with laughter.*

Reg (*turns, looks at Joey*) Oh, I see. The information for
all this drollery comes from you. Perhaps you'd better
sort him out. (*He walks back to the door.*)

Ben Reg! Coom 'ere, lad! You coom and sort me out.
Coom on, lud, it's mun's work!

Reg stops, walks slowly towards Ben.

Cloomp, cloomp, cloomp, aye, tha's they moother's feet,
Reg!

*Joey lets out another gasp. There is a silence, Reg
standing in front of Ben.*

Reg I don't like these games, Joey. You know that.

Joey (*spluttering*) I'm sorry, I didn't mean . . .

Ben Going to cook my kidneys after all then?

Reg Is that what you want?

Ben Ah coom on –

Reg No, I'm not playing with you. So don't say one
more word, eh? Not a word. (*He turns to go.*)

Ben (*steels himself*) Ah Reg, lud –

Reg turns around.

Coom on then.

Joey Ben!

Ben Owd sod, feery, punsy –

Reg hits Ben in the stomach, not very hard – he falls to the ground.

Joey Don't!

There is a silence, then a shape at the door.

Reg There. Is that what you wanted?

Edna knocks, puts her head in.

Edna Oh sorry.

Ben Living theatre. Next time around in Polish.

Edna Oh. (*to Reg*) I'll come back later. (*She goes out.*)

Ben For a kick at my balls. Why should she be left out?

Reg (*calmly*) But you're pitiful, pitiful. This man you've given me all the talk about. That you made me jealous of. (*He turns, goes to the door.*)

Ben Still, couldn't take it, could you, butcher's boy!

Reg (*to Joey*) It was silly. You'll have to outgrow that kind of thing, Joey.

He smiles at Ben, and goes out, closing the door quietly. There is a long moment. Then Ben goes and leans on the edge of the desk, smiles at Joey.

Ben (*touches his chin*) Your bugger's made me bleed again. (*Laughs.*) You're beginning to get little wrinkles around your eyes. Are they laughter wrinkles, or is it age creeping up you, on little crow's feet? (*Pause.*) You'll be one of those with a crêpe neck, I'll be one of the fat ones with a purple face, Reg will be . . . (*Pause.*) I was watching you while you were shaving the morning you were going to Leeds. If you'd moved your eyes half an inch you'd have seen me in the mirror. I was standing behind you studying your neck and my jowls.

Joey I saw you.

Ben Ah! Well, what did you think of all that, with our Reg, eh?

Joey I thought it was creepy.

Ben I wonder what your next will be like? Don't be afraid to bring him home, dear, will you? (*genteel*) I do worry so.

Joey There isn't going to be a next one. At least, not for some time.

Ben Ho, reely? I think that's a good plan, h'abstinence makes the 'eart grow fonder. (*He sits on the desk.*)

Joey I'm moving in with Reg.

Ben (*after a pause*) I don't think he'll have you, dear, after your indiscretions and sauciness.

Joey Yes he will.

Ben You'll go running after him, will you? How demeaning!

Joey Possibly. But it's better than having him run after me. I've been through that once, I couldn't face it again.

Ben You love him then, your butcher's boy?

Joey Actually, he's not a butcher's boy, in point of fact. (*He picks up his briefcase and returns to his desk. Little*

87

pause.) His father teaches maths at the university. His mother's a social worker. They live in an ugly Edwardian house . . .

Ben (*after a pause, nods*) Of course. Quite nice and creepy. Creepy, creepy, creepy, creepy!

Joey I'm sorry.

Ben Well, thank you anyway for the fiction. (*He sits on the hard chair by his desk. There is a pause.*) So you love him then?

Joey No. But I've got to get away from you, haven't I?

Ben Really? Why?

Joey (*sits at desk*) For one thing, I'd like to get some work done. During your married year I did quite a bit. I'd like to finish it.

Ben What?

Joey My edition of Herrick.

Ben If the consequence of your sexual appetites is another edition of unwanted verse then you have an academic duty to control yourself. Could I also mention, in a spirit of unbecoming humility, that if I hadn't taken over your studies when you were an averagely dim undergraduate, you'd never have got a first. Your nature is to settle for decent seconds – indecent seconds, in Reg's case.

Joey I know. But those were in the days when you still taught. Now you spread futility, Ben. It creeps in, like your dirty socks do, into my drawers. Or my clean ones, onto your feet. Or your cigarette butts everywhere. Or your stubble and shaving cream into our razor. Or your voice, booming out nursery rhymes into every corner of this department, it seems to me. Or your –

Ben Shut up! That's rehearsed.

Joey Thousands of times.

* [**Ben** (*after a pause*) He's going to get it published for you, isn't he?

Joey (*shrugs, after a pause*) Yes. He said he'd help.

Ben (*laughs*) And Appley Dappley has sharp little eyes. And Appley Dappley's so fond of pies.

Joey I can't help it. It's the only way I'll get ahead.

Ben Into what? There's nothing left for you to get ahead in, it's all in the past, and that thins out as the years go by. You'll end up like Edna, sending out Dean's Reports on any student you haven't killed off, and extinguishing a poet or two in the library. While it all rots away around you.

Joey Perhaps it won't rot away if – (*Pauses.*) I'd rather end up like Edna than like you. Once you talked to me of literature as the voice of civilisation, what was it, the dead have living voices –

Ben I hope not. I may have quoted . . .

the communication
Of the dead is tongued with fire beyond the language
    of the living.

I can still quote it when the moment's right.

---

* The passage in brackets was cut from the production the night before we opened. I am reinstating it because it now seems to me a passage that, whether it should be played in performance or not, conveys a great deal of useful information about Butley's relationship with Joey and about his sexual nature. In the first performance and all subsequent productions, this passage was replaced by the following stage direction:

A long pause – during which Ben goes to his desk chair and sits – the whisky bottle in his hand.

Joey And when will it be right again? It hasn't been with me since your marriage – since before it, really. It's been Beatrix Potter and passages and pastiches from Eliot . . .

Ben I adjust my selection to the context. Why did you move back into the flat with me, then?

Joey Habit, I suppose. I'm fairly feeble, as both you and Reg point out to me. I don't like being alone, and I couldn't resist – I was actually quite pleased when your marriage broke down.

Ben That's called friendship. (*Laughs.*)

Joey You should have stuck it out. With Anne.

Ben Should I?

Joey But at least you slept with her. You sleep with women –

Ben Not when I can help it. Mankind cannot stand too much reality. I prefer friendship.

Joey But it's the sort of friendship people used to have with me at school. Abuse, jokes, games . . .

Ben It's only a language, as good as any other and better than some, for affection.

Joey But I've got these wrinkles around my eyes, and my neck will crêpe, just as you said. And you're fattening and thirty-five, just as you said, and we don't belong in a school or nursery any more. Reg is right. We're pitiful. We're pitiful together.

Ben We're all pitiful, together or apart. The thing is to be pitiful with the right person, keep it from everybody else. And from yourselves whenever you can.

Joey Well then – well then – I can't keep it from myself any longer. I've been trying to keep you and Reg apart

because I knew this would happen. But I've been longing
for it, all the same. (*Pause.*)]

I'm sorry it had to be today, what with Anne and Tom.
I would have waited . . .

Ben (*in senile professional tones*) Which shows you have
no sense of classical form. We're preserving the unities.
The use of messengers has been quite skilful. (*Pause.*) All
right. All right. It doesn't really matter very much.

Joey What will you do?

Ben (*after a pause*) Could you, do you think, staunch
the flow of blood? (*He lifts his chin back.*)

Joey (*comes over reluctantly, takes the piece of cotton
wool Ben holds out to him*) It's just a bubble. (*He
hesitates, then bends forward with the cotton wool.*)

Ben The trouble with – all these confessions, revelations,
clean breaks and epiphanies – shouldn't we call them
these days? – is that – cluttered contact goes on. For
instance, we still share this room. (*as Joey steps away*)
You're going to have to live with your past, day after
day and as messily as ever. I'll see to that.

Edna (*knocks, opens the door, smiles*) May I?

Ben Of course. (*Laughs.*) Of course you may, Edna. It's
your turn.

Edna Now you'll really be able to spread yourself. It's
much more sensible. (*To Joey.*) I've moved out all my
files. What can I do now?

*A pause – Ben sinks into the chair in realisation of the
news.*

Joey I can manage down here. (*He moves away, goes to
the shelves, takes down his books.*)

Edna I'm glad I made one of you take advantage.

Joey goes out with a load of books.

I've quietened down, Ben, you'll be glad to hear. But I'd like to say I'm sorry about my – my little outburst just now. I must learn not to be so sensitive. I suspect it's the only way, with this new generation.

Ben They are rather frightening.

Edna Oh, I don't imagine you're frightened of them.

Ben I haven't enough pride. I shall continue to throw myself on their mercy. (*He goes to Joey's shelves – takes down a pile of books and puts them on the desk.*)

Edna They weren't very merciful to Aristotle in the Senate House.

Ben He had too many advantages. They couldn't be expected to tolerate that.

Edna (*laughs*) Well . . .

Ben (*watches her*) I haven't congratulated you on your book.

Edna Wouldn't it have been awful if someone had got in ahead of me? Twenty years – I'm really rather ashamed.

Ben Will you go on to someone else now?

Edna I don't know. (*She sits on the hard chair by Ben's desk.*) You know, last night I played a little game – I closed my eyes and turned over groups of pages at a time – and then I looked at a page. It was in the commentary on a letter from his sad wife. And I remembered immediately when I started working on it. It was in Ursula's cottage in Ockham, Surrey. I was still working on it when the summer term of the following year was over. I finished it during my first week back at Ursula's.

I can even remember the weather – how's the book on Eliot, by the way?

Ben It has a good twenty years to go.

Edna I'm sure that's not true. James is always saying that you get through things so quickly. I'm sure you'll be finished with Eliot in no time. Anyway, don't dally with him. Let me be a lesson to you –

Ben (*watching her*) Do you still go to Ursula's cottage?

Edna Oh, not in the same way. Ursula got married during chapter six. (*She laughs and goes to the door, stops.*) Oh hello. No, don't run away. (*She puts her head back in.*) Mr Gardner's here.

Ben Oh! Right.

Edna Will you go in, Mr Gardner?

She goes out. Gardner comes in. He is wearing a hat with feathers in it, a white Indian shirt, sandals, no socks.

Ben (*stares blankly ahead, then looks at him*) Well, Mr Gardner – you're here for your Eliot.

Gardner Yes, please.

Ben Tell me, what *did* I say in the pub?

Gardner Well, I told you I couldn't stand Miss Shaft's seminars and you told me I was interesting enough to do Eliot, and that I ought to go and see James. You said he'd pass the buck back to you because whenever he had a problem he converted it straight into a buck and passed it. Actually, you called him Cottontail.

Ben Did I? (*After a pause, he smiles.*) And here we both wonderfully are.

Gardner Yes. (*Smiles.*) Thank God.

Ben Well, let's get going. (*He goes to the shelf, gets a copy of Eliot, brings it back.*) Can you start by reading me a passage, please? Don't worry if you can't understand it yet. (*He hands him the book, open.*) There. Do you mind?

Gardner No, I'd like that. (*He sits on the hard chair by Ben's desk.*)

Joey (*comes in*) Oh, sorry. (*He goes to his desk and begins to pack the contents of the drawers.*)

Ben This is Mr Gardner, celebrated so far for his hat. Do you like it?

Joey Of its style.

Ben Once – some years ago – I taught Mr Keyston. During our first tutorial we spent a few minutes discussing his clothes. Then he read me some Eliot. Today I'm actually wearing his socks. Those are the key points in a relationship that now goes mainly back.

Joey (*opening drawers*) So you see, Mr Gardner, you'd better be careful. If you value your socks.

Gardner looks at his feet: he is not wearing socks. Ben and Joey look at Gardner's feet, then Joey goes on putting papers into his briefcase.

Ben Please begin.

Gardner (*reads*)
                    'In that open field.
    If you do not come too close, if you do not come
        too close,
    On a summer midnight, you can hear the music
    Of the weak pipe and the little drum
    And see them dancing around the bonfire
    The association of man and woman

In daunsinge, signifying matrimonie –
A dignified and commodious sacrament.

Joey, finished clearing, looks at Gardner.

Two and two, necessarye coniunction,
Holding eche other by the hand or the arm
Whiche betokeneth concorde. Round and round the fire

*Joey looks towards Ben, they exchange glances, then
Ben looks away. Joey goes out, closing the door gently.*

Leaping through the flames, or joined in circles,
Rustically solemn or in rustic laughter
Lifting heavy feet in clumsy shoes,
Earth feet, loam feet, lifted in country mirth
Mirth of those long since – '

Ben So you're Gardner, are you?

Gardner (*stops, looks at him in surprise, smiles*) Yes.

Ben
Ninny Nanny Netticoat,
In a white petticoat,
With a red nose –
The longer he stands,
The shorter he grows.

Gardner What?

Ben I'm moving on, Mr Gardner. I'm breaking new
ground.

Gardner Oh. (*He laughs.*)

Ben Furthermore, I hate your hat.

Gardner I'm sorry.

Ben Did you wear it when you bombed the Velium
Aristotle? And are you going to wear it for your raids on
Dappley and *Parsley*, eh?

Gardner What?

Ben It won't do you any good. Aristotle in his Velium stood alone, vulnerable, unreadable and so unread. But *Dappley* and *Parsley* are scattered in nursery consciousnesses throughout the land. They can still be tongued with fire.

Gardner What are you talking about? – I wasn't anywhere near the Senate House when that happened. I don't even know what it was about, properly.

Ben No, you're a personal relationships type of chappie, I can sense that. Please go away. Go back to Miss Shaft.

Gardner What? But I can't – after all that trouble –

Ben Trouble for you, fun for me. Go away, Gardner, and take your plumage with you, I don't want to start again. It's all been a ghastly mistake. I don't find you interesting, any more. You're not what I mean at all, not what I mean at all. I'm too old to play with the likes of you.

> *Gardner puts the Eliot down, goes out. Ben puts the book back, sits at the desk, turns off the desk lamp and tries feebly three times to turn it on again.*
> *Curtain.*

WISE CHILD

Wise Child was first performed at Wyndham's Theatre, London, on 10 October 1967. The cast was as follows:

Mrs Artminster Alec Guinness
Mr Booker Gordon Jackson
Jerry Simon Ward
Janice Cleo Sylvestre

Director John Dexter
Designer Motley
Lighting Richard Pilbrow

Characters

Mrs Artminster

Mr Booker

Jerry

Janice

Act One

Interconnecting rooms in a hotel. The one left of stage (facing) is small, with a single bed, a large cupboard, a hard-backed chair, a heavy lamp on the bedside table. The one right of stage is large, with a double bed, a handbasin, an armchair, a large cupboard.

Mrs Artminster enters the large room, hurriedly. She is stout, tall, dressed in a fur coat, has a small hat perched on top of her head, the rim of which comes over her forehead, a veil hanging from it. She is in her fifties. A small cluster of rinsed blue curls is visible, also heavy make-up. She is burrowing into a large handbag, with a zip. She takes out a quarter of a bottle of Scotch. Begins to uncork it when a door bangs offstage, and there are feet in the hall. Jerry comes into the other room, and Mrs Artminster thrusts the bottle into her coat pocket. Jerry is slight, very pretty, with his blond hair cut short. He looks about seventeen. He takes something out of his long raincoat pocket, throws it on the bed, takes off his raincoat, throws it over the chair, goes towards the connecting door, when the door bangs again offstage. He freezes, then tiptoes to the connecting door. There is a knock on his door and he opens the connecting door softly, enters with a finger to his lips. Mrs Artminster has been taking off her coat and folding it so that the pocket is out of sight, over the armchair. She turns with theatrical innocence as Jerry enters, begins to say something, sees his signal and stops. He clicks the door shut. There is another knock on his door, which then opens. Mr Booker looks in.

*Mr Booker is about forty, plump, about the same build
as Mrs Artminster and the same height. He wears
spectacles, moves slowly as if afraid of knocking into
things. His spectacles are bifocals. He looks around the
room, several times, withdraws his head. Then puts it
back in. Looks at the object Jerry has thrown onto the
bed, and advances towards it. He trips against the chair,
nearly knocks it over, turns around in a panic, and goes
out. Jerry, who has been standing by the connecting
door, listening, then opens the door and slips in, just as
there is a knock on Mrs Artminster's door. He sees the
object on the bed (which is a wig) hurries over and stuffs
it under the pillow.*

Mrs Artminster Come.

Mr Booker I'm just popping my head in to wonder how
you are this evening, Mrs Artminster.

Mrs Artminster Still turning dizzy and faint now and
then, I'm afraid to say, Mr Booker.

Mr Booker Oh, I'm sorry to hear that. (*Little pause,
stares at her.*) But you've been out, I see.

Mrs Artminster Yes, I did try a few steps down the
street, until I was overcome.

Mr Booker Oh. Well, perhaps tomorrow you'll feel
stronger and more like it. (*Little pause.*) Well.
(*Withdraws head, puts it back in.*) I didn't see you go by
my office, by the by.

   Long pause. They stare at each other.

I must be getting lax. I'm usually in the habit of keeping
an eye out for passing guests, even when there aren't any.
(*Little pause. Withdraws with a laugh, puts his head
back in.*) Has Garfield come in yet, by the by?

Mrs Artminster No, unless he's snatching a little doze. He may be very tired.

Mr Booker Been up to Little Munstering again, has he? I hope they're not giving him trouble. It's hard for a boy to control workmen, judging by my own experiences of the last month.

Stares at Mrs Artminster. She makes no reply.

Well, perhaps I'll see him later on, if I pop up later, if I may?

Mrs Artminster Oh yes. That would be agreeable.

Mr Booker If I'm not intruding, that is?

Mrs Artminster No.

Mr Booker Well . . . (*Smiles, goes out.*)

Throughout all this Jerry has been standing by the door of his room, listening. When the door shuts he tiptoes into Mrs Artminster's room. She begins to speak. He raises a hand and she stops. There is a knock on his door, and Mr Booker puts his head in again. Looks around, looks at the bed, goes over to it, stares at it puzzled. Puts his hand on the pillow, then goes out. Mrs Artminster and Jerry stand facing each other, then, when the door closes in the hall, Jerry crosses the room and sits down on the bed.

Jerry So you went out then?

Mrs Artminster Yes, I did. Think I can spend the whole day in here, nodding and chattering to myself like one of your Dutch harlots?

Jerry Where did you go?

Mrs Artminster Never you mind. (*Little pause.*) I went out, that's where.

Crosses to the bed and sits down, back to Jerry, who is staring straight ahead of him. She turns and looks at him, shrugs, turns away.

But it wasn't far because my dogs are barking, I can tell you. (*Takes off a shoe, sighs.*)

Jerry (*viciously*) Ooooh! Do you mind! They make my stomach jump!

Mrs Artminster What's the matter, dear, you can't stand your old mum natural you should have left her where you found her, shouldn't you? (*Takes off other shoe, massages foot, puts shoe back on.*) He's a bit – (*Tweaks her ears.*) Our Simon B. is, the way he's up after you every evening like a weasel for his rabbit.

Jerry He makes me sick.

Mrs Artminster Yes, and who doesn't make you sick? Your old mum with her feet, Simon Booker with his smiles and helpfulness, the poor nigger Janice you sneer at too – you get above yourself, Jer, that's your problem. Not everyone finds you a sweet little tease. I don't, for one, and Derek doesn't for another, and that's two that count.

Jerry Derek, he doesn't count, not as far as I'm concerned.

Mrs Artminster Well, Simon Booker does. You keep dodging him and denying him and he'll be demanding the rent and throwing us out. (*Little pause, chuckles.*) He's a good man, and don't you forget it. There's not everyone would take us in just because I fainted in his lounge from shock and you begged him on your tiny knees. He's got the right to put us out on the pavement with a boot in each arse and don't you forget that either.

Jerry I'm not worried about him.

Mrs Artminster Well I am, Jer, it's me that's got to stay in here facing him while you dart in and out. He nearly said again about no guests officially until next week, I could see it from the way he was working his mouth, and he smells something's wrong, I could see it in his eyes.

Jerry Eyes! He hasn't got any eyes! That's double glass in those spectacles of his, he can't see far enough to blink at it.

Mrs Artminster He can see you all right, oh, I've watched his features light up at your mere voice. He hasn't heard it raised like I have, in spite. The soft-hearted don't like being deceived, Jerry. It kills the goodness in them.

Jerry Yes, well, you're right about him smelling something wrong, you make sure you stand three feet from him, or why don't you have a wash? The convenience's laid on. (*Indicates the washstand.*) You turn that knob and hot stuff comes out, called water.

Mrs Artminster Shut your mouth, I've had enough.

Gets up and picks up her coat from the chair. The quarter-bottle half slips out; she tries to thrust it back casually, her back to Jerry. He watches her.

Jerry I can see you.

Mrs Artminster What? What can you see?

Jerry You know what I can see.

Mrs Artminster None of your business, what you can see.

Jerry Yes, it is my business what I can see. (*Gets up, goes over, stands in front of Mrs Artminster with his hand out.*)

Mrs Artminster I don't care what you can see, you're not having it.

Jerry Yes I am, Mum. (*In a sinister voice.*) Nine counties, Mum.

> *Mrs Artminster turns, stares at him, then slaps the bottle into his hand, crosses to the bed, sits down. Folds arms. Jerry stares at her, she unfolds arms, strikes her knee savagely, then refolds arms.*

And where did it come from? (*Long pause.*) You stole it. (*Long pause.*) Where did you steal it from? (*Pause.*) Not from – not from Booker! You – you stupid old bitch.

Mrs Artminster He won't miss it. He wasn't in his office, he was peering down the street looking for we know who. (*Pause.*) He doesn't know it was there, it was in the back of his cupboard, I just plunged my hand in and that's what it wrapped itself around, so whose fault is that? (*Pause.*) There was bottles on bottles of it.

Jerry He'll miss it all right.

Mrs Artminster No he won't. And what if he does? There's always the nigger to blame it on. Niggers are thieves aren't they? (*Pause.*) Anyway, he can't stand the sight of her.

Jerry How do you know?

Mrs Artminster He likes you, doesn't he?

> *They stare at each other. Then Jerry throws the bottle on the bed and goes and sits down. He puts his head in his hands. Mrs Artminster looks at him tauntingly.*

Derek would have understood.

Jerry (*viciously*) Derek isn't here, is he? (*Looks at her.*) You've still got gravy on your blouse from yesterday, what's the use my telling you to sponge it off?

Mrs Artminster Yes, the mention of Derek always brings

the poison out in you. Just because Derek was a man you can't stand him.

Jerry leaps to his feet. They stand staring at each other, Mrs Artminster tauntingly, Jerry in a rage.

Jerry (*after a pause*) I didn't hear that, lucky for you.

Looks at Mrs Artminster, then goes into his room, takes a quarter of a bottle of Scotch from his jacket pocket, comes back.

Here you are. (*Gives it to Mrs Artminster.*) I was looking forward to giving it and now you've spoilt it.

Mrs Artminster Thank you, Jerry.

Jerry (*in a martyred voice*) But you don't want it now, do you?

Mrs Artminster Don't want it? Oh, I want it all right. Course I do.

Jerry But not like you would have if you hadn't stolen yourself one of your own.

Mrs Artminster (*after a pause*) I'll tell you what, Jer, you take this one and keep it for me – (*gives own bottle*) and I'll start in on this one, and you can give me the other one when I need it.

Jerry It's not the same.

Mrs Artminster No, it's better. It's two presents instead of one. (*Pause.*) Thank you, Jerry.

Jerry (*after a pause*) That's all right.

Mrs Artminster takes a swig. Jerry gets up and goes out to the washstand, comes back with a glass. Gives it to Mrs Artminster. Smiles, then sits down beside her.

Mrs Artminster Jerry.

Jerry What, Mum? (*This has to be said half ironically, half tenderly.*)

Mrs Artminster Guess what?

Jerry What?

Mrs Artminster I saw in Simon B.'s office.

Jerry What?

Mrs Artminster I'm just telling you this, Jerry, I'm not saying anything. (*Long pause.*)

Jerry Well, what?

Mrs Artminster There's a safe in there, Jerry.

Jerry doesn't answer.

Well?

Jerry Well, what?

Pause, turns and stares at her.

Mrs Artminster You all over. If I had my Derek along – a quick in, a swing of the jogger if Booker was fool enough to be hanging around, and out. That's the way Derek does things.

Jerry Not any more he doesn't. Derek doesn't, does he? Not any more, Derek doesn't. So don't Derek me, you know it makes me sick to hear his name repeated without mercy. It's *me* that keeps you free. Me. Not Derek.

Mrs Artminster Free! You call this free! The only ideas that run in your head are to keep me in confinement, oh, you enjoy yourself at my expense.

Jerry Well, I'll tell you one thing, I wouldn't talk if I was taken. I'd lay all the blame on my own head, I wouldn't

have you hunted across England. Would I? Would I?
(*Glares at her.*)

Mrs Artminster (*after a pause*) No, Jerry, you wouldn't.
I know that.

Jerry And Derek – what is Derek? Big teeth and fat,
that's what Derek is. Isn't he?

Mrs Artminster There's no denying he's big built.

Jerry Fat, you mean. Don't you?

Mrs Artminster He likes his food, and where's the harm
of that?

Jerry It's no good his liking his food where he is, is it?
Because there's only slops and hard bread, isn't there?

Mrs Artminster That's what you tell me, Jerry, yes.

Jerry And you like your food too, don't you?

Mrs Artminster I'm only human, Jerry.

Jerry So you're better off where you are, aren't you?
(*Long pause.*) Aren't you?

Mrs Artminster I expect I am, Jerry, yes, as you say so.

Jerry And Derek's no good to you, is he? He never was,
was he? I'm the one you need, aren't I?

Mrs Artminster (*after a long pause*) Yes, you're the one
I need, Jer. Ever since you brought yourself to me with
your golden hair and cheeky smile I knew you for the
one. (*Sarcastically.*)

> *Jerry gets up, walks around the room, slapping his
> hand against his thigh. Then he goes out, into his own
> room. Mrs Artminster takes a long swig of whisky,
> braces herself. Stares at the door. Jerry comes back in.*

Jerry I got that feeling when I was out this afternoon.

Mrs Artminster (*carefully*) Did you, Jerry, what feeling?

Jerry (*pathetically*) You know.

Mrs Artminster Where your bones are china, and people are going to knock into you and you'll turn to powder.

Jerry Glass, and it's not me they'll break, it's my bones.

Mrs Artminster Well, Jer, as long as you're all right, what do your bones matter then?

Jerry But my bones cut me up from the inside. *My own bones.* Every way I move I slice a bit more out of myself. That's the worst feeling. China doesn't cut you up like that.

Mrs Artminster What you need is a bit of fun, Jerry, to take you out of yourself. You've got no feeling of fun.

Jerry (*shaking his head, paying no attention*) Yes, and supposing it gets worse even? Because it doesn't matter what you know, it's what you are. I know my bones aren't made of glass, I know that.

Mrs Artminster That's right, they're not. They're made of bone, dear.

Jerry But they'll cut me if I break up. I know that, don't I? *That's* why I've got to move delicate, because of what I know *could* happen. It doesn't make any difference, it's all the same, what the doctors and magazines say. Have you noticed me when I'm moving delicate, Mum?

Mrs Artminster (*after a pause, looks away from him*) Yes, I have, Jer, and it's very ugly. You walk about me like spiders, I thought it was because you'd got corns.

Jerry No, it's because of my glass bones, which I am, Mum, I am.

Mrs Artminster Corns are worse, dear, they're there and wishful thinking won't get rid of them. High heels bring *them* up.

Jerry Yes, and then one day there's someone coming at me, because of the risks I take, and what do I do? I couldn't hit him, could I, I'd just be tearing myself open from inside, and what if I fell? What if I fell, Mum?

Clutches Mrs Artminster.

Mrs Artminster Derek doesn't have dreams like that, Jerry –

As Jerry stirs angrily:

Yes, I know – but I've got to say his name, Derek doesn't have dreams like that. He sleeps at night, because he knows when he wakes up in the morning nobody's going to wonder at him. And if they do he shows an arm. It's people looking at you you can't stand, Jer, and you can't stand it because you can't look back at them from as good as they are thank you very much whoever you are. You keep a watch instead, and it's like my heart was tethered the way you keep it on me. (*Long pause.*) Was it my fault? Tell me the truth, was it my fault? No, one blow from Derek's jogger, he disabled himself that postman did, falling like a cripple in the wrong places. Is that justice? Is that what you expect? Derek was an expert, and don't you forget it, no, Jer –

As Jerry walks impatiently about:

You listen to my piece until I've done. You nagging and nine countiesing me, you think of Derek and what he was and still is if I know Derek, and then you think of those glass bones you talk about. Yes. (*Long pause.*) Oh Jerry. Jerry. Last month you was dreaming of being an eagle, why can't you go back to that? (*Long pause.*) Yes, an eagle it was, Jerry, in Staines. Then Slough, Hitchin, Baldock, it changed itself to glass bones. Reading, glass bones and cut up from the inside. What next? (*Pause.*) That's why I say, find us a Little Munstering and lie quiet. (*Long pause.*) Why don't you want a girlfriend, that's what I want to know? (*Long pause.*) You tell me that, boy?

Jerry Twits.

Mrs Artminster What?

Jerry Twits. I said they're twits.

Mrs Artminster That's not the word. (*Pause.*) Oh, Jerry, Jerry, Derek was everywhere with his muscle at your age, he couldn't help himself. He built himself up with practice. He was small and dainty when he was young, but he didn't despise muscle. (*Pause.*) And he'd have their skirts up and their panties down as soon as look at them.

Jerry He was taken on top of one, wasn't he? The police hammering at the door and smashing the windows to get him, and he just lay there, eyes glazed and grinning his pegs out all over his fat face, if I know Derek.

Mrs Artminster *You* don't know Derek. (*Laughs.*) You don't know Derek. (*Laughs again.*) Who do you know? You know what they say, Jerry?

Jerry What? What do they say?

Mrs Artminster It's a wise boy that knows its own, Jerry. That's what.

Jerry (*after a pause*) Well, I know my own mum all right, don't I, on account of the police of nine counties would help me find her if she was ever lost to me, wouldn't they?

Mrs Artminster There you are, that's what I mean. (*Gets up.*) You have your dreams and I've got to listen to them even if they're nightmares and not worth the bother. But me, me, what about me and my hopes for rest? I say Little Munstering and what, do you help me towards that? Oh, it's one-way traffic with you, Jerry, all your way, and to hell with me, you treat me to threats and police to make me beg. That's your feeling.

Jerry Little Munstering. There isn't any Little Munstering. You've done enough harm with your Little Munstering, with that Booker. *I've* got to answer the questions. *Me.* Because you can't shut up. Derek and Little Munstering. Little Munstering and Derek. You make me sick.

Mrs Artminster Yes, you're sick all right.

Long pause. They sit in silence, staring down at the floor.

Jerry It's my nerves, I can't help it.

Mrs Artminster I know you can't, son.

Jerry I always shout when my nerves are down. (*Long pause.*) It's the way they get at me. And you don't even ask me how I did.

Mrs Artminster Well, it's a funny trick you're up to, Jerry, and although I admire the brains of it, I don't understand it. And what I do understand, I don't like.

Jerry Course you don't like it, I don't swing any of your joggers so the law can't touch me. And that's where the brains is. (*Long pause.*) But I still get nervous, don't I?

Mrs Artminster And that's what's funny about it. You don't like being looked at, and you earn your keep by showing yourself off. It's bound to get you down, son.

Jerry Yes, well, it's no good your telling me that, I know it, don't I? (*Long silence.*) Why don't you help me?

Mrs Artminster (*cautiously*) Help you?

Jerry (*in a low voice*) Give me a test then.

Mrs Artminster (*after a pause*) No, Jerry, you're too quick for me. I couldn't test you.

Jerry Go on. Please.

Mrs Artminster To tell you the truth, Jerry, I'm not in the mood. I couldn't stand one of your tantrums.

Jerry I won't. (*Long pause.*) I promise. Please.

Mrs Artminster No, Jer, I'm not in the mood, I've told you.

Jerry But you're in the mood for the sozzing you'll get into yourself, aren't you? You're in the mood to let me go off and do it tomorrow, it doesn't matter how my nerves are down, aren't you? You're in the mood for the pain and humiliation, because of the benefits, aren't you? You're in the mood to lie there and get fat, that's the only mood you're in, all the time. You're in the mood –

Mrs Artminster All right, Jerry. All right. There's one of your tantrums you promised we wouldn't have, but all right, anything for peace.

Jerry goes out of the room, takes the object out from under the pillow.

But it gives me the creeps, and that's my mood.

Jerry comes back into the room just as Mrs Artminster stops talking.

Jerry Well, you can't test me lying on a bed with a bottle at your lips, like a baby. Get up then.

Mrs Artminster gets up and goes reluctantly to the chair, which is facing the other door. Jerry puts his

*head into the hall, obviously to see that the coast is
clear. Looks back in.*

Go on, you've got to stiffen up. You're power. Talk
power.

*Goes out as Mrs Artminster readjusts herself in the
chair, turning it so that the back is almost to the
audience. During the following scene she talks with two
voices, one pitched low and manly, with grotesque
upper-class intonations, the other the voice she
normally uses with Jerry. There is a knock on the door.*

Mrs Artminster Come, come.

*Jerry comes in shyly, wearing a blond wig which falls
to his shoulders. As he advances there is silence.*

Good God, what the hell is this?

Jerry No, no. (*Takes the wig off and throws it to the
floor.*) No. They don't say that.

Mrs Artminster Well, I'd be buggered, wouldn't I?

Jerry Polite. They're always polite.

*Picks up his wig, goes out into the hall, shuts the
door. There is a knock.*

Mrs Artminster 'M'in.

Jerry enters as before.

(*After a pause.*) Name, old chap?

Jerry Artminster, sir. Garfield Artminster.

Mrs Artminster 'M'in, Artminster, and have a pew, old
chap.

Jerry comes in, sits down.

Now, Artminster, handsome of you to come along, see us
today. About a position in – in –?

Jerry Technical side, sir.

Mrs Artminster 'Nical side, glad to have you aboard, 'trested to know, before we begin personal stuff, what experience in technical side you've had, Artminster, wasn't it?

Jerry Well, sir, I put in my application form that I did two years at Hornsey Tech, sir, of the three-year course.

Mrs Artminster And didn't finish the course, Artminster, old chap?

Jerry Well, sir, I – (*Shakes his head.*)

Mrs Artminster Come, come, boy, speak up. No need to be 'fraid.

Jerry shakes his head again. There is a long pause.

Speak up, boy. (*Another pause.*) You don't just sit there blushing red, do you?

Jerry Yes, I do.

Mrs Artminster Well, what am I supposed to do?

Jerry Get embarrassed.

Mrs Artminster Oh, I am, yes I am. Well, old chap, so you're 'fraid you didn't finish the course. Now no need to be 'fraid of me, old chap, you just tell me about why you got sacked.

Jerry I wasn't sacked, sir, they asked me to rest, for a little, sir.

Mrs Artminster Good, good, very good. Excellent. Now let me get your particulars down.

Jerry I'm very willing, sir, like Mr Hempting says in his letter.

Mrs Artminster Hempting? Who's Hempting?

Jerry He's a reference.

Mrs Artminster Who is he?

Jerry Me.

Mrs Artminster Well, what do you say?

Jerry He says I'm very intelligent and hard-working, and a bit of an individualist. (*Long pause.*) Then they ask me about my, you know – (*Pause.*) Go on then.

Mrs Artminster Now, I can see that you're an excellent chap, Artminster, and just what we want and all that, but there is a little problem here about your hair, which is too long for the kind of chap we have in mind for the position, I'm 'fraid, you'd have to get it cut, short back and sides sort of thing.

Jerry No, sir.

Mrs Artminster Sorry, old chap.

Jerry (*mumbling*) A free country, sir.

Mrs Artminster Free country, cod's balls, old chap, what do you mean, free country, you think you can walk into my office, your hair hanging down your shoulders, old chap, and tell me that it's a free country. Well, I'll tell you something, Artminster or whatever your name is, this is a free country, not because chaps like you want to get jobs with chaps like me with your hair hanging down to – (*Stops, and in own voice.*) What you doing, then?

Jerry I'm crying.

Mrs Artminster Cry— Haven't you any respect for yourself?

Jerry I can't help it. (*Pause.*) Get on with it.

Mrs Artminster (*after a pause*) Now look here,
Artminster, old chap, no need for you take on, what
I'm trying to say is, this is a country where people can
be people, no holds barred, but there's got to be decency,
there's got to be order, I know it and you know it. And
there are people on one side, like me, we keep things
together and make things go, and we love our country,
go down to our cottages in places like Little Munstering
and we sit there and dream of decency and order, and
that's all right, that's what it's all about, trees and an
orchard of plums and a river with bridges over it, Jerry,
and – and – Artminster, there's the other people who try
to take it away from us, what we've put up and what
we're holding together, want to get into my cottage in
Little Munstering and loot it empty, or one night when
I'm in the town flat with wife and kids, come through
one of our windows in the basement, where the bad
catches are, come slipping up the stairs as easy as shadows,
come like grease into the office, muscle the guard, smash
the furniture, rob the desks, the safe, get away with what
we've made, and start in again somewhere else. (*Pause.*)
They're the other people, Artminster, and that's fair, we
know them and they know us. They got their joggers,
we got our police and it's all part of the same thing. But
Artminster old chap, there's a third sort of people, just
one or two of them, thank God, they're not with *them*,
they're not with *us*, they wear their hair to their shoulders
and they snivel and con where the law can't touch them
and the joggers are – what I mean, old chap, is you don't
fit in anywhere, with your funny ways and your hair and
that's why we can't give you the job, see, old chap? Now
I don't mean to be hard, but what I'm trying to say is,
where's the police if the police can't cure you? Where's
the joggers – like the Peasbury Postman's attacker and
his accomplice – if they can't take you in? I mean, who's
to look after our wives and our kids from chaps like

you, Artminster? You ruin everything. (*Long pause.*)
That's why I can't give you the job.

> *Jerry, after a long pause, and wiping his eyes, gets up,*
> *goes to the door.*

(*As Jerry stands at the door, waiting.*) Well, is there
anything else, Artminster? (*This in a very cocky voice.*)

Jerry My expenses, sir. (*Long pause.*) I've got the chit,
sir, you sent me. One rail fare to Reading from London,
sir, first class, comes to two pound twelve, return; one
lunch on train, sir, twelve shillings; one night in the
Great Southern Hotel, two pound two shillings, sir; one
lunch in Reading, sir. Seven shillings and sixpence. Five
pound thirteen and sixpence, sir.

Mrs Artminster Five pound thirteen and six. You can't
get five pound thirteen and six for wearing a wig and
snivelling. I mean, that seems a bit steep, Artminster.

Jerry Well, sir, and then there's my mum, sir.

Mrs Artminster (*after a pause*) Your mother, Artminster?

Jerry Yes, sir, she's sick, sir, and she has to come with me
wherever I go, as she needs constant attendance owing to
her habits, which she can't help, sir, being a polio victim
from the neck down, and someone's got to feed her and
bath her and – *other things*, sir, that's why I had to bring
her with me. Up in the hotel. In a wheelchair, sir.

> *Long pause.*

Mrs Artminster Jerry, you've got more ice-cold nastiness
in you. I mean, why don't you put her in a home,
Artminster, there are houses for old ladies in her sad
condition.

Jerry Yes, sir, I know, sir, people are always trying to get
her into a home but there are *things*, sir – (*Long pause.*)
I love my mum, sir, I couldn't see her taken away from

me and clapped into a home. I love her, sir, and she needs
me and relies on me, she's got faith in me. I couldn't be
myself again if I let them catch her, sir, and put her away.
Because she loves me back. (*Long pause.*) That's why
I don't belong, that's why people are always after me, it's
not because of the way I look, sir, it's because I've got
this love in me for my mother that no matter what she'd
done or who she was, I'd demean and humble myself to
keep her free and happy, and they can see that and they
don't like it, that love in me for Mum, they don't want
to cut my hair off, they want to take the love out of me.
So I don't care what you say about me, sir, there's no
need for you to insult my mum because she can't help
herself.

Mrs Artminster (*after a very long pause*) And they
believe you?

Jerry Course they do. Me being a bit off is one thing, it
makes them cocky, but toting a wheelchair mother about
and setting her on and off the toilet turns their stomachs.
They imagine me doing it, see, and they think of their
own mums, and themselves lifting them on and off the
toilet, and their hands feel different. They pay me the
double expenses to get rid of me. (*Long pause.*) And they
feel the feeling in me, about my mum, like I said, and
they don't like it. I tell the truth, see. (*Long pause.*) See.

Mrs Artminster Yes, I admire it, Jerry, but I don't like it.
That's the truth.

Jerry That's because you don't know it, the way you do
it, breaking in. Now let's do it straight.

There is a slight knock on Jerry's door.

Then you feel it.

Mrs Artminster No, Jer, honest I'm not up to it, I'll tell
you what, we'll do it . . .

Voice fades as Jerry goes into the hall, and Mr Booker comes into Jerry's room. Both doors close simultaneously. Then Mr Booker crosses to the communicating door, raises his hand to knock, goes back, stares around the room, goes into the hall as Jerry enters Mrs Artminster's bedroom.

You must be Artminster, old chap.

Jerry Yes, sir.

The door of Jerry's room opens again, and Mr Booker steals in. He goes to the communicating door and puts his ear to it.

Mrs Artminster Good of you to come along, Artminster, hope you had a good trip, poor weather I'm 'fraid.

Mr Booker stands up, hesitates, then knocks on the door. Mrs Artminster and Jerry stare at each other, then Jerry goes to the hall door, and out. Mrs Artminster gets up.

Enter.

Mr Booker enters through communicating door. Jerry goes into his own room.

Mr Booker I'm not disturbing, I trust.

Mrs Artminster Oh no, I was just saying to Garfield that you'd be up shortly, as you'd promised.

Mr Booker Garfield?

Mrs Artminster Yes, he just went down the hall a minute to the toilet.

Jerry, who has been listening at the door, slips to the hall door, opens it and closes it, then walks to the communicating door. Puts his hand on the knob.

Mr Booker It's very odd, I thought I heard some voices, it must be me. (*Looks at Mrs Artminster.*)

> *Jerry begins to open the door, realises he is wearing the wig, takes it off, throws it out of sight, and enters.*

Oh, hello, Garfield, there you are.

Jerry Hello, Mr Booker. May I come in a minute, Mother, unless you're busy?

Mrs Artminster Of course, dear, Mr Booker has just popped in for a chat, he knows how I like my bit of company and a gossip in the evening.

Mr Booker Well, how are things in Little Munstering?

Mrs Artminster Yes, how are things, dear?

Jerry Oh, the place is coming along very nicely, thank you, they expect we can move in soon.

Mr Booker That's good news, good news indeed. Although not for me, of course, I shall be sorry to lose you.

Mrs Artminster You spoke to the gardener about the plum trees, Garfield?

Jerry Yes, Mother. (*Little pause.*) He's planted them.

Mrs Artminster And how do the plums look?

Jerry Lovely, Mother.

Mr Booker At this time of year?

Jerry Well. (*Laughs.*) They're special plums. Early.

Mrs Artminster Why don't we make ourselves comfy? Mr Booker, you sit down on the bed, and Garfield, stop your fidgeting, dear, and take a pew.

They sit down, Mr Booker on the end of the bed, Jerry on the side.

Now – (*Little pause.*) What about the plumbing, Garfield, what do they say about that?

Jerry Oh, they've fixed that.

Mrs Artminster Put the trimmings in, have they, dear, like I instructed?

Jerry Yes, Mother.

Mrs Artminster That's a relief, seeing as they're so slow these days.

Mr Booker Oh they *are*, the way they stop for a smoke and a cup every five minutes. It's a wonder to me we're not all living on the streets, holding us up to ransom.

Mrs Artminster I know. I say the same to Garfield, it's the war that did it. Before the war, service was service, work was work and money was money, they had to look to their jobs then, or unemployment and the dole was staring them in the face, instead of our being the beggars of Europe as we are now.

Mr Booker You can't tell me anything about plumbing and plumbers, there's a week left before we open and have you noticed the toilets? It doesn't matter what I say – and the overtime? I go down on my knees to them.

Mrs Artminster Overtime! Overtime from what, but having a good time at our expense, that's what I say.

Mr Booker *And* they use the guest toilets. There are perfectly good, clean toilets in the basement, I pointed them out and said that was one thing I was very strict on. But no, I catch them coming out of all the guest toilets without so much as a by-your-leave or a may-I.

Mrs Artminster I know what you mean, Garfield, I hope you showed them the outside toilet by the bridge.

Jerry Yes. Mother, I did.

Mrs Artminster And what did they say to that?

Jerry They're using it, Mother.

Mr Booker Well, you must have a way with them, Garfield, I wish I could get that from our plumbers, they spend all their time winking at Janice. (*Little pause.*) By the by, if I could just ask, where did you say Little Munstering was exactly actually? (*Pause.*) I was glancing at a map of the area just last night, to while away my insomnia, and I couldn't see a Little Munstering.

Jerry It's outside Andover.

Mr Booker Oh, yes, very pretty countryside, lovely landscapes out there. That's where I was looking, by the by, from Reading right through to Wiltshire. Is it to the south or north?

Mrs Artminster North.

Jerry (*overlapping*) South. (*After a pause.*) No, Mother, it's to the south, you're always bad on direction.

Mr Booker (*shakes his head*) And I haven't even heard of it, that's the shameful truth. I like to know pleasant spots and nearby villages, for the guests' sake. They're not all travellers, you know, some of them have a real love of visiting the pretty places – how do you get out there, Garfield, by the by?

Jerry In a bus.

Mr Booker Oh dear, you don't have to tell *me* about our local bus service, the rudeness! Which number, by the by?

Jerry (*after a little pause*) 726.

Mr Booker Oh? To Hayler's Pond? It's out that way, is it?

Jerry nods.

That's to the north. (*Little pause.*) Directly to the north. The 726. It's called the North Line Service. It even stops at Northlynne, North Hill and North Junction. The 726.

Jerry Mother, I owe you an apology.

Mrs Artminster I always tell you, you should listen to your old mother, dear.

Mr Booker So Little Munstering's that way, is it?

Jerry Yes.

Mr Booker On from the end of the route, I suppose. Up Hindley Lane –?

Jerry I can't remember the name.

Mr Booker It'd have to be Hindley Lane. The rest is by-pass and the tracks to London, as I recall. Yes, and then you'd go along the field – Johnson's Field – and it'd be some way there, wouldn't it?

Jerry Yes.

Mr Booker (*after a pause*) By the by. (*Pause.*) I've been wondering if you remembered to telephone the Great Southern and explain about booking in here. They'll never believe it was a mistake – (*Pause.*) They'll think I stole you from them, especially as I don't even reopen for another week – (*Pause.*) Although we're too humble to compete with the Great Southern. (*Laughs.*) Did you telephone?

Mrs Artminster It was the first thing I made him do as soon as I came to myself again.

Mr Booker I hope you don't think I'm fussing or nosy. I hate people who are nosy. (*Little pause.*) By the by –

There is a knock on the door. Jerry gets up and opens it. Janice enters. She is a tall, very pretty West Indian girl. She is smiling.

And what's on today, at The Three Musketeers?

Janice Sausage. And there's liver, Mr Booker, sir.

Mr Booker Didn't you find out about the soups, Janice, you know Mrs Artminster's been ill. She won't want liver, will she?

Janice Oh no, sir.

Mr Booker Well then?

Janice Mrs Arminst, she always like the sausages, sir. Six sausages, sir. Every night, sir. (*Smiles at Mrs Artminster.*)

There is silence.

Mrs Artminster And don't forget the Worcester, Janice, tonight.

Mr Booker Well, it's good to see you've recovered your appetite, Mrs Artminster. Go then, Janice, Mrs Artminster's hungry. (*Looks at Mrs Artminster.*)

Mrs Artminster (*after a pause*) I like that girl.

Mr Booker Yes, she's a nice girl. (*Pause.*) Bit slow, though, in some respects. (*Little pause. Then taps his forehead.*)

Mrs Artminster Oh, you won't find the intelligent ones over here, oh no. They stay in the sun, where they belong.

Mr Booker Yes. They're very happy, a happy people. I'll say that for Janice, she may be a bit – (*taps his forehead*) but she's happy.

Mrs Artminster Yes, I like her.

Mr Booker Oh, I've nothing against her personally, she can't help her habits after all, they're bred into her.

Mrs Artminster (*in an excited voice*) And you know what they say about them and the way our white boys –

Jerry Mother, I've –

Gets up, stands staring at her while Mrs Artminster and Mr Booker stare at him.

Mrs Artminster What is it, Garfield? I must say you're very nervous tonight, the way you keep hopping about and gaping, it's rude, dear.

Jerry doesn't move.

Come on then, you go and have a little nap – he's had a hard day, a mother can tell. Come and give your old mother a kiss and lie down. (*This in a significant voice.*)

Jerry Yes, Mother.

Comes across and gives her a kiss. Goes towards the connecting door.

Mrs Artminster Garfield was always the sensitive, delicate one in our family, his brother Derek now, as tough as six wrestlers, and no holding him. But Garfield needs holding and looking after, he'd wither without it, he's got a loving nature, haven't you, Garfield?

Jerry I don't know. (*Smiles with awkward shyness.*)

Mrs Artminster Oh, he has, I tell you. Come and give your old mother another kiss, dear.

Jerry stands awkwardly, then comes over. Gives Mrs Artminster a kiss. Goes back to the door, opens it, goes through.

Mr Booker Well, you'll want to eat in peace. (*Having watched Jerry exit.*) So I'll leave you. Goodnight, Mrs Artminster.

Mrs Artminster Goodnight, Mr Booker, it was kind of you to cheer me up.

Mr Booker leaves the room. Mrs Artminster fishes for her whisky bottle, begins to nuzzle it. Meanwhile Jerry is sitting on the edge of his bed, his hands clasped between his legs. There is a low knock on his hall door, and Mr Booker enters.

Mr Booker I just wondered if you were all right, Garfield.

Jerry (*getting up*) Yes. Yes thanks.

Mr Booker Because I thought something upset you. (*Little pause.*) And if it did, I think I know what it was.

Jerry No.

Mr Booker You're not upset?

Jerry No.

Mr Booker Oh. Well – I didn't know you had a brother, Derek?

Jerry Yes, but he's dead. Derek was a – he was a – he had a heart attack.

Mr Booker I'm sorry to hear that, Garfield.

Long pause. Meanwhile Mrs Artminster has come to the other side of the door, listened for a minute, nodded, and gone back to her chair.

I had a close friend once. He wrote a book. (*Long pause.*) I'll tell you about him some day.

Jerry Who?

Mr Booker The friend I was telling you about.

Jerry Oh. Thank you very much, Mr Booker.

Mr Booker Yes, he wrote the book when he was a priest.

Pause. Mr Booker is staring at Jerry intently.

Do you ever go to boys' clubs, Garfield? I was just wondering, because my friend did a lot of work in the boys' club on Martin Street. I don't want to force you into anything, I hate people who do that, but I could show you around, if you like. (*Little pause.*) When you've settled into Little Munstering, I mean, and if we still – should happen to see each other. (*Laughs.*)

Jerry Thank you very much, Mr Booker.

Mr Booker Garfield – (*Little pause.*) Is there any reason why you shouldn't call me Simon?

Jerry Simon.

Mr Booker Called Peter. (*Little pause.*) The Fisher of Men. I'd rather you called me Simon. (*Little pause.*) After all, we've known each other for a week, haven't we, and that's a long time for a fisher of men. (*Little pause.*) I'm sorry, I'm a bit nervous myself tonight, I don't know why.

Little pause. Mrs Artminster has come back to the door to listen. She swigs sometimes from her bottle.

By the by, did you know our Gaumont was doing a festival of religious films shortly?

Jerry No.

Mr Booker The truly great ones. I'd love to see them, but I hate going to the pictures by myself. (*Little pause.*) Do you like pictures?

Jerry No, I – they hurt my eyes.

Mr Booker Oh? Have you got bad eyes too? We *are* in a poor way between us, what with our nerves and our eyes, aren't we? (*Little pause.*) Garfield, if there's any little problem you think I could help you with, you will come to me with it, won't you? No matter what it is. (*Glances towards the door.*) I know how difficult things can be.

Jerry Thank you.

Mr Booker I mean it, Garfield. (*Stares at him.*) Would you like to borrow that book, then?

Jerry What book?

Mr Booker The one my friend wrote. The priest. (*Little pause.*)

Jerry Thank you very much.

Mr Booker I think you'd like it. (*Little pause.*) I think you'd understand it. (*Stares at Jerry.*) Well, goodnight, Garfield.

Jerry Goodnight.

Mr Booker I'll get that book now, if you like.

Jerry Well, I'm a bit – I don't think I could concentrate now.

Mr Booker I see. (*Little pause.*) Well, I won't lend it to you if you're not interested, you'd be liable to forget it, or put it away in your luggage, and it's a personal copy. Guests are very careless about our towels and soap without so much as a thank you. I'm sorry if I've been forcing myself on you, Garfield, I hate people who do that. I must have misunderstood. Goodnight.

Jerry No, it's not that, I'm just a bit – I'd like to read the book, honestly I would, Simon, but as it's so precious to you I'd be frightened of losing it.

Mr Booker I see. (*Looks at him.*) Well, perhaps tomorrow night then. (*Coldly.*)

Jerry Yes, I'd like to borrow it tomorrow night, really I would, I'd be up to it then.

Mr Booker All right, Garfield. Goodnight then.

Jerry Goodnight, Simon.

Mr Booker Goodnight. (*Goes to the door, opens it, stands looking into the hall.*) I'm sorry if I turn a bit funny sometimes, Garfield –

Jerry makes obscene gestures at him.

It's that I'm out of the habit of talking, really talking to people since my friend –

Turns. Jerry manages to check a gesture.

I mean people I might care about – Goodnight, Garfield.

Exits. Jerry makes one magnificently obscene gesture at the door, goes toward Mrs Artminster's door as she moves away from it to the bed.

Mrs Artminster Oh yes, he really delights in you, I could hear his voice, it was leaking under the door like oil. What'd he want then?

Jerry He was going on about some priest, I don't know.

Mrs Artminster Oh yes, I bet his hands were up those skirts all right. But no, I mustn't sneer, I've got religious feelings too, and I don't like sneering at the chosen. I used to say to Derek he had the makings of a priest, he had strong thoughts about God, so our Simon Booker's entitled to his friend.

Jerry What's the matter with you? Didn't you see the way he was asking us questions?

Mrs Artminster Because he's interested, Jerry, that's why. (*Little pause.*) It wouldn't hurt if you asked him a few questions, in politeness.

Jerry What about?

Mrs Artminster *You* know what about.

Jerry Now you keep your mind off that, I told you we're not doing anything like that.

Mrs Artminster Where's the harm in finding out, for the interest? Derek would have beaten it out of him in three minutes, but you've got your own way, Jerry, I'll give you that, you've got a way with homosexuals, you could wind him about your fingers and have the truth. A smile would get it for you.

Jerry Shut up.

Mrs Artminster Yes, that's how you talk to me, isn't it? I'll tell you something, Jerry, I'll tell you what you are.

Long pause, swings legs off the bed. Janice comes in with a tray. Mrs Artminster looks at her, looks at Jerry, smiles.

Oh hello, there you are, dear, how kind.

Janice smiles at Jerry, walks across the room with the tray, puts it on the table by the bed. Mrs Artminster looks at Jerry, then at Janice.

Why, what lovely earrings those are you've got on, Janice, I didn't notice those before, may I see them from closer to, dear? Sometimes a pretty object does more to rouse me than pills.

Janice stands by the bed, smiling.

Oh yes, they look very fetching in those little lobes of yours, where did you purchase them? The only thing is, I can't make out the design, could you bend a bit?

Janice bends over the bed. Jerry glares, Mrs Artminster looks at him, then takes one of the earrings between fingers.

Janice Mr Booker, he gave them – ow! (*Straightening with a cry.*)

Mrs Artminster I'm sorry, dear. It seems to have caught itself in my fingers. Here it is, now let me punish myself by putting it back on. You start, Garfield dear, I know how peckish you get. Yes, Janice, bend a little lower, dear, it's nice to know there's no colour feeling in Mr Booker's hotel, black and white mix in, and how else are you going to raise yourselves – oops, now isn't that clumsy, my fingers have always been my weakest part for a lady, they're so chubby they make me blush, now I wonder where did it go?

Jerry, who has been watching, comes over to the bed. Janice steps away, Jerry bends over the bed, there is a sort of tussle between them.

Jerry Here it is, Mother.

Mrs Artminster Oh, thank you, dear. (*Little pause.*) You put it on for Janice, there's a good boy, to make up.

Jerry I don't know how.

Mrs Artminster Janice will show you, won't you, Janice?

Janice giggles. Stands offering the side of her face to Jerry. Jerry stares at Mrs Artminster, who stares back.

The girl's waiting, dear.

Jerry goes forward, stands a long way from Janice, holds the earring up.

Just pop it into the hole and screw, dear, you can work it out for yourself.

Jerry holds the earring out and seizes the lobe of Janice's ear.

Janice Ow! (*Giggles.*)

Mrs Artminster Closer, my dear, closer, you look as if you're fishing without a pole. You've good eyes, don't worry about pricking her. You move in on him, girl.

Janice moves a little closer to Jerry, who shies away, then braces himself and screws the earring in. Janice smiles at Jerry, who moves back.

You've got him eating out of your hand, dear. Well, goodnight, and we'll see you tomorrow.

Janice goes towards the door, turns, smiles.

Janice Goodnight. (*Exits.*)

Mrs Artminster What's the matter, son, you look a trifle pale?

Jerry You know what's the matter.

Mrs Artminster No, I don't, are you poorly again?

Jerry You know how I hate their smell.

Mrs Artminster Do you, dear? I'm very fond of it myself, it makes my head swim, and Derek used to chase them till he had them by the tail. Pass my sausages, I'm ravening.

Jerry (*taking the sausages over*) Derek's dead.

Mrs Artminster What?

Jerry I told Booker he's dead, I'll tell everyone, and he's dead all right, you won't be seeing him again for twelve years.

Mrs Artminster Oh you evil boy, you'd like to see him dead, wouldn't you? (*Eats a sausage.*) And you've never set eyes on him.

Jerry Oh yes, I set eyes on him every time you talk about him, I see him before me with every word, pegged-toothed, fat, bullying all the small ones, oh, I've set eyes on him all right. Besides, I saw that photo in the papers.

Mrs Artminster His head was covered by a coat and he was stooped over to get into the car. (*Eats another sausage.*) Aren't you hungry?

Jerry No.

Mrs Artminster Pass your plate, then.

Jerry (*viciously, watching Mrs Artminster eat*) Can't you watch where the Worcester goes? Talk about ladylike.

Mrs Artminster If you don't like what you see, turn your eyes away, dainty-pants.

There is a silence. Jerry takes the plate away and puts it on the tray. Goes and sits down. Mrs Artminster looks at him.

(*Taunting.*) Well, give your old mum a kiss then.

Jerry looks at her.

Well, you won't look at Booker, can't stomach the juices smell of Janice, who'll you kiss, Jerry? Not even your old mum? Go on, Jerry, give your old mum a kiss. (*Pause.*) Like Derek used to do.

Jerry (*leaping to his feet*) He never.

Mrs Artminster Oh no? Oh no? *You* don't know what fondness is, for all your talk. (*Takes a swig of Scotch.*) Come on, Jerry, a kiddle, a cuddle, a knickery muddle, oh a cuddle, Jer, my youngest and prettiest won't give me a cuddle when I need one, oh he says he loves his mum, but no cuddles, no kisses.

Jerry puts his hands to his face.

(*Watching him.*) Had enough, have you?

Little pause, as Jerry doesn't move.

Oh, come on, Jer. (*Pats the bed.*) It's all right. What's the matter, son?

Jerry shakes his head.

What? Tell me.

Jerry I don't know. I don't know. The way you go on at me.

Mrs Artminster Well, I don't mean harm, do I? (*Pause, then in a very gentle voice.*) You know I don't mean harm, don't you, Jer?

Jerry shakes his head.

(*Putting a hand on his shoulder.*) Fond is fond, Jer, and that's what counts.

Jerry (*taking his hands away, looks at Mrs Artminster*) Will you play then?

Mrs Artminster (*after a pause*) What?

Jerry You know what.

Mrs Artminster What's the time?

Jerry (*looks at his watch*) It's early.

Mrs Artminster No it isn't, Jerry, I can tell by my craving.

Seizes his wrist, looks at the watch.

Jerry Just once. Three goes. That's all. Just three goes. (*Little pause.*) You said fond was fond, you did.

Mrs Artminster All right, but come on quick.

They hold out their fists, raise and lower them three times. Jerry has stone and Mrs Artminster has paper.

Jerry You win.

Holds out his hand, palm up, and Mrs Artminster hits him hard across it. Then they do it again; this time Jerry has scissors and Mrs Artminster has stone.

You win.

Holds out his hand, palm up, in excitement. Mrs Artminster stares at him a moment, then again hits him hard across it. Then they do it again, and this time Mrs Artminster has scissors and Jerry has paper.

You win.

Holds out his hand, palm up, head thrown back.

Mrs Artminster I'm not saying anything.

Jerry What do you mean?

Mrs Artminster You know what I mean.

Looks at him, then strikes him across the palm of his hand. Jerry holds out his fists again, Mrs Artminster shakes her head.

Jerry One once, once, once, please, please.

Mrs Artminster (*gets up, slaps hands together*) Fair's fair. Fair's fair.

Jerry looks at Mrs Artminster pleadingly, then gets up, goes into his room. Locks the door to the hall, opens a case. Takes a chamber pot from under the bed. Meanwhile Mrs Artminster is taking off shoes and stockings. Jerry returns, hands the box to Mrs Artminster, puts the chamber pot under the hot tap, goes to the hall door and locks it. Mrs Artminster has taken a cigar out of the box, unwraps it. Jerry goes to the window, opens it wide. Collects the chamber pot from the sink, hands Mrs Artminster her whisky.

Aaah. Aaah. Where's a light then? (*Sniffing at the cigar.*) There's one in my handbag, fetch it over.

Jerry goes over, gets the handbag, gives it to her.

Jerry The trouble with you is you've got no control.

Mrs Artminster Control, don't talk to me about control.

Jerry crouches down and begins to swab at Mrs Artminster's feet.

I could burst out, Jerry, burst out at any minute and expose myself. (*Sighs contentedly, begins to hum.*) One day I'll do it, and where'll you be then?

Jerry Well, I'll know where you'll be, won't I?

Looks up significantly, but Mrs Artminster is lying back, smoking and sipping from the Scotch. Jerry goes back to swabbing her feet. Mrs Artminster's hum rises into 'On a bicycle made for two'.

Curtain.

Act Two

SCENE ONE

Jerry is standing before the mirror in the wardrobe, with a case open at his feet. He takes out the blond wig, tries it on, takes it off, puts on a tight black one with curls. Takes that off and puts on a long red one. Simultaneously Mrs Artminster is sitting at a table, pouring tea from a pot into a cup and lacing it with whisky. Finishes the bottle, looks at it in dismay, puts it down. Then starts to put on lipstick and face powder from her handbag, occasionally taking sips from her cup. There is a knock on Jerry's door. He stuffs all the wigs back into the case as the door knob is turned, goes towards the door, remembers his wig on his head, whips it off and is stuffing it into his pocket as there is the sound of the key in the lock. The door opens and Mr Booker enters behind a large portrait in oils of a Jesuit of about forty-five – the colours of which are almost grotesquely vivid. The Jesuit is florid and bald.

Mr Booker Oh. (*Stops.*) Good morning, Garfield, I didn't mean to disturb. I thought you must have gone out as you didn't answer to my knock. May I come in, if that's all right?

Jerry Yes.

Mr Booker Thank you, because today's the day I hang the pictures. This is the one I've specially chosen for your – this room. What are your feelings about it?

Jerry It looks very nice.

Mr Booker Just right for – here, don't you feel? I'm very proud of it myself for personal reasons.

*Props it against a chair and comes around, to stand
beside Jerry.*

My pride is in the feeling that it catches the priestly
qualities in particular. People don't use these words now,
I know, but to my eyes he was a beautiful man on account
of his saintish face. He knew the meaning of compassion.
It's there in the eyes. (*Points to them.*) It's that friend of
mine I think I mentioned to you, done when he was a
priest.

*Picks the painting up, stumbles against the bed, comes
back, picks up the chair and almost falls with both.
Manages to hang the picture on a hook. Jerry watches
coldly. The painting dominates the room.*

Yes, the gift of myself he called it, which he said must be
an ordained gift because of my optical weakness.

*Mrs Artminster has got off the bed and has been
listening to this. Now leaves the room.*

Now that he's gone, it's as if he'd taken the gift with him.
(*Little pause.*) He said it would happen, he said I would
have to wait, until it was risen up. (*Little pause.*) The gift
I mean. (*Little pause.*) I telephoned last night, Garfield,
by the by.

Jerry What? (*Looks at the picture.*)

Mr Booker To the Great Southern, Garfield. (*Stares at
the picture.*)

Jerry Oh? (*Little pause.*) Well, thank you very much.
Actually I've got to go now, because I've got an
appointment at ten in Little Munstering.

Mr Booker That still leaves you time for a little talk,
Garfield.

Jerry Yes, well, I like to be a bit ahead, you see.

Mr Booker I think you'd better spare me five minutes. (*Turns his head, to look at Jerry, then looks back at the picture.*) Because of my telephone call to the Great Southern. (*Pause.*)

Jerry Well, what did you call about?

Mr Booker I think you know, Garfield.

Jerry No, I don't.

Mr Booker I think you do. (*Turns head, looks at Jerry, turns back to the picture.*) It was about your reservations. There *were* no reservations, Garfield, in the name of Artminster. (*Little pause.*) Last night, when we were talking easily together, before you turned cold, I said to you that if you had any problems I would help you. In spite of your coldness I still want to help you, Garfield, because I think your coldness came from your problems. (*Turns his head.*) Why did you lie to me, Garfield?

While this has been going an, Mrs Artminster has put down her mug and comes over to the door. She listens, bends down, looks through the keyhole, then quickly leaves the room, by the hall door.

Jerry There must have been a mistake. Mother!

As he hurries over to connecting door, opens it, stares around an empty room, enters, followed by Mr Booker.

There must have been a mistake.

Mr Booker No mistake, Garfield. (*Turns his head.*) I should mention that being in the hotel world, I know how to speak to other hotel managers. No mistake, Garfield. (*Turns back to the picture.*) What is the problem that causes you to lie to me, Garfield?

Jerry (*after a pause*) I – I have to do it, Simon, I have to.

143

Mr Booker Why? Why do you have to lie to me?

Jerry Because of my mother. (*Goes and sits down an the bed.*) All my life, she's – (*Shakes his head.*) When I was little she was a clippie for the thirty-one bus route, Simon, and evenings she waitressed in Ned's Sandwich, all because of me. Derek didn't do anything, he was off with his friends, swilling down beer and getting into bad company, Simon, and doing things – I can't talk about them, they cause me pain, the things he did to me, I've never told her about them. So she had to bring me up herself, slaving to keep me in good clothes so that I could face the teachers at school, slaving to give me the best in the way of food, oh no, *I* never went short, not for anything, and *she* never said a word. Of course I didn't know when I was little what it meant to have a big boy like Derek who never cared for her although she cared for him, I didn't know what it was to be looked after like I was looked after.

Mr Booker Of course you didn't, Garfield.

Sits down on the bed beside Jerry, puts a hand on his shoulder. Jerry edges away slightly.

Jerry Then when I was ten I got this thing in my bones, they were always breaking, like glass almost. And she – she asked Derek to help, and he wouldn't. So she borrowed money to have me sent to the most famous bone specialist in London. I spent two years in hospital, Simon, two years, and there wasn't a day she didn't come by with some toy or box of allsorts or a bag of tiger's tails for me. Then out to slave at Ned's, and clippying, and cleaning at night, to pay back the money. (*Puts his face in his hands.*)

Mr Booker (*putting his hand an Jerry's shoulder*) Don't blame yourself, child. Of course you can't.

Jerry (*taking his hands away*) And last year she got a turn, a bad turn, and when she came out of it, with me nursing her night and day, she was talking of – of – how there was this place we had, that had been left to her by Derek when he died of his heart attack, a cottage in Little Munstering, and we had to get to it. I can't tell her the truth, I can't, it's her dream of peace this cottage is, so I've had to pretend about it, and bring her here. What else could I do?

Mr Booker Nothing, child, nothing. (*Little pause.*) And how did you come to find *me*?

Jerry Well, there were Great Southern Hotel advertisements, Simon, all over the station, and I said Little Munstering was near here because it was all I could afford out of London, and she said, stay at the best, Garfield, we can afford it. So I pretended to look up the direction and saw the Southern, and I brought her here, that's when she – well, when she saw the lobby, because it wasn't what she thought it would be like at the Great Southern, and you said no guests until next week, that's why she fainted in the lobby. (*Little pause.*) I just chose it out of the book, Simon, because it was the same name.

Mr Booker Your moving finger stopped, Garfield.

Mrs Artminster throws open the door of Jerry's room, arm raised in angry astonishment. Sees room is empty, drops arm, goes over to connecting door, takes fresh bottle of whisky out of pocket and begins to sip at it.

Jerry What?

Mr Booker All your travelling and worrying have carried you here, here to the Southern, like Fate or – or – (*Looks at the picture.*) I'm glad you told me the truth, Garfield. Was it a pain to you to lie to me, child?

Jerry Yes, Simon, it was.

Mr Booker She's a great burden to you, isn't she?

Jerry Who?

Mr Booker Your poor mother.

Jerry No, Simon.

Mr Booker I understand, Garfield, I understand what you feel. But let me say one thing to you, child, a most important thing. There are two kinds of human love, child, the love of gratitude and obligation, and the love that rises in us, free and spontaneous. The second love is the love that lifts the spirit up and out, against the tight bonds of life that seem to press us down and confine us in servitude. When this lifting comes we know the second love, the love that is freedom, the spouting forth of the heart, that buried fountain.

Mrs Artminster comes over and listens by the door.

But we must never confuse the first love, of duty and obligation, which is imposed by dependants, child, with the second love, of spontaneous youthfulness in the spirit, which arises mysteriously; and which is a step towards the third love, which is the love of God in humility and therefore above the human. I myself was taught that by one who could stand straighter and pour himself more fully into those he loved, the word from the mouth that enters the mouth, the mouth that closes around the word and drinks the word in, the mouth and the word become one. In his case. (*Little pause.*) And by the by, Garfield, there are homes for the sick and ageing, there are doctors and comfort, on the medical health.

Jerry (*after a pause*) But I – I couldn't – after all she's done for me – (*Swallows, covers his face again.*)

Mr Booker Lumps in the throat, Garfield, are compassion. Compassion merely. (*Little pause.*) By the by, child, how were you planning to pay my poor bill?

Jerry I'm going to work it off. Every morning, when I say I've gone to Little Munstering, I go out and look for a job. That's where I'm going now, to find out about a chance of a position in an office. And I thought if I worked hard and saved, I could get enough, one day, after I've paid you, Simon, for a little cottage –

Mr Booker stands up, raising Jerry up by the shoulders, putting his hands on them, while Mrs Artminster, who has been watching through the keyhole, also rises, puts her hands on the door knob, thinks,

Mr Booker You will have a position, Garfield.

Mrs Artminster opens the door.

There is a place for you. In Reading. I promise you that.

Mrs Artminster Oh you promise him, do you? What do you promise him, and may I ask why you're resting yourself on his shoulders?

Mr Booker (*stepping away*) Oh, good morning, Mrs Artminster. (*Laughs.*) Garfield and I were having a little talk.

Mrs Artminster About what, may I be permitted to be so bold as to ask?

Mr Booker Oh, merely about a great friend of mine, who's passed. (*Looks at the picture.*)

Mrs Artminster steps forward and also looks at the picture. There is a long silence. Then Mrs Artminster steps away, turns her back on Mr Booker.

Mrs Artminster It's time you were running along, Garfield dear, you've got a busy day in Little Munstering.

Jerry Yes, Mother. (*Makes for the door.*)

Mrs Artminster Garfield!

She holds her head sideways, offering a cheek. Jerry comes back and kisses the cheek. Mrs Artminster straightens his tie, brushes at his lapels, feels in his jacket pocket, takes out a comb. Gives it to him.

You know what Derek always says, about flat hair and respect.

Jerry begins to comb it flat.

Mr Booker I must say, I thought the fashion these days was for wild hair.

Mrs Artminster (*turning, studies him*) You don't follow it yourself, do you?

Mr Booker I mean for the young lads.

Mrs Artminster That's as may be. (*Turns back to Jerry.*) Garfield wears his hair flat as long as his old mother's around to see to it, no matter what advice other people may give. Now that looks very nice, dear, and off you go. (*Gives him a kiss on the cheek.*)

Jerry Goodbye, Mother.

Mr Booker Goodbye, Garfield. Perhaps we'll have a chance to continue our chat later.

Jerry looks at Mrs Artminster, who turns and looks at Mr Booker. Goes out.

Mrs Artminster I see. (*Continues to stare at Mr Booker.*)

Mr Booker Yes, madame, what may I do for you?

Mrs Artminster Whose room are you in, dare I ask?

Mr Booker One of my hotel rooms, I think, madame.

Mrs Artminster Oh pardon me, I thought it was my son Garfield's room, as you'd let it out to him. I didn't know hotel owners were allowed into the rooms to caress the boy guests.

Mr Booker I beg your pardon?

Mrs Artminster Pardon is too weak a word. Mercy is what you should be begging for. What is it you're after with my Garfield? Fondling him.

Mr Booker Fond – fond – I, fondle!

Mrs Artminster Did you have your arms around him, or did my eyes deceive me? Where were you when he was getting into his clothes? Crouching at the keyhole?

Mr Booker (*after a pause*) I'll tell you what I was doing, madame, since you force it from me with accusations. I was getting the truth from him. The truth, madame.

Mrs Artminster The truth? What truth? And what right have you got to have it?

Mr Booker The truth, madame, in answer to some questions. About – it's you who compel it out of me – yourself, madame.

Mrs Artminster Who is this? Who is this before you?

Mr Booker (*confused, after a pause*) You, I presume, madame.

Mrs Artminster You, you presume, madame. Well? Well? (*Pause.*) Where are your questions, madame?

Mr Booker (*after a pause*) I couldn't bring myself to torment you with them.

Mrs Artminster No? Would you prefer me to torment you with some of my own? Like about what I've just seen?

Mr Booker Very well, you leave me no alternative. I asked Garfield why he had told me an untruth about reservations at the Great Southern.

Mrs Artminster Untruth? What untruth?

Mr Booker (*holding his hand*) And his answer, madame, was that because he loved you, you had to be deluded. Yes – (*Gesturing silence.*) Because, madame, of the shock of discovering that there wasn't any money, in spite of the bill you've been running up here, and that there isn't any cottage in Little Munstering, and that there isn't even a Little Munstering. And never has been and never will be.

Mrs Artminster sways, with a hand to her head.

I'm sorry you've wrung this out of me, madame, and that it's caused you pain, but truth is truth, and even mercy can't temper it.

Mrs Artminster No money?

Mr Booker Not a penny.

Mrs Artminster My cottage!

Mr Booker Not a thatch. (*Pause.*) Nothing but a son who is wasting his life away for you.

Mrs Artminster You lie, you lie. (*Little pause.*) I can't believe it.

Mr Booker Can't, madame, or won't? Which is it?

Mrs Artminster reels across the room. Mr Booker grabs her by the shoulders and they tumble onto the bed. Mr Booker clambers up, stares down, then runs out of the room. Mrs Artminster gets up, goes into the other room, takes a gulp of Scotch from the bottle in the bag. Goes back, falls across the bed, waits.

*Mr Booker comes back with a bottle of Scotch,
unscrews it, holds it to Mrs Artminster's lips. She
gulps some whisky down. Moans. Straightens. Looks
around the room. Looks at Mr Booker.*

Mrs Artminster What happened?

Mr Booker You had a turn.

Mrs Artminster Why? Did I receive a shock?

Mr Booker No.

Mrs Artminster Are you sure? I only get one of my fits
from a bad shock, like when we came to the wrong
hotel. (*Looks at Mr Booker.*) You didn't shock me then?

Mr Booker No. (*Pause.*) We were chatting here,
pleasantly, about Garfield.

Mrs Artminster (*looking around wildly*) Garfield.
Something's happened to him? Where is he?

Mr Booker He's all right, quite all right, madame.

Mrs Artminster But where is he?

Mr Booker (*after a little pause*) He went to Little
Munstering.

Mrs Artminster Oh. Yes, well he's a good boy. (*Pause.*)
What were you saying about him?

Mr Booker Merely that he was a most pleasant and
modest lad, unusual in these times. And devoted to his
mother. Also unusual.

Mrs Artminster And nothing more?

Mr Booker (*after a pause*) No.

Mrs Artminster (*putting her hands to her head*) But
voices sound in my head, words and insults. Lies to hurt.
I hear lies in my head.

Mr Booker Oh no, madame, we even had a little laugh together. (*Little pause.*) Unless the lies come from deeper in, and are trying to force their way out.

Mrs Artminster And there's this evil picture of – of Garfield and some – some, can it be man? Cuddling up together? Can it be?

Mr Booker (*handing her the bottle*) Here, madame, another drop to clear your brain.

Mrs Artminster takes a swig.

How do you feel now?

Mrs Artminster Clouded. Troubled and clouded. Who is that creature? (*Points to the picture.*)

Mr Booker My – spiritual father, madame.

Mrs Artminster Spiritual – and yet you're here, aren't you? (*Studies the picture.*) Why's he smirking in purple? (*Long pause.*) What did you say my Garfield went out for?

Mr Booker walks to the picture, looks at it, turns to Mrs Artminster.

Mr Booker I think you know, madame. The clouds and troubles in your mind are truth obscured. You know, madame. (*Stares at her.*) Because of the possibility of his taking up a good position here, in my hotel, which we were discussing before your spell.

Mrs Artminster A position here? When he has an income and a cottage in Little Munstering? (*Long pause.*) And what were you offering? (*Contemptuously.*)

Mr Booker You were too delicate to ask. You only expressed your gratitude and your interest. (*Little pause.*)

I was helping you to see the truth, which could be useful to you.

Mrs Artminster You're after something, Booker, and it's poison to me and my Garfield, whatever it is.

Mr Booker Madame, madame, at this very minute your son is standing before an interviewing board, cap in hand.

Mrs Artminster My Garfield is *proud*.

Mr Booker Yes, madame, he's proud. And that's why he's selling himself to the highest bidder. He wants to keep your delusions alive.

Mrs Artminster Why are you doing this, Booker? I thought you were my friend, the way you came up to me every evening and helped to keep me cheerful. Now you go on and on, over and over, you tell me my Garfield's coming to work for you, why? Why do you want him? You've got that Janice, haven't you? Why do you want my Garfield? What good can he do you?

Mr Booker (*after a pause*) Modesty is what I need at the desk. (*Sits down in chair.*) Breeding. Someone with the gift of quietness. *She's* no Garfield.

Mrs Artminster Who?

Mr Booker Janice.

Mrs Artminster Who said she was?

Mr Booker I said she *wasn't*.

Mrs Artminster Why?

Mr Booker Well, she isn't, is she? I was comparing her to Garfield in quietness.

Mrs Artminster What's he got to do with it?

Mr Booker He's quiet.

Mrs Artminster Who said he wasn't?

Mr Booker I didn't.

Mrs Artminster Why? Why didn't you, Booker?

Mr Booker What I said was what I particularly admire about Garfield and what qualifies him for a post on my desk was that he wasn't like Janice, and what I said was that he was quiet. (*Pause.*) For his sake, madame, face the truth. That boy has gone out to get a position, and I can help him. Face it, madame, face it.

Mrs Artminster Oh yes, the sun rises and sets on my Garfield to hear you speak his name, but there's one thing I can't face because you won't tell me, and that's what you're after. But I can smell it.

Mr Booker (*leaping to his feet*) Well, you've gone all the way down and shown yourself at last, haven't you, madame? (*Pause.*) But I couldn't expect you to understand. (*Pause.*) There's no one could understand, except someone who helped me once and took me under his wing.

Mrs Artminster And where is he now, this wing of yours?

Mr Booker He was persecuted. By people like you. (*Walks to the picture.*) Oh yes, they're against it in all the places, in all the godless world. Even his own church turned against him. If a man has a loving heart they crucify him – as the Testament shows us. He – (*pointing to the picture*) that man, had to go to Canada.

Mrs Artminster Didn't take you along, eh?

Mr Booker We keep up a correspondence. And there are celebration cables – at Christmas and birthdays, on the blessed rising and transfiguration of Easter. He remembers, though the world forgets.

Mrs Artminster Well, you're not desperate, are you, or you'd go to him.

Mr Booker (*turning*) The time came for me to suffer my own way, without going unto him.

Mrs Artminster Well, keep your suffering off of my Garfield.

They look at each other. Mr Booker turns to the picture, turns away from it.

Mr Booker There's no point in making an offer even, then?

Mrs Artminster An offer? For my son? Do you call him cattle, that you can buy or sell?

Mr Booker A fish, for the fisher of men. A lamb for the shepherd. Fish, fowl and soul, immortal soul, to work at my desk.

Mrs Artminster You offer me *money*?

Mr Booker I offer *you* money, as I offer *him* life.

Mrs Artminster Money?

Mr Booker nods, goes to the picture.

You haven't enough money to buy my son from me.

Mr Booker turns, stares at Mrs Artminster.

Where? Where do you keep this money of yours, you keep boasting about? In some safe or other, I suppose, you'll be telling me next.

Mr Booker nods. After a long silence.

Oh, you monster. How much do you think I'd sell him for?

Mr Booker I do not buy him. I buy you. I buy *from* you. I buy his liberty from you, it is you that I buy, and cast away. (*Pause.*) Never to return. (*Little pause.*) You may write, of course, on open postcards. (*Little pause.*) Two bottles of my Scotch are missing, by the by.

Mrs Artminster Don't ask me, accuse the nigger. (*After a pause.*) Oh, I could say yes, just to have him set up in a position, to ease a mother's worry. (*Pause.*) Don't think I don't know what's the matter with me, with my dreams of Little Munstering and money to keep us on. Do you know what I want, Booker? Just a view of bridges over a river from a little window, and orchards to tend as I get old. Do you think I haven't worked for it, Booker, worked and worked? (*Pause.*) I love my boy, and he loves me. We're bound together by it. And that's the trouble, because even if I listened to you, *he* wouldn't. He would fret after me. I'm not saying he wouldn't be better off, but he won't take up a position without me.

Mr Booker I'll talk to him. I'll make him understand. We know each other, Garfield and I. Two hundred pounds. If you help me.

Mrs Artminster How?

Mr Booker Tell him he needs to be free. Tell him you need his freedom for him. Tell him in a mother's love. And mention the satisfaction it would give you to know that he worked here, at my desk.

Mrs Artminster (*after a long pause*) I'll tell him. I'll tell him how much it means to me, this freedom. (*Pause.*) You know, Booker, once I had another boy. His name was Derek. Derek would have understood. He was muscle, Derek was, knew how to do a job and stay in himself. He didn't need me to look after him. He didn't need to be looked after by me, Derek didn't. That was where our strength was – Derek and me. Now I'd like a look at him again, to remind me before it's too late. I'm old, Booker, old. I need my Derek now. (*Little pause.*)

Mr Booker Garfield will remember you.

Mrs Artminster What will he remember, Booker?

Mr Booker (*going towards the door*) He will remember that you helped to set him free. I must go now. I have other rooms to visit, other pictures to hang.

Mrs Artminster And what about my two hundred?

Mr Booker When the choice is made. I'll be up this evening, as per.

Mrs Artminster You're a babe, Booker. I warn you that now, you're a babe in the wood, if you think it's going to be easy. I'll want that two hundred on the spot.

They stare at each other. Mr Booker exits. Mrs Artminster gets up, looks at the picture, goes into the next room, comes back for the whisky bottle, goes back into the next room. Then goes to the bed, lies down with the whisky bottle, begins to hum. Hums louder – 'On a bicycle made for two'. Stops humming. Drinks.

Curtain.

SCENE TWO

Mrs Artminster is lying on the bed, dozing. The bottle of Scotch, a quarter empty, is cradled in her arms. Jerry's room is in darkness. The door of Jerry's room opens. His light goes on. Jerry enters. Mrs Artminster jerks awake, blinks, conceals the bottle under the mattress. Jerry takes the blond wig out of his pocket and puts it in one of the cases. Meanwhile Mrs Artminster is arranging herself on the bed.

Jerry comes in. He sniffs, looks at Mrs Artminster suspiciously, sniffs again, then goes to the window and opens it. Turns. Mrs Artminster, who has been pretending to be asleep, now wakes.

Mrs Artminster Hello, Jerry. (*In a tender voice.*) Had a hard day, son?

Jerry I've had a terrible day, terrible. (*Sits down in the chair.*) Load of twits think just because I sit there in my goldilocks I don't have feelings. Laugh and clown and slobber their pity, for the sake of five-pound expenses. (*Little pause.*) There was a little twit with Jew eyes and big lips and a fuzz of white hair. I knew what he was up to, all right. They offer me a position and I turn it down, then I don't get my expenses, do I?

Mrs Artminster What did you say?

Jerry I said yes, sir, I wanted to be helped, and I kept looking at his white fuzz, silky and noble, and I said of course I couldn't cut my hair and the bit about a free country and nothing in the advertisement. He said that was all right. *That* stopped me.

Mrs Artminster You took the job?

Jerry Had to, didn't I? But I kept my eye on his fuzz, all the same. And he said twenty pound a week, starting Monday.

Mrs Artminster Twenty pound a week. That's high, Jerry, very high, for someone without particulars.

Jerry Oh yes, he was a bright Jew all right. I couldn't say no, could I?

Mrs Artminster (*after a pause*) So you've fixed yourself up then, Jerry, after all? I always said you were meat for the soft-hearted. All that cleverness and you got yourself caught. (*Shakes head.*) I knew it was coming.

Jerry Wait a minute, can't you, because he said, did I have any questions? He was waiting to see what I'd do, he knew I'd never turn up and he'd saved himself a five, and got himself some cheap laughs at my expense. And I said I was very grateful for the chance, and I'd be there nine sharp, a bit earlier because I'd want to get down to it straight away, a lot to learn and that, and he said no need, come at nine, and I said no, it was all right, I'd be there at eight because you needed to be set on the toilet and washed at seven, and fed your tea and porridge, and then I could leave you. That's when he began to get a bit worried, about whether I meant it, and there I'd be on the doorstep with my hair down my shoulders and eager, but he kept up his nodding and Jew grinning, and said anything else, and I said there was one thing, very personal, I didn't want to make him angry, and I sort of lay across the desk and whispered shyly into his face, still watching his fuzz, 'Pardon me, but yours is lovely, where did you get it? Was it made by hand?'

There is a long silence. Mrs Artminster stares at Jerry, who is looking tense.

Mrs Artminster So what did he do?

Jerry Shouted at me.

Mrs Artminster What did you do? (*Looks at him.*) You –?

Jerry Cried. (*Begins to slap his hands together, as if in agony.*) I cried. I couldn't help myself. I told you I can't help myself. It just came out. Any minute my bones was going to break into pieces and I'd be skin on his floor, with jagged ends showing through, I kept thinking of that, and what you'd say when you heard, and you crying over my box being lowered, these things kept going round and round, and then next thing I was out on the street, my expenses in hand and more, and wiping my eyes, and I could feel them watching from the windows, and people on the street staring, so I got down a siding and out of my wig. Then I went to Dewbury and Son. They took one look at me and signed the chit.

Mrs Artminster So how much did you take, in the whole day?

Jerry Thirty pounds. But that's Reading done with. Word'll get round. I'll write some letters tomorrow, there's hundreds of firms in the north looking for boys with technical training. They're warm in the north, I've heard that. Friendly and hospitable.

Mrs Artminster And how much did it take off of you, this thirty pounds? (*There is a silence.*) What I mean, Jerry, is look at the state you're in, ragged and clenched up, you don't know where you are? (*Little pause.*) Do you, son? You've got a trick, and it's killing you off. What's the good of it, son, what's the good of it?

Jerry I don't know anything else, do I?

Mrs Artminster I could teach you.

Jerry What could you teach me? Some of your joggering? So I'd be like Derek, and end up where Derek is? No thank you. No thank you.

Mrs Artminster You'd only have to do it the once. (*Little pause.*) It'd be easy, no need for a real jogger. (*Little pause.*) I'd do the joggering.

Jerry Like you joggered the Peasbury Postman?

Mrs Artminster Derek did that, he forgot his own muscle, I got more experience than Derek. I'd aim right. Jerry, Jerry, all you'd have to do is keep a watch, give me the signals, we'd be away. We'd find a place in the country, lie low, be peaceful. He's got money in that safe.

Jerry Who –?

Mrs Artminster You know who.

Jerry No. I've told you no. He'd have them after us in ten minutes. He *knows* us.

Mrs Artminster No he doesn't.

Jerry Well, he knows us like this, and they know you the other way, you'd have nothing left. Everybody'd know us then.

Mrs Artminster We'd have a chance. We'd have a man's chance, more chance than Derek had.

Jerry Shut up about him. I've told you, the police –

Mrs Artminster The police! Sometimes I'd rather be in a room with the police of nine counties than just you, Jerry, and that's the *truth*. I tell you I don't know myself, I'm lost, funny things happen to me when you're here. Woman's tricks I use now, and handbag cunning. Derek wasn't the only one famous for his muscles, and I'm not boasting. Where have *my* muscles gone, Jerry, and don't I have instincts? Don't I? You tell me, go on, tell me. There's that Booker downstairs sitting on a safe with a fortune in it, he told me as much, and what's my instinct about that? Mine. My instinct.

Jerry (*getting to his feet*) You're free, you're free and you're fed and you're looked after, that's your instinct, happy, and you want to throw it away just for the pleasure of joggering Booker. Where'd your instinct be *inside*, *you* tell *me* that.

> *There is a long silence. Then Jerry sits down, his hands clasped, Mrs Artminster punches the bed, stops, looks at Jerry.*

Mrs Artminster You could do it, Jerry. You could do it with a smile and your nerve. You could get into that safe, clean it out, and leave him babbling his nonsense while he watched you. He'd help you, he's that drunk with love. No need to jogger, no risks, nothing. You'd have something on him, if you did it right. (*Little pause.*) Just a drop of tenderness, you could keep your eyes shut.

Jerry (*clasping his hands over his ears*) I can't hear you.

Mrs Artminster For my sake, Jerry.

Jerry I can't hear you.

Mrs Artminster All right, Jerry, but I've given you the chance. (*Quietly.*)

Jerry I can't hear you.

> *There is a long silence. Then Mrs Artminster gets up, Jerry watching, with his hands still over his ears. Mrs Artminster lifts up the mattress and takes out the Scotch. Takes a long drink. Jerry takes his hands away.*

Where'd you get it from?

Mrs Artminster I'm not talking to you, so don't ask questions. (*Takes another drink.*)

> *There is a knock on the door. Jerry stares at the door, gestures at the bottle, Mrs Artminster puts the bottle on the table, in full sight, stares malevolently at Jerry.*

Enter.

Janice enters, smiling. Stands just inside the door.

Janice Sausage and wooost from the Three Musketeers?

Mrs Artminster (*looks at Jerry*) Come in, my dear, come in for a moment.

Janice advances into the room. She smiles at Jerry, who pays no attention.

Garfield, what's your fancy tonight?

Jerry I don't care.

Mrs Artminster Don't care was made to care, dear. (*To Janice.*) You're looking very ravishing tonight, my sweet, and you've got those lovely doo-dahs on again. They especially go in black lobes, I envy you.

Jerry (*loudly*) I'll have the sausages. What do you want, Mother?

Mrs Artminster I'd like a little woman's talk with Janice. Come sit by me, dear. And have a sip of this. (*Shows her the bottle.*)

Janice Oh no, missus. Mr Booker, he say I've got to hurry your supper, he wants to come up.

Mrs Artminster How kind everyone is being. Do you hear that, Garfield? Mr Booker wants to come up. To see you, I'm sure of it. Because he likes you, dear, doesn't he, Janice?

Janice laughs.

Does he like every stray boy who comes into this hotel, Janice?

Janice Mr Booker, he love boys' movements, he say. (*Laughs.*)

Mrs Artminster Do you hear that, Garfield? You're not the only pebble on the beach, my dear. Tell me, Janice, what's that steel cupboard with a knob on it that Mr Booker keeps in his office?

Janice It's for valuable.

Mrs Artminster Is that where he wants to pop Garfield into, for safe keeping?

Janice Oh, he like Garfield. I hear him say to God, in his office.

Mrs Artminster Ah, it would be good for my Garfield to have a little taste of confinement. Perhaps he'd come to enjoy it, wouldn't you, Garfield, in Mr Booker's steel cupboard. Does the knob have a special number on it, Janice, for opening?

Janice Oh, big number. 3338967.

There is a silence.

Mrs Artminster What was that again, dear?

Jerry I thought you had to go downstairs straight away.

Mrs Artminster What was that number again, dear?

Janice Millions. 99999999. Very big number. (*Little pause.*) I don't know.

Jerry You'd better get downstairs or there'll be trouble.

Mrs Artminster Pay him no mind, dear. I can see that we've got a lot to say to each other. It's not often I get a chance to speak with another lady, what with having to keep my eyes on him all the time. Come sit by me. Just for a minute. That's all I ask.

Jerry Leave her alone.

Mrs Artminster I told you, dear, you're not being spoken to. (*To Janice*) Oh he's very jealous, that one, a nasty, sulky boy. Come drink, my sweet – (*pouring Scotch into the mug*) – and tell me what you think of the taste.

Janice Mr Booker, he say don't touch alco.

Mrs Artminster This isn't alco, sweet, it's cereal boiled down and will do you good. Try it, come on, a little sip, try it.

Janice laughs, comes over, sits down, takes the mug.

Jerry Peasbury Postman. (*Little pause.*) Nine counties.

Mrs Artminster Fetch them here, then. There's some things I could tell them about a little freak of my acquaintance. (*To Janice.*) Now my dear, have a swallow and savour it. That's not drinking, what you're doing.

Jerry I'll make trouble.

Mrs Artminster I thrive on it. So does a young lady like Janice.

Jerry (*in a whisper*) Please. Please.

Mrs Artminster (*puts her hands over her ears*) I can't hear you, Garfield.

Jerry stands there, trembling, then goes into the next room. Sits on the edge of the bed, bitterly.

Now what were you telling me about that Mr Booker? Go on, another little sip.

Janice takes one, giggles.

That Booker?

Janice He a good man. He read prayers. He speak to God.

Mrs Artminster Oh, does he? (*Pours more Scotch into Janice's mug.*) I know what he asks for, then. But what about his cash, and how much does he keep?

Janice I don't know about that. (*Giggles again.*) He don't speak to me, hardly. He's a good man, doesn't like my black girl feelings, he say.

Mrs Artminster Well, we can see why he doesn't like the likes of you, sweet, it's because you're too young and savage for the likes of him, too full of the female sauces.

> *Jerry gets up, goes to the door. Crouches down and puts an eye to the keyhole. Gets up, slams his hand against the door.*

Janice Oooh. (*Giggles.*)

Mrs Artminster He's shy before the ladies, he and Booker are two of a kind. He fancies you too much, white against black, it gives him nightmares to think of it. (*Pause.*) And he's probably thinking those bubbles of yours – another sip, sweet – (*pouring more into the mug*) those bubbles aren't real.

Janice (*holding out earrings*) Oh, they real. Mr Booker, he give them to me because of the boy he teaching to pray.

Mrs Artminster Oh, teaching him to pray, was he? You saw it?

Janice Yes.

Mrs Artminster Down on his knees, was he?

Janice Yes, Mr Booker, he down on his knees praying, and this boy Henry, he standing against him, arms out in Lord Jesus Christ, he praying too, and moaning out to God, God, then Henry, he very bad, he run off, and Mr Booker he say to me, 'Here are some earrings Janice,' and I don't to say he is a religious man who like to pray with Henry, because the people of this world, where is their heart and understanding. Yes, they're real, these.

Mrs Artminster And those other bubbles, what about those? Are they real?

Janice What bubbles? (*Takes a gulp of Scotch.*) Oooh. Where?

Mrs Artminster Those bubbles under your blouse, sweet.

Janice (*with a screech of laughter*) Course they are, yes indeed they are.

Mrs Artminster I love you already, my dear, as if you were white, but I don't believe you, no I can't. Because if they are I might have to consider you for a photograph study in *Hearth and Lounge*, wouldn't I? And then there'd be no stopping you.

Janice What you saying?

Mrs Artminster *Hearth and Lounge*, dear, it's a popular ladies' magazine, and a friend of mine is the owner. I promise to send her pictures of local beauties I meet on my travels. I don't like doing it, the girls get uppity, what with talk of film contracts and easy stardom. But they don't accept false bubbles, especially from darkies, they get police raids from that. And those bubbles are false bubbles, admit it.

Janice These no false. These real as the Lord.

Mrs Artminster Oh no, my sweet, I'm afraid I can't believe you, you're lying there, although it's no reflection on yourself, only on the colour of your skin, which you can't help.

Janice These real.

Mrs Artminster Now my dear, you'll anger me if you go on like that, it's well known that black girls are born without bubbles, it's your big flaw. If they was real you'd be on every hoarding in the country. (*Pours Scotch into her mug.*)

Janice They real. They real. (*Pushes herself forward.*) Feel, go on and feel.

Jerry comes over, his hand on the knob. Mrs Artminster stares at the breasts, gets off the bed, then goes over and pushes the catch on the door. Goes back to the bed.

Mrs Artminster No, because foam is firm and stuffing's soft, and whether they're soft or firm they could still be false. No, if they look right uncovered I may feel them as an extra precaution. Then we'll talk about photographs, but not a word of this to anyone else because I'll have all your darkie cousins at my door.

Jerry tries the doorknob, pushes, slams the wood again, goes and sits down on the bed. Puts his head in his hands.

Janice What you want me do? (*Giggles.*)

Mrs Artminster I was giving you permission, dear, to show me your bubbles.

Janice Oh, you want see? (*Begins to unbutton her blouse.*)

Mrs Artminster No, no, do it slow and graceful, dear, a button at a time and pausing often because it's more ladylike. Remember this is a magazine for the upper-middle-class type of person, and style is important. Now go to the far side of the room and count ten before you even begin. Can you count ten?

Janice One, two, three, fours –

Mrs Artminster pushes her off the bed and gives her a pat on the behind. Janice totters from the Scotch.

Mrs Artminster That's it.

Janice stands rigidly.

No, loose a little, girl, pluck idly at a button and smile about you.

Janice (*very loudly*) One. Two. Three. Fours.

Mrs Artminster Shh. Ladylike. Do it in your head, or have a guess. Start again.

Jerry rises, walks around the room, then goes to the door, grabs the knob, jerks viciously. Mrs Artminster pays no attention. Janice begins to unbutton her blouse.

No, on second thoughts, begin with the accessories. Ear bubbles off first. Just drop them on the floor, as if you had tons of them stowed away. Which you will have if you reach the fame I've in mind for you.

Janice reels slightly from the Scotch, straightens, giggles.

Janice Don't know what you want.

Mrs Artminster raises her voice. Jerry obviously hears and stands stock still.

Mrs Artminster I want you to strip, that's what I want. Now do it, and do it quiet. (*Lowering her voice.*) You know what poses is? Poses?

Janice Poses?

Mrs Artminster Natural body postures.

Puts a hand behind head, thrusts out bosom, turns her head. Janice imitates her.

Yes, that's good for a beginning, very good and talented. Now dear, ear bubbles first. (*Settles back on the bed.*)

Janice takes off her earrings, drops them. Jerry seizes

*the doorknob, shakes it. Lies against the door. Janice
stops for a moment, Mrs Artminster makes a half-
threatening, half-erotic gesture. Janice lurches, giggles,
begins to unbutton her blouse. Jerry walks around the
room, striking his fist against objects. Stops suddenly,
stares at the connecting door, runs towards it as if
about to smash it down with his shoulder, stops at the
last second. Turns around. Sits down on the bed,
covers his face with his hands.*

*Meanwhile Janice is peeling off her blouse and
doing poses. Mrs Artminster is lolling back. Jerry
suddenly gets to his feet, as Janice begins to undo
buttons on her skirt. He runs towards the hall door,
opens it, rushes into the hall, out of view,
Simultaneously there is a distant door banging. Jerry
runs back into the room, glares about him, peels back
the covers of the bed, leaps in, pulls covers up and
turns face to the wall. Sound of footsteps. His
bedroom door opens, Mr Booker puts his head in,
stares sightlessly around the room, withdraws. A
second later his head reappears. He stares at the bed.
Steps in very quietly, stands uncertainly.*

*Janice is now stepping out of her skirt, stumbles
mid-pose, recollects herself.*

*Mr Booker goes to the middle of the room, stares
intensely at the bed. Goes over to it. Puts a hand
down on the covers, moves his hand up the covers,
rests it on the pillow beside Jerry's head. He stares
down at the head, suddenly snatches his hand away,
goes across the room to the picture, looks at it, turns
around, goes back on tiptoe to the bed. Stands at the
head, hands folded in semi-prayer fashion across his
chest. Puts his hand down again, strokes the covers.*

*Janice has kicked off her shoes, clumsily, and is now
rolling down her stockings, also clumsily. Mrs
Artminster is less relaxed on the bed.*

Mr Booker (*in a long, yearning sigh*) Garfield. Oh Garfield.

He sinks to his knees beside the bed and rests his face on the bed, beside Jerry's, his hands folded into his lap.

Oh Garfield.

Jerry stirs under the covers, huddling tighter.

Mrs Artminster (*as Janice moves back and forth, in movements that are gauchely erotic*) Oooooh.

Janice giggles and begins to unclip her bra.

Mr Booker Garfield.

Puts his hand an Jerry's head, stares at him. A pause, then Jerry begins to stir under the blankets again, more urgently. Mr Booker gets up quickly, tiptoes rapidly across the room and out of the door. Jerry immediately gets off the bed and runs to the connecting door, stops, stares at it. Janice drops the bra, Mrs Artminster is sitting bolt upright, beckoning Janice across the room with both arms. Janice is walking towards her. Jerry turns, runs out of the room, into the hall, disappears, bursts into Mrs Artminster's room, runs in front of Janice. Stops.

Jerry Slut. Slut.

Mrs Artminster Jerry!

Janice (*overlapping*) What he say? (*Backing away.*)

Jerry Black-skinned white-toothed monkey-grinning, gibbering foul fur peeling off. Fur. (*This should be said in a low, almost muttering voice.*)

Mrs Artminster Jerry! (*Gets off the bed.*)

Jerry Filth and fur holes and filth nigger slut nigger slut.

He advances on Janice, who is backing away.

Mrs Artminster (*grabbing hold of Jerry by the arm and trying to drag him away*) Shut up.

Jerry You naughty. You naughty.

Janice runs past and out of the room. Mrs Artminster slaps Jerry's face. He reels back, then sinks on the bed, hands over his face. There is a long silence.

Mrs Artminster I told you. I warned you. You keep me choked up in what I want, I told you. What about my instincts, where are they? (*Little pause.*) You've only yourself to blame. There's things I need in spite of you. (*Pause.*) And to hell with the police. To hell with them.

She stares at him, then sits down beside him. She picks up the Scotch bottle and has a drink. Jerry sits with his face covered, then gets up, runs over to Janice's clothing, bundles it up and runs to the cupboard with it, stuffs it in. Turns, goes back into his own room. Walks around, straightens his bed, looks at it, turns again, goes back into Mrs Artminster's room.

Jerry I knew what you'd be doing, guzzling at your bottle.

Mrs Artminster looks at him. Jerry advances, stands before Mrs Artminster. There is a long silence.

(*Pathetically.*) Oh, I've had a bad shock, I came all over faint. They're so rude to me because of my hair, they laugh at me, and then I got that feeling about my glass bones and I had a nightmare or something. (*Sits down on the bed.*) There was darkness and smells and my heart stopped beating and inside I was splintering, and being cut and cut and I was bleeding, Mum, there was red running, I can't bear to talk about it. What can I do? (*Long pause.*) Mum.

Mrs Artminster looks at him.

Mum?

Mrs Artminster looks at the bottle.

Mum?

He rests back against Mrs Artminster, who sits rigid, then puts the bottle down and puts an arm around him. Stares blankly ahead. Jerry cuddles himself into Mrs Artminster.

(*In a muffled, contented voice,*) Mum.

Curtain.

Act Three

Mrs Artminster is lying on the bed, nuzzling from the bottle. Jerry is standing before her, in his blond wig. He has a case beside him. He takes a few steps across the room.

Jerry (*turning his head sharply, three times*) See what I mean? (*Swings head again.*) It doesn't swing. And if it doesn't swing, it doesn't look natural.

Mrs Artminster What?

Jerry You're not watching. (*Swings head again.*) I said it doesn't look natural.

Mrs Artminster Oh, pardon me, I didn't know you wanted to go in for looking natural.

Jerry It's got to swing out when I turn my head, see. I can't sit there looking straight ahead when they ask me questions, can I? But if I turn my head and my hair stays pointing in the same place, then they'll wonder. (*Swings his head again.*) It's got too big inside. It's stretched.

Mrs Artminster Probably nervous sweat.

Jerry I don't sweat, you know that. No, it's these cheap plastics they line them with.

Mrs Artminster Oh yes, well, you think of cheap plastics against my skin-line, and it doesn't stretch, it shrinks, on a hot day it's like I was a baking potato.

Jerry (*tenderly*) Don't you worry, I'll get you comfy soon as we're gone from here. The black one's nice though, isn't it, Mum? (*Takes a black one out of the box.*) And still fits a treat. (*Puts it on.*) But I don't know, I always see myself as blond or red, to swing over my eyes. I feel naked in this.

Mrs Artminster Yes, well you look lovely and untakeable in all of them, why don't you give it a rest, Jerry?

Jerry What's the matter with you then? (*Takes off the wig, puts it back in the box.*)

Mrs Artminster Nothing. (*Little pause.*) Perhaps I'm hungry, that's what.

Jerry (*shutting the box up busily*) Oh yes. Well, *I'll* slip out and get your sausages. (*Smiles.*) And Worcester. I'll pour half a bottle on.

Mrs Artminster You'll have to, won't you?

Jerry I don't mind. (*Little pause.*) You know I like getting you things.

Mrs Artminster Nobody else is going to do it, is she? (*Stares at him.*) Not now.

Jerry What do you mean?

Goes out of the room into his own, with the box, puts it away, comes back in.

It's no trouble, honest. (*Smiles at Mrs Artminster.*)

Mrs Artminster You know what I mean. What I mean is, Miss Black-Bubbles isn't going to get my sausages for me, not now she isn't. That's what I mean.

Jerry (*after a pause, slaps his leg*) You don't have to mention it.

Mrs Artminster Not mentioning it won't stop it from having happened. She'll remember it, won't she? And what's your Simon Booker going to say?

Jerry What's it matter what *he* says?

Mrs Artminster It'll put him off you.

Jerry What's that matter?

Mrs Artminster And I thought you was the one who didn't like trouble. We need Booker friendly, and you're the one that keeps him that way.

Jerry We can leave here tomorrow, he can't stop us. (*Pats his pocket.*) I've got enough to get us to Leeds. We can go First if you want. (*Goes to the door.*) Like some chips?

Mrs Artminster I'm not hungry.

Jerry You said you was.

Mrs Artminster Well, now I'm not. (*Little pause.*) You put me off my food, the way you talk about Simon Booker. There's something I like about that man, just because he's good and wants to help people doesn't mean you can go sneering at him.

Jerry What are you saying, help people? What's the matter with you, you gone mad? I had him in there while I was – I was taking a doze, sniffing around at me and stroking at me and praying –

Mrs Artminster And what does that matter? He's got needs like everybody else and he's got other feelings on top of them. That man Simon Booker's had a hard life, but he's got it in him to be a good friend. What's more, he's climbing to the top in the hotel world, and don't you despise him for it. (*Finishes off the bottle.*)

Jerry (*after a pause*) What you up to?

Mrs Artminster Nothing. I'm just telling you about a man, Simon Booker, who's got the makings.

Jerry Well, he hasn't got the makings of me, I'll tell you that.

Mrs Artminster Yes, you've got it against nigger that she's juicy woman and against Booker that he's bent –

Jerry Shut up. Shut up. Now what you up to?

Mrs Artminster Nothing.

Jerry Oh yes you are. Now what is it?

Mrs Artminster Nothing, I tell you. It doesn't matter. I just don't like to hear evil nonsense about Simon Booker, who's got a religious nature and's willing to help. That's all. That's all I'm up to.

> *There is a long silence between them. Then Mrs Artminster, avoiding Jerry's stare, gets up and goes to her bag, takes out the other bottle of Scotch and uncorks it. Jerry watches.*

Jerry Where did you get that?

Mrs Artminster This? (*Looks at the bottle.*) From a friend. (*Looks at him.*) Of a friend.

Jerry What friend? Booker?

Mrs Artminster I can't tell you that. He swore me to secrecy.

Jerry It was Booker, wasn't it? (*Little pause.*) You stole it.

Mrs Artminster I told you, I got it from a friend of a friend, and I can't say more. But he's got an interest in me, he was up here today making propositions.

Jerry Propositions? To you? (*Laughs theatrically.*)

Mrs Artminster Yes, to me, and why not? Don't you think your old mum's got charms? There's more where you come from, Jerry, who prefer a mature lady and are willing to give her presents to prove it. (*Little pause.*) Perhaps Janice's got a brother she introduced me to, while you was out peddling your wigs. A sweet black boy, more like someone whose name you can't bear the sound of than he's like you, colour apart.

Jerry (*stares at her uncertainly*) You stole it.

Mrs Artminster Oh did I? What's the matter, can't you stand a little competition, son? It's you who made your mum this way, and if she catches other people's fancy, you've only yourself to blame, haven't you?

Jerry You stole it. (*Whispered.*) You did, didn't you? You did.

Mrs Artminster What's the matter, son, got some more of the jelly-belly?

Jerry runs to the bed, flops on it, face down. Mrs Artminster goes over to him.

Course I only said perhaps – (*Little pause.*) And I didn't say it was my friend, did I? I just said a friend. Perhaps it was your friend. (*Little pause.*)

Jerry Who? (*Beats his hands on the bed.*) Who? It was Booker, wasn't it? Wasn't it?

Mrs Artminster (*after a long pause, sighs*) Course it was Booker. (*Little pause.*) I stole it. (*Little pause.*) It doesn't matter.

Jerry (*sitting up*) I knew it all the time.

Mrs Artminster (*sitting down, takes a drink, looks down at the floor*) Oh Jerry, Jerry. (*Long pause.*) Aren't I entitled to anything except what you make up for me? Where's my past, Jerry, gone along with my hope, that's where. (*Pause.*) We did twenty-seven jobs together, I taught him from when he was a green thug and nothing, till it took them a week to catch him, out in those fields where he ran about like a hunted animal. There's honour in that, I see it now. Four men held him down, and then they had to use handcuffs. He went silent.

Jerry Oh did he? (*Little pause.*) They want you, though, don't they? They haven't stopped looking, they're not going to stop – it said in the paper that postman was having his milk from a bottle like a baby. (*Little pause.*) They've been watching nuns in Andover. Where'd you be, without a son to show you're a mother? (*Pause.*) So he must have talked, for the remission.

Mrs Artminster You're a liar. You're a liar.

Jerry No I'm not, Mum, and what's more you know it.

Mrs Artminster (*intensely and vindictively*) I hate you.

Long pause. They stare at each other.

No, Jerry, I don't hate you, if I hated you I wouldn't want to see you happy, and worry about you, I'm sorry I said that.

Jerry shakes his head.

I'm sorry I said that, Jerry, I take that back, because it's not true. (*Pause.*) You know that, don't you?

Jerry hangs his head.

What about a game of scissors and papers, Jer? (*Sits on the bed, with fists out.*) Come on, Jer, I feel just like a game. (*Pause.*) Jer?

Jerry looks up, puts his fists to his eyes.

J-e-r-r-r.

He comes over, sits down, puts out his fists sulkily, then lowers them and shakes his head.

(*Very tenderly.*) Yes, Jer, come on. Come on. (*Sharply.*) All right, if you don't want to, that suits me.

Jerry raises his fists.

Now.

They raise and lower their fists three times, Jerry just a fraction behind Mrs Artminster. Mrs Artminster does scissors, Jerry does paper.

Jerry Scissors cut paper.

He holds out his hand and shuts his eyes. Mrs Artminster looks at him, at his hand, then gets a piece of wood which is by the window, and comes back. Sits down. Hits him hard across his palm. Jerry receives the blow with head thrown back, in martyrdom. They ready themselves and do it again. This time Mrs Artminster has stone and Jerry has scissors. She hits his hand again. The game is repeated twice more; each time Mrs Artminster wins and hits his hand. On the fifth time:

Mrs Artminster I'm watching you.

Jerry What?

Mrs Artminster I'm watching you.

Jerry Well, I like that, who's winning then? You are.

Mrs Artminster Am I? Jerry, you're a cheat.

Jerry Cheat! Look at my hand!

Mrs Artminster Yes, that's what I mean. We'll do it eyes closed, then we'll see.

They close their eyes, do it, although it's evident that Mrs Artminster is watching. Jerry has stone and Mrs Artminster, a fraction behind, has paper. She hands him the wood.

Go on.

Jerry looks at the wood without taking it.

Go on. (*Menacingly.*) I'm waiting, Jerry.

Jerry shakes his head.

Jerry.

Jerry I can't.

Mrs Artminster Why not?

Jerry Because I – because I hate violence, that's why.

Mrs Artminster (*after a pause*) Derek would.

Jerry stares at her, grabs the wood, turns his head away, swings down. It strikes Mrs Artminster hard on the arm. She lets out a roar of fury, grabs the wood and flails him with it. Jerry crouches away, giggling and crying out.

Jerry I'm sorry, I'm sorry, I didn't mean it, Mum, I didn't mean it. I'm sorry, Mum.

Mrs Artminster (*striking more savagely*) I'm not your bloody mum. I'm not your bloody mum.

Stops, looks at the stick, then throws it across the room in disgust, stares at Jerry, who is still curled up on the bed, giggling and whimpering, then shakes head.

It's no good, Jerry. It's no good. (*Little pause.*) It's wrong.

Jerry (*stopping*) What?

Mrs Artminster (*standing up*) It's wrong, Jerry, you and me. We're wrong for each other. (*Long pause.*) I've got to take my chances and make my run, Jerry. I need a go for my freedom.

Jerry You can't. You'll be taken.

Mrs Artminster I don't care any more. It's not worth it. Look at you. Jerry, look at you. And look at me. In these togs, at these games. I am fifty-three years old, Jer, and I'm lost to myself. Lost. (*Little pause, then pleadingly.*) All I need is a little cash, say two hundred, to help me get a start. (*Little pause.*) You help me, Jerry. (*Little pause.*) Please. (*Little pause.*) Please.

Jerry (*gets to his feet*) But – we're happy together, aren't we? We're happy. (*Little pause.*) I'll be better, honest I will. I won't do it again. I was only joking.

Mrs Artminster It's not the doing, Jer, it's the feeling behind it, and that's no joke. All the feelings, all of them. Glass bones, nigger smells, scissors and paper. (*Pause.*) It's just that I got to make my run, Jer, and finish like I started off. It's right. (*Little pause.*) Please.

> *There is a long silence. Jerry turns away, stands with his back to Mrs Artminster. Shakes his head. Mrs Artminster moves towards him, his hand out. There is a knock at the door. Mr Booker puts his head in. Coughs. Then comes in, holding Janice by the arm. She is wearing a man's dressing gown. Mr Booker looks at Jerry.*

Mr Booker I'm very sorry to interrupt, with Janice, the truth is something unpleasant has blown up.

Mrs Artminster The truth is I told that girl never to darken our room again. What does she want now? (*Stares at Janice scornfully.*)

Mr Booker The unpleasant fact is, I found her sobbing in one of the cupboards with nothing on virtually, I must say. She was sobbing and her breath was filthy with alcohol, which I don't and can't allow. Garfield, I'm sorry to make suggestions. She seemed to be saying something about being attacked by, the unpleasant truth is, Garfield, by you, although I confess it was difficult to make out.

Mrs Artminster Oh she did, did she? That's what she said, is it? (*Little pause.*) And you'd take the word of this – this – over my son Garfield you pretend to worry over? Well, I'll give you the unpleasant facts of the truth, if she can bear to stay in the room to hear it, and don't blame me if it's too strong for you, it's not my fault your present company is a nigger and a slut, even if she is decorated in your dressing gown. Or do you want to tell it, Garfield, can you bring yourself to open your mouth on it, my dear?

Jerry (*shakes his head*) No, Mother.

Mrs Artminster *She* came cavorting into my son Garfield's room when we were in here calmly waiting for our supper, and was going through my son's belongings with an open bottle of whisky he had purchased for me as a little gift. Oh yes, she was rolling with it, and singing one of her songs when Garfield found her at it, and accosted her with the truth about herself. And do you know what she did, oh yes, she began to strip herself down and offer herself at him until he was forced to come running in here to me, and I had to deal with her myself. *He* couldn't bear to look at her brazen nudity, he was that ashamed, could you, dear?

Jerry shakes his head.

He was took sick with the sight of her.

Mr Booker I knew it. I knew it. I knew you were lying to me, how dare you, you animal. (*Shakes Janice.*) Where are her clothes, by the by?

Mrs Artminster Clothes? On her body, the last I saw them. I made her put them back, every stitch and tittle, before casting her out. What she's done with them since, I wouldn't know, and yes, animal is the word. It's the word Garfield used to me, and the word I used back at him. Animal. Garfield and I have been up here ever since, upset and sick, waiting for an apology from the animal. Haven't we, Garfield?

Jerry Yes, Mother.

Mr Booker Well, what do you say? (*To Janice*) What do you say?

> *Janice, dazed and in tears, begins to cry audibly, shaking her head.*

They're waiting for an apology. (*Shakes her again.*) You'd better say sorry, or there'll be no mercy for you. Even from where mercy's infinite and ever-abundant. (*Shakes her.*) Say you're sorry. Sorry, say sorry.

> *Janice begins to scream and jerk. Mrs Artminster comes across and takes her by the other arm.*

Mrs Artminster My son Garfield's waiting for the word.

> *Janice thrashes about, and they control her by forcing her to her knees. She crouches with her head lowered, in front of Jerry. They have her arms forced up painfully.*

Mr Booker Now, Janice, say after me – 'O Lord, I do in my deepest sincerity repent for the blackness of my heart' – say it, 'O Lord I do –'

Janice O Lord, I do –

Mr Booker 'In my deepest sincerity repent –'

Janice In my deepest sincerity repent –

Mr Booker 'For the blackness of my heart.'

Janice For the blackness of my heart.

Mr Booker 'And furthermore, O Lord –'

Janice And furthermore, O Lord –

Mr Booker 'For the foulness and depravity of my thoughts –'

Janice For the foulness and depravity of my thoughts –

Mr Booker 'And my behaviour to your faithful servant –'

Janice And my behaviour to your faithful servant –

Mr Booker 'Garfield Artminster.'

Janice Garfield Artminster.

Mr Booker 'Amen.'

Janice Amen.

They release her, she falls on the floor.

Amen Amen Amen Amen Amen –

Mr Booker (*opening the door*) Now go to the basement room, where you will stay, until I see fit to redeem you. Go. Go, I say.

Janice crawls out of the room, Mr Booker steps into the hall to watch her go. Jerry is now standing close by Mrs Artminster. Mr Booker comes back into the room.

(*To Jerry.*) I never doubted for a moment, Garfield. I hope you believe that. I knew you to be innocent. I only hope you were satisfied with the confession and apology that were wrung out of her.

Mrs Artminster Yes, and it was no pleasure, I can tell you. But you had it coming to you, Garfield, and I'm glad we got it for you.

Jerry (*looks at Mrs Artminster, comes to her, kisses her on the cheek*) Thank you, Mother.

Mrs Artminster (*who has moved away*) Course it was Mr Booker's apology mainly, Garfield. He thought it up.

Jerry (*turns to Mr Booker*) Thank you.

Mr Booker (*gently*) That's all right, Garfield. I was glad to do it for you. You know that, I trust.

Mrs Artminster goes towards Jerry's room.

Jerry Where are you going, Mother?

Mrs Artminster I felt one of my turns starting up just now, Garfield, and I thought I'd just lie myself down on your bed –

As Jerry advances toward her:

No, no, dear. I'll be glad of the quiet. You two men carry on without me.

Looks at Mr Booker, goes into Jerry's room. Jerry stares at the door, turns.

Mr Booker Well. (*Takes a nervous step forward, stumbles against the chair.*) Well, I'm glad that unfortunate nastiness has been cleaned up. I hope you're not too upset.

Jerry (*looks at him, looks at the door of his room, sits down on the bed*) No.

Mr Booker Good. That's good. (*Long pause, sits down in the chair.*) May I?

Jerry What?

Mr Booker (*gets up, gestures towards the chair*) Sit down.

Jerry Oh. Yes.

Mr Booker sits down.
Mrs Artminster is sitting by the door, listening. Suddenly she gets up, comes into the room, walks across the room, collects her bottle of Scotch, goes back to Jerry's room. Jerry and Mr Booker watch her. Jerry gets to his feet as she goes out, then sits down again. There is a long silence. Mrs Artminster sits by the door to listen, and sips from her Scotch.

Mr Booker I was just wondering how you'd got on?

Jerry What?

Mr Booker In your interview.

Jerry Very well, thank you.

Mr Booker Oh, I see. (*Little pause.*) You've got a position then?

Jerry (*gets to his feet, sits down*) No.

Mr Booker (*eagerly*) Then you didn't accept?

Jerry Yes.

Mr Booker You did accept?

Jerry Yes.

Mr Booker I see. (*Long pause.*) You got on very well in your interview in which you accepted a position, but you didn't get the job?

Jerry Yes.

Mr Booker I see.

Long pause, while Mr Booker takes off his spectacles, wipes them. Jerry sits staring at the floor, sometimes at his bedroom door.

(*Putting his spectacles back on.*) What actually happened then, if I can take on myself the right to ask, Garfield?

Jerry What?

Mr Booker With respect to the position you accepted but weren't offered, as I understand it.

Jerry They didn't want me.

Mr Booker (*after a pause*) I know how you must feel, to feel rejected. That's the worst of all feelings. But Garfield, Garfield, this rejection will be for the best, others have been rejected before, as the Testament proves. (*Little pause.*) Why didn't they want you, by the by?

Jerry shakes his head. There is a pause.

You're upset, my child. I know it.

Jerry (*laughs*) Upset? I'm not upset. (*Raises his voice.*) I don't care any more, I don't.

Mrs Artminster nods, sips from the whisky bottle.

Mr Booker (*intensely*) Yes, Garfield, you care. That's where you're like me – (*Gets up.*) And that's where you suffer. (*Walks to the picture.*) It's called passion, after a sacred event of love. Garfield, there are only a palmful of us, he used to say, who can be naked before each other and face the darkness. The dreadful darkness.

Jerry Yes, yes, that's all right, isn't it? But what about the smell, how can she face that? (*Raises his voice.*) You know how, because she smells of it herself.

Mr Booker (*little pause*) Yes, Garfield, you're right, of course, I wouldn't have mentioned it for the world if you hadn't brought the matter up. But we must be merciful and remember that she can't help herself, although I've noticed it personally every time I go in for a chat, and remember too what cleanliness is next to.

Jerry (*looks at the door*) Peasbury. (*In a raised voice,*) That's all I have to say. Postman. At the top of my voice. (*Little pause.*) Little Munstering – (*Spit.*) That's what'd be left of Little Munstering. And who'd be free then? Who?

Mr Booker (*stepping towards him*) Yes, Garfield, you're right. You *are* free. You're already free. She has a claim, of course, and I won't forget it, don't you worry. (*Stops.*) Where's Peasbury, by the by?

Jerry What?

Mr Booker Why did you say Peasbury?

Mrs Artminster is sitting transfixed by the door.

Jerry Because there was an attack at Peasbury, a bad attack, that ended in a death almost.

Mr Booker (*excitedly*) There'll be no danger of that in a home, I promise you. Professional nurses, and a sum arranged and put aside, for her tastes.

Jerry It was death, as good as. You think of it, drooling food out like a baby, helpless, dependent on a bottle. *That's* what they say.

Mr Booker No, Garfield, *I* haven't said it, and I wouldn't say it if you hadn't said it first. But the professional nurses will wean her away from it, they've got new methods. (*Little pause.*) You did say postman, by the by.

Jerry (*who is facing the door, swings his back at Mr Booker*) Yes, I'll tell you about the postman. In Peasbury. Yes.

SIMON GRAY

Mrs Artminster scrambles to feet.

Why shouldn't I?

Mrs Artminster enters the room.

I know what she's up to, and I don't care, see.

Mrs Artminster (*entering the room, points finger at Jerry*) Jerry! You utter, and Derek will get out special to see you.

Jerry Derek out? (*Laughs.*) You know where Derek is? (*Looks at Mr Booker.*) You know what you've got here?

Mrs Artminster Jerry!

There is a long silence. Mrs Artminster and Jerry stare at each other, Mr Booker stares at Jerry.

Mr Booker Garfield, please.

Jerry Well, now I know you, don't I? I really know you.

Mrs Artminster Perhaps you do, and perhaps it's time you did.

There is another silence. Then Jerry turns and goes towards the door of his room.

Mr Booker (*to Jerry's back*) Garfield, listen to me, I beg you.

Jerry slams the door.

Mrs Artminster You've got to be tough, Booker, and deaf to his ravings. For his own good. He'll cling like a leech unless you use a box of salt.

Mr Booker But he's so upset, I don't understand.

Mrs Artminster Course he's upset, I warned you, didn't I? But it's no good simpering at him like a lady. Now get at him.

Mr Booker But I – (*Wrings his hands.*) Where *is* Derek, by the by? I thought he was dead.

Jerry (*entering*) All right, you don't have to worry about me, any more. I'll leave you alone. I'm going.

Mr Booker Listen to me.

Jerry (*to Mrs Artminster*) I mean it. I'm off.

Mrs Artminster Are you, dear, then walk ginger on those bones.

Jerry And you needn't worry, I'm not coming back.

Mrs Artminster (*turning away from him*) Course not, or why say goodbye?

Mr Booker Garfield, let me speak to you for a moment, that's all I ask.

Jerry looks at Mrs Artminster and turns away.

Mr Booker Please, Garfield.

Mrs Artminster Jerry, the manager of this hotel wants a word with you. I advise you to answer up, boy.

Jerry slams the door.

(*Whispering.*) I told you. Force. Use force.

Mr Booker (*strides to the door, knocks on it*) There's a little matter of fifteen pounds ten shillings outstanding before you can depart from these premises, Mr Artminster. One pound five per night, per cheapest rates. (*Waits.*)

Jerry is packing.

You are answerable for tonight, as you've stayed past checking out time, two p.m.

Jerry pays no attention.

Fifteen pounds ten shillings, Mr Artminster. (*Pause.*)
Garfield, I don't mean to be hard on you, I know what
bad times you've gone through. I'm on your side, Garfield.
I just want to talk to you about the possibility of a
position on my desk.

Mrs Artminster Jerry, dear, this man is serious and to be
trusted. I vouch for it.

Jerry stops packing a moment, and then goes on.

Walk in on him, you're the owner, aren't you?

Mr Booker You don't have to do anything you don't
want to, Garfield. (*Opening the door as he talks.*) Just let
me speak to you, and then say yes or no when you've
heard out my heartfelt proposal.

Jerry (*turning, as Mr Booker enters the room*) You get
out. I know what you want, and you're not having it
from me, see. I've been followed by the likes of you all
over Victoria Station, except *they* weren't blind.

Mr Booker Garfield! (*He stumbles forward, falls on the
bed.*) Oh God, oh God.

Jerry Don't God me any more your Gods, homo blindie.

*A long pause, during which Mrs Artminster comes
to the door. Mr Booker buries his face in his hands,
shakes his head, then looks at the floor.*

Mr Booker It's not fair. It's not fair. What have I had
since he left me? I stand behind the desk with that slut
of a nigger to talk to, and my weeks are garbage and
godless. Sad in the evenings, the afternoons dead to me,
and the mornings I can hardly get out of bed from shame
of my dreams. And then you came, Garfield, you came
unto this hotel by accident that was Fate, and there were
feelings again. I can't help my feelings, that are given to

me. I've watched you, Garfield, as you've passed me towards the street, and I've come up here just for the gift of a chat with you. And you tell me that's evil and that I follow you all over Victoria Station in my blindness. And so I would, Garfield, I would follow you wherever you bid me, just so I can help and look after. That's my feeling, that's my feeling. (*Little pause.*) I want to be a good man, Garfield. Good. There's faith in me, to be brought out and put to service. (*Little pause.*) That's all I want, Garfield, and you talk to me as if you hate me for it. It's wrong.

Jerry Wrong, oh yes. It's wrong. (*Looks at Mr Booker.*) I've got my feelings and they're different from yours. What about her, and what she's just done to me? What about my feelings, do you think of them in your slobberings? My own mum.

Mrs Artminster (*quietly*) I don't know the meaning of the word where you're concerned, Jerry. I look at you and I see Stonehenge around my neck.

Jerry stands up and faces Mrs Artminster, who comes over to him and puts her hands around his face.

Now I'll tell you something, boy. You're going to do what I say, because the time has come for me to make my run. And the time has come for you to show you've got real feelings for me, son, and let me go when I'm dying from lack of my freedom. Because whatever you think now, I've done my best for you, Jer, I have. Do you think I've come along with you from blackmail? Do you think you could contain me if there wasn't other feelings to hold me close? But now, Jerry, now I know, and you know too, and soon the whole nation will know and be after me for myself, and that's the way it should be, that's the way I want it. If you've ever trusted me before, you trust me in this. (*Steps away.*) You could do worse than Simon Booker. He'll look after you, he's promised me that.

As Mrs Artminster and Jerry face each other:

Mr Booker I will, Garfield, I will. I've already forgotten your words to me. They'll never be mentioned between us.

Jerry All right. (*To Mrs Artminster.*) All right. You know I couldn't speak out. You know that.

Mr Booker (*standing between Mrs Artminster and Jerry*) What do you say, Garfield? What do you say?

Mrs Artminster It's the best for all of us, Jerry.

Mr Booker A position at my desk –

He reaches up his hands to put them on Jerry's shoulders, withdraws them.

And your freedom to be as you like. (*Little pause.*) Garfield? (*Little pause.*) I'll do anything you say. (*Little pause.*) Full board and lodging, of course.

Jerry (*turning away, sits on the bed*) All right. (*In a dead voice.*) All right.

Mr Booker You say yes?

Steps forward, stands in front of Jerry with hands clasped.

Oh Garfield.

Jerry (*in a dead voice and shaking his head*) But you won't last without me.

Mrs Artminster But I'll be going in myself, Jerry, whatever the end. (*Draws a deep breath.*) Booker, do you know who you've been dealing with? No, you don't. You've been dealing with the Peasbury Postman's assailant's accomplice. Derek Stewbat's accomplice.

*Little pause, while Mr Booker sits gingerly down
beside Jerry and stares at him, and then at the ground.*

And now, Booker, I'm counting on you to let me have
my two hundred, and give me the chance to get clear of
here, as was agreed.

Mr Booker I'm a small establishment, Garfield, you
know that. You've seen it for yourself. But if there's faith
between us, Garfield, there could be miracles.

Mrs Artminster Jock Masters, Booker. Me. (*Laughs,
points to his own chest.*)

Mr Booker (*looking at him*) What?

Mrs Artminster Jock Masters.

Mr Booker Who's that?

Mrs Artminster The Peasbury Postman's assailant's
accomplice.

Jerry stares at Mrs Artminster.

Mr Booker Who?

Mrs Artminster Jock Masters.

Mr Booker Oh. (*Nods, turns back to Jerry.*) Yes, I don't
deny that there are just the travellers, Garfield, and one
or two from a better class who might stray in now we've
got the decorating done.

*While he is talking Mrs Artminster has taken off her
wig and comes to stand beside Jerry, looking down at
Mr Booker. Mr Booker keeps his eyes fixed on Jerry's
face.*

And there's things I've been thinking on, Garfield, like
travellers' specialities, which would be Janice for instance,
sent up to the rooms.

Mrs Artminster Now about my two hundred you promised me, Booker.

Mr Booker But only with your permission and consent, Garfield. Nothing without that.

Mrs Artminster Look, if I'm to make my run, I want to get started. (*Puts her wig back on, angrily. It slips over one eye.*) Jerry, ask him for my two.

Mr Booker And I've often had a little dream, Garfield, vision like, of a room set aside as a chapel.

Mrs Artminster Jerry?

Jerry (*looking up*) You said I wasn't yours. You said I was his now.

Mrs Artminster (*sadly*) Jerry.

Jerry You said you preferred Derek.

Mrs Artminster Oh Jer, how could you?

Jerry And I was Stonehenge around your neck, you said, when you looked at me, and you wanted me off with Booker.

Mr Booker (*looking at Mrs Artminster*) Why did you say that about the Peasbury Postman's assailant, by the by?

Mrs Artminster So you wash your hands off of me, Jerry, do you?

Jerry That's what you want, isn't it? Talk to him. (*Points to Mr Booker.*) He owns me, you said.

Mr Booker (*in a quiet voice, getting up, walking around Mrs Artminster, studying the wig closely*) By the by, didn't you say the name –

He jerks off Mrs Artminster's wig.

– of Jock Masters? (*Stands back.*)

Jerry leaps to his feet.

Mrs Artminster Thank you, Jerry. Thank you. I don't blame you for what you've done, no I don't. I just wish you hadn't done it so underhand, I just wish you'd let me have my run.

Mr Booker I think you said yourself that Jock Masters is the Peasbury Postman's assailant.

Mrs Artminster (*to Jerry, who is standing, frozen*) Course I knew I'd never make it, Jerry, just as you'll never make what you want. But I could have tried, couldn't I? (*Turns, makes for the door.*)

Mr Booker Oh no you don't. You're not going anywhere.

Mrs Artminster Keep your hands off me, homosexual, nobody mauls at Jock Masters.

He turns and grapples with Mr Booker, who overcomes him easily, and forces him into a chair.

Mr Booker Telephone for the police, Garfield.

Jerry I don't want the police.

Mr Booker Garfield, Garfield, this is a criminal I've got here. I couldn't let him get up and walk away, could I, in defiance of the law of the land?

Jerry Why not?

Mr Booker Think of reputation, Garfield, and what would happen to the hotel if it leaks out that we harboured knowingly.

Jerry I don't want the police. If you call the police, I'm leaving.

Mr Booker (*after a pause*) All right. But there must be no return, and no communications. You must pursue your own salvation and repentance, without reference to Garfield.

As Mrs Artminster gets up, Jerry takes the wig from Mr Booker.

Jerry You'll have to make your run in those togs. You haven't got a suit.

Mrs Artminster I know that, Jerry, I'll take the risk.

She goes into the next room, collects zipper bag.

Mr Booker It's all over now, Garfield, the end of that has come. One day you'll look back on it and see what it was you had here, with this person. And the guilt will have cleansed itself out of you, and your restless spirit will be safe and settled. How did you come to be mixed up with him in the first place, by the by?

Mrs Artminster, who has come back into the room, walks slowly and heavily as if worn out. She stands with her bag and bottle, staring at Jerry.

Mrs Artminster It was in Ned's Sandwich, down by the Stepney Graveyard, where I was hiding myself over a cup of tea. Just after Derek was taken and there was descriptions in the papers, and an Identikit likeness. I'd walked past three police that morning, but he knew me at once – (*Shakes head.*) He knew me at once, this one did. He came to the table and whispered to me that he could help or cry out, whichever I preferred, it was like he was on the lookout. He took me back to his room behind the Mile End Tube and there were the togs in a cupboard and a wig prepared, and a box of lipstick and powders. I was garnished and out again before I could think, and all the time he was talking to me, cool and gentle. It was like he'd been waiting.

*Puts the bottle into the bag, and zips it shut. Then
walks across the room, with the same dull tread, puts
a hand to Jerry's face.*

And he's done his best by me, I won't deny it. However
far or little I run, Jerry, there won't be a word about you
in it when I'm taken. You'll read about me in the papers,
how I was hunted and trapped, and there'll be questions
and pain down at the station, when the boys light into
me, but I'll talk about every minute I was free and there
won't be a word about you in it. There's no shame in
being fond, Jerry, and I'll tell you now that I'm fond of
you. I always have been. I always will be.

Jerry (*sobs, straightens*) They're not checking the nuns
at Andover. I made it up. They haven't been looking
hard for weeks. (*Little pause.*) Derek didn't talk. (*Little
pause.*) Just a few more weeks and you'd be clear.

Mrs Artminster The time is come, son, as it was bound
to come. (*Turns away.*)

Mr Booker (*taking him by the arm*) Yes, Garfield, let the
thief walk in humility. There's a future to think of.

*Mrs Artminster walks slowly towards the door. Jerry
makes an effort to run, Mr Booker hangs on to him
and holds him tight.*

Let him go, Garfield. (*Gently.*) It's what he wants.

Jerry But she won't last without me, I know it.

Mr Booker He's in God's hands, Garfield.

Jerry She hasn't got a chance.

Mr Booker (*to Mrs Artminster, who is standing with
hand on knob*) Go. Go on. Go.

Jerry (*struggling across the room*) What'll happen to her?

Mr Booker (*holds on to him*) God will protect him. (*To Mrs Artminster.*) Get out.

Mrs Artminster opens the door and goes out. Shuts the door. Jerry stares at the door for a second, listens to the sound of Mrs Artminster's feet, then swings around, dragging Mr Booker after him, clasps the heavy table lamp from beside the bed, and swings it into Mr Booker's face.

Jerry It's your fault –

As Mr Booker staggers back:

It's your fault –

Hits him again, and when he falls, crying out, kicks him in the face.

You spoilt it, homosexual. You spoilt it.

Mr Booker lies on the floor, arms spread out. Jerry stands staring down. Drops the lamp.

Mum. Mum.

There is a long silence, then the sound of feet coming down the hall. The door opens and Mrs Artminster stands there. Looks at Jerry, looks at Mr Booker, comes over. Bends down.

Mrs Artminster Now you've done it. He's dead, Jerry. You've done him.

Jerry Well, Derek would have done that, wouldn't he? (*Looks at Mrs Artminster.*) Yes, there's my muscles for you.

Mrs Artminster (*takes a step back*) But you joggered him dead. This one's dead, Jerry. This Simon Booker's dead.

Jerry You told me. You told me to jogger, didn't you? You told me to. Mum. Mum.

Steps towards Mrs Artminster. Mrs Artminster sits down on the bed.

What'll I do? What'll I do?

Mrs Artminster Do? (*Little pause.*) Why run, Jerry, run. Make for the crowded towns, or the open country. Cover yourself in twigs from ditches like Derek did, or sit on the bottom of London buses at rush hour like I did. Go where you're not known, or there's too many to care. Run, Jerry, run, that's what you do. Run while you got the time.

Gets up, advances cautiously on Mr Booker, begins to strip him at increasing speed.

Jerry I don't know how.

Mrs Artminster You'll learn.

Jerry (*as Mrs Artminster goes on with the undressing*) Please.

Mrs Artminster You've said your last pleases to me, Jerry, I can't hear them any more. Save yourself, boy.

Jerry (*sits down on the bed*) I won't.

Mrs Artminster (*turns, looks at Jerry*) Then you'll be took.

Turns back, begins to undress.

Jerry I don't care.

Mrs Artminster (*beginning to swap clothes*) Don't care was made to care, Jerry. Can't you see I've had enough of it, locked away like one of your Dutch harlots in chains, my needs suppressed. Well, not any more. Look at me, Jerry, and what do you see? Jock Masters, that's what you see, boy. And that means I'll visit his safe on my way down, that's Jock Masters' way, and I'll find a way to open it, don't you worry. And I'll take half of what's there, and leave the other half for you, because that's Jock Masters' way too, and always has been.

While he is talking Jerry has been staring at him, then he gets up, goes into the next room with his case, goes to the wardrobe, takes out Janice's clothes and begins to exchange them, at speed, for his own.

Then you can go back to your wigs and whining, Jerry. I'll tell you again what I always told you, that game of expenses gives me the creeps, the thought of you sitting there, I don't know how you could do it. (*Stops.*) Scissors cutting paper, stones smashing scissors, eagles, glass bones – my own muscles going, tears spring up – there's no life in that, Jerry, and what you got against smells anyway? It wouldn't work, Jerry, I've got my own dreams, haven't I? What about Little Munstering then? (*Bends over and does up his shoes.*)

Jerry comes back into the room and stands waiting.

Yes, you see me now and know what I say. See who's back, Jer. (*Straightening.*) Jock Masters, that's who's back.

Turns. Stares at Jerry. There is a long silence between them.

Curtain.

DUTCH UNCLE

Dutch Uncle was first performed at the Aldwych Theatre, London, on 17 March 1969. The cast was as follows:

Mr Godboy Warren Mitchell
May Godboy Megs Jenkins
Eric Hoyden John Alderton
Doris Hoyden Frances de la Tour
Inspector Hawkins Patrick Magee
Police Constable Hedderley Nigel Anthony

Director Peter Hall
Design and Lighting John Bury
Costumes Sheila Russell

Characters

Mr Godboy

May Godboy

Eric Hoyden

Doris Hoyden

Inspector Hawkins

Police Constable Hedderley

Act One

SCENE ONE

The year is 1952. A living room in a decaying house in Shepherd's Bush. The wall, right (the audience's right, that is), has a door leading into the hall. The wall, left, has a door leading into the bedroom. The back wall, left, has a door that leads into the kitchen. There is a door in the kitchen that also leads into the hall, but is not visible to the audience. Parts of the kitchen – the stove, sink, and parts of the hall, a door, opposite, that leads into the lavatory – are, however, visible to the audience when the appropriate doors are open. The furniture is as follows. Back stage, centre, a shabby sofa. An armchair to the right of it and slightly forward. Two hard-backed utility chairs, one left of sofa, one well away from the armchair and in front of it. On a small table, left, and close to the bedroom door is a gramophone and a pile of records. In the right corner of the room there is an enormous wardrobe, sticking out and carelessly placed. It is tall and deep, freshly varnished and covered with curlicues, etc. Next to it, against the wall and to the left, is a more conventional wardrobe, shallower and slimmer. Both wardrobes have drawers in their bases. On the other side of the enormous wardrobe and to its right, against the wall and close to the door that leads to the hall, is an alcove covered by two curtains that don't quite meet and don't quite reach the ground. The heels of shoes and a few inches of boxes are therefore visible, also sleeves of jackets, etc. The room is very messy. Bits of newspapers and women's magazines scattered about, a pair of woman's high-heeled shoes near the gramophone table, two empty packets of cigarettes on one of the utility chairs.

The curtain rises on the room, empty. There is a long silence, then a slight thumping noise from the large cupboard. The door opens and Mr Godboy steps out. He is carrying a gas cylinder with a length of rubber tubing, very long, attached to its nozzle. He puts this into the alcove, hangs the rubber tubing so that it sticks out a fraction from between the curtain, goes to the door, looks casually around the room, then walks forward very quickly. With his left hand he slams the door shut, with his right hand he seizes the length of tubing, plunges it into a hole on the right side of the cupboard; then, pulling the cylinder out, pretends to turn the nozzle with his right hand. Takes the tube out, puts it back as before, puts the cylinder back behind the alcove curtain, unlocks the cupboard door. Takes out of his coat pocket an enormous padlock, shut, with the key in it. Checks the padlock against the bolt, then, holding the padlock, opens the cupboard door, steps inside, out of view, shuts the door behind him. Bangs on the cupboard door. The noises are muffled. Stops.

There is a short silence, then the door, right, opens and May Godboy comes in. She is wearing a baggy dress and flattened shoes and an overcoat. She is carrying a basket with a greasy package on top. She puts the basket down, bends over it. While she is doing this the cupboard door opens a fraction. May stiffens, turns, stares at the cupboard, puts her hands on her hips in amazement. Then the door opens wide and Mr Godboy steps out, falters a fraction of an instant. The padlock, closed, is in his right hand. He closes the door fussily, keeping the padlock out of sight.

Godboy Oh hello, dear, I wasn't expecting you for another hour, you said.

May What's that?

Mr Godboy slips the padlock into his right jacket pocket, drops it to the floor, picks it up with a –

Godboy Whoops! (*Laughs.*) It's a cupboard, dear.

May (*still staring at the cupboard*) What's it doing in here?

Godboy Oh no, dear – (*Stuffing the padlock into his pocket.*) It's not for us – (*Laughs.*) It's for Eric and Doris. (*Little pause.*) As cupboard space was conditional on acceptance of terms for the upstairs apartment, legally furnishings have to be approved as adequate.

May Who by?

Godboy Um, Eric and Doris that would be, dear.

May And have they come complaining?

Godboy It's a matter of conscience also, dear.

May Whose?

Godboy Mine, that would be, dear.

May If it's for Eric and Doris, what's it doing down here?

Godboy It's merely for the time being, dear.

May (*looks at him, turns, picks up the basket, turns again*) And what was you doing inside it then?

Godboy Investigating it for capacity, dear, merely. (*Long pause.*) Would you like to have a look-see?

Opens the cupboard door, makes a formal ushering gesture. May walks closer to it, stares in suspiciously. As she does so Mr Godboy's right hand moves from the pipe hanging out of the alcove.

May What for?

Godboy It's very capacious, dear.

May Perhaps it is.

She steps away. Mr Godboy drops his hand.

But that doesn't mean I have to live in it.

Walks across to the sofa, settles on it, takes off her coat, flings it onto the utility chair. It slides off, falls to the floor.

What do you think I am, some class of hermit? (*Chuckles.*) Because no, I'm not, no, I'm not. (*She stares at him significantly.*)

Godboy (*comes over, picks up her coat, folds it over the back of the chair*) Well, dear, to tell you the truth, I've already been and placed some of your garments inside it. Your nightie and a frock you're fond of plus your comfy carpet slippers, dear, and other odds and ends.

May Why?

Godboy Well, I thought we'd avail ourselves of the use of it, while we had it. Legally it's our cupboard until it's theirs. (*Looks at her.*) Anyway, if there's any article you can't find, it's likely to be in the cupboard waiting for you, you could peer in now for a check.

May swings her legs up onto the sofa.

But if I'm not here, give me a call so I can help you sort through . . .

May Ooo, the headaches you give me, you make a fuss out of breathing.

Mr Godboy goes back to the cupboard, shuts the door, turns to the guppie case, scatters food from a packet into it.

Godboy I'm sorry, dear, it was just a little idea of mine.

May reaches down to the basket, picks the package up, opens it. It contains chips. She begins to pop them into her mouth. Mr Godboy turns, stares. She stares back at him, goes on eating.

Tasty?

May Is that what you been doing all afternoon, then?

Godboy (*smiling*) Pardon, dear?

May Messing about with cupboards?

Godboy Yes, dear.

May (*knowing*) You sure?

Godboy There was a lot to be looked after, dear. It had to be purchased first, then arrangements had to be made for its delivery, myself accompanying in the van, no laughing matter as you can imagine, then various matters arose in connection with the padlock I insisted on for security measures . . .

He hesitates, then boldly takes the padlock out of his pocket, flashes it at her, stuffs it away. While he is talking, May gets off the sofa and goes into the kitchen, leaving the door open. Mr Godboy hurries over to the sofa, picks up her coat, takes it to the cupboard, puts it in, shuts the door, as May comes back in, sprinkling vinegar over her chips.

(*Coming back to the centre of the room.*) And on top of that I had to supervise the placing of the cupboard, also no laughing –

May Doris or Eric didn't drop down then?

Godboy No, dear, as I was explaining, I was compelled to be out all afternoon.

May Well, Eric was down looking for you while you was gadding about with cupboards; he wants to know when you're going to do some work on his Doris, if you're still up to doing work on anyone, that is . . . (*Settling back on the sofa.*) Seeing as he says as he's asked you five times.

Godboy (*after a pause*) Yes, dear, it's been a matter of waiting until the time is right, which it now is.

May And there I was thinking you'd be glad to get your hands on her shy little toes; think of the liberties – (*making prising gesture with a chip*) while you was knocking off a corn.

> *Mr Godboy looks at her, then goes to the kitchen door, shuts it, comes back, sits down on one of the utility chairs, laughs, shakes his head.*

Godboy I hope you don't joke like that around the neighbourhood, dear, on account of what you know it could do in the way of damage to my professional standing.

May (*sucks her fingers*) Oh and would it? (*Wags her head.*) What standing?

Godboy It might give people the unfortunate impression that everything wasn't right between us, dear.

May It's unfortunate where the truth is, then. (*Pause.*) What about the standing that never stands because it's already had damage done to it according to your story and as I was the last to know?

Godboy (*after a long pause.*) Pardon, dear?

May I've been thinking. How's your wound today? Throbbing, is it? Throbbing away?

Godboy It's merely been causing me a trifling pain, dear, thank you for asking. I managed to get down to the chemist for a prescription refill that'll assist me to doze off at night.

May (*sarcastic*) Well, that'll bring me some peace at last, won't it. (*Little pause.*) Your passion's been on the doze since the day we was married. (*Gets up, looks irritably around the room.*) And so's your foot-doctoring, so's your everything.

Godboy (*watching her alertly*) As you know, dear – are you looking for something?

May Where's my coat?

Godboy I popped it in the cupboard. (*Gesturing towards it.*) I believe it would be fatal for me to practise full time owing to the effect on my pension and side benefits, even my little family legacy would suffer.

As May goes towards the cupboard, he gets out of his chair.

And the fact that I'm perfectly willing to assist out on the wife of a tenant doesn't mean I have to go begging for it, merely, dear.

Sits down again as May walks past the cupboard to the alcove, pulls the curtain back, heaves the cylinder out of the way, scrambles about on a shelf, knocking down bits and pieces of clothes, then comes back wiping her hands on a large handkerchief. May blows her nose, settles back on the sofa as Mr Godboy goes to the alcove, puts the cylinder right while pretending to be putting the clothes back.

May What's that?

Godboy Pardon, dear?

May Those tubes and pipes?

Godboy Oh. (*Laughs.*) Merely a little device I was offered at the chemist to try out a little experiment with, merely, dear. (*Straightening, he closes the curtain.*)

May (*looking at him*) All day I've been thinking about you. I've got a surprise coming for you.

Godboy Pardon, dear? (*Brushing at his clothes.*)

May When we got started together you was brimful of talk about how you was going to swell up until you was too big to handle on your own, as feet was feet and would always cause pain and need doctoring, and all I seen you do in two years of marriage is monkey about on that pension of yours and go on about your wound and bother them down at the police station. (*Points a finger at him as he comes back.*) Where else was you this afternoon? (*Nods.*) Where was you? At the police station, that's where you was, wasn't you?

Godboy (*sits down*) Indeed, dear, I did drop in for a chat this morning.

May (*kicks off her shoes, sighs*) And what was you doing down there this time?

Godboy Merely discussing, dear, as I said.

May What?

Godboy (*after a pause*) Murder, merely, dear.

May What murder?

Godboy James Ryan O'Higgs, the Dublin accountant and wife- and female-tenant-murderer, dear. The one who polished off his wife and tenant in a week, and how he kept the police at bay with clever lies, although they was – were suspicious after the first. But still he kept on at it . . .

As May gets up, he watches her.

Chat merely, dear.

Getting to his feet as May goes to the cupboard.

What you might call shop.

Moving towards her as she opens the cupboard door, he takes the padlock out of his pocket. May turns, looks at him. He has been walking furtively, now walks nonchalantly to stand beside her.

May (*looks at him with contempt*) No wonder you need medicine, the way you fill your brain up with stuff like that.

She moves closer to the cupboard as Mr Godboy slips behind her to the alcove.

Where did you say my slippers was?

He puts his hand against the cupboard door to shut it, takes the pipe in his right hand. He cannot of course see May, as the cupboard door blocks her from view.

Godboy That's right, dear, in there, dear.

May steps around from the cupboard, stands behind Mr Godboy, who is still poised, holding the pipe in his right hand, the door in his left.

(*In a shout.*) He did it by gassing, May!

He slams the door as May puts a hand on his shoulder. He whirls around, laughs.

May (*as Mr Godboy drops the pipe*) What's the matter with you, I don't care if he did it by eating them raw; let me through, and why can't you leave my things alone?

As Mr Godboy steps away from the alcove, she bends down, knocking aside the cylinder, then comes out carrying a pair of slippers.

Godboy Those are mine, dear. Yours are in the cupboard.

May They'll suit.

She puts them on. He watches her malevolently.

And talking of gas, you be careful; the number of times you left the oven taps on for no reason, it's a wonder you're still here. And now it's tubes and what.

Godboy (*laughs*) Merely a device . . . (*Slips the padlock back in his pocket.*)

May (*turning her back on him*) Not that it matters. I've got a surprise for you.

Godboy Indeed? What sort of surprise?

May You'll find out when it comes. (*She settles again on the sofa.*) And who was you having this chat with? Your Inspector Hawkins?

Godboy With Duty Officer Larkins, dear. (*Shuts the door, comes back.*) Although it's funny you should mention Inspector Hawkins, dear, as he did come in while I was talking to Duty Officer.

May And has he remembered you yet?

Godboy His eyes were red-rimmed with fatigue and there was stubble on his chin; I garnered from Duty Officer's hints that he's been working twenty-four hours on the Merrit Street case – he wasn't in a condition to remember me.

May But he's been at that station two months now, and you been down there every day of the week, how is it he don't remember you if you was so close to him in the war?

Godboy (*stiffly*) I never said I expected him to remember me, May, I merely said in my capacity as Special Constable we'd come into contact before he was posted.

May Ooooh! Well, to hear you tell it, sometimes you was always at his side.

Godboy I admire him, May, yes, and I've followed his career, yes, and I'm proud to have been in contact, yes, and that's all I've said, May.

May And yet he don't remember you even! Yes?

Godboy (*looks at her coldly*) Inspector Hawkins will remember me all right, May, when the time comes.

May (*stares at him*) It's funny to me the way your voice changes at the mention of his name, why didn't you marry him instead?

  Long pause. Mr Godboy is sitting stiffly.

And from what I hear you're not the only one's coming into contact with Hawkins. Who was he with?

Godboy (*coldly*) Pardon?

May Who was your Hawkins with?

Godboy He was in the company of a female constable.

May That sounds like the Hawkins I've been hearing about.

Godboy (*still coldly*) Doubtless she has a key part to play in the Merrit Street case, May, given the nature of the offence.

May As long as she's female that's not all she'll have a key part to play in, constable or no constable, from what they say about Hawkins.

Godboy (*after a little pause*) There's always gossip about inspectors of a filthy nature.

May Oh, he's of a filthy nature all right, ladies and Hawkins are never out of each other's sight, that's what I hear.

Godboy You're talking about Inspector Hawkins, May. There's not, nor never has been no stain on his record.

May That's not where the stains would be. Manly Hawkins!

Mr Godboy sits staring straight ahead.

Isn't that what they call him?

Godboy That nickname was acquired because he's got the looks and manners of a born policeman. At first it was Irish Hawkins, but he soon put a stop to that, and then it was Mannerly Hawkins, from the respect he'd earned with his politeness, and then people got careless with it and it slipped into Manly, which only a few proven constables ever called him to his face and was – were allowed to get away with it in my hearing, if he thought highly of them to be on intimate returns. (*Little pause.*) As for the female constable, if she's working under Inspector Hawkins, and has been brought in special to do it, it's because she's developed a reputation in her own right. (*Little pause.*) I'm under oath to Duty Officer not to divulge what she's been requested to do in the Merrit Street case, I can only say she's in danger up to the hilt.

May (*laughs tauntingly*) If she's hanging about hoping the Merrit Street attacker will rip off her skirts to get in her up to the hilt, then that's Hawkins's idea of pleasure too, from what I hear, oh yes, what the Merrit Street attacker don't give her, Hawkins'll make up for.

Long pause. Mr Godboy sits staring straight ahead.

And I'll tell *you* something, I wouldn't mind being in her shoes. With *either* of them.

Godboy May I ask, May, may I ask where this gossip you've been hearing's been taking place?

May Never you mind where.

Godboy Because I don't believe you've had the pleasure of seeing Inspector Hawkins in the flesh.

May And he hasn't had the pleasure of seeing me the same way. (*Laughs.*) It's a wonder to me they let you come snooping around the station, you've got no business there, and as for Manly Hawkins, he'd order you back to the corns and bunions, which is where you belong, if he noticed you at all, which he won't.

Godboy (*laughs softly*) He'll notice me, May, when the time comes.

May Well, I won't be here to see it. (*Significantly picks up and shakes the cigarette packs.*)

Mr Godboy looks at her, looks away.

And you remember I said that. (*Little pause, feeling irritably under her.*) Where's my coat then?

Godboy Oh, I do believe I hung it in the new cupboard, dear.

May sighs, gets up, tramps across the room to the cupboard.

May I have to do everything for myself in the place, why can't you leave me alone?

As Mr Godboy follows her, she opens the cupboard, stands thinking as Mr Godboy comes up behind her, then, leaving the door open, goes out of the hall door, right, leaving that open also. Mr Godboy is fumbling for the padlock.

Godboy No, dear – (*Laughs.*) It's in the cupboard here.

Shakes his fist, then goes out into the hall after her. As he does so the door, left, opens, and May comes tramping in holding some cigarettes and matches, lights up as she settles back on the sofa. Mr Godboy reappears through the kitchen door.

May What you doing, following me about like a mongolese idiot?

Godboy I thought you wanted your coat, which is in the cupboard, dear. (*Shuts the kitchen door, comes over to his chair, sits down.*)

May What for? I'm not going anywhere – yet. It was me fags I wanted. (*Taps ash on the floor.*)

Mr Godboy sits staring at her. After a minute he gets up, picks up an ashtray from the gramophone table, puts it on the floor beside her, makes to sit down, then goes across, makes to shut the cupboard door, looks quickly at May, leaves it open and shuts the hall door. Comes back. Sits down. There is a silence.

My Number One would have laughed, he hated the police.

Godboy I know he did, dear, but your first husband and myself was – were comparatively speaking two different kettles of fish.

May Yes, he was.

She draws on the cigarette, reaches down, stubs it out on the floor beside the ashtray without looking. Mr Godboy watches, then goes across, picks up the butt, puts it in the tray. May watches him.

He enjoyed himself, that one did. For one thing he liked goodbye parties.

Godboy (*sitting down*) Pardon, dear?

May Nothing. I've got a shock in store for you, that's all. And the first of it is that Eric and Doris is coming down later.

Godboy (*after a pause*) Eric and Doris, dear? (*In a controlled voice*) Indeed? Tonight, dear?

May That's right, but I'm not telling you why, because it's got pleasure in it, and you don't know what that is.

After another pause, Mr Godboy gets up, walks over to the cupboard door.

Godboy I was under the impression we was – were having a quiet night all by ourselves, dear. (*He shuts the cupboard door, comes back.*)

May Was you? (*Points to the cupboard.*) Clear it out.

Godboy (*sitting down*) Pardon, dear?

May Clear it out. Kindly clean that cupboard out of my things, Number Two. (*Claps her hands.*) That you been kind enough to fill it up with. I'm going to be needing them later.

Godboy I don't understand, dear.

May You will soon enough.

There is a long pause. May claps her hands again. Mr Godboy gets to his feet, walks to the cupboard. Stops before it.

Godboy You want me to get your things out, dear, you actually mean?

May That's right, and why should *I* do it? (*Lights another cigarette.*) I'm not your slave.

Godboy (*standing before the cupboard*) Dear?

May What now?

Godboy Couldn't this trifling chore be left until later, dear?

May No.

Godboy There's a question of fetching something in for Doris and Eric.

May It's fetched, don't you worry.

There's a pause. May claps her hands again. Mr Godboy steps inside the cupboard.

I'm leaving you.

Godboy (*puts his head out*) Pardon dear?

May claps her hands. Mr Godboy goes back in.

(*Shouting.*) Are you still in love with me, dear?

May (*laughs*) What?

Mr Godboy steps fluently out of the cupboard, shuts the door, hurries over to May.

Godboy I've been meaning to inquire for some time, May? (*Sits down beside her.*) It's particularly important for me to know the answer; I'd like to think there's been happiness for you this last two years.

May That's what you like to think, is it?

Godboy (*folds his hands into his lap*) You've got such an amusing wit, dear. (*Laughing.*) Oh dear.

May I have, have I? (*Little pause.*) What you think you're doing then?

Godboy (*smiling*) Pardon, dear?

May Get back into that cupboard. I'm not going near it and don't you think I am.

Godboy (*sits*) The truth is, dear . . .

May claps her hands. Mr Godboy leaps to his feet, hurries over to the cupboard, steps inside. There is a pause.

May (*half singing*) Oh, I'm leaving you, leaving you, leaving you.

Godboy Pardon, dear? (*Head appearing around the cupboard door.*)

May I said, if you was the same kettle of fish as my Number One, you wouldn't have no wound, and if you had, it wouldn't stop you.

Godboy (*steps out of the cupboard*) Specialists have done their best for me, dear, and still I defeat them all.

May If you was like Number One, you'd learn to handle me. (*Little pause.*) Once he give me a tanning, and I loved him the more for it.

Godboy (*after a long pause*) I have my own way of doing things, dear. Violence to a living creature is not in my nature.

May What you up to, in and out of there like a rabbit from a top hat? (*Claps her hands.*) Come on, Perkins, come on.

> *Mr Godboy wheels around, goes back into the cupboard. Steps out again almost at once.*

Godboy The truth of the matter is, dear, I'm not feeling exactly on top of myself.

May Oh yes, it's about time for that, isn't it? And something else I've been thinking, if that wound's down there, why does it hurt you up there?

Godboy That's what defeats the specialists, dear. (*Clasping his head, comes over, sits down.*) All they know is, if they solve the one they solve the other.

May (*gets up, trudges over to the cupboard*) I knew I'd have to do it myself.

Godboy No, don't do it, dear, we can do it together after Eric and Doris have left. I'd enjoy that. Just the two of us.

May By then it'll be just the one of us. (*Looks at him.*) I want everything to my hand. (*Nods.*) Besides, knowing Eric, he'll forget to come, if there's something at the pictures he wants to see.

She goes into the cupboard. Mr Godboy comes over, stands in indecision, looking yearningly in at her.

Godboy You say he's gone to the pictures.

He half reaches for the padlock, takes his hand out, empty. May comes out with an armful of clothes, drops them on the floor.

May That's where he'll be, if I know Eric, he'd be at the pictures if Doris was dying and the world was changing to mud.

Goes in, comes out with more clothes, drops them down as Mr Godboy comes closer.

You must be mad, filling this up with my things, then turning on your wound to get off it. (*Goes in again.*) Oh yes, and it's only the thought of seeing him . . .

Mr Godboy, sidling to the alcove, plunges his hand in behind the curtain.

Godboy Yes, he forgot last time, didn't he, dear?

He slams the cupboard door shut, simultaneously there is a knock on the hall door, right, and Mr Godboy opens the cupboard door again. The shutting. The knocking. The opening. All should come at almost exactly the same instant. Mr Godboy stands holding the cupboard door open, having let go of the pipe. He is smiling courteously. May comes out, looks at him, steps very close, points a finger into his face.

May Now what are you . . .?

The knock comes again. She turns to the hall door, goes towards it. Mr Godboy bends down, picks up armfuls of her clothes, puts them back in the cupboard, shuts the cupboard door, as May opens the hall door.

I knew you wouldn't forget your May.

She stands aside, to let first Eric, then Doris pass. Smiles at Eric. Eric is about twenty-five, thin-faced and pale. Black hair slicked back. Doris is about twenty, taller than Eric, her lips are bright red, her fingernails scarlet. She is wearing a New Look cotton dress, nylon stockings with seams, and stocky, high-heeled shoes. She walks gingerly, with a slight suggestion of a limp. She is holding a handbag pressed close to her stomach. Eric is wearing a raincoat and scarf. He walks across the room with one shoulder slightly hunched.

Eric Hello, May.

Doris Hello, May.

She is watched closely by Mr Godboy, who is standing now to one side, his hands over his crotch.

May You're a relief for sore eyes, if you hadn't come I'd have killed you.

Godboy (*following Doris, who has sat down on the sofa; in a low voice*) This is a pleasure, Doris.

Eric sits down in one of the utility chairs, adopting a slouched, tough-looking posture. May comes to stand beside him, puts a hand on his shoulder.

May See anything different in here?

Eric What? (*Stares around the room, shakes his head.*) No.

May (*bending her face close to his*) Go on, something extra.

Eric stares at Mr Godboy, who is standing between the armchair and the sofa.

Eric Him.

There is a pause.

I mean, last time he wasn't here, when we come down.

May laughs.

Doris Yes, there's a –

May (*sharply*) Don't spoil it, Doris, let him guess.

Eric (*shakes his head*) What?

May puts her hands around his neck, pretending to throttle him. He hunches up, makes cinematic gagging sounds.

May (*jerks him upright*) Come on then.

Eric What?

May points Eric's face to the cupboard, pretends to throttle him further.

May Ooo you! What's that then?

Little pause, as Doris and Mr Godboy watch.

Eric Oh. (*Little pause.*) A shed.

May screams with laughter, wags Eric's head with her hands, as Mr Godboy sits down beside Doris. Folds his hands into his lap, looks at her, looks at May and Eric.

May It's a cupboard we got for you, you midge, what do you think of it?

Eric (*after a pause*) It's big.

Godboy It was the most capacious obtainable.

Doris nods. Eric looks at the cupboard, puzzled.

May Is that what you could do with?

Eric What for?

May For locking Doris up in when she's naughty.

She laughs, sits down in the chair opposite Eric, then pulls it close to him. Mr Godboy says something to Doris in a low voice.

Eric What?

Godboy I was merely saying to Doris that I'd be able to deal with her tomorrow, if things go as planned.

Eric Oh.

Eric looks at Doris, who looks down into her lap.

May (*to Eric*) She's lucky, he hasn't touched a foot in six months, except his own, but he'll make an exception out of Doris, and if *you've* got anything coming up, I'll handle it. (*Slaps his knee, laughs.*)

Eric Oh, I'm all right, aren't I, Doris?

May That's just the way of it, it's the poor ladies that suffer, it's a good job we don't get corns on our heels. (*To Doris.*)

Doris On my heels?

May On your heels. (*Nods solemnly, then bursts out laughing.*)

Eric (*joins in*) You can't get corns on your heels.

Godboy (*to Doris*) It's a fact that corns can cause as much distress to the whole system as ulcers, which is why I've made arrangements to attend to you properly, Doris.

Doris Well – (*Little pause, looks at Eric.*) I get a bit nervous at being tampered with, see?

Eric She's always been like that. Won't go near a doctor.

Doris Last time I went he – he – hurt me somewhere.

May Where?

Doris Somewhere, that's all.

Godboy There's no cause for concern, Doris, I can assure you of that.

May (*leans over, slaps Eric's knee*) You been doing any more your night walks, then?

Eric What? (*To May, then to Mr Godboy*) Can you do for her, then?

Godboy Indeed. (*Nods at Doris.*) I'll do for you, Doris.

Doris What will you do then?

Godboy There'll be a preliminary examination, Doris, to ascertain the extent of its growth, how deep in the imbedment goes, which will be followed by some probing.

Doris Probing? Oh.

May (*nodding her head at Eric*) Here, Eric, I heard you come in the other night, it was morning, almost.

Eric Oh. (*Nods. Then to Mr Godboy.*) She won't like too much probing, she dead against being tampered with.

Godboy Probably a mere lotion will do the trick, or I could administer a little whiff, Doris.

May (*bends forward to tap Eric on the knee*) What you do out there at night?

Eric (*looks at her*) Nothing. (*To Doris*) That sounds all right, Dorrie.

Doris That's all I'm having.

Eric Yes, that's her lot.

Doris A little whiff of what?

May wags her head irritably.

Godboy (*after a pause*) That will depend on what other symptoms it's been giving you, Doris, otherwise than its throbbing and its size.

May That's enough, isn't it?

Eric What?

Godboy (*to Doris*) Any other inconvenience above the pain?

Doris (*shakes her head*) Whiff of what, what'll you –

May (*simultaneously with Doris and to Mr Godboy*) Isn't that enough?

Godboy In which case the lotion applied on sterile pads, or a little whiff.

Doris Well, whiff of what?

May (*to Doris*) Why don't you show it to him now? Go on. (*There is a pause. Doris looks down at her handbag, which she is clutching to her stomach.*)

May Go on, give us a look.

Eric (*to May*) Here, she don't want to do that.

Godboy I appreciate that, Doris.

May Oooo. (*Slaps Eric on the knee.*) Aren't they the bashful two?

Eric She's like that. She don't like showing herself off.

May It's only a corn we want to see. Go on, slip off your stockings, dear.

Godboy (*to May*) A chiropodist isn't permitted to take public liberties with his customer's feet, dear.

May 'A chopidist isn't pitted to show his customer's feet, dear.' (*Imitating contemptuously.*) Ooooh dear. Don't worry, chopidist, nobody wants to see people's feet at a party, it's music we want. Put a record on, Eric.

Eric What? Oh. Righto.

> *Gets up, walks over to the gramophone, picks up a record, scans the cover closely and uncomprehendingly, puts it down, picks up another.*

May (*to Doris*) You going to have a fling with the chopidist?

Doris (*who is staring straight ahead*) I can't.

May Course you can, what do you mean, can't?

Doris (*voice quavering*) I can't dance with that foot.

May Dance with the other one, then. (*Laughs.*) Or borrow one from the chopidist.

Godboy (*to Eric, who has been watching him*) Eric, old boy, if you'll excuse my mentioning it, that one's not for dancing to.

Eric (*who has been about to put the needle on*) What?

May (*to Mr Godboy*) What do you know about what's for dancing to? Eric and me can dance to anything.

Gets up, goes to the centre of the room, makes dancing movements.

Put it on, Eric.

Eric Oh. Righto. (*Looks at Mr Godboy, looks at May, puts the record on.*) We'll just have a quick one, Dorrie.

The record begins. It is one of Churchill's war speeches. Eric stands by the gramophone, bewildered. Doris looks down at her handbag, May stands still. Mr Godboy gets up, walks right across, takes the record off, puts it back in its cover, goes back, sits down.

Who was that then?

Godboy (*after a pause*) That was Winnie, old boy.

May goes to the record pile. Eric joins her, they begin to sort through the records.

(*To Doris.*) Five years ago there wasn't a man in this country wouldn't have laid down his life for Winnie, and glad to do it.

May whispers something to Eric, laughs.

Of course, the war wouldn't mean much to Eric, as he was safe out of it, I'm glad to say for his sake.

Eric (*turning*) What?

Godboy I was merely wondering, Eric, where were you precisely when the V-2s commenced dropping?

Eric Me?

Godboy In 1944 to be frank, old boy. Where were you precisely?

Eric (*thinks, looks at Doris*) I was in Wales, wasn't I, Dorrie, in that home?

Godboy Now refresh my memory, old boy, were there V-2s dropping in Wales?

Eric V – what? (*Little pause. Indignantly.*) Here, I never had nothing like that.

May (*puts a record on the gramophone*) What you going on at him for – you'd have ridden on a V-2 if they'd let you wear your Special Constable uniform. (*As the music starts.*) This one was too nice and young to get messed up in that.

> *She holds out her arms, they start to dance, Eric glancing apprehensively at Doris. May leads Eric further into a corner of the room, dancing amorously, Doris and Mr Godboy watching.*

Godboy Indeed, Eric was too young for combat, and I don't hold it against him, Doris.

> *Doris goes on watching the dancing, tense.*

But there was – were some youths on the other side who weren't too young. Mere children of nine were issued with pitchforks and ordered to stand and resist. Those were the sort of people Winnie had to stamp out – (*stamping his foot*) to make the country safe for the likes of Eric, who is a very pleasant boy, as I'm the first to admit. They didn't teach him to read in Wales, then?

> *Little pause. Doris shakes her head.*

So frankly, between you and me, Doris, as May and Eric wouldn't understand as they naturally like to enjoy themselves, that's why I'm against having that record put on for joking at. Those were terrible days. (*Little pause.*) And that record brings back happy memories of them. How's your toe now?

Doris shrugs.

I hadn't forgotten about it, Doris, there was something I had to get out of the way first, which I'm dealing with now. (*Looks at May.*)

The music stops. May does a grotesque curtsy. Eric laughs, looks towards Doris, sees her face, stops laughing. May looks at Doris and Mr Godboy, keeps a hold on Eric's arm.

May What's he off on now, the double Dublin tenant and wife gasser?

Eric What?

May His head is filled with murder, that's all he thinks about, isn't it, chopidist? That and Inspector Manly Mannerly Irish Hawkins.

Godboy Indeed, dear, I keep in touch, merely.

May (*to Eric*) Come on, let's get our hands on something I've got special in the kitchen.

Leads Eric towards the kitchen. He looks at Doris, who glares at him.
  Doris and Mr Godboy sit stiffly on the sofa, staring straight ahead. There are noises from the kitchen, a crashing sound, a scream of May's laughter. A pause. Then Mr Godboy gets up, goes to the gramophone. As he does so, Eric comes in, his coat and scarf over his arm, looks at Doris, who turns away from him, plods across the room to the cupboard, opens it.

Godboy (*with his back to Eric and Doris*) My interest in murder is connected to my interest in police work, Doris, needless to say, which goes back a long way. My years as Special Constable during the war naturally heightened my interest. That's all there is to it, in spite of May's hints, I hope you won't . . .

Mr Godboy turns, as Eric, having shut the door of the cupboard, walks back across the room to the kitchen door. Watches him. Eric looks at Doris, whose face is still averted, stands at the kitchen door.

Eric Well, I'll just . . .

He shrugs, nods, goes into the kitchen, leaves the door open. Doris sits staring ahead. Mr Godboy looks towards the kitchen door, from which comes a scream of May's laughter; goes towards it to shut it when it slams noisily from inside. He stops. Goes back to the sofa, sits down. There is a pause.

Godboy May has a funny sense of humour, she makes me chuckle out loud sometimes. (*Little pause.*) You can't understand the workings of murder until you understand the workings of the police. The two things are connected. (*Little pause.*) Do you follow me there, Doris?

Throughout the following conversation there are noises from the kitchen, mainly of May's laughter, but gradually with Eric's joining in.

Doris (*shrugs*) I don't like the police.

Godboy (*swings his head around, looks at her*) Indeed? I'm sorry to hear you say that, Doris, very sorry. Have you any grounds?

Doris shrugs. After a long pause, she looks down at her handbag.

Doris They searched me once. In front of – people.

Godboy (*after a pause*) Well, Doris, justice has not only got to be done, it's got to be seen to be done. That's what makes our country great. (*Pause.*) I'm sure you'll admit they did a good job of it.

Long pause, as Doris continues to stare down.

Pardon a little ignorance, unfortunately searching wasn't one of my duties, how far exactly did they authorise themselves to go?

Doris (*whispering*) Everything. They took off me everything.

Godboy Indeed? (*Long pause.*) That would include, pardon my asking, to get the details straight in my head – (*putting a hand to his head*) stockings, undergarments such as for instance camiknicks and bra, naturally? (*Little pause.*) Am I right in my guess?

Doris Me everything.

Godboy Yes, they've got to be thorough. (*Little pause.*) It was male officers took part in this.

Doris They was peeking. One of them was.

Godboy Superintending the legality, Doris, merely, that's all. Can you remember who it was precisely? Did you see his face?

Doris I don't know, I kept me eyes down.

Godboy (*after a pause*) Indeed. (*Little pause.*) As a matter of interest, Doris, and strictly privately, May's likely to go off on a little trip.

Sudden scream of laughter from May.

Doris Oh? She never said.

Godboy No, I intend it to come as a complete and utter surprise to her. She won't know about it until she's on her way, virtually.

Another scream of laughter.

She's got it coming to her, she deserves a long rest.

Doris When's she going then? (*Little pause.*)

Godboy I've got it planned so that with luck she'll be gone by tomorrow.

Waits through another scream.

I think I can promise you that.

Doris That'll be nice.

Godboy (*turns his head, looks at her*) I'm glad you've said that, Doris.

The kitchen door opens, and Eric puts his head around it. He is grinning.

Eric Who's for stout, then? (*Little pause.*)

Godboy No thank you, Eric.

Eric looks straight at Doris. She stares ahead.

Eric Dorrie?

She continues to stare ahead.

Dorrie?

Eric looks at her a moment longer, withdraws, closes the door.

Doris Is she going a long way away?

Godboy Purley, probably. (*Little pause.*) I only mention it now merely so you won't wonder at her abrupt disappearance tomorrow.

The door opens again. Eric, grinning, puts his head in.

Eric Who's for a drop of something else, then?

Mr Godboy looks at him, Doris stares straight ahead.

She's got a bottle of gin in there.

Godboy No thank you, Eric.

Eric Dorrie?

She continues to stare ahead.

What?

Withdraws his head, shuts the door. There is a burst of laughter from May.

Godboy (*after a pause*) How do you feel about that surprise news, Doris?

Doris (*after another scream*) It'll be quiet without her.

Godboy Indeed. (*Nods.*) That's one thing I'm expecting. (*Little pause.*) It would be best if I was to arrange our appointment now. (*Takes the padlock out of his pocket, puts it back hurriedly, takes out a diary.*) As you now realise, I shall be free as of tomorrow on. I'll be ready to get down to it before it's too late. (*There is a silence.*) I'm referring to your toe, Doris. What do you say to tomorrow teatime?

Mr Godboy looks at Doris, who shrugs nervously, looks down.

Righto, tomorrow teatime?

Doris What is, I mean, this whiff you was – whiff of something . . .

The door opens. Eric comes in. He is slightly drunk.

Eric Comfy? (*Long pause.*) That May. (*Laughs.*)

Doris (*looks at him vindictively*) May's going away tomorrow.

Mr Godboy looks at her.

Eric She hasn't said nothing.

Godboy Only you're to keep it quiet, old boy, it's a surprise to May, don't let anything drop.

Eric thinks. Laughs.

Why do you laugh, old boy?

Eric Well, she keeps saying she's got a surprise laid up for you.

Godboy Indeed? What type of surprise precisely, Eric?

Eric She won't tell, she keeps tapping her nose and laughing over it, but I got a part in it.

Godboy Indeed, Eric, what's that?

Eric You got to wait. (*Holds up his hand.*) Eh, Dorrie?

She stares ahead. There is a silence, then the sound of a lavatory flushing off, right, and the door, right, opens. May enters the room, one arm raised, she looks at Eric, they lower their arms simultaneously and begin to sing.

May (*as May advances on Mr Godboy*) 'Now is the hour.'

Eric 'When I must say goodbye.'

They sing the song through, Mr Godboy and Doris sitting staring straight ahead, until the last few lines, when Mr Godboy begins to sing. He sings the last line by himself as May throws herself laughing into Eric's arms and lights dim.

SCENE TWO

Lights up. Half an hour later. Doris and Mr Godboy still sitting on the sofa, staring directly ahead. There is a sound of a door slamming, the kitchen hall door, left. May comes in through the kitchen door, left. She is carrying a glass. She sits down on one of the utility chairs, left, drinks from her glass. Mr Godboy and Doris watch her.

Doris (*after a pause, voice quavering*) Where's Eric then?

May (*sipping from her glass*) Gone, dear.

There is a little silence.

Doris Where?

May Don't know. (*Little pause.*) Last I saw he was lurching down the hall. (*Looks at her sharply.*) Where's he go most nights, I hear him coming in all hours.

Doris (*after a pause*) For walks. (*Pause.*) He said he'd stop. He said he wouldn't any more.

Godboy Doubtless he'll come straight in up to the flat, Doris.

May Doubtless. (*Little pause. Looks at Doris.*) What for? (*Little pause.*) Oh, drink puts Eric in a talking mood, we got the same problems, Eric and me. (*Shakes his head.*) But I'm getting over mine.

Godboy Pardon, dear?

May She knows what I mean. (*Stares at Doris.*)

Doris, after a pause, gets up, stands for a moment with her handbag, half opened, clasped to her stomach, then walks limping to the door, right.

(*Silkily.*) Bye, dear.

Mr Godboy gets up, follows Doris, holds the door open for her.

Godboy Goodnight, Doris.

Doris He said he wouldn't go out nights any more.

Godboy Don't you worry about him, Doris, he'll be back in no time. (*Little pause.*) And see you as arranged – (*Slapping his pocket.*) Teatime.

> *Doris goes out. Mr Godboy puts his head into the hall, watches for a second, then shuts the door, comes back. May drinks from her glass and watches him.*

May Coming tomorrow, is she?

Godboy Pardon, dear? Oh, yes, tomorrow seemed best.

May Well, you'll have a free hand tomorrow.

> *Mr Godboy looks at her.*

Not that a free hand with her's worth a eunuch's while.

Godboy Pardon, dear?

> *May looks at him, shrugs, drinks. After a pause:*

Well, dear, that was a pleasant evening, I must say.

May Must you? Why?

> *Mr Godboy stares at her.*

Why must you say it?

Godboy I thought you must be enjoying yourself. (*Long pause.*) Who's for bed, dear?

May Pardon, dear? (*Mimicking.*)

> *Mr Godboy laughs. There is a pause. He goes to the cupboard, swerves on to the guppies. May sits watching him. He turns, looks, nods, smiles.*

Godboy Well, dear – (*Stretches.*) Well – (*Yawns.*) I need my bed, I must – (*Stops himself.*)

May What for?

Godboy Why, for a good night's sleep, dear.

May That what you think I need?

Godboy Par—

May (*simultaneously*) Pardon, dear? A good night's sleep which is you curled up and clinging to the edge of your side like a winkle. A good night's sleep, which is me blinking into the darkness and thinking about what I had with Number One and how it won't never come no more. (*Little pause.*) Why do you wear two pair of pyjamas?

Godboy Merely, dear, because I'm susceptible to cold, just as you prefer your hottie, why do you ask?

May My hottie's got more bed-life in it than you have. (*Pause.*) You know what I'm trying to say to you?

Godboy No, dear.

May Can't you even guess?

Godboy (*after a little pause*) No, dear.

May (*slowly, significantly*) More fool you, then.

She gets up, goes to the kitchen, leaves the door open. Mr Godboy looks at the cupboard, then towards the kitchen door. Goes on tiptoe to the kitchen door, shuts it. Then hurries to the cupboard.

(*Flinging open the kitchen door.*) Leave it open.

Mr Godboy stops, turns around.

Leave it open. I've had enough of you closing things up on me, now I'm after space.

She goes to the door, left, opens it, goes into the bedroom. Mr Godboy stares after her, then goes quietly to the cupboard, opens it. Goes to the alcove, checks the cylinder, then turns around, goes to the guppies.

243

Godboy Don't forget your night-things in the cupboard, dear. I've left the door open for you to make your selection from.

May appears at the bedroom door, holding a suitcase open. She stares at him. He stays bent away from her, gestures with his hands backwards.

I was merely reminding you of your nighties.

May (*significantly*) Yes, I'll be needing those.

She walks across to the cupboard, steps in. Mr Godboy whirls round, suddenly remembers padlock, snatches it out, turns the key to open it, opens it, drops the key, picks the key up, makes a go at putting it back, then frantically puts it in his mouth, steals across, puts the padlock open and ready in the door-jamb hook, then, key still in his mouth, whips to the alcove, grabs the tubing, reaches for the door with his left hand, as May steps out with the clothes. Mr Godboy slams the door, whirls around. May turns as he holds the tubing behind him, walks up to him, puts her face close to his.

(*Shouts.*) Stop slamming, I said.

She gives him a push with her arms. Mr Godboy steps back, swallows the key, as May turns away.

Open it up again.

Mr Godboy stands watching, swallowing and coughing slightly as May disappears into the bedroom, then gagging a little, opens the cupboard door, stands with the pipe held down, waiting.

(*Calling.*) You wouldn't notice if the house was collapsing around your eyes.

Godboy True, dear, very true.

He swallows experimentally. May reappears, begins to hum 'Now is the hour . . .'

May (*stares at him*) What you doing then?

Godboy (*holding the pipe behind him*) Thinking merely, dear.

May About murder merely, dear?

Mr Godboy laughs.

Or about how much you'd miss me merely, dear?

Godboy (*laughs again, wags his head*) Oh May!

Coughs again. May comes towards him, stands in front of him.

May Oooh *you*. (*Shakes her head.*) Ape!

Turns, plods back towards the door, left, stops, turns, goes back to the cupboard. Mr Godboy watches tensely. She stands in front of it, half enters it. Mr Godboy moves forward. May turns.

No. (*Holds up a hand.*) No, not now you don't, no help from you, thank you. Go nurse your wound. (*Significantly.*) You're too *late*.

Mr Godboy stops, takes a pace back. May enters the cupboard. Mr Godboy leaps forward. There is a knock on the door right. He stops, stares towards it.

(*Now bending down, her buttocks sticking out of the cupboard.*) Answer it, then.

Mr Godboy hesitates, then thrusts the pipe back into the alcove, goes towards the door, opens it a fraction.

Godboy Oh. (*Little pause.*) Hello.

May is now down on all fours, buttocks sticking out of the cupboard.

Doris (*but not distinct*) I can't find him.

Mr Godboy stares in agony at the cupboard, into which May has vanished. Holds the door open. Doris walks gingerly a few steps into the room.

Godboy (*stares at Doris*) I should tell you in all fairness we was – were just preparing ourselves for beddy-byes. (*Laughs.*) Doris.

Doris (*frightened*) Eric's not there!

Godboy Indeed!

He glances towards the cupboard. May's buttocks reappear, slowly. Doris watches.

Well, I can assure you he's not with May or me, I'm afraid to say. (*Holds the door open wide.*) Have you glanced in your toilet?

Doris (*shakes her head*) He's not there.

Godboy In which case I gladly give you permission to knock on our toilet.

Doris He's not there.

Mr Godboy watches May back out of the cupboard, an armful of clothes held to her waist. She looks at Doris, shakes her head contemptuously, then goes across to the room left.

Godboy Indeed? Not in the toilets you say. You do surprise me, but it merely means he must be somewhere else.

He watches May come out of the room, go into the cupboard again.

Doris He said he wouldn't any more, he said, he does funny things when he's had too much.

She stares at May's back accusingly. Mr Godboy's head moves in anguish between Doris and the cupboard.

Godboy Not to worry, Doris, my advice to you is to phone the hospitals from the corner call box.

Doris Hospitals!

Godboy (*as May comes out again*) They have the authority to put you in touch with the latest accident cases and mortuary victims. So not to worry – May, dear!

Doris No, he doesn't get hurt, he goes round and round, he says his head does.

Godboy Now Doris, that covers hospitals, mortuaries, toilets, which is all I can think of at the moment.

Desperately, as May comes back:

So pop upstairs and get a good night's rest.

He steps in front of the cupboard with his arms out.

May, dear, did you hear that? Eric has mysteriously vanished!

May stops, looks at him, looks at Doris, shakes her head contemptuously.

May What a pair, oooh, you lovely things, he's gone to clear his head, like I told you. (*Stares at Doris.*) And if he *had* gone for a bit of something else, I wouldn't blame him.

Mr Godboy resolutely stands before the cupboard as May tries to pass.

Godboy But we have reason to believe that the situation could develop into something more seriously tragic, dear. Doris is thinking in terms of fatal accidents.

May (*after a moment, looking from one to the other*) I'll tell you something, the same what I've been telling him.

She nods to Mr Godboy, who, as she goes to stand close to Doris, is attempting to shut the cupboard door behind his back against a piece of hanging-out cloth.

Because this is the last chance I'll get as things down here have come to a head at last, and that's if you made your Eric welcome, he'd be up there, inside, and you know who I mean, who a man ought to be inside of. You don't give him what he needs, Doris Hoyden, and he'll do what I'm doing to him, who doesn't give me the same.

She nods at Mr Godboy, who has now turned around and is wrestling with the cupboard door face on.

Godboy Indeed, dear, there's no doubt about that.

May Or you'll end up like him, hanging about the police station and chasing after an Inspector Hawkins as if he'd do his work for him.

Godboy (*shuts the cupboard at last, turns around, stands against the door grinning*) Exactly what I say to you, Doris, let the police handle it.

There is the squeal of tyres outside. Pause. They listen.

Doris Oh no, no, I'm not going near them.

May Ooooh, what a pair!

She turns, goes to the door, stops, looks back, shakes her head, goes into the room, left.

Godboy Now Doris dear, as May says, not to worry, not to worry. Also as May says, there's the police outside near at hand, you could go and bother them, I merely mean – (*goes to the hall door, right, opens it*) this tramping about isn't doing our corn any good, and the best thing for you all said and done is to aim for some shuteye. (*He holds the door open, gestures usheringly out of the door, stops, cocks his head.*) And who's that coming in now if I'm not mistaken.

He steps out into the hall, Doris behind him. Hawkins, as yet unseen, says something inaudible. Mr Godboy backs into the room, forcing Doris back behind him.

That is my name, yes.

Hawkins says something else. Mr Godboy stands at the door as Doris peers over his shoulder, stares in alarm, then hurries away, goes to sit down in a corner of the sofa, her face turned away.

Godboy Indeed, sir, indeed.

He stands aside to let Hawkins in. His face wears an expression of bemused reverence. Hawkins steps in, steps out again. His voice audible in a shout:

Hawkins All right, boys, wait out in the car there and keep the engine humming, boys.

He enters. He is wearing a smart suit, a carnation in his buttonhole. And is carrying a trilby. He is a tall, broad-shouldered, flush-faced, tough-looking forty-five. He comes past Mr Godboy into the centre of the room, looks at Doris, who is facing away, nods.

Evening ma'am.

Doris nods, mumbles, without looking at him. Mr Godboy stands staring at Hawkins's back in a kind of rapture. Then holds out his hand, advances around him at the precise moment that Hawkins revolves, so that again Mr Godboy's hand is held out to Hawkins's back. Drops his hand, clears his throat as Hawkins turns again. They face each other.

Godboy Pardon me, sir, but it is Inspector Hawkins, sir, isn't it? This is an honour, sir. (*Little pause.*) Indeed.

Hawkins Thank you, Mr Godboy, Duty Officer Larkins said I'd be known on the premises if I took the liberty of dropping in out of the night. (*Looks at Doris.*)

Godboy (*nodding*) We was colleagues during the war years, sir, in a manner of speaking, and recently since you've been back I've exchanged nods at you down at the station, sir, although doubtless you've been too much on the job to pay them much attention.

As he holds out his hand again tentatively, Hawkins goes smoothly over to Doris, at whom he has been smiling.

Hawkins And is it Mrs Godboy then?

Doris shakes her head, looks away.

Godboy (*coming over*) No, Mrs Godboy is busy in the bedroom, her work there is never done, as they say. (*He picks up quickly a few of the clothes May has dropped*), Although I'm particularly anxious for her to meet you. (*Straightens.*) This young lady's from the upstairs premises, she's lost her husband for the moment. (*Laughs.*) May, dear! May! (*Goes over, knocks on the door.*) May! (*Opens the door, shoves the clothes in while calling out.*) There's someone here I'm anxious for you to meet.

Hawkins has been standing close to Doris, who sits tight, staring ahead.

Hawkins Lost your husband, have you, if he's missing too long, you call on us then.

Godboy May, dear, there's Inspector Hawkins himself in the parlour.

Hawkins (*winks, nods at Doris*) The husband we can't return, we replace. (*Laughs.*)

Doris (*in a whisper*) Thank you.

May appears at the door, Mr Godboy in front of her. She has a mountain of clothes in her arms. Mr Godboy steps around her, puts an arm around her waist, clears his throat to attract Hawkins's attention. May stares at Hawkins cynically.

Hawkins (*turns*) I was just saying to the young lady, there's a pick of the boys at the station.

Godboy (*laughs*) I've been hoping that you two was – would come face to face before too late, too long, I merely – the idea of it means a lot to me, this is my wife, Inspector Hawkins, May Godboy.

Hawkins (*nods, smiles, revolves his trilby in his hands*) It's a great pleasure ma'am.

May drops a few clothes from the top of the pile which Mr Godboy tries to catch, then bends down to pick up.

May It's the dream of his life, to show you off at me.

Godboy (*straightening, puts the clothes back on the pile*) Pardon, dear? (*As a few more clothes drop from the bottom of the pile, laughs, bends down again.*)

May And he only just pulled it off, a day later you'd have missed me.

Hawkins Now I call that flattering. (*Little pause.*) You're taking a trip, are you?

Godboy (*now fishing between May's legs for an article of underclothing*) Pardon, sir? A trip? (*Laughs.*) No, not that she knows of, eh, May dear, oops, pardon, dear.

May I might be. (*Nods.*)

Hawkins (*laughs*) Ah, the ladies need little trips as much as the ladies' husbands.

> *He turns, does a nod-wink at Doris, who is still staring desperately ahead.*

Godboy Pardon? (*Straightens, looks smiling from one to the other.*)

May Have you come to arrest him? He spends all his time down at that station of yours, he'd be better in the nog behind it.

Godboy (*laughs, takes all the clothes out of May's arms*) Not even Inspector Hawkins can arrest me *before* I commit my offence, May dear. (*He goes into the bedroom.*)

Hawkins No, the truth is, ma'am, that cruising around in the neighbourhood, with a spot of waiting ahead of me, I remembered Larkins mentioning Mr Godboy's name, and thinking to meet some of the people on top of it all – (*turns, nodding at Doris*) I thought to myself, why not look in for a minute as the lights from your home were cheering up the darkness, like an invitation it seemed. (*Turns, nods to Doris again.*) If I'm not intruding, that is.

May Well, where's this female constable they're all talking about that's turned up so sudden, don't I get to see her?

Hawkins (*little pause*) Is it Constable Hedderley you mean?

*As Mr Godboy comes back out of the room and
stands beside May again.*

Well, to tell you a secret – (*turning to look at Doris*)
Constable Hedderley's out on a very special duty just a
minute or two away, so if you hear a strange commotion,
as will be the ringing of police bells, the blowing of
police whistles, the barking of police dogs, it'll be that
Constable Hedderley's pulled it off and I'll be on my way
in a hurry.

Godboy The Merrit Street case!

Hawkins (*after a pause, looks at Mr Godboy*) Well, and
so it is. There's the mind of a natural policeman for you.

*Mr Godboy swells proudly, looks at May, who turns
her face from him.*

I gave orders there was to be no gossip, so I'll be
having a word or two that'll boil Larkins' ears in the
morning. (*Laughs, nods at Doris.*) But there's no harm
in mentioning it now, as you're under my personal eye.
(*Nods to Doris again.*) The truth is that Constable
Hedderley's under a street lamp and fiddling in the line
of duty with suspenders and stockings and generally
behaving temptingly, and all about Merrit Street the boys
are scattered, waiting for the attacker to start his indecent
assault on our provocative piece of bait, who's also
carrying a handbag to tempt him further.

Godboy Masterly, Mannerly, masterly.

Hawkins looks at him.

May Yes, that's nice, but what if he gets into this
Hedderley before they get there, or can't stop him once he
gets going? There's some men I knew, one in particular
I was married to once – (*Looking at Mr Godboy.*)
Couldn't have been bombed off a lady he'd get that –

Hawkins laughs, winks-nods to Doris.

Godboy Now, my dear, all of Inspector Hawkins' finest combined can handle any man going.

Hawkins Don't you worry, ma'am, Constable Hedderley will toss him off as soon as look at him.

May Oh, will she! (*Lets out a screech of laughter.*)

Hawkins laughs, nods towards Doris. Mr Godboy, baffled, chuckles. After a silence:

Yes, it's not only from him I heard about you, Manly.

Hawkins looks at her. Chuckles. May chuckles. Hawkins looks towards Doris, who smiles awkwardly, goes on chuckling.

Hawkins Well, no, no, I have to keep myself free to move in any direction. I can be to Hedderley's side in thirty seconds with the car waiting, so don't you disturb yourself on Hedderley's account, ma'am.

Godboy That's what they mean by springing a trap, dear.

May Yes, well I got to do some springing myself, out of my own trap.

She unwinds Mr Godboy's arm, which has replaced itself around her waist, goes back into the room, slams the door. Mr Godboy turns, stares after her, then opens the door, puts his head in as Hawkins goes over, stands near to Doris, smiles at her, nods.

Godboy What about a cup for Inspector Mannerly Hawkins, dear?

May says something inaudible but clearly abusive. Mr Godboy emerges, embarrassed, looks towards where Hawkins was, then turns to where he is now, standing beside Doris.

254

As I say, her work is never done. (*Little pause, then significantly:*) Although it soon will be, if I finish off a little plan of mine.

Pause. Hawkins continues to smile at Doris, who sits stiffly, smiling, staring ahead.

Would you care for a – (*looking about him*) stout, sir?

Hawkins (*shakes his head*) Oh, no, no, thank you very much, only if there's one available.

Godboy Indeed there is. (*He hurries to the kitchen.*)

Hawkins (*to Doris*) I hope I haven't been frightening you, ma'am, with my talk of the Merrit Street rapist?

Doris shakes her head.

We come into contact with such terrible things, we forget the peace of mind of the innocent. (*Little pause.*) Ah, but still the city's a place at night, a violent place, and there's not a corner in it you can't hear its horror come screaming for you, if you stand there listening still as a nun. (*Little pause.*) Do you know what I mean?

Doris nods.

(*Looks at her.*) When I was a boy, and yourself a girl, we wouldn't have believed it then –

Doris looks quickly up again, then down.

Would we? (*Little pause.*) And now I go about like all the nuns that ever were, waiting for the messages or listening to the screams, and it's only when I'm talking with someone like yourself, ma'am, that I remember there was a time of innocence for all of us. (*Little pause.*) And that's the truth.

Mr Godboy enters, carrying a bottle of stout and a glass. As he pours the stout:

Godboy This is indeed good news about the Merrit Street case. It'll mean another feather in your cap, Man— Inspector, rape rates almost as high as murder in some quarters –

Hawkins is still looking at Doris.

(*Significantly, handing Hawkins the drink.*) Although not in my own personal opinion, frankly.

Hawkins (*takes the glass, nods*) My best to you, Mr Godboy, ma'am.

Holding the glass in toast, quickly to Mr Godboy, then a fraction longer to Doris, sips, stares about the room, sees the guppies.

Godboy (*clears his throat*) In –

Hawkins (*saunters over to the case*) Goldfish, now?

Godboy Um, no sir, in fact known as guppies, sir. (*Laughs.*) Gups we call them.

Hawkins And what nimble little fellows they are, darting this way and that. (*Bending over.*) I like them, I like them for their speed.

Mr Godboy comes over to the guppie case, stands on the other side, bends over it.

Godboy Yes, they are quick, very quick. (*Puts a finger in reflectively.*) Inspector, there's a question, um, I'd be interested to hear your personal view on.

As Hawkins moves smoothly back to Doris, sits down in one of the utility chairs next to her.

Do you think of your top murderer as a basically common or garden chap?

Hawkins whimsically offers his glass to Doris, who shakes her head, looks down into her lap.

I merely ask, because there's no doubt that some types of it are on the increase, although I've got no sympathies for the wounded veterans back from the front who lay about harmless old ladies for petty cash.

As again Hawkins offers Doris his glass, with insistent nods and smiles.

No, I've no time for them, that's a mixture of bad experiences and bad upbringing on the part of soft parents.

As Doris is finally forced to take a sip.

No, I'm referring to a different specimen altogether, your cool-blooded killer who has the nerve and is prepared to go through with it to the final consequences, as in the case of O'Higgs, the wife- and female-tenant-gasser, for instance, merely.

He looks up, looks around, sees Hawkins sipping from his stout, stares at him. There is a pause.

As you may remember, sir, I've had a little time on the force to my credit.

Hawkins Oh yes, a Special Constable, wasn't it? (*Sips.*) Not quite a fully paid up street-beater like myself.

Godboy Indeed. Unfortunately I was disqualified from submitting a full application owing to a mixture of age and a wound sustained in an accident. A rough house that got beyond itself. (*Little pause.*) Children will be children, no blame was officially attached, although malice was definitely involved. (*Comes over, sits down beside Hawkins in the other utility chair.*) Pardon me. Of course, a lot of it was checking padlocks in the evening, Mannerly, giving tea to the bombed-outs, which between you and me – and is no secret – made nuisances of themselves when in a state of shock and had to be

SIMON GRAY

restrained, and added to which there was molest-arrest –
taking into custody. (*Shaking his head.*) I merely mean
aliens who had no business in the country in the first
place and had to be locked up in the interests of the
security of the nation.

*Little pause, as Hawkins sips again, looks towards
Doris.*

But mainly on the whole I was called on to assist in
breaking the news in cases of fatal disasters. (*Little
pause.*) I sometimes spent six hours a day in breaking
tragic news, Inspector Manly, as you can imagine, I tried
to do it politely but firmly.

*May comes out of the room, left, walks around to the
cupboard, opens it, looks in. Mr Godboy watches,
then as May looks in the second cupboard:*

Hawkins (*slowly*) So you might say you did all our
dirtiest work for us?

Godboy (*watching May*) It was an honour, Hawkins,
Manly, Inspector Hawkins. (*Laughs.*) Can I help, dear?

*As May comes back across the room, leaving the
cupboard doors open, and entering the room, left.*

Her work is never –

Interrupted by the slamming of the door.

Um . . . (*Little pause.*) Indeed, it's because of my time on
the force that I'm never likely to be one of those who'd
forget our Pierrepoint . . .

Hawkins Pierrepoint?

Godboy Winnie, I merely mean, Inspector. (*Shakes his
head, gets up, goes to the cupboard doors, shuts them.*)
Pardon me, or runs about like lots of them do nowadays

making a mockery out of due procedure in the country
especially . . .

*Comes back, stops, as the door, left, opens, May
stands there for a second, then slams the door.*

Her work is never – (*Laughs.*) Especially when it's an
established fact – (*sits down*) that it's always properly
and ceremoniously carried out with chaplains, doctors
and officials in attendance.

Pause, looks at Hawkins, who stares at him.

Hawkins (*after a pause*) Is it hanging you're talking
about, then?

Godboy Indeed, sir. (*Nods.*) It's my own personal
considered opinion now you bring the subject into the
open, frankly, that a man who is going to end up that
way knows about it long before, from daydreams and
other symptoms, as in the case of – (*little pause, looks
at Hawkins hard*) the gasser O'Higgs, for instance.

Hawkins (*after a long pause, drains off his glass, stares
into it*) Mr Godboy – (*Slight pause.*) Mr Godboy, would
you have something I could wash this down with, now?

Godboy Oh. Well, I'm sorry to say that was the last of
the stout, there's nothing left in the kitchen except some
gin and of course water.

Hawkins Now that would be very nice, that's very kind,
a glass of gin and water would do the trick for me nicely,
Mr Godboy.

Godboy (*gets up, takes Hawkins's glass*) An honour,
Mannerly. (*Goes out into the kitchen.*)

Hawkins (*after a pause*) Tell me, ma'am, I think I've
forgotten your name already, or never asked in my
rudeness.

Doris (*in a low voice*) Doris Hoyden.

Hawkins Ah. (*Little pause.*) And I've never seen you before, Doris Hoyden?

Doris shakes her head.

It's as if I'd had a peep of you sometime, there are little pictures going on in my mind, of a peep.

Doris shakes her head.

It's the way you sit with your eyes down, lowered, that recalls – (*Little pause.*) Well, it recalls all the girls of the village of my boyhood in Mayo, and none of the girls of the lonely policeman's life in the City of London. (*Leans a little closer.*) Are you one of those that likes to dance, now?

Doris shakes her head.

Ah, but you'd be a natural dancer, I can see that, Doris, not one of those that leads a man, you'd know enough to give in to him in his movements.

He leans a little closer. The door, right, opens and May comes out. Looks at Hawkins and Doris, crosses in front of them.

(*Straightening away from Doris.*) Ma'am.

Nods, smiles. May stares at him, goes on out through the door, right.

Now there's a lady would dance a man back out through the doors of the Mother Church herself. Doris Hoyden.

He looks at her. Doris stares down into her lap.

I've got a great feeling about you, let me ask you now –

Stops, as the door, right, opens and May comes back in, carrying a lavatory roll. Simultaneously Mr Godboy comes out of the kitchen, carrying a glass of gin. He stares at May as she looks at Hawkins. May continues across to the door, right.

Godboy Can I help, dear?

May slams the door. Mr Godboy nods, smiles, hands the glass to Hawkins, sits down. There is a pause as Hawkins drinks.

I think you was mentioning the gasser O'Higgs. (*Little pause, stares at Hawkins.*) In relation to which, it's my own personal opinion that a man like O'Higgs prepared himself for the rope in the knowledge that it was going to go off ceremoniously without a hitch. To snatch the noose away from him with talk of specialists is to take the first step back into the jungle as far as I'm concerned. It puts an end to his heritage. (*Stares at him.*) May I say again, Mannerly, what an honour it is to have you in my home at last while I'm on the subject. (*Little pause.*) Did you ever mingle with someone similar to O'Higgs, before the event, so to speak, socially?

Hawkins O'Higgs? The only O'Higgs I ever knew had the purest tenor voice in the whole world, you could hear that voice through the screams of the City of London itself. (*To Doris.*) And what does your presently missing husband do, Doris, if I can ask?

Doris (*after a pause*) He's between.

Hawkins Between?

Godboy Between jobs, she means. Eric's being a bit unlucky at the moment, through no fault of his own, naturally, as he's totally unqualified.

Hawkins But still there's a great luck if he has you to come home to, Doris, for that's what a marriage means. Has he been missing from you long?

Doris shakes her head.

A little bit of night wandering he goes in for, does he?

Doris shrugs.

When the mood comes over him to count the stars of the sky and the blessings of his home? (*Laughs.*)

Godboy Eric is one of those who have – has – who succumbs to a weakish head for alcohol, I'm sorry to say.

Hawkins (*to Doris*) Well, he has a habit of turning up in the end, does he?

Doris nods.

And that's a very pleasant habit for both of you, I think?

Doris looks down. There is a long silence. Hawkins stares at Doris, Mr Godboy stares at Hawkins.

Godboy Inspector, may I be so bold as to show you something? (*Gets up.*) It's merely this piece over here, a recent acquisition, in a manner of speaking, for which I've got interesting plans.

As Hawkins turns in his chair, goes to the cupboard.

Take a good look at it, sir, I'm particularly interested in your opinion.

Hawkins leans over, pats Doris on the knee.

(*Opens the cupboard door.*) I chose it myself. As you see, capacious. And around here, to the side, there's a hole, goodness only knows what for, Mannerly, originally.

Laughs, shakes his head, looks towards Hawkins, who swings his head away from Doris.

Doris (*sidling down the couch*) Um, I've got to be, um . . . (*In a low voice.*)

Gets up. Hawkins also gets up.

Godboy It's worth pointing out there's enough room to get a fully grown adult in here, even May Godboy, my wife, could be got in here, sir. (*Laughs.*)

Doris limps hurriedly to the door. Hawkins, following Doris sidles ahead of her by the cupboard, so blocking off her exit.

Hawkins It's big enough to get into, you say? (*To Doris.*) Now isn't that amazing?

Godboy Indeed it is, sir. (*Gets into the cupboard.*) As I was saying, capacious enough for May Godboy herself, who could easily be accommodated.

Hawkins (*as Doris goes around the back of him, opens the door, right*) May I just – for interest –

He closes the cupboard door, holds it closed with his left hand, catches Doris's hand with his right.

You're off upstairs, then?

Doris nods.

(*Stares at her.*) Well, perhaps we'll be seeing each other again, some people I see over and over again, and there's been a glimpse –

The door, left, opens and May comes out. Stops. Stares at Hawkins, who releases Doris's hand.

(*To Doris.*) Goodnight, ma'am, and my respects to your husband, I hope I'll be seeing him also.

As Doris pulls away, stares at May, who shakes her head knowingly, goes out of the room. Hawkins turns, looks at May, as knocking sounds come from within the cupboard.

There is a sudden blowing of whistles, yapping of dogs, shouts, from a few streets distance.

(*To May.*) And there's Constable Hedderley calling.

May Ooooh, everybody needs you so bad, don't they? Including my husband, where is he?

Hawkins Ah! (*Opens the cupboard door.*) I'm off to Merrit Street, Mr Godboy, I'll wish you goodnight and thank you. (*Leans in, shakes hands with Mr Godboy.*)

Godboy Merrit Street! You've done it then! Congratulations, Mannerly, congratulations, sir!

Hawkins Thank you, and goodnight.

Closes the cupboard door again, puts his hat on his head, goes out, right. His voice in the hall:

All right, boys, all right, get moving, boys, come on.

The front door bangs. May stands looking at the cupboard. It opens. Mr Godboy steps out.

Godboy Merely, um . . . merely . . . something I wanted Mannerly to see.

May shakes her head at him, then points her finger at her head, revolves it slowly.

Well, the Merrit Street attacker has been taken at last, dear. (*Looks at her.*) I wonder whose trail Mannerly will be on next? Perhaps some time he'll be up against someone who knows the game inside out, and can give him a real battle of wits.

May He's already on her trail, isn't he? And he'd have her inside out before your eyes and you wouldn't know what he was up to.

Godboy Pardon, dear?

May Do you know what I've been doing in there?

Godboy What, dear?

May I've been telling you something.

Godboy Indeed, dear? What?

May looks at him, goes over to the sofa, sits on it. She is now wearing shoes.

May What's the time?

Godboy (*looks at his watch*) Ten-thirty, bedtime, dear.

May Come sit by me.

Godboy (*stares at her*) Well, I noticed there was still – were still some things in the cupboard, dear, I thought we could do it together.

May claps her hands, points to the floor beside her. Mr Godboy comes over, sits down on the edge of the sofa, gingerly, at May's feet.

May You call that comfy?

Godboy (*nods*) Thank you, dear.

May Well, I don't.

Gives him a push with her feet. He stumbles off the sofa.

Come on, let me have a last fling at your sad old head, as that's the only part of you I'll remember as that's the only part I'm allowed to touch.

Points to the floor beside her. Mr Godboy sits down on the floor, his head level with the sofa. She starts to knead his head gently.

Godboy You've got a long night ahead of you. Tomorrow, I merely mean, dear.

May Oh shut up your niggidy-naggidy with your merely means. (*Little pause.*) Rest easy now and settle yourself back, because this is important. (*Slips her hand down his throat, then begins to undo his tie.*) It's your last chance.

Godboy Pardon, dear?

May The trouble with you is you won't let go, that's what's defeating those specialists – if you've ever been to any. (*Pulls his tie off.*) I got a lot of life in me yet, that's what I been telling you, and if you'd just let me have a last-minute go at you everything could still come right. (*Puts a hand down his shirt, begins to rub his chest.*) There's a lesson to be learnt with taking a high hand, we all want it except for the freaks like Doris.

Godboy Doris, dear?

May She won't give that boy what he needs. (*Shakes her head.*) But there's some men could make us follow after them like a wet puppy dog, and she'd better watch it, she's met her match, from what I see of Hawkins. What's this doing to you?

Godboy Making my chest nice and warm, thank you, dear. Can I take you to mean that Doris and Eric's marriage is definitely on a friendly type of basis?

May She's not my idea of friendly, nor Eric's. And is *this* doing you good?

Godboy Yes, dear, thank you, although not too warm, it tends to tingle then – so Doris is against –

May Tingle away, Number Two, tingle all over. Number One used to like this more than anything.

Godboy Indeed, dear?

May Oh, you and Number One is poles apart, One always up, Two always down, and the horror of it is he's the one who's dead. (*Little pause.*) Does it make you green to hear me talk of Number One?

Godboy No, dear, I enjoy hearing you reminisce.

There is a crash of the front door outside. Mr Godboy leaps to his feet, hurries over to the door, looks down the hall.

May What is it?

Godboy It's Eric, dear. Eric.

Sound of feet in the hall, crashing.

Doris has been looking – what's happened to your trousers, Eric? (*Turns.*) He's gone.

May What was the matter with him?

Godboy Nothing dear, except he looked out of breath and his trousers was – were torn.

May (*chuckles*) There's a boy after my own. If he's in the mood to do a bit of that on Doris, perhaps he'll save them both. (*Claps her hands, points to the floor.*)

Mr Godboy, after a pause, comes back, sits down.

Don't it even make you green to see me having games with that Eric?

Godboy No, dear, I particularly wanted you to have a pleasant evening, which was magnificently rounded off by the appearance of Inspector Hawkins himself.

May Hawkins, O'Higgins, murder, wounds. I'd be better rubbing at a turtle. (*Removes her hand, lies still, stares at the ceiling.*) It's no go. No go. Last week it was my fiftieth birthday we was seeing out together and what did you do for it but spend the day creeping around them at the police station and the night sitting in your chair like a little white corpse. (*Long pause.*) I'm a warm woman, Perkins, everybody knows that, even your Manly Hawkins could see it in a wink, I'm a warm woman but the fire's going out. There's got to be hot coals to keep me banked, and you're turning me into embers, Perkins, embers. What'll happen to me if this goes on? What'll happen to me? (*There is a long silence.*) What do you say to me, then?

Godboy Dear. (*A pause. He sits staring ahead, his hands folded into his lap.*) If I haven't given satisfaction over the last two years, dear, it's because I've been waiting for me to see my path straight.

May And do you see it straight to me, Perkins? (*Pause.*) Is that where the path's leading, into me?

Godboy No, dear. Now that Inspector Manly Hawkins has now called, after I'd given up all hope and was going to go ahead anyway, it can only lead to him, dear. (*Pause.*) I'm sorry.

May (*gets up. Stands looking down at him.*) What do you want with him? He don't want anything from you, it's someone else *he's* after. (*Nods at ceiling.*)

Godboy And yet he came, dear, on time exactly. (*Looks up at her.*) To me.

May Well, I don't care no more. That was a chance I was giving you, Perkins, and I wanted you to take it. Remember that, it's all I ask now.

She goes to the large cupboard, flings it open, looks inside. Mr Godboy gets up, hurries over to the alcove, seizes the pipe, pulls it out, bends over, fishes for the cylinder, frantically pushes the pipe so that it falls into the guppie case, finds the cylinder, turns on the tap, drags the pipe out of the guppie case, turning around, as May steps out of the large cupboard, opens the door of the small cupboard, steps in. Mr Godboy slams the door of the large cupboard, pushes the pipe through the hole and simultaneously jerks out the padlock, puts it through, closes it, turns back to the gas cylinder. As he is doing this, May steps out of the small cupboard, with a hat on her head, glances at Mr Godboy, turns, stares at him, shakes her head, goes on into the room, left, reappears almost immediately with two suitcases, articles of clothing sticking out from under the lid, looks at Mr Godboy, who is now pressed flat, stomach first, against the cupboard door. Shakes her head again, walks through the kitchen door. Mr Godboy turns, his arms pressed back flat against the cupboard door.

Godboy (*quietly*) Haw-kins. (*Stares blankly ahead.*)

Curtain.

Act Two

SCENE ONE

The following afternoon.

The curtain rises on the same set as in Act One, but the room is now very neat. Mr Godboy can be heard and partially seen in the kitchen, moving about. He comes fussily into the parlour with a new feather duster, which he flicks here and there. He is wearing an apron. Suddenly he stops, stands alert, then puts the duster down and goes to the hall door, right. Stands listening, opens it a crack, peers out, opens it wider.

Godboy (*into the hall*) Doris. (*There is a little silence.*) I've just put the kettle on.

Little pause, He beckons with his hands. Doris appears, limping slightly more than in Act One. Her handbag is tightly clutched to her front. She stands at the door.

I thought you'd forgotten, it looked as if you were passing me by.

Laughs, ushers her in, makes to shut the door, is unable to do so. Opens it.

Eric (*walks past him in a pair of bright new trousers*) Hello.

Godboy stares at him for a long moment. Eric stares back at him, confused.

Godboy Oh, you're coming in for a moment too, are you?

Eric (*nods*) Yeah. (*Long pause.*) What? (*Short pause.*)

Got old May off all right then, did you? (*Looks around.*)
The place feels empty without her, eh, Dorrie?

> *Laughs nervously as Mr Godboy continues to stare at
> him.*

She certainly had a send-off from what we heard, eh,
Dorrie?

Godboy (*walks briskly to the guppie case, sprinkles food
on the surface, puts a finger in, waggles it*) Pardon, old
boy?

> *Eric watches him, then comes to stand beside him as
> Doris sits reluctantly on the sofa.*

Eric You calling out goodbyes to May.

Godboy Oh, pardon me for waking you, yes, I did shout
after her from the doorstep, I didn't mean to be heard.
(*Puts the package back on the table.*) There, there, my
little fellows, how's that for a feast?

Eric (*looks at them closely*) Why they lying on top like
that?

Godboy Because, old boy – (*Stares a little closer.*) They're
dead.

Eric Oh, is that it.

> *Doris lets out a little scream.*

Godboy (*picks one out, looks at it, drops it back in,
wipes his fingers on his apron*) This is very upsetting,
I don't mind admitting.

Eric How did it happen then?

Godboy Natural causes.

Eric Oh.

Godboy It can happen to anybody. Nevertheless it's a surprise. It's the last thing I thought would happen.

There is a long silence.

Doris (*who has been sniffing*) Gas.

Godboy (*swings towards her*) Pardon, old boy?

Doris I smell gas.

Godboy No there isn't, old girl.

There is a pause. Eric sniffs. Another pause.

Eric What is it then?

Godboy Merely an unfamiliar odour, old girl. (*Walking across and taking off his apron.*) I've been boiling up some cabbage heads. Perhaps it's merely that. (*Folds apron carefully, puts it on the gramophone table.*)

Eric Can't help feeling sorry for them though. (*Puts his finger into the water.*)

Godboy Indeed, that's only human. (*Goes over to Doris.*) Well, Doris, how are –?

Eric It's funny thinking of them, they was here last night when we was clowning around enjoying ourselves, they was swimming around then, back and forward and up and down, and now today they're gone. Dead.

Godboy is listening, although facing Doris, who is staring down into her lap.

Godboy (*with a smile*) Your husband Eric . . .

Eric Likely it was May's going did for them.

Godboy (*turning*) You're talking nonsense, old boy, if you don't mind my speaking frankly to you as between friends, grief is unknown to fish.

Eric Is it? Oh?

As Mr Godboy turns back to Doris.

What grief?

Godboy Pardon, old boy?

Eric What grief? You said grief.

Godboy I merely mean, old boy, that those guppies would hardly go away from grief of May's passing, pass away from grief of May's going I merely mean. (*Long pause.*) And if you work it out, if they knew enough to know May was going away they'd know enough to know she was certainly coming back as far as she knew.

Eric (*laughs*) Course they didn't know she wasn't coming back.

Godboy (*nods his head at him several times*) I'm glad we're agreed on that, Eric. (*Turns back to Doris. Stops. Turns back to Eric.*) They didn't know she was going, I also mean.

Eric Oh. (*Nods vaguely.*)

Godboy (*turning back to Doris*) How's it coming along today, Doris?

Eric What will you do with them?

Godboy The remains will have to be disposed of, naturally, old boy. (*Little pause.*) What kind of trouble has it been causing you today, Doris?

Doris It's all right today.

As Eric comes across the room, and sits down in one of the utility chairs.

Godboy Really, Doris, my dear, I was observing you closely as you limped across the room. We both know what needs doing to it. (*Turns to Eric.*) Eh, Eric?

Eric (*nods*) How will you dispose of the remains?

Godboy I will I will I will. (*Stops himself.*) Pardon, old boy?

Eric Them gups.

Godboy They will have to be sluiced, old boy.

Eric Oh. Down the toilet you mean?

Godboy (*nods*) Now, Doris –

Eric (*shaking his head*) Old May won't like that.

Mr Godboy stares at him.

No, she won't like having the remains sluiced, if I know May.

Godboy I wasn't talking about May's remains, I merely mean, old boy, I was talking about the guppies' remains if you take my meaning? (*Turning his head quickly.*) I like your dress, Doris.

Eric What?

Godboy I was admiring Doris's dress.

Eric Oh? Where's my raincoat then?

Godboy Pardon?

Eric Well, wasn't it down here last night? (*Looks at Doris.*)

Mr Godboy shakes his head. Stops shaking it as he remembers, then shakes it more vigorously.

Godboy It was not. No.

Eric Well, listen, me and May was having a dance and I was wearing it then, then me and May went into the kitchen for the stout and gin and I was wearing it then,

then May come up to me and took it off me . . . (*Looks around.*) 'Less she took it with her.

Godboy I don't mean to cause trouble, old boy, but May wouldn't be seen dead in that – in that – no, get that idea right out of your mind. (*Little pause.*) It'll turn up where you're least expecting it. (*Little pause.*) Righto, old boy?

Eric Oh. (*Nods.*) Righto.

Godboy Indeed you probably lost it when you went off in that strange way.

Eric (*after a pause*) No, I wasn't wearing it then, no.

Godboy Where did you go anyway, we all sat here worrying about you.

Eric Oh. (*Laughs, hunches a shoulder.*) Out. I went out.

Godboy Yes, well, Doris was in a state, it needed Inspector Hawkins himself to calm her down.

There is a long pause.

Eric What was he doing here?

Godboy Merely visiting myself, old boy.

Eric Oh. (*Nods.*) You haven't seen my scarf then?

Mr Godboy stares at him coldly. There is a long silence. Eric looks around him, stares at the cupboard, points at it.

I know, I . . .

Godboy Now I don't mean to cause offence – (*shouting*) but I'm getting tired of all these accusations of scarves and raincoats and sluicing May down the toilet, that is the guppies, where's your manners?

Long pause. Eric stares at him in bewilderment, Doris stares down into her lap.

Do I get my apology?

Eric shakes his head perplexed. There is another pause.

Doris (*in a whisper*) Say pardon.

Eric Oh. Righto. Pardon.

Godboy (*nods*) Least said, soonest mended, old boy.

He gets up, goes into the kitchen, leaving door open. Eric looks at Doris, who keeps her face bent. He looks away.

Eric finally crosses his legs, begins to jog a foot up and down, whistles tunelessly. Doris glares at him. He stops. Pause. Looks at her. She looks away.

Eric Honest, Dorrie, I was just walking.

Doris Walking?

Eric Just walking around, that's all.

Doris (*in a hiss*) And what about me, with that policeman, what was I meant to be doing while you was just walking around, with him walking around me? And them trousers you caught on barbed wire. What barbed wire?

Eric Well, I told you, there was this barbed wire –

Doris turns her face away.

Anyway, you heard him, that policeman was just visiting. (*Looks at Doris's face.*) I love you, Dorrie.

Doris pays no attention. Eric sits hunched. Begins to jog his foot again, looks around the room hopelessly, sees cupboard, gets up, goes over to it, stares at it

*closely, then tries handle. Pulls harder, then holds up
the padlock.*

Here, Dorrie!

*She pays no attention. He peers between the door crack,
gets down on one knee. Mr Godboy comes into the
room carrying a tray. Puts tray down on the floor, picks
up two cups, carries one to Doris, puts it beside her.*

Godboy Sugar, my dear?

Doris Yes, please.

Godboy What about Eric? Eric?

Eric Yes, please. (*Peering now with his face close to the
crack.*)

Godboy (*stirs Doris's cup for her*) There. Lots of sugar
to sweeten your outlook on things. (*Chuckles, pats her
shoulder.*) Not to worry, Doris. Not to worry.

*Nods, turns, walks across the room with Eric's cup,
puts it down on the floor beside him, turns, walks
eagerly back towards Doris.*

It's worrying does more harm than corns and ulcers put –
(*Stops. Turns, looks at Eric.*) Old boy?

Eric Yeah. (*Sniffing hard.*)

Godboy Haven't you got any respect, old boy? Haven't
you got any? Any respect?

Eric What? (*Turns his head.*) What for?

Godboy For – for – for property, I merely mean.

Eric Oh.

*Looks at Doris, gets up. Stares at Mr Godboy, who is
glaring at him.*

Doris (*after a long pause*) Say pardon, Eric.

Eric Oh. Righto. Pardon.

Little pause, as Mr Godboy nods slowly.

Godboy Granted, Eric, as soon as asked. Now – (*Gestures to one of the chairs.*)

Eric But I thought May said it was for us.

Godboy Indeed it is.

Eric Oh. (*Comes back to his chair. Sits down.*) But it's locked.

Godboy (*about to sit down, pauses*) Indeed it is.

Eric (*looks at Doris*) Well –?

Godboy It'll have to remain locked until further notice, thank you for reminding me.

Eric Oh. (*Looks at Doris again.*) But I remember, see, that's where I put my scarf and raincoat, see.

Godboy (*strikes his knee*) How many times do I have to tell you. (*Shouting.*) There's nothing in there except May's remains.

Long pause. They all sit staring ahead.

By which I merely mean the bits and pieces of May . . . (*Falters.*) which she couldn't take with her and had to leave behind. (*Little pause.*) If you take my meaning, old boy. (*Little pause.*) Have you got those facts straight in your mind?

Eric Righto, yes, righto. Pardon.

Godboy (*after a pause*) Granted.

There is a long silence. They drink their tea. Doris with her head lowered, Mr Godboy genteelly, Eric from the wrong side of the cup.

(*To Doris.*) Excuse me speaking sharpish to your husband, I don't mean you to take it personally. (*To Eric.*) It's just at the rate he's going on funny things will be turning up all over my parlour. (*Laughs.*)

Eric laughs. There is another long silence.

Eric This cupboard then, that's got all this stuff of May's in it and it's locked, are you still giving it to us then?

Godboy Indeed I am, yes, the sooner you get it up to your own parlour the happier I'll be.

Eric Oh. (*Nods.*) Well – (*Looks at Doris.*) That's a bit funny, well, I mean – (*Laughs, looks at Doris.*) You're giving us this cupboard and it's got May's stuff in it, and it's locked up so we can't get into it anyway, and it'll take up all the room in our room, won't it? And I mean that's a bit funny. As we can't get into it even.

Mr Godboy looks at him, goes over to the cupboard, bends down, opens the drawers at the base, turns, folds his arms, looks at Eric. Eric looks at Doris, who looks away.

Godboy (*quietly*) Any further complaints, Eric?

Eric shrugs. Mr Godboy comes back, sits down, sips from his tea. Eric looks at him, looks at Doris, looks at him again. Laughs suddenly. Mr Godboy puts his cup into its saucer, stares at Eric.

Eric No, I was just laughing because it's a bit funny getting a cupboard you can't get into except in a bottom drawer and it's as big as our room nearly and it's ponging away. That's all.

Pause, while Mr Godboy looks at him, and Doris looks down into her cup.

Well, you smell it, Dorrie. Go on, smell it.

Godboy (*folds his arms*) Doris, be a good girl and smell it, will you, Doris? As that's what your husband wants.

Doris (*gets up, limps across the room, smells the cupboard, limps back*) It's not too bad. (*In a low voice, looks accusingly at Eric.*)

Godboy Virtually odour free?

Doris I smelt far worse from that leak we had in the stove.

Godboy Thank you, Doris. (*To Eric*) Well, old boy? (*Little pause.*) Eric?

Eric Um. (*Looks from Doris to Mr Godboy.*) It's just that it smells funny to me. Gas in a cupboard. (*Little pause.*) It smells funny.

Godboy Oh does it, old boy, and if it does I'll tell you why, it's because you're turning a bit nosy, frankly speaking. Righto. (*Little pause.*) Righto.

Eric (*after a pause*) Pardon.

Godboy Granted as asked. Now to change the subject to something pleasant, did you hear the news about Inspector Mannerly Hawkins' success in the Merrit Street case? He was here last night, wasn't he, Doris, just prior to catching the man who's certainly helping him now down at the station, if I know Mannerly Hawkins. (*Laughs.*) Eh, Doris?

Eric Oh? (*Laughs.*) I heard something about that, yes. (*Looks around the room, begins to jog his leg.*)

Godboy Yes, if you hadn't run off like that, you could have met Mannerly too, Eric. Still, May and Doris met him, I'm glad about that. Eh, Doris? (*Smiles at her.*) He's got amazing instincts, Mannerly has. (*Turns to Eric.*) What did you hear?

Eric Nothing, no. (*Shakes his head.*) Only when I was down at the, um, 'bacconist's, there was something I heard about this girl undoing her stockings or something and this chap went up to her, or something like that.

Doris When did you go down to the 'bacconist's?

Godboy (*laughs*) That was no girl, Eric, that was Police Constable Hedderley.

Eric Who?

Godboy Hawkins' female accomplice, old boy.

Eric (*angrily*) What was she doing there, then?

Godboy Pardon?

Eric Well, what was she taking her stockings off for then?

Godboy Bait, Eric, she was bait in the trap.

Eric Well, what'll happen to him, then?

Godboy Further promotion. Or another favourable mention from a judge.

Eric No, this bloke. The one you say they, um . . .

Godboy With Mannerly Hawkins on the job, Eric?

Eric But suppose they get – got – I mean, it's the wrong bloke?

Godboy I repeat, Eric – we're talking about Inspector Mannerly Hawkins.

Eric (*thinks*) Well, but if he was a bloke coming home from going into the air to clear his brain for a moment, and happened to be in the area by mistake, see, and there was this girl pulling her stockings off and waving them at him, this – um, bloke, he might come up to her, just from – well, and asked what she was doing larking about and if his brain was a bit fogged she could have got hold of him and pitched him to the ground bruising his shoulder something – see what I mean, it could be an accident, see. (*Long pause.*) No, I'm thinking, that's all. (*Little pause.*) No.

Godboy I say it again, Eric – (*Laughs.*) We're talking about Inspector Mannerly Hawkins. Down there at the station he's dealing with a criminal second in value to a murderer himself. Mannerly doesn't make mistakes, Eric, as I ought to know.

Eric Oh. (*Little pause.*) That's all right then. (*Little pause.*) I mean, if he's got someone he thinks did it, and he doesn't make mistakes, that's all right then. He can't grumble.

Godboy Who can't grumble?

Eric This chap they got.

Godboy Oh, he'll grumble all right, there's very few know how to help the police, Eric, very few like the gasser O'Higgs. After he'd been trapped with the corpse of his wife in an airing closet, and the female tenant laid out on the kitchen table, stark, he knew his time was come. He sat down and wrote out a brilliant confession on the spot. Being in a lawyer's office he knew the language. There's very few men like O'Higgs, and an animal like the Merrit Street attacker wouldn't be one of them.

   Doris shudders.

What is it, Doris?

Doris I been having dreams about him, nightmares, I mean.

Eric (*looks at her, clears his throat*) Who?

Doris Him. People like him. The one was in Merrit Street.

Eric gets up, takes his cup over to the record table, then wanders to the guppie case, stops in front of it, peers in, turns, wanders towards the cupboard, stops in front of it, raps on the door, stops himself, looks towards Mr Godboy furtively, then stands by the cupboard listening to the conversation between Doris and Mr Godboy.

Godboy What sort of nightmares would those be, Doris?

Doris I mean, what could you do, if he got you? What could you do? And people, what would they think? There was one I was reading about in the States of America, he did things to girls with tape and shoe laces and stuffed their mouths with cotton wool so the girls was helpless, and was powerless to struggle, and then he did other things to them. It wasn't their fault.

As Eric abstractedly opens the bottom drawer of the cupboard, begins to unwind the length of pipe:

Godboy No, Doris, if you were rendered incapable first, you'd be cleared of any blame.

Doris And when I was little there was this one he used to wait at bus stops in his car, he was after us when we was little.

Godboy They're different, Doris. There's no excuse for that. I hope the authorities realise hanging's too good for them, what they need is medical treatment from specialists.

Doris But this Merrit Street one, he could've come through my bedroom window when I was all asleep and quiet, and done things to me, he could've bound me up and I couldn't have done nothing if he did it by force, while you – *(to Eric)* was walking the streets.

Eric (*shakes his head*) Not to you, Dorrie, I wouldn't do that.

Godboy (*looks towards him, leaps to his feet*) Now Eric, what you prying into now, Eric?

Eric Well, it was in this drawer. (*Holds out the cylinder.*) It's got that gas smell to it.

Godboy (*walking across to him*) Smell, smell, smell, all you talk about is smell.

> *Takes the cylinder away from Eric, thrusts it behind the alcove curtain.*

Now I'll tell you, old boy, I'm getting tired of telling you your manners in front of your own wife, you're interrupting a very pleasant conversation we're having. (*Turns, looks him in the face, very close.*) And there's another thing, old boy, what are your plans for the afternoon?

Eric What?

Godboy Because frankly, old boy, it's time Doris and me were getting down to it – her corn, I merely mean, and it's medically a trifle funny to have a patient's husband loitering about in my cupboards. (*Long pause.*) What about going to the pictures?

> *Eric looks at Doris.*

Doris (*looking down into her handbag*) Could we do it tomorrow?

Godboy No, Doris, I'm sorry to say I've got to get you over with, any moment now my time might not be my own.

Doris (*hesistates*) Well, can't he stay then?

Godboy Again I have to say no, Doris, on general grounds. This is between you and me, my dear.

Looks at her, then takes Eric by the arm, leads him to the door, right.

Now you go to the pictures, then you stroll about a bit, and then you look in on me, it'll be all over then as far as Doris is concerned, I merely mean we'll have had it off. (*Little pause.*) Righto?

Eric Oh. (*Shrugs.*) Well.

Looks at Doris, walks past Mr Godboy, kisses Doris. She turns her mouth away.

Well, ta-ta, Dorrie.

Doris (*in a low voice*) Ta-ta.

Mr Godboy ushers him out of the room, stares after him, watched by Doris, then shuts the door. Stands looking at Doris. There is a pause. He comes and sits by her on the sofa, folds his hands into his lap, clears his throat. Doris looks down at her handbag.

Godboy (*after a little pause*) How are you feeling now, Doris?

Doris Cold. I feel cold.

Godboy Cold, eh? That's a good sign.

Doris Is it?

Godboy It's when people get all heated up that inconveniences begin.

Doris Oh. (*Little pause.*) Can I have the fire on, then?

Godboy (*leaps to his feet*) Indeed, my – (*Sits down again.*) No, I'm sorry to say that might be a trifle risky under the circumstances. (*Long pause.*) Because of the little whiff I might be compelled to give you.

Doris (*after a long pause*) What for?

Godboy It's usual in these cases, Doris. (*Laughs.*) Never you mind your little head about that, dear.

There is a long silence. Mr Godboy turns his head and stares at Doris.

I'm sorry about my treatment of Eric, he's a good lad. Above all, most likeable. (*Little pause.*) What was it precisely that attracted you about him?

Doris Well, it was that he looks like that Humphrey Bogart.

Godboy Oh, indeed, my dear, you do surprise me there, my own impression of Humphrey Bogart on one viewing is of a trifle more educated man. But these things are a matter of personal taste.

Doris It's when he wears his raincoat.

Godboy His raincoat isn't in this room, Doris.

Long pause.

Doris Whiff of what?

Godboy Pardon?

Doris Whiff of something, you said.

Godboy Indeed. (*Nods.*) My own marriage to May was a blessing in its way. I didn't know what it was I wanted until I met her and found myself thinking about it. Fifty years a bachelor is a long time for a man, he dreams of what he is but he don't – doesn't do anything about it until fate compels him. (*Looks at Doris.*) I've followed Mannerly Hawkins' career since the moment I saw him, down at the self-same station he's returned to. There was something there that bound us together, Doris. Did you know O'Higgs was taken into custody by a man he'd worked with in his capacity as a lawyer's clerk? He

286

addressed some letters to him, personal letters, from his
final cell. They were eventually published in a newspaper.

Long pause.

Doris (*clears her throat*) Whiff of what, will it be?

Godboy (*looks at her*) Whiff of the same thing I had to
give to May, Doris. (*Little pause.*) If it hadn't been for
my wound, things would have been different. I'd have
been a different man on the force. Mannerly Hawkins
is a man. He's got the authority.

Pause.

Doris It's funny. (*Laughs.*) It's not hurting me now.

*Mr Godboy looks at her again, bends towards her,
pats her on the arm, gets up, arranges one of the
utility chairs so that it's facing to the left. He goes to
the alcove, takes out a cardboard box. Doris watches.
He comes back, clears his throat, stands holding the
back of the arranged chair. Bends over, pats the seat
with his hand. Doris watches. Pats the seat again.
Laughs. Doris limps over, sits down. Mr Godboy
squares his shoulders, turns, stands behind Doris.*

Godboy Kindly remove the shoe and stocking please.
(*Stiffly, then turns around and folds his arms over his
chest.*)

Doris slowly takes off her shoe, then her stocking.

Ready?

Doris (*in a low voice*) Yes.

Godboy (*walks stiffly around the chair*) Would you
mind just stretching it out, Doris, so I can have a proper
glimpse of it.

Doris stretches her leg out. Mr Godboy crouches down some distance from the foot, inspects it carefully. After a little pause, whistles. Doris looks at him in alarm.

We just got to it in time. It's burgeoning fast. There'll be danger if it's allowed to develop.

Gets up, goes to the alcove, picks out a box from the back, then another one. Comes back, opens the top box, takes out small knives, pads, lotions, puts them on the floor.

I've been a great admirer of yours, Doris. I expect you realise that.

Doris (*watching him*) What?

Godboy We share similar ideas about things, Doris, very similar. (*Stares up at her.*) I appreciate what you was – were telling me about your dreams. (*Gets up, holding the second box.*) As I said to May, violence to a living creature isn't in my nature. That's why I was a bachelor for fifty years. (*Opens the box.*) Now I have to administer a whiff of something mild.

Doris Well – (*in a shaky voice*) what is it?

Godboy It's to help you out.

Doris (*shakes her head*) I don't want that.

Godboy Now Doris, I wouldn't want to have myself having to counter serious opposition. There could be dangerous responses made by your reflexes which could throw me off my stride. (*Laughs.*) It's a case of too many cooks can spoil the broth, merely.

He comes around to stand beside Doris. She looks up at him. There is a long silence.

You won't give me any trouble, will you, Doris?

Doris shakes her head.

(*Puts a hand on her shoulder.*) Thank you, Doris.

Doris What's that, then?

Godboy This. (*Holds the box up.*) This will make you laugh when you see it. (*Little pause.*) I'll have to ask you to slip it on in a minute of your own volition. It'll facilitate matters dreadfully for you.

Doris (*makes a ghastly laughing sound*) But what is it?

Godboy It's an appliance you're familiar with. It'll even bring back childhood memories. I've done some alterations so that it comes in handy for what's got to be done. My own invention.

Opens the box, shows her the contents, laughs. Doris stares down into it.

Righto?

Doris shakes her head, starts to get up.

(*Pressing her down with his hand.*) Righto.

Doris subsides. Sits staring down into her lap. Mr Godboy comes round so that his back is to the audience, blocking her from view. There are slight struggling sounds. He keeps his back to the audience.

There you are, it's the right size, it suits perfectly.

Doris makes mumbling sounds. Mr Godboy stands stiffly for a moment, puts his hands behind his back, twists them, his head up. Then bends.

You look as right as rain.

Doris mumbles.

(*Shouting.*) You look as right as rain.

Little pause, further mumbling from Doris.

As *rain*, I said.

Sounds of footsteps in the hall, right.

Eric (*shouting*) I know, and I haven't got my raincoat.

Godboy (*stands frozen by the chair. There is a pause, then tentatively*) Pardon?

Eric Dorrie!

Godboy What do you want?

Eric It looks like rain, and I need my raincoat, that's all.

Godboy It isn't here. I told you.

Eric Oh. (*Pause.*) How's it going then?

Godboy Doris is in excellent condition. (*Holding her shoulders as she struggles to rise.*)

Eric I'll be off to the pictures then.

Godboy Righto.

Sound of Eric moving about outside the door, then a confusion of steps. Mr Godboy hurries over to the door, right, exposing Doris for the first time. She is wearing a gas mask. He opens the door, right, stares down the hall, then closes the door, turns the key in the lock. As he is doing this the door left opens, and Eric puts his head in. Stares at Doris as Mr Godboy steps away from the door, turns, sees him. There is a long pause.

Eric (*to Doris*) What are you doing in that, then?

He bursts out laughing. Doris makes mumbling sounds.

Godboy (*hurries back, puts a hand on Doris's arm*) You're interrupting a very important moment, Eric. This is no time for your jokes.

Eric stops laughing. Looks grave. Lets out another snort. Stops.

Eric I'm going to see *Flame and Arrow* with that Virgin Mayo and Burt Lancaster. (*Little pause.*) That all right?

Doris stares at him.

Flame and Arrow.

Bellows. Pantomimes drawing a bow. Doris nods.

(*To Mr Godboy.*) It's outlaws in the woods. She don't like them, she likes cities. (*Little pause.*) It's where he catches her and keeps her chained by a chain around her neck. (*Little pause.*) It'll be good. (*Little pause.*) Righto. (*Little pause.*) Ta-ta then.

Godboy Ta-ta.

Eric walks across the stage to the door, right, watched by Mr Godboy, tries the handle, finds it locked, steps away, comes back across the stage.

Eric Righto.

Mr Godboy, who has kept a hand on Doris's shoulder, hurries after Eric with a utility chair, puts it under the handle. Comes back, looks at Doris, pats her on the shoulder. Goes to the alcove, takes out gas cylinder, length of pipe, starts to come back. There is a knock on the door, right. He turns angrily, puts the cylinder down, goes to the door, right. Puts his ear against it. Sound of footsteps.

Godboy (*shouting*) I'm beginning to think your Eric is a trifle mad, Doris. If you'll pardon me for saying so.

Unlocks door, opens it a fraction, peers out, opens it wider, then steps out of sight into the hall as the door, left, opens inwards, thus causing the chair to fall over.

Hawkins enters, followed by Hedderley, in a long police skirt, tunic, curls, etc. Hawkins stares down at Doris, as Hedderley takes up a position by the record table, hands behind back.

Hawkins Well, and here's a pretty sight. (*Laughs.*)

Doris stares up at him, then down into her lap as Mr Godboy comes back in through the door, left, stepping carefully over the chair. Stops. Stares at Hawkins.

Godboy (*reverently*) So you've come again!

Hawkins I think we're interrupting something, Mr Godboy.

Godboy (*as Hawkins turns back to Doris*) No, Mannerly, no. Please pardon the mess.

Goes to the door, left, picks up the chair, Hawkins is now staring down at Doris's leg. She draws it up awkwardly, sits with her hands clasped around her handbag.

We was – were just about to get commencing down to a nastyish business. (*Little pause.*) Doris's corn, I merely mean.

Comes back, picks up the cylinder, carries it, with the tube trailing behind, to the alcove.

And a preliminary settling down I go in for as part of my technique. (*Comes back.*) Doris is a nervous girl – (*Bends over her. In a low voice.*) So I slipped this on in a reminiscent vein about the old days.

Takes the gas mask off. Doris looks around, looks down at her handbag.

Hawkins Ah, and so it's you, Doris Hoyden. (*Crouches slightly to stare at her.*) But you're not still waiting for the wandering husband? (*Little pause.*) He wouldn't still be on the wander now?

Godboy He's just gone this second, Mannerly.

Hawkins (*looks at Hedderley*) Now isn't that a pity, then.

Hedderley nods. There is a pause. Mr Godboy walks over to the alcove, the gas mask in his hands.

Godboy I'm merely, um, pardon me . . .

Hawkins Mr Godboy.

Mr Godboy stops, turns. Hawkins comes towards him, revolving his hat in his hand. Stands thoughtfully for a moment, then puts his hand on Mr Godboy's left shoulder. Mr Godboy comes to attention, as if under arrest. Then Hawkins moves to the cupboard, gives the padlock a flick.

Ah, and it's quite a lock you've locked your treasures up with.

Turns, smiles at Mr Godboy. Doris, during this, picks up her shoe and stocking and begins to limp towards the kitchen door.

(*Quietly, still smiling at Mr Godboy.*) Hedderley.

Hedderley shifts around, stands beside Doris. Doris stops. Hedderley stares at the side of her face. Doris is facing the wall, right.

Godboy Yes, sir. (*Little pause.*) Unfortunately I can't put my hand on the key at this precise moment, Mannerly, which has got itself unfortunately lost somehow.

Hawkins (*turns, looks down at the guppies*) And the charming Mrs Godboy?

293

Godboy Unfortunately May Godboy is no longer with us just at the moment, I'm sorry to say. She took that trip I was hinting about last night.

Hawkins Did she now. (*Puts his finger into the water.*) Not as sprightly as yesterday, I think.

Godboy (*after a pause*) A little run down, and in need of a rest, now you ask, Mannerly.

Hawkins (*still staring into the tank*) Not dead though?

Godboy No, Mannerly . . . It's a kind of holiday.

Hawkins A holiday. (*Stirs his fingers around.*) How strange the little creatures are, in their ways. How strange.

Godboy (*after a pause, laughs*) Very true, Mannerly, very true.

Hawkins Mr Godboy. (*Looks at him.*) What it is, Mr Godboy, is that there's a little matter we're trying to get to the bottom of.

Godboy Sir?

Hawkins (*comes over, puts a hand on Mr Godboy's shoulder again.*) And I think you can help us, Mr Godboy.

Godboy (*stares into his face*) Help you in your inquiries, Mannerly. Yes, sir.

There is a long pause.

Do you want me to accompany you to the station, Mannerly?

Hawkins (*shakes him gently by the shoulder*) Well, to tell you the truth, we're on a little game of cat and mouse, and sometimes it's better for the cat to sit beneath the mouse's lair. (*Tilts his head, smiles.*) Isn't that the truth?

Godboy I've been expecting another visit, Mannerly, but I didn't expect even you would be precisely – (*Shakes his head in admiration.*) May I say, whatever the outcome of your present inquiries, my congratulations are offered again on your Merrit Street attacker triumph. It will always be an honour, wherever I may end up, to recall that you sat in one of my chairs while it was happening. It'll be mentioned in my letters, Mannerly, from wherever I end up.

Hawkins is looking towards Hedderley and Doris throughout this.

And of course similarly congratulations to Constable Hedderley, if that is Constable Hedderley, that is.

Hawkins That is. Although Hedderley's a little modest about accepting congratulations this morning, aren't you now, Hedderley?

Hedderley Sir.

Godboy Even so, the Merrit Street attacker's a big feather to have had in her cap.

Hawkins laughs, shakes his head, walks towards the centre of the room, followed by Mr Godboy still clutching the gas mask.

Hawkins Hedderley wouldn't know how to receive a feather like that, would you, Hedderley? Your whole nature's against it, isn't it, Hedderley?

Hedderley Sir.

Godboy (*after a pause, looking from Hawkins to Hedderley and Doris*) That's in the best tradition, sir, of course. If I may say so personally, I think it's wonderful that the fair sex is being taken up, as long as they're not in it for the glamour merely, of course.

Hawkins Hedderley?

Hedderley Sir.

Hawkins Did you hear what Mr Godboy said about the fair sex? Are you in it for the glamour?

Hedderley Sir. (*Shakes head.*)

A long pause, during which Hawkins looks towards Hedderley, who continues to stare at the side of Doris's face.

Godboy Of course, even with the fair sex good officers are born and not made.

Hawkins Well, Hedderley, how would you answer Mr Godboy on that? Were you born, do you think, Hedderley, or were you made?

Hedderley Sir. (*Little pause.*) Made, sir.

Hawkins By whom were you made then, Hedderley?

Hedderley Sir. (*Little pause.*) By sir, sir.

Hawkins (*turns, smiles at Mr Godboy, tilts his head, turns back to Hedderley*) Now fill me in, Hedderley, on what you're doing at the moment?

Hedderley Sir. Nothing, sir.

Hawkins Well then, ask the young lady to turn around, it's rude to keep her on edge like that.

Hedderley says something in a low voice to Doris, who turns around slowly, clasping her handbag, her shoe and her stocking to her waist.

(*Goes up to her.*) Excuse our manners, Doris Hoyden, why don't you make yourself comfortable?

Gestures to the sofa. Doris looks at him, limps over to the sofa, sits in its corner, tightly.

No, no, Doris, right in the middle, the middle of the sofa's the most comfortable.

> *Doris shifts to the middle. Hedderley looks at Hawkins, who tilts head almost imperceptibly. Hedderley sits down next to Doris, on Doris's left. Hawkins turns one of the utility chairs around and straddles it, facing the other utility chair, which, after a hesitation, Mr Godboy turns around and also straddles. Hawkins begins to revolve his hat in his hands. Hedderley takes Doris's handbag from her, opens it, begins to go through it. Doris sits staring down into her lap. Mr Godboy begins to revolve the gas mask in his hands. There is a silence.*

Godboy So you're already on the trail of something else, Mannerly, after last night? (*Laughs.*)

Hawkins Ah. (*Shakes his head.*) It's not all the city's wickedness happens at night, Mr Godboy, as you'd be knowing yourself, I think. (*Stares at him.*) There's a loneliness that comes with daybreak that can turn a man's heart in his chest, isn't there? And fog the mind with the sorrow of us all.

Godboy Indeed, Mannerly?

> *Staring back at him, revolving the gas mask in time to Hawkins's revolutions.*

Hawkins The evil's done by daybreak, Mr Godboy. The morning has its own cries, and who can hear them if a policeman can't? How can a city live, if a city's lost its faith, and has its horrors locked in its households.

Godboy (*as Hedderley opens Doris's compact, tastes its contents*) I can assure you, Mannerly, that key will turn up eventually.

Hawkins No, Mr Godboy, the key was thrown away by the fathers of the nation. (*Rubs his eyes.*) There's not the difference I used to think, when I was in the care of the real fathers, between the vocation of the priest and the vocation of the policeman. We're both of us lonely from discipline. (*Laughs.*) And who is there, in this city, can tell them apart, the sinners and the sufferers, if the policeman can't?

Godboy (*confused*) There's no doubt that you can, Mannerly, your record shows it.

Hawkins leans over, takes Doris's stocking from her lap, runs his hands along it, his hat on his knee.

Hawkins But if loneliness can sour men into sinners, it's discipline can convert sinners into policemen. (*Begins to knot the stocking.*) Would there be something in the house can ease my throat from its preaching? (*Laughs.*)

Mr Godboy stares at him, puzzled.

A little drop of whatever it was you found for me last night, but only if you've got some.

Godboy Indeed, Mannerly. (*Little pause.*) Gin?

Hawkins Whatever it was, water and something or other, I think.

Mr Godboy gets up, goes into the kitchen.

(*Turns to Hedderley and Doris.*) Hedderley?

Hedderley Sir?

Hawkins Are you going through Mrs Hoyden's handbag, Hedderley? Is that what I'm seeing?

Hedderley Sir.

Hawkins And did you give Hedderley permission, Doris?

Doris shakes her head.

Well – and why don't you ask what Hedderley's up to then, as is your right?

Doris looks down, shakes her head.

Ask anyway.

Doris (*in a whisper*) It's all right.

Hawkins (*who has knotted the stocking several times, leans forward, letting it hang from his hand*) Ask Hedderley, Doris.

Doris (*in a whisper*) Why are you looking through my handbag?

Hedderley hands it back to Doris.

Hawkins (*to Doris*) Demand an apology, Doris. (*Pause.*) Doris. (*Little pause.*) Doris.

Doris (*in a whisper*) Say pardon.

Hedderley (*after a pause*) Sorry, ma'am.

Hawkins gets up, sits down on the right of Doris, stares at her intently as he unknots the stocking.

Hawkins Doris, it's slipped my mind, what did you say your footloose husband's name was, Doris?

Doris (*in a whisper*) Eric.

Hawkins (*glances at Hedderley, who shakes her head imperceptibly*) That's right, and that's it. (*Little pause, puts hand on Doris's knee.*) Between-Jobs Eric. (*Laughs, tilts his head.*) And tell me, Doris, aren't you perhaps suffering from loneliness with Between-Jobs always going away from you like that?

Doris shakes her head.

So you're expecting him back, then, sometime between now and never?

As Mr Godboy comes into the room, with a glass with water in it, and a bottle of gin:

Doris He'll be back for tea, he said.

Mr Godboy hands the glass to Hawkins, who looks at Hedderley, abstractedly takes the bottle from Mr Godboy, who is just about to pour, and pours himself a large gin.

Hawkins For tea?

Godboy Eric's a bit funny in his movements, but he's not one to forget his tummy, I'll say that for him.

Hawkins (*swallows from his drink*) As long as you don't prefer him gone, Doris, and send word to him to stay away?

Squeezes her knee with his other hand, laughs, tilts his head at her. Doris shakes her head.

Ah, but then you'd be having a mother to turn to, if you felt lost beyond yourself?

Doris shakes her head.

And no father either?

Doris shakes her head. Hawkins drinks some more, his hand still on Doris's knee.

Ah, and Hedderley's in the way of being an orphan too, aren't you, Hedderley?

Hedderley Sir.

Hawkins Which is why Hedderley took to the discipline of the policehood, isn't it, Hedderley? (*Laughs.*)

Hedderley Sir.

Hawkins (*tilts his head, laughs*) Ah, there's been a glimpse, Doris. Somewhere. I know it.

Hawkins hands the glass back to Mr Godboy, gets up, Hedderley also gets up. Looks down at Doris, puts his hand on her shoulder, then heads for the door, right, followed by Hedderley. Mr Godboy runs ahead, unlocks the door, opens it for them. Hawkins pauses by the guppie case, looks in, wags his finger about, looks at Mr Godboy, who is holding the door open.

I might be back, Mr Godboy, I might be back.

Godboy (*looks at him*) I know that, Mannerly. I'll be ready.

Hawkins tips his head, then goes out, followed by Hedderley. Mr Godboy goes out of the room after them. Doris looks towards the open door, right, then picks up the stocking, which Hawkins has left on the sofa, picks up her shoe and her handbag, tiptoes out into the kitchen left. There is a silence on stage, then Doris reappears through the kitchen door, followed closely by Mr Godboy. He escorts her back to the chair, sits her in it.

There's the officer in a million for you, Doris. Inspector Hawkins. Mannerly Hawkins. Did you notice his courtesy in interrogation? The way he established that May Godboy was absent was a delightful piece of consummate skill. (*Looks down at her.*) But you're pale, my dear?

Doris What's he want then?

Godboy (*after a pause*) He knows, Doris, and I know, but I can't tell you. It's between Mannerly and me. He's working in the dark but he'll get there in the end. (*Little pause.*) With him, cat and mouse is an art.

Doris What's he want with Eric then?

Godboy (*laughs*) Eric's got no place in this, he wouldn't bother himself with an Eric.

Doris Oh. (*Little pause.*) He had his hand on my knee, like last night again.

Godboy A red herring, Doris, that's known as. He had his hand on my shoulder, twice. (*Laughs.*) Twice.

He turns, goes to the alcove, comes back with the cylinder, locks the door, right, picks up the gas mask, walks purposefully back to Doris.

Doris No, I changed my mind.

Godboy (*looks at her*) It's too late for that, Doris. It's now or never.

Bends over her, again a short struggle, straightens. Doris is in the gas mask, sitting hunched.

He knows me for what I am, Doris, that's his secret, and soon he'll have the mouse, which is me, in his paws, and two's a better catch for him than one.

Mr Godboy picks up the end of the tube, thrusts it under the gas mask, turns the cylinder, wrestles with the knobs. As he is doing this, Doris snatches the tube out. The gas comes out as she holds it up. Mr Godboy turns.

(*In a long whisper.*) Manly. Manly.

Goes to Doris, puts his hand on her shoulder, bends over her, sees the pipe Doris is holding, grabs hold of it, takes a deep breath to exclaim, and still holding the pipe, reels away, grabs at the cylinder, turns off the tap, then crashing around the chair, sways to the sofa, watched by Doris, who gets anxiously to her feet.

Lights. Curtain.

SCENE TWO

A couple of hours later.

Lights on Mr Godboy, sitting on the sofa, his head lolling. He appears to be asleep, his hands are pressed into his crotch. He leaps suddenly to his feet, sits down again, stares ahead, slumps forward, buries his face in his hands. There is a knock on the door. It opens tentatively. Eric puts his head in, smiles at Mr Godboy, sniffs, makes a face. Mr Godboy stares slowly at him.

Eric Hello!

He comes in, carrying a small pail, smiles at Mr Godboy, who is still staring at him. Goes over, puts the pail on the guppie table, turns, sniffs again, coughs, makes as if to say something, checks himself, smiles.

Um, didn't you say she'd be done now then?

There is a long silence, Mr Godboy looks at the cylinder on the floor, looks back at Eric. Gets to his feet, walks over to Eric slowly. Puts a hand on his shoulder.

(*Laughs nervously.*) Where is she then? Is she upstairs?

Godboy Eric, I regret to inform you that your wife has met with a fatal accident.

Eric (*uncomprehending*) What?

Godboy She didn't suffer, sir, that must be the main consolation at a time like this. Her release was instantaneous.

Eric (*worried, looks at him apprehensively*) Where's Dorrie?

Godboy's shoulders jump, he goes back, sits down.
Puts a hand to his head.

Godboy My wound is playing me up something terrible.

Eric (*coming over to him*) Where's Dorrie?

Godboy An old wound. Pre-war. My dad did it to me, in a game with his belt.

Eric (*shouting*) Where's my Dorrie?

Godboy (*shouting back*) Don't you shout at me, old boy. A Special Constable's a Special Constable. (*Pause.*) Righto?

Eric (*whimpering*) Where's my Dorrie?

Godboy I keep telling you. She met with a fatal attack, mistake, I merely –

Eric begins to shake his head from side to side.

Would you mind restraining yourself, my personal giddiness isn't helped by it.

As Eric looks at him:

A great release must be your main consolation. Remember your manners.

Staggers to the window, opens it, sticks his head out, comes back, watched by Eric. Goes to the guppie case, picks up the food package, shakes it over them, pauses, then puts his hands into the water and bending down, splashes his face. Straightens. Turns.

Eric Where is she?

Godboy Whom?

Eric Dorrie!

Godboy (*looks around, confused, stares at Eric*) I have reason to believe that she must be laid out in the kitchen.

Eric turns, makes as if to run to the kitchen. Mr Godboy seizes his arm, they grapple, Eric falls to the floor. Mr Godboy sits on top of him.

This is bound to be a time of stress for you. I've had experience of grief in happier days. Kindly stop bobbing up and down, Eric, you're on my wound.

Eric Please, please, I've got to see her.

Godboy Why?

Eric I got to, she's my Dorrie!

Godboy There's nothing to see, merely her remains.

Eric Let me see her! (*Bucking frantically.*)

Godboy This is irregular. She's liable to be in a state of undress.

Eric (*stops, stares up at Mr Godboy*) What have you done to her?

Godboy Don't you attempt to incriminate me, boy.

There is a long pause.

How was your pictures, old boy?

Eric It was all right, it was good.

Godboy (*cunningly*) Can that story be checked out?

Eric What?

Godboy I'm in the clear on this, Eric, you're not good enough to play cat and mouse with me. And I'll tell you why. I left May –

Eric May?

Godboy Doris, I merely mean, alone in the cupboard –

Eric Cupboard?

Godboy Kitchen, I merely mean, don't keep confusing me, Eric, it's a cheap trick, left her alone in the kitchen when compelled to fetch an emergency refill of my prescription. When I came back, I found her already passed away on the kitchen table and a moment later, although myself laid low by my wound, heard you hammering at the door in a state. (*Little pause, cunningly.*) You are in a state, aren't you? We can agree on that?

Eric Let me go to her, please.

Godboy (*after a pause, gets up*) All right, Eric, I give you permission. I'm inclined to believe your story, but I'm not sure that a superior officer like Mannerly Hawkins would take a favourable view.

Shouting the last part of this after Eric, who has run into the kitchen. Then goes to the sofa, sits down. Noises come from the kitchen. Mr Godboy folds his hands into his lap, stares straight ahead. After a moment Eric comes out, stares at him.

I've been thinking, Eric, it would look strange to the police if your wife was found dead in my kitchen. Kindly carry her upstairs, to your own parlour, where she belongs.

As Eric sits down, as if in shock.

While you're about it please remove that cupboard I went to great annoyance to purchase for you. The ideal solution would be for you to cram May –

Eric (*listlessly*) Doris.

Godboy (*after a slight pause*) Doris, into the sea trunk I noted among your possessions. It would be best for your own sake if you could get her in completely, try not to have anything hanging over the edge, then hoist the sea trunk on top of May –

Eric Doris.

Godboy Nonsense, old boy, you can scarcely hoist Doris in the cupboard on top of herself in the cupboard, can you? (*Laughs.*) It's May that's in the cupboard.

Eric looks at him.

It's May's cupboard, I merely mean, Eric, old boy. So you hoist – (*pause*) Doris in the sea chest on top of – (*thinks*) the cupboard and then there'll be real cat and mouse with Mannerly when he comes calling. Those are my plans for you, I've thought them all out.

Eric continues to stare at him.

Now. (*Rubs his hands together.*) Did you get her garments?

Eric shakes his head.

What did you make of – (*thinks*) Doris's – (*nods*) appearance? (*Looks at Eric.*) Did she look serene?

Eric shakes his head.

(*Stares at him.*) Now, Eric, violence to a living creature –

Eric She isn't there.

Mr Godboy stares at him.

She isn't. No . . . (*Shakes his head.*)

Godboy Where is she then?

Eric I don't know.

Godboy gets up, goes into the kitchen, comes out again, carrying the gas mask

Godboy Something's wrong here, old boy. You looked in the larder, did you? (*Half turning.*)

Eric She isn't there.

Pause, as Mr Godboy stands uncertainly.

Now you tell me, you tell me – (*Slowly, raises a finger menacingly.*) You tell me where my Dorrie is.

Gets up, goes over, puts his finger close to Mr Godboy's face. Godboy walks past him, to the door, right, opens it, puts his head out, freezes as steps are heard.

Godboy Good evening, sir, this is an honour, although to tell you the truth I was just off for another of my refills. Prescription for my gammy . . .

Backs in, followed by Hedderley. As he does so, Eric backs out, in the kitchen, nearly closing the door. Mr Godboy enters, followed by Hedderley. They stand facing each other. There is a long pause. Mr Godboy's shoulders jump. He chuckles. Hedderley stares unblinkingly. Little pause. Hedderley sniffs.

A minor accident with some gassed cabbage-heads. Boiled over I merely – Mannerly not with you then?

Hedderley Soon.

Godboy That's very kind of him.

Hedderley I'm looking for Eric Hoyden.

Godboy Indeed?

Hedderley He's not upstairs.

Godboy (*in a low voice*) That's his story. Can it be checked out?

Hedderley I'm not empowered to force an entry. (*Little pause.*) Is there anything you can tell me about him?

Godboy He's a fine lad. (*Lowering voice slightly.*) In spite of a mild history of violence.

Hedderley takes out notebook, jots down. Then goes to one of the utility chairs, crosses legs, skirt slightly hiked, left stocking rumpled.

Hedderley Yes?

Godboy It's not his fault he doesn't know his own strength. To look at he's a reed, so if other people don't know his strength, and he's not so quick frankly – (*taps his forehead*) as other people, how can *he* know it?

Hedderley (*writing*) Yes?

Godboy Nothing is known against him in this house except his fondness for gas which he can't keep from talking about. (*Pause.*) In his quiet moments he's deceptively likeable.

Hedderley (*writing*) Yes?

Godboy (*coming closer*) His word's not to be trusted. (*In a low voice, then stepping casually away.*) He's got a wonderful sense of humour.

Hedderley (*writing*) Yes?

Godboy (*as Eric's face appears around the kitchen door, sees it*) I'll stand by Eric to the end. If you need a character witness, don't hesitate to call on me to speak out.

Eric shuts the door.

He can't help his habits, they're second nature.

Hedderley (*writing*) Yes?

Godboy You're conducting this investigation very quietly and firmly, officer, and I'll be glad to report that to Mannerly.

Hedderley stares at him, then puts the notebook away. Keeps staring at him.

The last I saw of Eric – (*coming closer*) he was off after his May. Doris. (*Little pause.*) What is the precise nature of the charges being laid against him?

Hedderley That depends on what he's done.

Godboy (*as Hedderley recrosses legs*) There's British Justice for you.

Hedderley (*quickly*) Where's your wife?

Godboy (*quickly*) Still away, sir.

Hedderley (*after a pause*) Why do you call me sir?

Godboy (*laughs, shakes his head*) Pardon.

Hedderley When do you expect him back?

Godboy (*quickly*) When she's rested.

Hedderley (*quickly*) Who's rested?

Godboy (*quickly*) Doris . . . May.

Hedderley (*quietly*) I was asking you about Eric Hoyden. (*Gets up, takes a step towards him. Stocking slipping.*) Where is he?

Godboy Well, Eric's a law in himself. (*Shakes his head.*) I must say I don't know why I confused Doris and Eric like that, they're quite different kettles of fish. (*Laughs.*) Naturally.

Hedderley Your wife Doris?

Godboy Doris Godboy, my wife.

Nods, begins to rock back and forth, sees that Hedderley's stocking is slipping. Stares as Hedderley flicks through the pages of the notebook, then stops.

No indeed. May. (*Slaps his forehead.*) May Godboy. Eric is Doris's wife.

The kitchen door opens softly and Eric puts his head in.

Hedderley (*steps very close to Mr Godboy*) Why are you staring at me?

As Mr Godboy begins to shake his head.

I need to adjust my clothing.

Godboy Pardon?

As the door opens wider, Hedderley throws her leg out, hoists up skirt. Mr Godboy stares, turns, hurriedly folds his arms.

Hedderley Kindly turn around, we're not permitted to interrogate from behind.

Mr Godboy turns slowly, stares straight ahead, a fixed smile on his face. Hedderley fiddles with suspender clip, then very sharply:

Where is your wife?

Godboy Purley.

Hedderley We may need her to testify. Where can she be reached?

Godboy Thatch Cottage, Mimosa Drive.

Eric is staring transfixed at Hedderley's leg. Takes a step inside.

Failing that, the YWCA. If she can't get into her auntie's house, she stays at the YW. They're very tolerant there.

Eric, his mouth hanging open, shuffles another step forward, begins to shake his head.

Failing that she may have gone to one of her other aunties. She likes to go from auntie to auntie indiscriminate.

Hedderley stands, as Eric is about to shuffle forward again. Eric turns, goes quickly back out of the kitchen. There is a long pause. Hedderley and Mr Godboy stare at each other.

(*Clears his throat.*) Does Mannerly use you often?

Hedderley Often.

Godboy (*after another pause*) How did you come to enter the force, may I ask?

Hedderley Inspector Hawkins picked me out during a certain period when I was frequenting coffee bars in the Notting Hill area. He took me in hand, dealt with me like a Dutch Uncle, and then when he'd finished showing me the ropes invited me to apply for special duties.

Godboy He's got greatness in him.

Hedderley stares at him, walks past to the door. Turns, smiles at Mr Godboy.

Hedderley What is your own attitude to violence?

Godboy I'm against some of it.

Hedderley Are you against discipline?

Godboy (*after a pause*) It's not in my nature to hurt a living creature.

Little pause, as Hedderley continues to smile at him.

Although my own sister used to apply it to me sometimes, when I was little. (*Stares at Hedderley as if transfixed.*) She used to compel me to roll down my trousers and she spanked me on my bare bottie. (*Laughs.*) She was only a few years older than me, but very strong. She wanted to join the force also. Unfortunately she fell victim to an unsavoury incident and had to leave for Dublin after the war. (*Long pause.*) She was like you in major respects.

Hedderley (*nods*) Inspector Hawkins is for discipline. We'll be back later.

Godboy Thank you, sir.

Hedderley looks at him, goes out, shuts the door. There is a long pause. Mr Godboy stands staring at the door, as if in a trance. Eric comes in left, goes up to Mr Godboy, tugs at his sleeve.

What do *you* want?

Eric I want my Dorrie.

Godboy (*blinking, shakes his head*) Do you, old boy, well I can't help you in that. All I know is that something funny's going on with regards to you as far as the police are involved. Things keep turning black for you.

Eric What?

Godboy They seem to be after you in connection with May. May Godboy.

Eric Well, I don't know about May, it's Dorrie –

Godboy (*laughs smoothly*) Eric, Doris is old enough to look after herself, if indeed she's alive. It's May the police are calling in my help for. Cat and mouse is warming up, Eric.

Eric (*shakes his head*) It's my Dorrie –

Godboy Now, Eric, if you've anything you wish to clear off your chest in respect to the gassing of May Godboy, tell me now.

Eric What gassing?

Godboy Where's her remains, Eric?

Eric What remains?

Godboy (*points dramatically at the cupboard*) Remains of May Godboy.

Eric You said she was in Purley, I heard you.

Godboy Then as long as Mannerly and I can find her there – (*walks away from Eric*) there's nothing for you to worry about, is there? (*Whips around.*) What did you do this afternoon?

Eric I told you, I went to Virgin Mayo and Burt Lancaster.

Godboy Cinema alibis can be broken into shreds, Eric. Who's your witnesses?

Eric I – I – (*Points to the pail.*) I got you those. Them gups!

Godboy Was Doris with you at the time?

Eric She was with you.

Godboy Oh, and was she here when you got back, Eric?

Eric No, that's what I'm –

Godboy Who's your witnesses, Eric?

Eric (*thinks*) You are. (*Nods.*)

Godboy Indeed? All I know is that I was laid out on account of my old wound and when I came to myself *you* was hammering about with loose questions of May having died in an accident. So who's your witnesses, Eric?

Eric Doris.

Godboy Hah. Hah hah. So it was *Doris* is dead.

Eric (*shaking his head*) No, no, what I mean is May –

Godboy May!

Eric I haven't seen her.

Godboy (*puts his face forward, hisses*) Witnesses, Eric, witnesses, you need a witness, Eric, who's your witness, Eric, who? Who?

> *He follows him across the room as he backs away. The door opens, right, and Hawkins steps into the room.*

(*Whipping around.*) Good afternoon, Mannerly, I was hoping you'd turn up, here's a real problem for you.

> *Eric makes for the kitchen door, opens it, a figure in blue is fleetingly visible. Closes the door, turns, faces the wall, left.*

Hawkins (*revolving his hat, walks towards Eric*) Good afternoon, sir, I don't think I've had the pleasure.

> *Eric coughs.*

Godboy Eric Hoyden, Inspector Hawkins is inquiring politely after your name.

Eric Eric Hoyden.

Hawkins Well, I'll say this for you, you're a difficult man to put a hand on, Eric Hoyden.

> *Puts his hand on Eric's shoulder, turns him around slowly. Eric stands with his hands sunk into his pockets, head lowered.*

And what do you know about all this, sir?

Eric What?

315

Hawkins And now what does *what* mean, sir, may I ask? (*Puts a finger under Eric's chin and lifts it up.*) What's *what* mean, sir?

Eric Nothing.

Hawkins Is it nothing, then, sir? You've no burglaries to tell me about? (*Gives Eric's jaw a little shake.*) No murders, sir? (*Gives Eric's jaw a little shake.*) No – (*little pause*) indecent-assaults-and-handbag-snatching to turn my ears with, sir?

Eric attempts to shake his head. Hawkins holds it steady. Eric points a finger at Mr Godboy, who is standing with his hands behind his back.

Eric He – he – he done something to my Dorrie, he did.

Hawkins (*still holding Eric's jaw*) And have you done something to *his* – (*slight stress*) Dorrie, Mr Godboy?

Godboy I wouldn't touch her with a barge-pole, Mannerly. (*Laughs.*)

Hawkins turns his head, looks at him.

I've got too much respect, sir.

Eric He did, he did, he told me himself she was dead.

Hawkins removes his hand from Eric's jaw, pats both his cheeks simultaneously.

Hawkins Well, sir, I can see you've nothing to fear from the law, and certainly you wouldn't mind a little inspection from one of my men. (*Little pause. Shouts.*) Hedderley!

Whipping Eric around to face the kitchen door as he does so. The kitchen door opens simultaneously, Hedderley comes in. Hedderley walks slowly towards Eric. Hawkins moves away to stand next to Mr Godboy. Eric stands transfixed. Hedderley stands

*facing Eric, then puts arms about his shoulders in a
hug, sways about with him.*

Eric Here! Here!

*Hedderley takes Eric's hand and presses it against her
right leg, moves it up under the skirt.*

(*Bending over.*) Here!

*Hedderley straightens, drops Eric's hand, turns, nods
once to Hawkins. Hawkins beckons with his head.
Hedderley goes to him, they walk to the other end of
the room, whispering. Eric looks towards them,
makes for the kitchen door, left.*

Hawkins (*without turning*) Would you be kind enough
to hang on a little, sir, thank you, sir.

*Eric stops. Mr Godboy looks towards Hawkins and
Hedderley, goes over, takes Eric's arm.*

(*Turns.*) Now that's a lovely pair of trousers.

*Eric looks down at his trousers, looks away. Hawkins
whispers to Hedderley. Mr Godboy fingers Eric's
trousers.*

(*Turning.*) Would you do Constable Hedderley the
kindness of permitting Constable Hedderley the use of
your toilet?

Godboy Indeed, Mannerly, it's across the hall, Hedderley.

Hawkins (*staring at Eric, repeats*) Would you do
Constable Hedderley the kindness of permitting Constable
Hedderley the use of your toilet?

Eric (*after a silence*) What?

Hawkins Your toilet, sir. Constable Hedderley's in
trouble.

Eric Oh. (*As Hedderley comes towards him.*)

Hawkins Oh now, sir, you wouldn't be one of those citizens who demands a search warrant from an officer desperate for a toilet, sir, would you?

Eric Um . . . all right.

Hedderley holds out a hand.

Hawkins Now where exactly did you say your toilet was, sir?

Eric Upstairs landing.

Hawkins Now there's great stress in the force on personal hygiene. Constable Hedderley will be wanting to wash her hands in your sink afterwards, could you let her have the keys to get in with, sir?

Eric (*after a pause*) I lost them.

Mr Godboy puts his hand into Eric's trouser pocket, takes out the keys, holds them triumphantly to Hedderley. Hedderley stares at them.

Hawkins Mr Godboy, I think those are Mr Hoyden's keys, and I advise you to return them to him immediately, Mr Godboy.

Mr Godboy looks towards Hawkins, gives the keys to Eric. Hedderley takes them from Eric.

Manners, Hedderley!

Hedderley (*to Eric*) Thank you, sir. (*Goes out.*)

There is a silence. Hawkins stands rotating his hat, smiling at Eric. Mr Godboy stands bewildered, looking from Hawkins to Eric. Eric stands hunched.

Hawkins (*to Eric*) Now I think, sir, you were saying something about *your* – (*slight stress*) Dorrie, I think.

Eric He knows, he knows. (*Nods at Mr Godboy.*)

There is the sound of an upstairs lavatory flushing. They all stare up at the ceiling. There are crashing sounds from above.

Hawkins Well, if anything's happened to that young lady, there'd be some answering would have to be done, to the law and to myself. (*Little pause.*) There was a young lady once, permitting herself to be humbly searched down at the station when she was innocent of everything but weakness of spirit, and I caught a glimpse of her through a crack in the door when she was standing with only her little hands for covering, and then I was called off to a breaking and entering and when I got back she was lost to me. Now I've been looking for that young lady –

The door, right, opens. Hawkins and Mr Godboy turn towards it. Eric stares quickly away as Hedderley comes in carrying armloads of handbags and a pair of trousers. Hawkins and Mr Godboy go on staring, as the door, left, opens. Doris puts her head in, Eric sees her, takes a step towards her. Doris looks around the room, sees Hawkins, shuts the door.

Eric She's – she's –

Eric turns, sees the handbags and trousers, stops. There is a long silence on stage. Hedderley drops the handbags, comes towards Hawkins, hands him the trousers. Eric turns around again. Hawkins takes the trousers, shakes them out. They have a large section missing at the fly. Hawkins strides across to Eric, turns him around, takes his chin in his hand.

Hawkins So now we know what you do between jobs, Between-Jobs Eric. You do the ladies of Merrit Street, sir.

There is a long silence.

Godboy You mean there were *two* Merrit Street attackers, Mannerly?

Hawkins Just one lucky one – (*turns Eric's face to the right, then to the left*) who must be thanking God – (*turns Eric's face up to the ceiling*) he's been taken at last. (*Releases him.*) We should have had you last night, Between-Jobs, all the misery of your guilt should have been over for you in the darkness of last night, if Constable Hedderley hadn't over-baited himself with heavy perfume and a skirt too tight it prevented him from running free. Isn't that so, Hedderley?

Hedderley Sir.

Hawkins Ah, while Constable Hedderley, coated in this perfume and hobbled at the legs, was throwing Between-Jobs around on the pavement, the dogs, unable to recognise Hedderley's natural body odours, sprang straight at Constable Hedderley. Except, that is, for an elderly bitch with dirty habits who plunged straight for Between-Jobs, preferring the male smell of *him*, and tore this –

Little pause. Takes out of his pocket the cloth from Eric's trousers, complete with fly-buttons, and holds it against the torn trousers.

– from the Merrit Street attacker. (*To Eric.*) So another day you had to suffer through, for your release.

Godboy And to think I left you alone in my kitchen with May!

Eric I wasn't going to – I wasn't going to – I'd made myself stop doing it. But she – (*looks at Hedderley*) he – she – was pulling her stockings up and smiling at me and winking and my head was buzzing from May's stout and

gin, and I just meant to help out with something and the
next minute she was whirling me about and holding me
on the ground and his knee was in my back and her arm
was around my throat and there was these dogs, these
dogs . . . (*Covers his face with his arm.*)

Long silence.

Hawkins There, there, boy, it's all right. It's all over for
you now. (*Little pause.*) Or will be when you tell us
where our Dorrie is.

Eric She's in the kitchen.

Godboy Don't tell lies, Eric, it won't serve. You took her
away somewhere this afternoon and gassed her or
something like that, and we both know it.

Hawkins (*takes a step towards Eric, restrains himself*)
Just tell us, son, and then we can have a good talk about
the other matter down at the station.

Eric She was here, he done it, I don't know, she's – (*He
stops, looks at the faces.*) I tell you.

*Hawkins looks at Hedderley, turns, walks to the front
of the stage. Hedderley takes Eric's arm, and leads
him to the sofa, makes him sit down, bends over him.
Mr Godboy stands somewhere between Hawkins and
Hedderley, his hands behind his back.*

Hawkins (*turns his head to Mr Godboy*) When I was a
little boy, Mr Godboy, over there in County Mayo –

Mr Godboy nods attentively.

I had a dream of devotion, a lonely life given up to
salvation. I dreamt that as a boy, I did.

*Hedderley bends over Eric, does something to him,
Eric cries out. Mr Godboy turns his head, looks
towards the sofa.*

And come Sundays there was a special pond I'd walk to, deep and calm it was, and there in the long afternoon I'd sit and think of what was open to me to be done.

Hedderley makes Eric cry out again. Mr Godboy again looks towards the sofa, takes a step back to it.

And of the little I have to give. And my dog Whiskers up to some doggy mischief at my feet or behind me in the bushes. (*Shakes his head, smiling.*)

Hedderley makes Eric cry out again. Mr Godboy takes another step back.

And somehow in those days the sun was always shining, yes it was, or that's the way I see it now, from the black heart of the big city. When I look back to it from no more Sundays in Mayo.

Mr Godboy, who has been standing, looking down at Eric, his hands behind his back, watches Hedderley bend over Eric again.

And yet somewhere in the back of my mind is the picture, I'll keep it there through disciplining and pain, of what it is I've lost.

Mr Godboy leans over and does something experimental to Eric. Then Hedderley does it. Then Mr Godboy. In a see-saw rhythm.

Eric (*screaming out*) I tell you she was there, larking about in the kitchen.

Godboy I won't have you telling lies about my kitchen, Between-Jobs.

Hawkins (*smiling*) Through disciplining and pain I hug it to me, that Sunday afternoon when I dreamed of devotion, by an eternal pond, in an eternal sunshine, and I –

Doris puts her head around the kitchen door, stares at the scene on the couch, takes a few frantic steps in, stops. Hedderley and Mr Godboy go on working on Eric.

(*Turns, sees Doris.*) – am boy eternal.

Goes over to Doris, takes her gently by the arm, leads her to the centre of the stage.

Godboy Where is she, Between-Jobs, where is she, where?

Hedderley Where? Where?

They bend simultaneously over him.

Hawkins (*puts a finger under Doris's chin, tilts her face up*) And I am boy eternal, Doris. I thought you'd been taken from us. (*Very gently.*) Where have you been, Doris?

Eric lets out a long shout. Hawkins looks towards them as Mr Godboy turns his face around. He is laughing, sees Doris, nods to her, turns back to Eric. Begins to do something, suddenly stops. Hedderley stops.

Hedderley. (*Nods to the kitchen door.*)

Hedderley helps Eric from the sofa, takes him into the kitchen.

Mr Godboy. (*Nods again to the kitchen door.*)

Mr Godboy hesitates, looks at Doris, follows Hedderley.

And Hedderley, there's to be only gentleness now, Hedderley.

Hedderley Sir.

Hawkins Mr Godboy?

Godboy Sir.

They go into the kitchen, shut the door. Hawkins stands looking at Doris, who clutches her handbag to her stomach, stares at the ground. There is a long pause. Then Hawkins puts his hand through Doris's arm, leads her to one of the utility chairs, sits her on it. Doris's handbag drops from her lap, its contents scatter over the floor. She makes a move to pick it up. Hawkins restrains her, pats her knee, crouches at her feet, begins to put her things back into the handbag.

Hawkins Are you frightened?

Doris sits hunched.

Of course you are. I think it's part of your nature, isn't it? (*Pause.*) Isn't it?

Doris nods. Hawkins shuts her handbag firmly, puts it back in her lap, stays on his knees.

And why has Eric been out in Merrit Street, grabbing at the ladies and their handbags then? (*Crooningly.*) Is it because you wouldn't let him near you, is it because he didn't know how to come near you, is it because you're frightened, Doris?

Doris (*after a pause*) He didn't mean it. Not Eric.

Hawkins (*strokes her foot*) Is he any good to you, Doris? (*Little pause.*) And is he, now? (*Takes her shoe off.*)

Doris (*after a pause*) Don't know.

Hawkins And what good are you, Doris, all by yourself while Eric's away from us all? Will you get yourself taken away again by another Eric, poor Eric. Will you?

Doris shrugs into a hunch.

What do you want, then, Doris?

Doris Don't know.

Hawkins And who knows what you're wanting, Doris? (*Stands up slowly, stands over her, looks down.*) Who?

After a long pause, Doris lifts her face to his. Pause.

Doris (*whispered*) You?

Hawkins And who'll make you a good girl, Doris?

Doris You.

Hawkins And who did I get a glimpse at, once, down at the station, and nude?

Doris (*staring up*) Me. (*Whispered.*)

Hawkins bends down, kisses Doris on the mouth. Raises her up by the arms, kisses her again, passionately.

Hawkins So what do you want, then, Doris?

Doris staring into his face, whispers something inaudible. Hawkins releases her slowly, looks at her.

Hah! (*Slaps her playfully on the rump.*) Hah! Hedderley!

The kitchen door opens. Mr Godboy enters, stands aside with his hands behind his back as Eric enters, Hedderley holding his arm up behind him.

Eric Dorrie, Dorrie, you all right, Dorrie?

Doris looks down, her handbag clasped to her stomach again. Hawkins nods to Hedderley. Eric is released, stands upright.

Hawkins Are you all right, Doris?

Doris looks at him, nods.

Eric I couldn't help it, Dorrie, I couldn't, it's 'cause I love you, Dorrie.

Hawkins Well, Doris, I think he's expecting an answer, have you got an answer for him?

Doris looks at Hawkins, shakes her head.

There's no answer for you, son. (*Goes to Eric.*) You were going to come to me in the end, you see, and you'll be glad of it, in the end, you see. (*Little pause.*) Think of it, while you were slipping through my net I was sitting here, beneath your home, waiting for you without either of us knowing it. Something called me here, it was your own cry that called me here, son, and that's why I came. There's always a reason for accidents. The reason was that you were waiting for me, what else could it have been? Think of that.

Godboy coughs. He has been standing restlessly during Hawkins's speech.

Godboy There could be other reasons, Mannerly, you could have come because someone –

Eric swings up an arm, points his finger at Mr Godboy, stares at him.

Eric It was you, you.

There is a long silence, then he cries out as if in revelation.

He done for May!

Another silence. They look at Mr Godboy, who puts his hands behind his back, swells his chest.

Godboy That's who it's been between, Mannerly, all along. Cat and – (*taking a step forward*) mouse.

Eric (*nodding*) He done for May!

Godboy Where do you think she's concealed then? (*Smiling at Hawkins, who is looking at Eric.*) All along?

326

Eric (*draws a deep breath, bursts out*) In the cupboard! In the cupboard, what's full of gas!

Godboy Mannerly? (*Smiling at him.*)

Eric That's it, the cupboard!

Godboy Quiet, rapist, people like you is two a penny nowadays.

Hawkins goes to Doris, takes a hairpin out of her hair, then, as Eric takes a step forward, without turning around:

Hawkins Hedderley.

Hedderley takes Eric's arm again. Hawkins goes over to the cupboard, bends down, fiddles the hairpin into the lock. Mr Godboy turns, smiles at Eric disdainfully, walks across to Hawkins, stands beside him.

Godboy I want to say, Manly, you've cracked open something big here, that'll be a feather in your cap in all the newspapers. I've waited for you to show up here, waited and waited, and you did, Mannerly, just on time. Our turn together was doomed. Cat and mouse, Mannerly, as you said yourself, the big mouse is in your paws at last.

As the lock clicks and Hawkins stands upright.

Permit me, Mannerly, it's all I ask now the moment is come. (*Takes the door.*) Here is what you've been waiting for, here is what was calling out to you.

Mr Godboy stands, stares Hawkins in the face, then flings the door open. Hawkins stares inside, then comes back to Doris, nods to Hedderley. Hedderley pushes Eric across the room past Mr Godboy, who is staring blankly into the cupboard. Hawkins follows, one hand resting carelessly on Doris's rump. She is

*limping, clutching her handbag tight. Eric suddenly
breaks free of Hedderley, and plunges into the
cupboard, comes out again, holds up his raincoat,
shows it to Doris.*

Eric I said it was in there, didn't I, Dorrie?

*Struggles defiantly into it. Hedderley takes his arm,
they go out.*

Hawkins (*to Mr Godboy*) There's a lot of confessing to
be made. And don't worry yourself about Doris, what
she needs is only a Dutch Uncle talking to. (*Looks at
Doris.*) I'll be showing you the ropes myself, Doris. (*Puts
his hat on.*) Goodbye, Mr Godboy, goodbye.

*Replaces his hand on Doris's rump. They go out.
Mr Godboy stands alone, staring after them. Then
goes and sits down on the sofa. Sits staring ahead.
A long wait. Then he gets up, goes forlornly over to
the guppie case, is about to shake some food in, checks
himself, picks up the pail, goes offstage, right. There is
a pause.
May appears through the kitchen door, carrying
her bags. Drops them on the floor, takes off her coat,
drops it on the sofa, looks about her, goes back into
the kitchen. Sounds of a lavatory flushing. Mr
Godboy comes in, puts the guppie case on the table,
pours the guppies from the pail into it, scatters the
food. Stands for a moment, back to the audience, then
turns, looks at the cupboard, goes to it, stares in, steps
in completely. May comes out of the kitchen door,
smoking a cigarette, looks about her, then walks across
the room towards the door, right, passing the cupboard.
As she does so she slams the cupboard door shut, goes
on out of the room, tapping ash.*

Curtain.

SPOILED

For Beryl

Spoiled was first performed at the Haymarket Theatre, London, on 24 February 1971. The cast was as follows:

Howarth Jeremy Kemp
Donald Simon Ward
Joanna Anna Massey
Les Peter Denyer
Mrs Clenham Pamela Pitchford

Director Stephen Hollis
Designer Anthony Holland
Lighting Joe Davis

Characters

Howarth

Donald

Joanna

Les

Mrs Clenham

Act One

SCENE ONE

The stage is divided. Three-quarters of the stage space, on the right, shows the living room and one quarter, on the left, shows a small spare room, referred to in the directions that follow as the bedroom. A wall with a door upstage, opening into the bedroom, divides the two rooms. The living room is large, comfortable, middle-class intellectual and casual. A table with books and a lamp stands in the window and against the wall downstage of the window a smaller table, also with books and a lamp. Against the wall upstage of the window is an old upright piano and piano stool. The main door to the rest of the house is facing us upstage right. Through this door can be seen the hall, with the foot of stairs upstage. The kitchen can be seen through a hatch, which is on the left of the main door in the living room. Running along the back wall of the living room, under the hatch, is a shelf unit with a lamp, a tray of drinks and a hi-fi unit on it. The speakers for the hi-fi are on a shelf above. Books fill other shelves on the back wall and shelves above the piano.

The bedroom area, left, has baby paper on the walls and is cluttered with a desk against the back wall, with a lamp and two single chairs, a carry-cot against the dividing wall downstage and parts of a larger cot upstage of the door. A folding bed, made up and hidden with a cloth cover is folded and stands against the wall, left.

The action starts in the living room.

Howarth and Donald are seated at the table, Howarth in the elbow chair right, Donald left. Donald has a bicycle satchel on the floor beside him, Howarth has textbooks

335

*on the table in front of him and a briefcase on the floor.
As the curtain rises Donald stoops to pick up three
textbooks which he has knocked onto the floor. Howarth
is eating a biscuit.*

Howarth In the event of almost any catastrophe 'je suis
desolé' will do nicely.

Donald Um, je suis desolé.

Howarth Yeah. A phrase like that's worth five marks in
the oral. It might be worth contriving a small accident,
like stumbling over the examiner's toes, to get it in.
Don't hurt him, mind.

Donald laughs.

OK. Expliquez-moi, monsieur Donald Clenham,
pourquoi vous êtes en train d'apprendre le français?

Donald (*nervously*) Um, um, parce-que je veux
apprendre le français.

Howarth (*waits, smiles*) Elaborate. Don't be afraid of
boring him.

Donald Um, um, parce-que je veux voyager en France et
parce que il est, um, c'est une langue très intéressant.

Howarth Now Donald, think. (*Pause.*) Une langue
intéressant?

Donald Oh, um. (*Laughs.*) Um, un langue intéressant.
Um . . .

Howarth (*looks at him, eyebrows raised*) Well, at least
now you're consistent. But wrong.

Donald (*after a ghastly pause, tentatively*) Une langue
intéressante . . .

Howarth Mmm, huh. OK. (*Smiles.*) Can you relax?
You're terribly tense today. Why?

Donald No, I'm all right. Well . . .

Howarth Is it because the exam's on Monday?

Donald (*shakes his head*) Well . . . I suppose I keep thinking about it, sir.

Howarth Don't make it worse than it is. Look, today's Saturday. You've got all day tomorrow. Don't suffer before you have to. What are you going to do for the rest of the weekend?

Donald (*shrugs*) Nothing really. Go for a bicycle ride with a friend and . . . well, do some work.

Howarth Fine. But don't do too much, eh? Get your mother to throw you out of the house, to the cinema or something, eh?

Donald nods.

No, really. I'm all for your translating a few passages, but for God's sake don't work yourself into a state. In fact, I'll give you a ration of passages to take home, and you stick to those. (*Rises, goes up to hatch, brings out a biscuit tin, helps himself to a biscuit.*) Mm? (*Looks at him, smiles.*) By the way, there's something I've been meaning to ask you. What have you been using for a dictionary?

Donald Just a, um, little one.

Howarth Got it with you?

Donald nods. Then, clearly embarrassed, he bends over, picks up his satchel, fumbles in it and picks an exercise book out of the satchel. A folded picture from a magazine drops from the exercise book onto the floor.

Donald The thing is, my mum got it for me. (*Picks a very small dictionary out of the satchel, holds it up.*) She

337

just went into the shop and asked for one and this is the one they, um . . .

Howarth Keep it for a weekend in Paris.

Hands him the little one and picks up an enormous Cassell's dictionary from the table.

But you borrow this one for this weekend, eh?

Hands him the big one. Donald notices the photograph on the floor and hurriedly puts his foot over it. Howarth sees this.

It's an extremely lucky dictionary. Even if you don't use it, it'll communicate a certain impressive confidence. I've lent it to hundreds of boys at school just before exams, and always with satisfactory results. Let it calm you down.

Donald Thank you, sir. I'll bring it back afterwards, straight away.

Howarth OK. Are you up to a dictation?

Donald grabs the photo from the floor and puts it in his satchel. Howarth notices this. Donald nods, draws an exercise book to him.

Let's see. (*Flicking through the pages of a textbook.*) What with you twice a week and five classes at school twice a week, I can never remember.

Donald puts the dictionary in his satchel and looks through his exercise-book.

'Ce matin-là Jean avait parlé beaucoup de blés et de ce qu'il appelait la "culture intensive" . . .'?

Donald Yes, we've done that one, sir.

Howarth 'Un homme voyageait dans un pays de montagnes . . .'

338

Howarth looks at Donald, Donald nods.

Yeah, I remember that, um, 'Il y a, à Vérone, des jardins.'

Donald shakes his head.

All right. (*Gets up, saunters to the window, puts his hand in his pocket.*) Ready?

Donald nods, pushes his satchel clumsily aside.

'Il y a, à Vérone, des jardins a l'italienne où l'on monte par une série d'escaliers et de terrasses. J'y passai l'après-midi dans un terrible perplexité. D'en haut, je découvrais . . .'

Donald, as Howarth reads, is still clumsily attempting to get ready . . . He knocks the satchel off the table, kneels, shoves papers and books back inside.

Donald (*gets up, is desperately scrabbling*) Sorry, sir.

Howarth stands watching, as Donald sits down, and gets a pencil out of his pencil case.

Um, sorry sir.

Howarth All right? 'Il y a, à Vérone . . .'

Howarth continues to read the dictation piece. Donald breaks the point of his pencil, scrabbles in the pencil case for a sharpener and starts to sharpen his pencil over the satchel. Howarth notices this and breaks off.

This isn't a good idea. Not now, anyway. Shall we give it a rest?

Donald (*sits looking down at the table, mutters inaudibly*) Sorry, sir.

Howarth Mmmm. (*Looks at him thoughtfully.*) Donald, if the worst comes to the very worst, and you don't *feel* like it on Monday morning, you can always take it the next time around, can't you?

Donald nods.

So why does it matter so much? You know, I'm generally telling boys at this stage that they've got to care more. In your case perhaps you should really try caring less.

Donald (*nods again*) Except, well. (*Looks at him.*) It's my mum, sir. She's expecting me to get it, and – because it's the third time and that. (*Laughs.*)

Howarth She'll be angry with you?

Donald No, no, she won't – no, but she, well . . . worries.

Howarth Parents do tend to. Especially mothers.

Donald Yes, sir.

Howarth (*pause, looks at him, as if thinking*) Look, do you think she'd spare you for the weekend?

Donald Sir?

Howarth Then we could take things at their own pace, eh? We could get through a bit of work, and calm each other down. I'd hate to think that all we've done over the last six weeks is going to slip away in a nervous weekend. (*Pause.*) Eh?

Donald Well . . . (*Stops, stares at him blankly.*)

Howarth Do you think she'd mind?

Donald shakes his head.

Or would *you* rather not?

Donald (*looks down, mutters shyly*) Don't want to put you out, sir.

Howarth I wouldn't have asked you if I thought you'd be putting us out. We'd both be delighted to have you. So the question for you to answer, frankly and fearlessly, is whether you want to. Do you?

Donald (*nods, looking down*) Thank you very much indeed, sir.

Howarth Good. Very good. Now we *can* relax . . . although, first you'd better phone your mother.

Donald Sir. (*Gets up.*)

Howarth It's just in the hall there.

Donald Sir. (*Nods, walks across the room.*)

Howarth stands for a moment, stroking his chin, then makes a sudden face, as if grasping that he's done something he hadn't really intended. He spots Donald's satchel, looks down at it, starts to bend to pick it up. Donald reappears at the door.

Um, the only thing, um, we're not on the telephone.

Howarth Oh. Well, you'll have to let her know, of course. Is there anyone else you could phone? You could ask *them* to ask *her* to phone us or . . . (*Shrugs.*) It's very complicated, isn't it?

Donald Well, there's some people next door – sometimes they let us use their phone.

Howarth There you are then.

Donald Sir. (*Goes out.*)

Howarth shakes his head, bends down and takes out the folded paper, opens it, looks at it, makes a little whistle of amused surprise . . . is about to put it back into the satchel, when the door opens and Donald reappears. He shoves the folded paper into his back pocket.

I just remembered, um. (*Laughs awkwardly.*) They're away this weekend. They've gone to visit her auntie . . . she lives in Bexhill.

Howarth Oh dear. Well, perhaps we'd better think again. I can't keep you here without letting your mother know, and it's scarcely worth your cycling all the way home and back again.

Donald I don't mind, sir. I mean, it wouldn't take me long.

Howarth Your mother might not be in.

Donald Oh yes, sir. She doesn't go out until later. She's doing the matinee . . . that's at two-thirty.

Howarth (*reluctantly*) Well, in that case . . .

The sound of the door slamming.

Joanna (*off*) Hello!

Joanna opens the door. She is carrying a bundle of clothing – scarlet, curtain-like – and a plastic carrier bag.

Howarth Though it seems rather a business . . .

Joanna (*entering between them, looks at Donald*) Hello, Donald – it is Donald, isn't it?

Howarth (*as Donald smiles, nods awkwardly*) Yes. Donald Clenham.

Joanna (*shaking hands with Donald*) Well, hello, Donald.

Donald Um, hello, um . . .

Joanna I've got your gear. (*Drops the stuff on the couch.*) I've just got to nip up to the butcher for the joint. I won't be long.

Howarth OK.

Joanna smiles, goes to the kitchen door and through.

Well, what do you think? (*To Donald*) If it *is* going to be difficult. Mmmm?

Joanna (*reappearing from the kitchen*) Have you finished, or are you going on a bit?

Howarth Actually, we were just deciding that very question. Why?

Joanna Well, I just thought if you *were* going on, why doesn't Donald stay and have a bite? (*To Donald.*) Only scrambled eggs on Saturday, I'm afraid.

Donald Mmm, well . . . mmm . . . (*Laughs, looks at Howarth.*)

Howarth As a matter of fact, darling. (*Laughs.*) The question we were attempting to decide was whether or not Donald should stay for the weekend.

Joanna (*looks at him, a fractional pause*) Oh, lovely. (*To Donald.*) Do.

Howarth That is, if we're all right for sheets and things.

Joanna We are. (*Smiling over-politely, directly at Howarth.*)

Howarth Actually, there are *other* problems. We can't think how to get hold of Donald's mother.

Joanna Donald's mother? (*After a pause.*) She'd be very welcome too, of course.

343

Howarth (*laughs again*) No no . . . to let her know where Donald is.

Joanna (*laughs*) Oh, I see. (*Suddenly, naturally.*) Oh, manage it somehow please, Donald. We'd love you to.

Howarth (*in relief*) Yes, come on now, Donald, let's think.

Joanna (*looks at Howarth*) Well, I'll see you later. (*Looks at Donald.*) Both of you, I hope.

Severe look at Howarth as she goes out, shutting the door.

Howarth (*smiles*) There you are, you see. My old lady isn't a problem, I'm sure yours won't be.

Donald No. Well, I'll go around on my bike then.

Howarth Good. That *is* settled then, isn't it? At last. (*Pause.*) Do you want to go now, or shall we have another go at that dictation?

Donald (*pause*) I don't mind. I mean, well, the dictation . . . if that's all right.

Howarth goes to the box and picks it up. Donald sits down at the table.

Howarth 'Ce matin-là Jean avait parlé beaucoup de blès et de ce qu'il appelait la "culture" . . .' No, that wasn't the one. Ah, 'Il y a, à Vérone, des jardins à l'italienne . . .' (*Stops.*) Have you ever thought that the major stresses in life come from the most minor embarrassments? Mmm – I mean, that we spend an enormous amount of energy and feeling on the most trivial worries . . . the ones that we forget about almost immediately. Mmmm?

Donald smiles, bewildered.

A random thought, and not worth interrupting a dictation for . . . Now – 'Il y a, à Vérone, des jardins à l'italienne où l'on monte par une série d'escaliers et de terrasses. J'y passai l'après-midi dans une terrible perplexité. D'en haut, je . . .'

Donald, during this, has secretly looked anxiously at his watch. He holds up his hand for attention, like a child in class, looking towards Howarth in a panic. Howarth stops and looks at him.

Donald She leaves for the cinema at two, for the matinee.

Howarth Yeah?

Donald Well, if I go later, I may be too late.

Howarth Oh. Well then, you'd better go now, hadn't you? (*Snaps the book shut, smiles.*) Get it over with once and for all, anyway. This could go on all afternoon.

There is a ring at the bell.

Is that all settled, then?

Smiling, goes out of the room. Donald puts on his jacket and looks hurriedly through his satchel.

Howarth (*off, at the front door*) Yes?

Les (*off*) Sorry to interrupt. My name's Les. I'm looking for Donald Clenham.

Howarth (*off*) Oh, come in, come in.

The door opens. Howarth comes back in, accompanied by Les.

Howarth For you, Donald. Les. (*Looking at Les.*)

Donald puts down the satchel.

Les Hello, Don. I'm sorry to interrupt. You said half past and I thought perhaps I'd missed you . . . that you'd already gone. There was another turning you could have meant. I thought I'd been waiting at the wrong one.

Donald I'm sorry. I – I . . . (*Looks at Howarth, then at Les again.*) forgot.

Les That's all right. (*Pause.*) Do you want me to wait on a bit, then? Or what?

Donald Well, I can't come, you see.

Les Oh. (*Little pause.*) That's all right.

Howarth (*who has been looking at Les*) I'm sorry, the fault is entirely ours. We persuaded Donald to stay for a bit, and in the confusion of arrangements *everything* got forgotten.

Les That's all right. It doesn't matter. We were only going for a ride. (*Pause.*) It doesn't matter.

Howarth (*to Les*) I know you, don't I?

Les I was at St Martin's for a while, sir.

Howarth Yes, I thought you were. About three years ago.

    Les nods.

Grant. Leslie Grant.

Les (*nods*) I never had you for French, I was in Mr Wales's class. I was only there for two years . . . and Mr Holliday's.

Howarth You left early, didn't you?

Les (*slightly embarrassed*) Sir.

Howarth (*pause*) What are you doing now?

Les Same as Don . . . I'm in Crabtree's.

Howarth Oh. Which part?

Les (*laughs, embarrassed again*) Well, in cutlery . . . at the moment. Mainly I'm on sales in cutlery, sometimes in toys.

Howarth And do you like that?

Les Well, not too much. (*Looks towards Donald.*) Eh, Don?

 Donald laughs awkwardly. Pause.

Howarth I'm sorry. Still, you'll probably be able to move on . . . or out.

Les We hope so. (*To Donald again.*) Eh, Don?

 Donald again laughs awkwardly.

Howarth Well, I'm sorry I've mucked up your Saturday ride.

Les No, it doesn't matter. We can go tomorrow, can't we, Don? (*A slight pause.*)

Donald Well, I'll be here tomorrow, Les, actually.

Les (*pause, still quite easy*) Oh. (*Pause.*) Oh well, that's that, then. It doesn't matter.

Howarth But look here, if you're going to be in this area – I mean, if you feel like coming out – do drop in for a cup of coffee or tea.

Les Oh no, I wouldn't want to interrupt . . .

Howarth (*pause*) You wouldn't be. We're bound to need a break. The idea is to get a bit of French into Donald in as relaxed a way as possible.

Les Oh, well, that's very kind of you. Thanks very much. I don't know if I will be in the area . . .

Howarth No, but if you are.

Les Well, thank you, sir.

Howarth How extraordinary, you two knowing each other. You never told me you knew an old St Martin's boy, Donald.

Donald Well, Les said . . .

Les I said I was sure you wouldn't remember me.

Howarth You see, I do. I was sorry you . . . had to leave.

Les Yes. (*Little pause.*) So was I. I might have learnt some French. (*Laughs.*)

Howarth (*laughs*) Well, um, Donald, if you're going to see your mother . . . We've been trying to think of ways of letting Donald's mother know that he's staying with us.

Les Oh, I'll tell her. I might as well go back anyway.

Howarth looks at Donald.

Donald Oh, well, thanks, Les. Thanks.

Les No trouble. It's only just around the corner from us. (*To Howarth.*) If she's not there, I'll put a note through the letter box, OK?

Howarth Perhaps you'd better give her our phone number . . . 6371.

Les 6371. I always remember numbers. (*Smiles at Donald.*) Good luck for Monday if I don't see you, Don.

Donald Thanks.

Les Goodbye, then.

Howarth Goodbye.

Les goes out.

Perhaps under the circumstances, you should see Les down the path, eh?

Donald nods, and hurries out. Howarth stands for a moment, then moves up to the hatch, reaches through for the biscuit tin and takes a biscuit. There is the sound of the front door. He crams the biscuit into his mouth, gulps it down hurriedly. Joanna comes in with the shopping bag, stands looking at him ironically.

(*Swallows furtively.*) I know. Don't say it.

Joanna But has he mysteriously doubled? I passed two of him cycling down the path.

Howarth (*laughs*) No, just a friend he'd arranged to meet.

Joanna Ah, gone to get more friends for the weekend perhaps? Will they come back as four? (*Goes out into the kitchen.*)

Howarth Darling, I'm terribly sorry. But I did apologise.

Joanna (*returning*) Did you? How?

Howarth I kept glancing at you abjectly.

Joanna Well, what came over you?

Howarth I don't know.

Joanna Richard, I ask compassionately.

Howarth (*pause, shakes his head, takes her hand and speaks directly to her, kindly*) Well, I do know. He's got his O level on Monday – he's failed twice already – and he's in a state about it. He lives alone with a repressively anxious and Catholic mother, who'll almost certainly demoralise him thoroughly before the weekend's out. So,

I thought . . . (*Shrugs.*) It might just make the difference. (*Pause, kisses her hand.*) Do you mind?

Joanna Yes. (*Hand on his shoulder.*) But I'd be a bitch if I made a fuss, wouldn't I? When the cause is so good. (*Kisses him.*)

Howarth Well, how are you, then?

Joanna Roughly as you see me. I've had a very stimulating morning. I asked Matthews why there was a layer of beef around the fat, like a blanket to keep it warm, and at the supermarket I caused – and then took part in – a scene about the size and colour of the eggs. I wanted large brown ones and they had tiny white ones, that look as if the chickens have stamped them out with machines. In other words, I succeeded in making myself into a harridan, and in the fridge I've got beefy fat, and a dozen shiny, white little eggs.

Howarth Poor darling.

Joanna Yes. How did you get landed with him in the first place?

Howarth Who? Donald? He's the one that Catholic priest wrote to the school about – O'Toole, Father O'Toole. His dad died when he was three, his mother's had to work to keep them both. He didn't do too well at school, is now doing something or other at that shop you hate – Crabtree's – and wants to better himself, I suppose. After his French he's going to try for maths and a few other subjects – with Father O'Toole's letters to help, no doubt . . . if he gets his French.

Joanna And will he?

Howarth It depends, I should say, almost entirely on his nerve, and whether he knows enough. No, probably not. His nerve is bad and he doesn't know enough.

Joanna But you're going to have a go?

Howarth Yes.

Joanna All right. But you shall make it up to me. What with vanishing for rehearsals while I sew up your costumes, introducing nervous boys into the house, and no doubt a briefcase full of marking . . .

Howarth I shall – make it up to you.

Joanna But there's something else. (*Sternly.*) You've been at the biscuits.

Howarth What?

Joanna What? (*Imitating him.*) The crumbs are clustered around your lips. (*Pokes him in the stomach.*) You're . . . (*poke*) . . . not . . . (*poke*) . . . to . . . (*poke.*) It's bad for you to be fat. (*Slaps him.*) And it's self-indulgence, and on top of which . . .

The door opens, Donald comes in, stops and looks at them awkwardly.

(*As Howarth steps away.*) Oh, hello. How did you get in?

Donald (*pause*) The door was on the latch.

Joanna Of course it was. (*Laughs.*) Well, you've fixed it all up, which is lovely.

Howarth We really must do that dictation. Come on, Donald, we'll go next door until lunch.

Joanna It's very cluttered in there.

Howarth It's all right. Besides, we'll be out of your way.

Joanna (*as Howarth and Donald go out*) But you don't have to be.

SIMON GRAY

Howarth appears not to have heard.

Blackout.

SCENE TWO

That evening.
In the small room, Donald kneels searching in his
satchel, takes out a copy of Mayfair *and shakes it, puts*
it back, goes quietly to dividing door and opens it very
carefully. He sees there is no one about, so enters and
looks on table, sits left of table and starts silently to
rehearse the moment when he dropped the photograph,
putting his foot out in the way he did before. Still puzzled,
he kneels left of the table to look under it. As he does so
Joanna enters.
Donald starts, rises.

Joanna (*closing door*) Did I frighten you?

Donald Um, pardon, I didn't know. I was looking for
Mr Howarth . . . I mean, whether he was back yet.

Joanna, behind the sofa, takes one of the cushions
from the left end to the right end, preparatory to
sitting there.

Joanna No, he's still rehearsing – at least I presume he is.
These school plays are meant to be for the students, but
every year he always seems to grab a small, but plum,
part for himself. This time he's one of those bishops in
Henry V, which means a lovely costume for him and
hours of needlework for me. Were you looking for him
under the table?

Donald (*laughs falsely*) No, there was a bit of paper,
um, it must have fallen out of my satchel.

352

Joanna (*looks around the floor*) In here?

Donald No, it's probably in there. It wasn't anything important. (*Little pause, then goes back into room.*)

Joanna Where are you going?

Donald Well, I'd better get back . . .

Joanna Oh, do sit down. You can't spend the whole time here working, and besides, we've scarcely exchanged a word all day.

Donald Well, I haven't finished that translation passage he set me.

Joanna (*smiles*) Sit down, please. (*With quiet authority.*)

> *Donald looks at her, comes across, sits down. Joanna picks up the edge of the material and the needle, begins to sew, suddenly laughs.*

Very satisfactory. I'm trying out a completely new technique – quiet authority – and it works . . . at least, it does with you. You can go now if you insist.

Donald No, that's all right.

Joanna Are you very on edge? Before an examination is hell, isn't it?

Donald No, I don't feel too bad this time. Not really.

Joanna Good for you. (*Smiles, pauses.*) You work at that big shop – Crabtree's.

Donald Yes.

Joanna It's very grand. I only go there on days when I feel impregnable. Which I'm certainly not at the moment. What do you do exactly?

Donald Well, I help out in accounts.

Joanna Oh, *do* you? You must have a very good head for figures, then?

Donald No, I just, you know, take the letters around and – that.

Joanna I see. Anyway, you're not one of the supercilious salesmen – the ones who put people like me in their places?

Donald Um, no. No.

Laughs. There is a silence.

Joanna I did have one very nice experience in Crabtree's. When I was working on the *Argus* – which, come to think of it, was up to three months ago – being pregnant makes me feel that anything before that was about six years away.

Laughs, Donald smiles dimly.

Well, it was my first year as a reporter, a real reporter, and I remember I went in to buy something very ordinary – spoons, I think – and they only had these Swedish things at about nine and six each, and the boy said why didn't I try Woolworth's. So, I made one of my scenes, and it ended up with my seeing the manager, who was very snooty –

Donald laughs.

– and said much the same thing. I really could have murdered him. Well, the next week I got my first real assignment, which was to interview the manager of Crabtree's about a special fair or sale they were having. It was delicious, strutting impassively into his office.

Donald laughs again, evidently realising it's expected.

354

Unfortunately, I was far too green and nervous to take advantage. *Now* I would have murdered him this side of libel.

There is a long, appalling silence.

I don't know what on earth he's up to. He was meant to be back . . . (*Looks at her watch.*) half an hour ago. I expect he's got involved – some lame duck – (*Embarrassed.*) I mean, some wretch who can't get his lines right – um, tell me. (*Hurriedly.*) What's he like as a teacher? I always hear from him what his pupils are like, but never from them what he's like.

Donald (*looks at her, looks down*) Well, he's very good. (*In a mumble.*)

Joanna I don't mean he's ever gossiped about you – except in the most flattering way. (*Laughs.*) God, how awful. It must sound as if I'm fishing, but I can't help taking advantage. You know, you're the first of his pupils I've ever had a chance to grill. (*Waits.*)

Donald Well, he's got a very good accent.

Joanna (*laughs*) Yes, that must be quite a help.

Donald (*pause*) And, um, well, it's when he explains something, then I understand it. When my teachers at school used to explain things, I didn't always understand . . . not really.

Joanna Ah, I see. He makes you want to learn, is that it?

Donald Well, if I go on getting it wrong, then it's like I'm sort of – well, you know, letting him – Mr Howarth – down.

Joanna There you are, you see. I've been married to a teacher for three years. My teachers . . . I either hated

355

them and ragged them unmercifully, or I had the most
ghastly crushes on them. (*Laughs.*)

Donald, puzzled, laughs.

Which is why I'm probably so uneducated.

Donald (*nervous laugh*) Yes . . .

Joanna Oh dear. (*Yawns.*) I feel sleepy all the time these
days. It's because I eat so much. I hope you haven't been
letting him pilfer cakes and biscuits from the kitchen.
He's on a diet this term – next term he's doing the
football, so I can let him relax a little.

Donald nods.

Does he? Steal from there? (*Gestures towards the kitchen.*)

Donald Steal? No, no. Well, I don't know.

Joanna Mm. He's very sly. I find chocolate and biscuit
crumbs in his pocket. (*Pause.*) Well, I could find worse,
I suppose.

*Donald gives a little giggle. Joanna looks at him – she
yawns again.*

Oh dear, I'm sorry. I suppose I might as well go to bed,
if I'm going to. (*Stretches.*)

Donald gets up.

No, why don't you stay here. It's much more comfortable.

Donald Well, I've got my stuff in there, um . . .

Joanna Oh. Well, in that case, *I'll* stay on the sofa.
(*Swings her legs up.*) There!

Donald (*uncertainly*) Well. (*Sits down.*) Um . . .

Joanna You *can* go, if you want. I shan't take offence.

Donald No, it's all right.

Joanna Well. (*Smiles.*) It's very nice of you. (*Pause.*) You will excuse me if I just close my eyes . . . and you pop off the second you want to.

Closes her eyes, keeps them closed. Donald, after a moment, looks at her, kneels and looks under the table again. The sound of a door closing downstairs. Donald retreats back into the bedroom with the satchel. He sits at his desk and writes out a translation during the following scene. Joanna sits up. Howarth comes in, with his briefcase.

Joanna Well? (*Looks at her watch.*)

Howarth I'm sorry. There was a bad case of stage fright. I had to do some soothing down. How are you, then?

Joanna Intolerant.

Howarth Oh. Not of me, I hope.

Joanna Only by association.

Howarth Oh. Where is he?

Joanna Oh – smoking pot in the kitchen, or out in the fields raping a peasant . . . Or, yes, possibly next door in one of his more serious moods having a go at his French, do you think?

Howarth Well, I'd better go in.

Joanna No, you don't. (*Takes him by the wrist.*) He's only just gone – you can spare me five minutes. *He* did.

Howarth Oh? What did you talk about?

Joanna pulls him down beside her, puts her arms around him.

357

Joanna Well, he wanted to know about our sex life. (*Taking his arm.*) Very prying, and slightly coarse in his approach. Lost his temper and called me a swollen tart – said he was looking forward to the day when you and me and our kind were swept aside. Frankly, some of his ideas struck me as a little wild, but he'll probably settle down in a few years' time and have babies like the sad rest of us.

Howarth You don't like him, then?

Joanna How would I know? He's been here all day, in a trance of shyness at lunch and supper, and concealed from view for the rest of the time. But I do just wonder why, of all the pupils you've ever taught, this is the only one I get a chance to look at.

Howarth He's a special case. None of the boys at school need this sort of attention – for obvious reasons.

Joanna Really, I'm not against him, you know. It just seems odd, in this day and age. It's not as if I was being *de haut en bas* to him. He was being *de bas en haut*, or whatever it is, to me.

Howarth He wasn't. It doesn't exist.

Joanna Don't schoolteach me, thank you.

Howarth Sorry.

Joanna You are prickly, aren't you? All through lunch you behaved as if I were going to assault him – warning glances at me, protective smiles for him.

Howarth Well, it was an ordeal for him.

Joanna Thank you. (*Laughs.*) Oddly enough, he makes *me* feel quite shy – which is why I chattered at him. Does he have any girlfriends?

Howarth I don't know. (*Mitigatingly.*) He's just as inaccessible to me, darling.

Joanna Well, you're not inaccessible to him. He managed a few words about you.

Howarth Oh? (*Little pause.*) What?

Joanna He said he liked to please you. That's why you're a good teacher. (*Pause.*) No, that's what it came to. What he really meant, of course, was that you've got a sexy personality. (*Little pause.*) And you're very self-indulgent.

Howarth Self-indulgent? It's . . . (*Looks at his watch.*) Ten-thirty on a Saturday evening. I've been cramming Donald all day, and ever since supper I've been rehearsing a school play and shortly I shall have to mark exercises for Monday – after, that is, a spell with Donald again.

Joanna You're not!

Howarth I've got to.

Joanna Can't you do them tomorrow?

Howarth Yes, but I shall have to do a few of them tonight as well. Donald's not the only one taking his O levels next week.

Joanna Well, bloody hell, it sounds like self-indulgence to me. It's only because it's a respectable activity that you get away with it. You know, I could, if I were feeling nasty, remind you that last weekend, which you spent almost entirely at rehearsals, you only managed to calm me by promising me this weekend – all to myself.

Howarth (*stacking exercise books in a pile on the table*) I know. I have apologised.

There is a silence.

Joanna Doesn't he have any friends at all?

Howarth Friends? Who? Donald? (*Looks through O-level dictation book.*) I don't know. He's got one – the one that came this morning. I suppose he's got friends, like any other ordinary young man.

Joanna Not so ordinary. He's too pretty to be ordinary. Even if he's totally innocent about his looks now – of course, when he finds out, he'll probably turn into a monster.

Howarth Then I shall have to watch him with you, won't I?

Joanna Oh, don't worry. I'd never have fancied him.

Howarth Poor Donald. Why not? (*Starts to correct an exercise book.*)

Joanna Perhaps because he'd never have fancied me. He seems to get on best with the older man. (*Giggles.*) Anyway, this is a bit strong – I'm meant to be the one in the interesting condition and we spend all our time talking about how –

Donald opens the door, coughs awkwardly.

– uninteresting your house guest is.

Donald Um, I'm – I've finished that, sir.

Howarth Poor Donald, I didn't mean to keep you, uh . . . (*Gets up.*) Anyway, I'll join you now.

Joanna Donald can join you – in here. It's much more comfortable, and I'm going to bed. And, by the way, Donald, I've made him confess – he eats cakes and biscuits with you, doesn't he?

Donald, as Howarth smiles irritably, stares at her, then at him.

You might as well come clean too.

Donald Oh no, he doesn't eat anything.

Joanna You've never even seen him eat *one* biscuit?

Donald No. No, I haven't.

Joanna (*looks at him, slightly startled*) You know, I don't believe you, though thousands would. (*Laughs.*)

Donald laughs and looks at Howarth, who raises a stiff smile.

Joanna Anyway, you're to be my ally tomorrow. You're to leave fatter than when you came, and he's to be . . . (*punching Howarth's stomach*) thinner when you leave.

Howarth (*sharply, to Joanna*) It sounds like a very good way to reduce me. You'd better go and get your books then, Donald.

Donald goes out, leaving his door open. Howarth turns away, walks to the table, and sits.

Joanna (*sotto voce*) You're not prickling again. I was only trying to cover up.

Howarth It's all right.

Joanna Do you think he heard?

Howarth I hope not.

Joanna You're not very reassuring.

Howarth Well, I can't *be* sure, can I?

The door opens again. Donald comes in, carrying his satchel. He comes to the table. Joanna sits on the sofa and starts to sew.

Joanna By the way, Donald, did you find your bit of paper?

Donald Um, no.

Joanna I'll keep my eye open for it.

Donald No, it doesn't matter, it's nothing. Just a stupid picture. (*Violently.*) *I* don't want it.

Joanna I see.

Howarth smiles slightly. He holds out his hand for Donald's exercise book. Donald takes it out of his satchel and sits.

Howarth (*looks at the exercise book*) Well, we wouldn't say, would we, that the sun was about to go to bed, even if the French do. What do we say?

Donald Mmm – it . . . (*thinks*) sinks.

Howarth Or sets, or goes down. Mmm-huh, well, all right, but you don't really, do you? 'Mount' a hill – I mean, one mounts a horse in English and that's about all these days. What do you do to a hill?

Joanna looks for her scissors in her work basket.

Donald Oh, climb it.

Howarth Yeah. You see, you're still being a little lazy, really.

Joanna looks in a tin on the piano. It rattles.

When you know what a word is – I mean, its literal translation – then think from that to the word we'd use. Do you see? . . . So. Mmm-huh, a little *wave*, a little grey *wave* on the horizon?

Donald Cloud, I mean. (*Laughs.*)

Joanna goes into the bedroom, opens and shuts a drawer in the desk.

Howarth Course you do, it's common sense. He's standing on top of a hill and he's looking across the plains, so even if the first word that comes to mind is a wave, then think about it. What is a wave, by the way?

Donald Um, um, um . . .

Joanna returns. Opens a drawer in the shelf unit. Looks in a tin which rattles.

Howarth We had it just the other day.

Donald Um, orage. Orage.

Howarth (*correcting his pronunciation*) L'orage is the storm. Well, it was in that piece – and it sounds –

He breaks off as Joanna rattles the tins again.

– sounds roughly like, um . . .

Turns, looks at Joanna, who has opened the tin, is looking inside it.

No?

Donald It's um, um, um –

Puts his hands to his face. Howarth watches him.

Vague. (*English pronunciation.*) Vague. (*French.*)

Howarth (*laughs*) Good boy!

Joanna shuts the drawer, turns and goes out of the room.

Now.

Folds his hands, smiles at Donald.

Est-ce que vous voulez parler avec moi un peu, monsieur?

Donald (*tensely*) Oui, monsieur.

Howarth (*more relaxed*) Take it easy. Whoever does it with you, just imagine it's me, and we're amusing ourselves

for a few minutes, mmm? This really *is* marks for jam.
OK? Où habitez-vous?

Donald J'habite en Angleterre.

Howarth D'accord. Vous vous appellez Donald Clenham
et vous êtes de quelle nationalité?

Donald Anglais.

Howarth Êtes vous sûr?

Donald (*hesitates*) Oui, monsieur.

Howarth Bon. Mais vos parents sont de quelle
nationalité?

Donald Ma mère est anglais – (*remembers the gender*) -se,
mais, mon père etait . . . (*Pause, desperate guess.*) Eer-
eesh.

Howarth Irlandais.

Donald Irlandais.

Howarth C'est ça que j'ai pensé. En ce cas, vous avez
une imagination bizarre, non?

Donald Um – um –

Howarth Bizarre, curious, extraordinary, extravagant.
(*French.*) Bizarre!

   Donald laughs.

Mais, c'est vrai. Tous les Irlandais sont très imaginatifs,
non? Et vous avez, vous-même, les yeux, les cheveux et
la charme d'un irlandais, non? Est-ce que tu pense que tu
as la charme d'un irlandais?

Donald (*laughs*) Je l'espère.

Howarth Et qu'est-ce que vous aimez faire, pour vous
amuser?

Donald J'aime bien à chanter.

Howarth Et vous chantez bien?

Donald No, sir . . . Non, monsieur.

Howarth Bien sur, vous chantez bien. Tous les irlandais chantent bien parce qu'ils sont très sentimentaux.

Joanna enters. Howarth turns to her.

Hello, I thought you were going to bed.

Joanna When I've finished your costume. (*Sits on the sofa.*)

Howarth Why don't you leave it till the morning?

Joanna I'd rather find some other way of amusing myself in the morning, thank you.

Howarth Well, I'm sorry it's such a job.

Joanna Well, it wouldn't be if you'd try it on.

Howarth Well, I can't right now, can I?

Joanna Well, it would only take a moment.

Howarth (*turning to her irritably*) We're in the middle of some French.

Joanna Yes, I realise that, but as I've spent three hours sewing it together, I thought you might spare me thirty seconds trying it on. (*Pause, angrily.*) After which I'll take myself off to bed.

Howarth (*sharply*) OK.

Joanna Oh, don't bother.

She throws the robe onto the sofa and goes out.

Howarth (*as she goes, making peace*) I don't mind . . . (*Pause, turns to Donald.*) Oh dear, I seem to have disgraced myself.

The door bell rings.

Oh, God! (*Goes off to answer the door.*)

Mrs Clenham (*off*) Good evening, I'm Mrs Clenham, Donald's mother.

Howarth (*off*) Oh, come in.

Mrs Clenham (*off*) I'm sorry to bother you like this.

Donald, recognising his mother's voice, rises.

Howarth (*enters, holding the door*) Donald, your mother.

Mrs Clenham (*stepping in*) Pardon me for coming like this. I tried to contact you on the telephone but Les must have given me the wrong number. I brought some things over for – my son.

Howarth Well, we're very glad to see you. I'll just tell my wife.

Goes out, closes door, calls offstage.

Darling!

Mrs Clenham Hello, Donnie.

Donald Hello, Mum.

Mrs Clenham (*in a low voice*) Are you all right?

Donald Yes, I'm fine.

Mrs Clenham It was a bit of a shock, getting Les's message.

Donald I'm sorry, Mum, I couldn't think how else to let you know. They . . . you know – it was a bit difficult.

Mrs Clenham Then Les giving me the wrong number . . . I dialled and dialled down at the shop, and I kept getting this man . . . He was very rude in the end. I was getting very worried.

Donald I'm sorry. (*Slightly irritable.*)

Mrs Clenham That's all right, Donnie. It doesn't matter. Anyway, you're all right then? It's very kind of them to ask you.

Donald Well, he's giving me a hand with revision – dictations and that. Right through. We were just in the middle of an oral.

Mrs Clenham Well, I'll be going straight back. (*Puts the brown paper carrier bag she has been carrying on a chair.*) Here, I've brought your pyjamas and toothbrush and your razor. (*Getting a cake box out of the bag*) And here's a cake. It's one of those orange gateaux.

Donald (*looks down at the cake*) Oh.

Mrs Clenham You give it to them, Donnie, as you know them.

Howarth and Joanna re-enter. Donald puts the cake in the carrier bag, puts the bag on a chair.

Howarth Mrs Clenham, this is my wife. (*Shuts the door.*)

Joanna How do you do? (*They shake hands.*) Oh, do sit down. Would you like some tea or coffee or a drink?

Mrs Clenham (*after a quick glance at Donald*) No, thank you. There's a bus back in a minute, it's the last one.

Joanna Oh, what a shame you've got to rush off.

Mrs Clenham I'm sorry I came up so late, but it was difficult because Les gave me the wrong number. And then I didn't get his note until I was off in the evening from my work.

Joanna Oh, I see . . . what do you do?

Mrs Clenham Well, I'm at the Rex. At the cinema.

Donald giggles nervously.

(*After a glance at Donald.*) I'm the usherette there.

Joanna Oh, I've always thought that must be lovely, seeing films as part of your work.

Mrs Clenham Oh yes, well most of them I see ten times in a week.

Joanna Yes, that must be a bit boring. (*Pause.*) Are you sure you haven't time to sit down?

Mrs Clenham No, thank you. I've got to get the bus. It's the last one. I just wanted to give my son some things.

Joanna I do hope you don't mind our stealing him for the weekend.

Mrs Clenham No, it's very kind of you to help him. (*Turns to Howarth.*) Thank you very much.

Howarth Not at all. It's a pleasure.

Mrs Clenham (*turning to Donald*) Well, goodbye Donnie.

Donald Goodbye, Mum.

Mrs Clenham And I'll be thinking of you on Monday.

Donald Thanks.

Mrs Clenham (*crossing to Donald*) Goodbye, Donnie. (*Kisses him.*) And don't forget tomorrow's Sunday.

Donald No, Mum.

Joanna Why don't you walk your mother to the bus stop?

Mrs Clenham Well, it's very cold. You'll need your coat, Donnie.

Donald Yes, Mum. (*Goes into the bedroom and collects his jacket.*)

Mrs Clenham (*crossing towards Howarth*) Do you think he has a chance, then?

Howarth Yes, yes, I certainly do.

Mrs Clenham But not certain to pass, then?

Howarth Well, these things are slightly in the lap of the gods, unfortunately, Mrs Clenham. But we're doing our best.

    Donald returns, waits nervously.

Mrs Clenham If anybody deserves to pass the exam and better his chances, Donnie does. He's not one for pushing himself forward, more's the pity. Of course I'm glad of that but he's . . .

Donald (*a nervous laugh*) Yes, Mum.

Mrs Clenham Well, thank you very much.

Joanna Not at all.

Mrs Clenham Thank you.

Joanna Goodnight.

Mrs Clenham Goodnight. (*Goes out.*)

Donald (*to Howarth, out of nervousness*) Goodnight.

    Donald follows Mrs Clenham out.

Howarth Well, there goes the lady who's responsible for the state of Donald's nerves.

Laughs and watches Joanna, who is touching the costume.

Shall I try that on as we seem to have a moment?

Joanna No thank you.

Howarth Oh, come on, Jo.

Donald enters, stays by the door, closes it.

Joanna (*to Donald*) That was very quick.

Donald Um, she made me come back. She said it was too cold.

Joanna Oh, very wise. You can't afford to get anything now. Well, I'll leave you in peace.

Joanna goes off and closes the door. Donald comes to the table and sits. Howarth sits on the arm of the sofa.

Howarth I think we've done enough for one evening.

Donald Yes, sir. (*Pause. Puts the book in his satchel.*) I'm sorry about that, sir.

Howarth What? (*Looks at Donald.*) About what?

Donald My mother. (*Pause.*) Her coming out here like that.

Howarth But you've got nothing to apologise for. She just wanted to make sure you were all right.

Donald Yes, sir. It's because she worries, sir.

Howarth Yes, you've already told me that.

Donald Sir.

Howarth Having parents is terribly difficult, one of the most difficult things in life – up to a certain age, anyway. Very few boys, in my quite extensive experience, aren't

370

mortified by their mothers or their father or both, but they wouldn't feel mortified if there weren't a muddle of other feelings as well – protectiveness and, well, love and sheer irritation, which generally comes from vanity. We want those we love to be admired, and we feel for ourselves as well as for them when we suspect they aren't. (*Pause.*) From what I can make out, I think your mother is an admirable woman. (*Little pause.*) It must have been very hard for her.

Donald (*nods, and in an emotional whisper*) I know that, sir.

Howarth Yes, I'm sure you do.

Donald nods again, emotionally.

Mmmm. (*Little pause.*) By the way, tell me about our mutual friend, Les.

Donald looks at him.

Are you two very friendly?

Donald Well . . . yes, well, as he's at Crabtree's and he lives near us and that –

Howarth I got the *impression* you were quite close.

Donald Yes, well, I see him more than anyone else. He comes around in the evenings and we have lunch and that. (*Shrugs, smiles.*)

Howarth Uh-huh. You must like him then?

Donald Yes. (*Now slightly worried, and defensive.*) Well, he's all right. (*Little pause.*) We're going to go to France together next holidays.

Howarth Really? What does your mother think about that?

Donald Well – (*Laughs.*) I haven't told her yet. She doesn't like Les too much. I think she quite likes him, but his parents are divorced – he lives with his mum – and as we're Catholics . . .

Howarth Ah, yes. I remember the business about the divorce. It was *one* of the reasons he left us – his mother took him away. His father was bad about maintenance, and Les had to go out to work. There are two little brothers, aren't there?

Donald Sisters.

Howarth Yes, of course – it would be sisters. (*Smiles. Pours himself a whisky.*) What's he like now?

Donald Well, he's very nice. I mean, he's always, you know, helping me, doing things for me. Lots of times, things I don't even think about – or well, even need – you know, he does them.

Howarth But you don't always enjoy it as much as you feel you ought to?

Donald looks at him, as if not understanding.

Donald Sorry?

Howarth I just mean that people – friends – sometimes get on our nerves, like parents. They do more than we want them to do.

Donald Well, once or twice . . . Once, I couldn't go into Crabtree's because Mum hurt her back, and I had to take her to the doctor's, and Les, he thought I was just swinging it because he didn't know about Mum, and he went around telling people I was ill, that he'd seen me the night before and I had a temperature with the flu. So, when I phoned up and said it was my mum that was ill, *they* thought I was swinging it too. But he was only trying to help, that's all.

Howarth Were you angry?

Donald Well, he got a bit upset.

Howarth So you apologised? (*Smiling.*)

Donald He was a bit upset. It didn't matter. I mean, I shouldn't have lost my temper.

Howarth Why not? (*Pause.*) If he did something bloody silly and interfering . . .

Donald I don't know. He takes it very hard.

Howarth Les never told you about St Martin's?

Donald No, well, just that he was there.

Howarth One of the reasons Les left St Martin's was because of the difficulty between his parents. But there was another reason.

Donald turns and looks at Howarth.

He was getting – well, a little too fond of one of the other boys. He kept writing him letters – love letters, in fact – and generally behaving . . . desperately. The other boy took the letters to the Headmaster – at least, his parents did. They'd found them in his satchel, and the Head was – he's a kind man, but not the world's most proficient psychologist – and he was a little clumsy about the whole thing. Unfortunately – or from some points of view, perhaps, fortunately – Les's mother said she wanted to withdraw him while all this was going on, and the Head, who, as I've said is a kind enough creature, and normally under the circumstances would have done something to keep the boy on, let him go. So . . . (*Looks at Donald.*)

Donald (*after a long pause, in horror*) D'you mean he's a homo?

Howarth It's not the word I'd use – ever, no. But boys, particularly at that age, can be sexually very confused. They're as much homosexual from necessity as they're heterosexual in their – (*gestures*) dreams. Mmm. The point, as far as their future happiness is concerned, is whether they grow out of it. The world, thank God, is learning not to judge homosexuals as if they were criminals. *But*, homosexual boys – men – (*shrugs*) do have a tendency to make emotional claims, to develop habits of dependence that can lead – if the other person is normal – to difficulties. Do you see?

Donald nods.

Relationships in even the most ordinary of circumstances can be difficult enough, God knows – (*laughs*) *and* depend upon habits. Joanna and I have the dieting thing, for example. It doesn't mean very much – at least, as far as actual eating goes – but it's become a familiar part of our lives, a habit that's a kind of reassurance, really. All right, but other habits – and in less ordinary circumstances – habits, say, where Les makes a nuisance of himself – like that little business at Crabtree's, because he's possessive, well, cares too intensely, let's say, and then gets too upset when you're quite rightly irritated, so that *you* apologise – that sounds a little too like a marriage to me. You might be drawn in further than you want. I'm only telling you all this because at school it's a part of my job, perhaps the most important part, to pass on what little information my experience has given me – and because you said you and Les were going to Paris together – perhaps I shouldn't have told you this – I thought I ought to warn you about possible complications. I certainly don't want you to do anything more than think about it all.

Donald (*pause*) I didn't know about that – about Les, sir – except my having to apologise to him all the time.

I mean, that used to get on my nerves, but I didn't know about that.

Howarth (*pats Donald's arm, relaxed*) Oh, don't worry. I know you like girls. (*Smiling.*)

Donald Sir?

Howarth Well you do like girls, don't you? I know you like looking at them.

    Donald laughs, looks at him; is overcome with embarrassment.

I'm trying to be exquisitely tactful – (*takes out of his pocket the folded picture*) and return your property to you without a fuss. It fell out of your satchel in all your comings and goings this morning.

Donald No, it's not mine, sir.

Howarth Oh, Donald. Come on, take it. I know it's yours.

    Donald goes to take it.

Just a minute, there's something you can explain to me. (*Takes the picture back, opens it out.*) The boots. What's the appeal of the boots? (*Points to them.*) The rest of it gets to me, in my own thin-blooded way. Proud breasts, pertly up-tilted – (*tracing lines with his finger*) saucy little nipples, suave hips, an exciting sheen on her flanks and a vee of shadows, which is what she wears instead of pubic hair. I always wonder whether it's rubbed out on the negative or shaved off before they take the photo. But the boots – what's the appeal of the boots?

    Donald stares down, transfixed . . . makes a giggling noise.

Mmmm?

Smiles slowly, then laughs. Donald also laughs.

It's not fair. I know exactly what the appeal of the boots is. Here. (*Hands the photo back to Donald.*) The real thing, of course, is trickier. It tends not to go about nude in boots, with all the embarrassing bits removed – unless you specifically ask it to – and it's very much in love with you. The real thing tends to be hairily human, with all that that implies.

The door opens. Joanna comes in in dressing gown and slippers.

Et voilà, c'est tout pour ce soir, Monsieur Clenham.

Joanna And high time. If Donald's going to keep fit for Monday morning, he'd better get his sleep.

Donald gets up, carries his satchel into the bedroom, leaving the door open.

Howarth Goodnight!

Joanna Goodnight!

Donald puts his satchel down on the desk in the bedroom and returns to the main room.

Donald Oh, my things. (*Collects his mother's carrier bag from the chair.*)

Joanna You do know where the bathroom is?

Donald goes to take the cake box out, half lifts it from the bag, then, too embarrassed to give it to Joanna, puts it back and hurries out of the main door.

I'm a bitch. I've been brooding in my bath and you are a terribly good teacher, aren't you?

Howarth Quite good.

Joanna (*hand on his shoulder*) And it's because you're all the things I blame you for – a liar, self-indulgent, lovable, sexy and exhibitionist.

Howarth Am I lovable?

Joanna (*caresses his head*) Well, quite lovable. But you're very lovable with him. I admit it. He's not very bright, is he?

Howarth No, not very.

Joanna And you make him brighter than he is, which must be one of the gifts of a teacher.

Howarth points ruefully to the pile of exercise books and reaches for one.

Oh you're not, are you?

Howarth Darling, I've got to.

Pause. Howarth starts correcting the exercises.

Joanna Do you think I'm more like a flower or a cow? I've been reading novels about pregnant ladies, and when they're written by men we're languid and dream-like, curiously beautiful, in touch with the mystery and other balls about creation. Our faces open as flowers, etc., etc., but when they're written by other ladies, especially the ones with degrees, we're always cow-like, sow-like, lumpish and clumsy. Which do you think I'm like?

Howarth Mmmm?

Joanna Cow, sow or flower?

Howarth Flower.

Joanna A flower with a urine test on Monday. You know, that Doctor Lafflin treats my bottom half like his wife's handbag, and my top half like an idiot son – but he does accept my little glass jar with a twinkle. The only time he's at all personal, is when he twinkles at me, and as I'm either holding or have just handed him a glass of my pee, I can scarcely twinkle back at him, can I, without seeming insane or obscene. Which do you think I am? Insane or obscene?

Howarth You're not insane.

Donald comes back in, wearing pyjamas and slippers and carrying the bag and a pile of his clothes with the cake box on top. He smiles at Howarth and Joanna and goes into the bedroom, puts his clothes on a chair.

Joanna What has he got in that cake box?

Donald turns on his bedroom light. Joanna goes to the bedroom door and knocks.

Donald (*puts the cake box on top of the folded bed*) Yes?

Joanna Donald? Are you all right in there? Got everything?

Donald Um, yes, thank you. It's very nice.

Joanna Good.

Donald (*coming into the main room*) The only thing is – um – is there a bed?

Joanna and Howarth laugh and Joanna goes into the bedroom, followed by Donald. Howarth follows to the door.

Joanna I'm so sorry, it's all made up. It only takes a second.

Joanna hands the carry-cot to Donald, who puts it against the wall.

378

I'm sorry about all the baby stuff, I was afraid you'd take all the nappies and rubber knickers as a joke in bad taste.

She hands the cake box to Donald, takes the cover off the folded bed and wheels it into the centre of the bedroom.

It opens this way –

Donald puts the cake box on the chest of drawers, unfolds the bed, which is ready made-up. Joanna puts away the bed cover and brings out a rug.

Howarth (*stepping forward to help*) Can you manage?

Donald Yes thank you, sir.

Joanna Donald, you're to stop calling him 'sir'. You're a guest, and besides, it ages me.

Howarth Yes, we're Richard and Joanna from now on.

Joanna Now, is that all right then? There's an extra blanket if you want it.

Howarth goes out of the room and sits at the table again, Joanna follows. Donald straightens the rug on the bed then comes into main room.

Donald Um – the only thing – is there a church?

Howarth Yes, there is. St Mark's – it's next door to the post office, a one-minute walk.

Donald Oh yes, I saw it.

Joanna What time have you to be there?

Donald Well, seven o'clock.

Joanna Seven!

Donald Well, I could go to the eleven o'clock mass, I suppose.

Joanna Is that all right? Lovely. We'll remember.

Donald Um, well, goodnight, sir. Goodnight, Mrs . . .

Joanna You've forgotten already!

Donald (*with difficulty*) Night then, Richard. Goodnight . . .

Joanna Joanna.

Donald Goodnight, Joanna.

Joanna Goodnight, Donald.

> *Donald goes into the bedroom and closes the door. He turns out the light and gets into bed.*

And what about you? I've suddenly realised I'm very neurotic, and only a cuddle will cure me.

Howarth (*having turned back to his exercises*) Say half an hour?

Joanna That's no use to me. I'll be asleep in three minutes, as you well know. Give me one now, on account.

> *Howarth turns and draws her to him. He cuddles her.*

Mmm, well, all right, if you promise to cuddle me if I'm asleep. I need some basic soothing.

Howarth I promise.

Joanna Mmm. (*Suspiciously, goes towards the door.*) Night, Richard. (*Imitating Donald.*)

> *Howarth looks after her, then goes back to his exercise book, then gets up. He goes to the hatch, brings out the biscuit tin, takes about four biscuits out. He sits down, takes a biscuit and continues to mark the exercise book.*

The lights dim to suggest the passing of about half an hour, then the one light by Howarth's table up, and Howarth still marking.

Donald, from his bedroom, has begun a low, keening sound. He is sitting up hunched together and rocking backwards and forwards in his sleep. Howarth, at first not noticing, goes on working. The keening noises get louder. Howarth looks up, looks at Donald's bedroom door, as the stage fills with the noise. Howarth gets to his feet, goes to the bedroom door.

Howarth (*knocks*) Donald, Donald. Are you all right?

The noise stops, then starts again. He opens the door and turns on the light.

(*Tenderly.*) What's the matter? Are you all right?

Howarth goes into the bedroom, bends over the bed, gently pushes Donald back on to the pillow. Donald stops moaning and sinks back, still asleep. Howarth straightens the blanket.

All right then, there you are. There. Now go to sleep.

Comes back to the door, is about to shut it.

Donald (*in a strange voice, intimately insolent*) Night, Richard.

Howarth stands with his hand on the knob, then turns out the light and closes the door gently.

Curtain.

Act Two

SCENE ONE

The Howarths' living room. The following morning.
   In the bedroom the bed has been made neatly and a chair from the desk has been placed by the door.
   The action starts in the living room. Donald is sitting at the table, pen in hand, exercise book before him. Howarth is standing by the window, the dictation textbook in his hand.

Howarth And you say you can't remember it?

Donald Um, I don't think so.

Howarth Sure?

Donald Yes.

Howarth Mm. I must have done it at school. Right – I'll read it through again. By the way – (*smiling*) did you sleep well?

Donald (*looks at him, slight pause, almost apprehensive*) Yes, thank you, um, Richard.

Howarth You gave me quite a turn.

   Donald looks at him, smiling awkwardly.

(*Smiling*) Don't you remember?

   Donald shakes his head.

You were – I don't know what you were doing. Keening.

Donald I – I'm sorry.

Howarth Don't be silly. There's nothing to be sorry

382

about – but did you know you do it?

Donald Well, sometimes I – I make this noise, Mum says.

Howarth Actually it's very effective – quite eerie.

Pause, as Donald looks down, mortified.

Have you ever seen anyone about it? A doctor?

Donald I think Mum mentioned it once to, um, Father O'Toole.

Howarth And what did he say?

Donald That I'd grow out of it.

Howarth (*little pause*) Then just when I thought I got you quieted – (*smiling*) you said, with a really quite unnerving lucidity, 'Night, Richard.' You don't remember that, either?

Donald shakes his head.

(*Laughs.*) It actually chilled my blood. (*Laughs.*) You sounded so – accomplished. Well, I'll read it through again. Ready?

Donald nods. As Howarth reads, he runs his pen along the top of the lines.

'Ce matin-là Jean avait parlé beaucoup de blès et de ce qu'il appelait la "culture intensive", mais il ne possédait aucune notion sérieuse d'agriculture. (*Looks up sharply.*) D'agriculture. (*Repeating it, with a slightly knowing exaggeration.*) Félicie haussait parfois les épaules. Philibert – (*looks at Donald*) jetait de temps en temps vers elle un regard de sympathie, et une fois il avait chucoté: "Ne vous fachez . . ."'

Joanna comes in, goes to the sofa for her handbag.

383

She smiles at Howarth. He smiles back at her. She looks in her handbag.

'"Ne vous fachez pas. Votre frère dit des bêtises, mais cela fait passer le temps." Mais Félicie l'arrêta . . .'

Joanna makes an apologetic gesture, goes over to the shelf and picks up a bunch of keys.

'Mais Félicie . . .' (*Stops.*)

Joanna Sorry, darling. I'm going to try and get a cup of coffee from the Haywards. I'll be back at lunchtime. The joint's on.

Howarth OK. See you then.

Joanna smiles at Donald, who smiles back, withdraws.

'Mais Félicie l'arrêta court. "Chut! Faîtes-moi donc le plaisir de vous occuper de ce qui vous regarde!"'

Sound of door closing. Howarth glances out of the window.

'Elle s'était mise en colère. Elle était bonne mais vive, et toujours prête a s'emporter . . . (*Waves out of the window.*) À s'emporter, surtout quand il s'agissait de sa famille.' OK?

Donald nods. Howarth saunters towards him.

You didn't make any corrections, did you?

Donald No.

Howarth (*leans over him, runs his finger rapidly along the lines*) You were quite right not to. Well, that's very good, isn't it? Except for this. One little mistake. But otherwise very good. (*Pause.*) Well done.

Donald Well – it seemed easy – I don't know why.

Howarth Don't you? (*Pleasantly, with a hint of underlying menace.*) Really? Probably just a matter of confidence, eh?

Donald nods.

(*Pointing at the exercise book.*) Of course, your little mistake was a stupid one. 'Une fois' – not only did I say it quite distinctly, but you know perfectly well that 'fois' is feminine.

Donald Well, um, that's meant to be an 'e' there. (*Points.*) It's just splodged.

Howarth So it is. Well, that makes it perfect. Something to be proud of. Could you stand doing another? A very short one.

Donald (*nods*) The only thing is – (*in a mumble*) I'm supposed to be in church.

Howarth (*as if not having heard, overlapping Donald's speech*) No, I think you'll find all these too easy. Have a go at this. Just a few lines – no splodges, mind. (*Smiles.*)

Donald sits listening. Howarth recites from memory.

'Ange plein de gaieté, connaissez-vous l'angoisse,
La honte, les remords, les sanglots, les ennuis
Et les vagues terreurs de ces affreuses nuits
Qui compriment le coeur comme un papier qu'on
    froisse?
Ange plein de gaieté, connaissez-vous l'angoisse?

'Ange plein de beauté, connaissez-vous les rides,
Et la peur de vieillir, et ce hideux tourment
De lire la secrète horreur du dévouement
Dans des yeux où longtemps burent nos yeux avides?
Ange plein de beauté, connaissez-vous les rides?'

OK?

He looks at Donald, who has clearly not understood a word.

Donald Well . . . (*Shrugs.*)

Howarth Have a go, anyway.

Howarth speaks at dictation speed, pausing between every two or three words.

'Ange plein de gaieté, connaissez-vous l'angoisse,
La honte, les remords, les sanglots, les ennuis
Et les vagues terreurs de ces affreuses nuits
Qui compriment le coeur comme un papier qu'on
   froisse?'

Donald writes, clearly completely confused, shaking his head.

Am I going too fast?

Donald No.

Howarth Good.

'Ange plein de gaieté, connaissez-vous l'angoisse?'

How's it going?

Donald Well, not really – (*Laughs nervously.*)

Howarth Well, perhaps I'd better stop there. Eh? Look through it then.

Donald does so.

'Ange plein de gaieté, connaissez-vous l'angoisse,
La honte, les remords, les sanglots, les ennuis . . .'

Crosses the room, looking down at Donald's attempt to do the dictation.

'Et les vagues terreurs de ces affreuses nuits
Qui compriment le coeur . . .'

Donald abandons the attempt, sits staring blankly down at his book.

> '. . . comme un papier qu'on froisse?
> Ange plein de gaieté, connaissez-vous l'angoisse?'

Pause. Donald looks at Howarth.

Well?

Donald I, um, got a bit lost.

Howarth Could you understand it?

Donald Well, some of it.

Howarth Then translate what you've got, and see if you can work backwards, filling in the blanks, so to speak. Not exactly examination practice, but a test of your – um . . . (*Gestures.*)

Donald Well, that'd take a bit of time.

Howarth (*looks at him*) We've got time.

Howarth picks up a newspaper from the sofa and stands by Donald, reading. Donald stares at his exercise book, rocking backwards and forwards slightly as he did in his sleep. Howarth turns back to look out of the window. Donald bends over his exercise book helplessly, picks up his pen, frowns, scratches down some words, shaking his head, shrugging, then looks towards Howarth. Howarth pays no attention. Donald writes down a few more words. There is a long pause, Donald staring towards Howarth.

Well?

Donald (*in a mumble*) Well, I got some of the words . . .

Howarth Mmm – huh. (*Picks up Donald's exercise book.*) 'Ange' – hip. My pronunciation must be a joke. 'Hanche' – hip. 'Ange' – (*drawing the word out*) angel.

(*Laughs again.*) Your first sentence appears to read, then, 'Hip plan of the limp' – 'limp?' – oh, I see. (*Laughs.*) 'Gaieté' – gait – limp – ingenious, 'do you know,' 'connaissez-vous', *well* done – 'l'angoisse' 'the English'. Didn't you even grasp, from its rhythms and rhymes, that it was a poem?

> *Donald shakes his head. Howarth takes down a*
> *copy of* Les Fleurs du Mal, *opens it at the poem*
> *'Reversibilité' and puts it down contemptuously in*
> *front of Donald.*

Look at it.

> *Donald does.*

(*Pointing out each word.*) Literally – 'Angel, full of gaiety, do you know the anguish, the shame, the remorse, the sobs, the tedium and the vague –' what did you put for 'vagues'?

Donald (*in a mumble*) Um, 'waves'. (*Starts to weep.*)

Howarth Of course. 'The tedium and the *vague* terrors of those frightful nights which compress the heart like a paper that one crumples. Angel, full of gaiety, do you know the anguish?' Mmmm? There's only one word there, actually, that you don't know – 'froisser' – to restrain or crumple – eh? There are no grammatical difficulties?

> *Donald shakes his head.*

And the fact that it's a painfully beautiful *poem* shouldn't have worried *you*, should it? As you didn't *register* it was a poem?

> *Donald shakes his head. Donald stares at him, puts*
> *his hands to his eyes. There is a silence.*

Well – do you think I'm being unfair?

Donald shakes his head. With his back to him, still looking out of the window:

Do you think I'm being cruel?

Donald shakes his head.

Well, I am. And do you know why? (*Turns around.*)

Donald shakes his head.

(*Crossing to Donald.*) Oh yes you do.

Leans across, picks up Donald's exercise book, flicks back through it, hands it to Donald.

What's this?

Donald (*after a pause*) That dictation, sir.

Howarth I do five of these a week, so it's scarcely surprising that I can't remember which I've done with whom. But *you* remembered, didn't you? From the first sentence. (*Little pause.*) Didn't you?

Donald sits hunched, looking down.

Didn't you? Mmm?

Donald Sir.

Howarth (*contemptuously*) Because you wanted me to give you good marks?

Donald shakes his head.

Because you wanted to impress me?

Donald (*after a pause, in a mumble*) Sir.

Howarth But it's cheating. And that's a very serious matter. (*Gently.*) I don't mean cheating *me*, about which I care not one damn, but cheating yourself, about which I do care. Don't you see?

Donald Sir.

Howarth You don't have to impress *me* with anything. At least, not in this way – that's something one keeps for one's girlfriend, or whatever.

Donald weeps, uncontrollably.

Even so, I was unfair, wasn't I?

Donald shakes his head.

I think I was insulted, and the very last thing you wanted to do was insult me. In fact, you wanted me to praise you – and what, after all, could be more flattering that that? Mmmm? (*Very gently.*) Donald?

Donald goes on looking down, crying.

Donald. (*Pause.*) Donald.

Donald looks up slowly.

I'm sorry. (*Smiling.*)

Donald (*his voice shaking*) Sorry, sir.

Howarth No, you're not to be. Not now. And the 'sir' you already know about.

Donald looks up, attempts to smile at Howarth's smile.

Donald, you do worry me, you know.

Donald begins to say 'sir', checks himself.

You're very attractive – my wife says you are – and you're not at all stupid, although I think you think you are, and you laugh – when you laugh, which is not nearly often enough – terribly nicely. But you give off an impression of – what? Well, as if you're permanently frightened. (*Pause.*) You are, aren't you?

Donald (*in a whisper*) Yes.

Howarth Of me?

Donald (*looks down*) Yes.

Howarth But not badly frightened of me? At least, not frightened in a bad way?

Donald shakes his head.

Well, that sounds about right. (*Laughs.*) But your trouble is – may I tell you what the trouble is?

Donald nods. Looks at Howarth.

Your trouble is not that you're frightened but that you don't realise that, on the whole, other people are frightened too, you see. They are. Always. Why, I'm even a little frightened of you.

Donald looks at him, laughs slightly.

But I am. I expect you judge me, don't you, in the way that we half-consciously judge *everyone* we know. Perhaps you find me pompous, silly, boring, fat? A trifle fat? Anyway, putting on weight?

Donald sniffs and laughs simultaneously.

But I am. Joanna tells me, and I feel it, other people – my students – must notice it. Well, that doesn't matter – there are other things I could be judged for – humiliated because of – just like you. That's the point, you see. But where I have a slight edge over you is that I know that other people are as frightened as I am. Of being found out. We all are. It's the great human secret. Do you believe me?

Donald is staring at him as if hypnotised.

But perhaps we go some way towards overcoming it by talking of it. Perhaps you and I needn't be more than a necessary little bit frightened of each other again?

(*Smiling.*) Eh? (*Little pause.*) How do you feel?

> *Donald looks at him, looks down. There is a long pause. He begins to cry again very slightly.*

You're not unhappy, are you?

> *Donald shakes his head. Howarth puts his hand on Donald's shoulder.*

You're not crying though, are you?

> *Donald shakes his head, puts his arm to his eyes. Howarth goes over to Donald, puts his arm around his shoulder.*

Donald, don't.

> *Donald sits, his arm still over his eyes. Howarth removes his arm gently.*

Got a handkerchief?

> *Donald fumbles in his pocket, takes out a handkerchief, blows his nose, wipes his eyes, draws a breath, then in a brave, trembling voice:*

Donald I'm sorry.

Howarth You're not to say sorry to me – ever again. People who say sorry all the time are, simply, doing dirt on themselves, mmm?

> *Joanna opens the door, comes in, stops. Howarth steps away from Donald. Donald blows his nose.*

Joanna I'm sorry. (*Little pause.*) Only it's gone eleven. (*She is carrying a basket of shrubs.*)

Howarth Gone eleven?

Joanna Donald's church.

Howarth My God. (*Looks at Donald.*) I completely forgot.

Donald Um, it doesn't matter, it was my fault.

Joanna (*advancing into the room*) Well, hadn't he better get along? He won't be too late.

She goes on out of the door, leaving it open. Donald looks at Howarth.

Howarth (*in a low voice*) All right?

Donald nods and fetches his coat from the bedroom.

OK. See you then (*Smiles.*)

Donald goes out. Howarth stands for a moment, looking towards the door, then goes over to it. Joanna comes, in, carrying two vases.

(*Taking one from her.*) Here, let me.

He takes the larger of the two vases from her and places it on the table. Joanna closes the door and puts the smaller vase on a stool.

How are you, then?

Joanna (*busy*) Preg-nant.

Howarth Poor darling. How were Peter and Sally?

Joanna Out.

Howarth Out?

Joanna Yes. Not in.

She takes the vase Howarth has placed on the table over to one by the window.

Howarth Well, it looks as if we have the house to ourselves for a change. (*Goes over to the table, starts arranging the books.*) What shall we do?

Joanna goes over to the sofa.

Joanna Peel. Peel the potatoes. Top and tail. The sprouts. In a minute.

She picks up the other vase of flowers and takes them into the lounge.

Howarth Poor darling. Can I help?

Joanna What was that all about?

Howarth What all about?

Joanna In here. Between you two. He was crying, wasn't he?

Howarth Yes. I was a little tactless. I pushed him a bit harder than I meant to.

Joanna I see. (*Little pause.*) Does it happen often?

Howarth Happen often?

Joanna With your other boys. At school.

Howarth With my other boys?

Joanna (*sharper*) You're developing an extraordinary trick of repeating all my questions. Did you know?

Howarth Well, you're asking some extraordinary questions. Did you know?

There is a pause, Joanna looking at the Sunday paper, Howarth looking at her.

Well, what do you mean, 'happen often'? If you mean, do I usually reduce my boys to tears, the answer is no, I most certainly do not. If you mean, is there occasional tension between us, the answer is yes, when the other party is someone like Donald.

Little pause. Joanna puts down the paper and listens.

There *have* been tears in my time. As in the time of any schoolmaster, I should think. The boys are vulnerable and the masters impatient. The resulting concussion is – sometimes – unpleasant. It's one of the hazards of the profession. It generally means I lose a perfectly clean handkerchief, as I did with Donald. (*Little pause.*) As a matter of fact, I merely caught him doing something silly – a kind of useless cheating – and nagged at him because of it more than I should have, and his – his nerve broke. Not his strongest point at the best of times, as his 'mum' warned us. It was my fault. And I said so. (*Little pause.*) I feel upset enough about it, you needn't worry. And I particularly dislike showing myself a brutal bungler in front of you. OK?

Joanna (*looks at him – there is a pause*) Come here.

Howarth What?

Joanna Come on. Please. OK?

Howarth goes over, Joanna takes his hand, raises it to her lips, kisses it.

Howarth (*sits on the sofa with his arm round her*) Have you noticed it's when people apologise to each other that the tears come?

Joanna (*gives him a kiss*) I'm sorry.

Howarth (*gently, after a moment*) But where are the tears?

Joanna Oh, I can manage them if you want?

Howarth No thanks. (*Indicates Donald's door.*) Enough is as good as a feast.

Joanna Feast? With all those biscuits inside you? (*Prods his stomach.*)

Howarth I – (*Laughs.*) We had a sort of elevenses.

Joanna Give us a kiss, pig.

Howarth does so, then straightens up.

But why should he cheat?

Howarth What? (*Shrugs.*) Why do boys ever cheat? Because it's easier than not.

Joanna But it's not an examination or anything. Why should he cheat with you?

Howarth Well, I don't know, I suppose because he wanted to get a good mark, I suppose. Or for his self-esteem, which, God knows, needs boosting.

Joanna You mean, to win your approval?

Howarth Not mine necessarily – at least, not personally. Probably just because his nerve is weak – and it's not tested when you do well.

Joanna Perhaps his nerve is weak because his feelings are strong. He wanted *you* to respect him – after all, if he cries when *you* find him out –

Howarth Well, I expect I'm the only teacher ever to take the mildest interest. (*Sits at the table.*) The question is, what would he have done if Father O'Toole had caught him cheating? (*Starts to mark exercise books.*)

Joanna (*looks at him*) When I was out, I suddenly got frightened.

Howarth turns to her.

I didn't go to the Haywards at all.

Howarth (*looking at her anxiously*) Oh, why not?

Joanna It was stupid, but I suddenly remembered the last time I went. (*Swings her legs off, looks at Howarth.*) And Sally talked all the time of her forceps delivery – did you know Tom was a forceps? They caught his head with the forceps and tugged it out. Although you wouldn't think so to look at him now – his head's enormous. This last week all I can think about is what could go wrong.

Howarth But you're supremely healthy – everyone keeps saying so.

Joanna Yes, but is he? Or she? Or – I don't know. I don't know if I'm up to what every woman's meant to fulfil herself in. The Americans just put you under about a week before, and you wake up with a baby or two, all sluiced down and probably gift-wrapped. (*Stands up.*) God, I'm boring. You've no idea how nervy I feel, from how boring I sound.

> *She bends down with a sigh, turns on the radio. It is Bach. She smiles at Howarth, goes out.*

Howarth (*listens to the music, then goes to the door, shouting*) Darling – you're not at all boring.

Joanna (*returning*) Sprouts or peas?

> *Howarth goes over to her, kisses her on the cheek, cuddles her.*

Peas or sprouts?

Howarth (*they kiss, he laughs*) Both, possibly?

Joanna All right, but you do the potatoes then. The elephant and the pig.

> *She does a few steps of a lumbering dance. There is a ring at the door bell, only just audible. Joanna looks at her watch.*

Back already? I always heard that was the Catholic system – little but often. (*Goes out.*)

> *Howarth returns to the table. Sound of voices, then footsteps. Joanna enters with Les.*

Darling – a friend of Donald's – Les.

Les Sir.

Howarth (*getting up*) Oh – hello. (*Little pause.*) I'm afraid Donald's out – he's gone to church.

Les Oh, I thought he'd go to the early morning mass – he usually –

Joanna We've been corrupting him, I'm afraid. We always sleep late on Sundays.

> *There is a pause. Joanna glances at Howarth, puzzled, then back to Les.*

Anyway, do sit down.

Les Oh, well, thank you. (*Sits down.*)

Howarth (*still standing*) Um, well, you cycled, did you?

Les Yes. (*Little pause.*) I wasn't sure what time you meant me to come exactly, you said coffee or tea and I thought that's either eleven or in the afternoon. (*Laughs.*)

Howarth (*to Joanna*) Um, I suggested to Les that if he should be cycling this way today, he look Donald up. They were going for a ride together yesterday.

Joanna But if you cycled, you must be exhausted.

Les No, I'm used to it, we go out every week almost.

> *There is a pause.*

Howarth That's two of your rides I seem to have messed up.

Les Oh, it doesn't matter. We can go next week. Well – (*Makes as if to rise.*)

Joanna Darling, what about a drink? Or would you prefer tea or coffee, Les?

Les No, well, that's all right, thank you very much.

Joanna Well, *I'd* like a drink.

Howarth goes to the door, shuts it, goes over to the shelf, pours a sherry, brings it back, gives it to Joanna.

You work in Crabtree's too, do you?

Les Yes, in the cutlery.

Joanna Oh, really? I tried to get some spoons there once, but they were so expensive.

Les Yes, I know. I always tell people to try somewhere else.

Joanna (*laughs*) Like Woolworths?

Les Yes.

They both laugh.

Joanna (*taking her drink*) Darling, I'm sure Les could be persuaded. Have a *small* sherry – you know it makes sense.

Les Oh, well – thanks very much.

Howarth, after a fractional hesitation, pours Les a very small sherry.

Joanna Have you known Donald long?

Les Well, since just after I left school.

Joanna You weren't at school together, then?

Howarth No, actually Les was at St Martin's for a short time.

Joanna Really?

Howarth (*handing Les his drink*) Although we scarcely knew each other.

Les Yes, I was only there two years, I had to leave early.

Joanna (*interrogatively*) Oh?

Howarth Which is how he came to miss me.

Les (*with sudden intensity*) That was one of my regrets.

Joanna (*to Howarth*) How very flattering.

Howarth Yes. (*Laughs.*) The best way to keep one's reputation is not to have it put to the test.

Les Everybody at school said you were marvellous and – well, Don says the same.

Joanna I must have more of this – hang on a minute. (*Goes out.*)

Howarth (*after a pause*) Well, I'm sorry Donald isn't here, after all your exertions.

Les He'll be gone a long time then, will he?

Howarth I don't know how long these things last – but I'm afraid I'll have to do a bit of French with him –

Les Oh, I see.

Howarth He's getting such a lot done – I'm terrified of breaking the spell. (*Little pause.*) I'm sorry.

Les (*finishes his drink*) No, it doesn't – (*Shakes his head, gets up.*) Well, perhaps I might as well get back anyway.

Howarth Well, at least you've got the weather, mmm?

Les looks at him uncertainly.

Still, I'm glad you could drop in.

Joanna (*comes back in*) Oh, you're not going?

Les Well, I've got to get on.

Joanna Oh, what a shame.

Howarth Les wants to get as much of the sun as he can.

Joanna Well, it's been *very* nice . . . (*Holds out her hand.*)

Les Oh, well, thank you. (*They shake hands.*)

As they do, there is the sound of the door closing, footsteps.

Joanna Ah!

Donald comes in, stops when he sees Les.

Les Hello, Don.

Joanna You got back just in time. That was lucky.

Donald Well, there wasn't an eleven o'clock mass.

Joanna Oh dear, I am sorry. Let's all sit down again, at least, and have another drink.

Les Oh, well, thanks, but if you're going to be working? (*Looks at Howarth.*)

Joanna Surely you're not going to do anything before lunch?

Howarth Um, no, no, not now – (*Looks at his watch.*) I shouldn't think. Do have a drink.

Joanna Do sit down.

SIMON GRAY

Les sits down again, Howarth pours sherry for Donald.

Les was just telling us that he never got to do French with Richard at St Martin's.

Les (*contemptuously*) Of course, we don't need French at Crabtree's. But we're going to France next holiday, and now Don'll have to do all the talking, eh, Don?

Joanna To France? How exciting!

Howarth gives Donald his sherry.

Les Yes, we thought we'd take our bikes, you know, just put them on the boat and then sort of cycle off – we thought we might even get to Paris, eh, Don?

Donald nods.

Joanna It sounds marvellous. You know, I think Donald's having you on, darling. He's really getting up his French so he and Les can have a naughty holiday together. (*Goes into the kitchen.*)

There is a silence, then the sound of saucepans from the kitchen. Donald sits. Les lifts his glass, sees it is empty and sets it down again.

Les (*to Donald*) I thought I'd ride up to Farlington.

Donald Oh. (*Nods.*)

Les But I won't if you want to go up there next week.

Donald No, that's all right.

Les Anyway, I can go and see what it's like, and we can go up again. Just take a quick look this time, you know, find out where the café is. (*Laughs.*)

Donald nods. Pause.

Well, um, I suppose I'd better be getting on. (*Gets up.*)

Howarth Yes – that's quite a trip, Farlington. (*Gets up.*)

Donald Yes. (*Also gets up.*)

Joanna (*raises the hatch and speaks through it*) Darling, ask Les if he'll stay to lunch.

There is a pause.

Howarth Les was just saying he was going to cycle up to Farlington.

Joanna Well, he'll be having lunch on the way, won't he? So why not have it here?

Howarth (*pause*) Yes, do.

Les Well, I don't want to cause trouble.

Howarth No trouble.

Joanna Well? Is he, or isn't he?

Howarth Yes, he'd love to.

Joanna Good. (*Shuts hatch.*) Potatoes, darling!

Howarth goes out.

Les How's it going, then?

Donald All right.

He goes into his room, hangs up his coat on a chair. Les looks at him, clearly worried, and follows him to the doorway of the bedroom.

Les Is this your room then?

Donald comes out, sits down at the table and starts to get on with his work.

I met your mum on the street – she was just coming back from church.

Donald Oh?

Les (*laughs*) She said to find out how they liked the cake.

Donald Oh. Yes, well, they liked it.

Pause.

Les (*sitting opposite Donald*) Well, it's all right then, is it?

Donald What?

Les Well, you know – everything.

Donald shrugs, looks at Les. Les looks at him, looks down.

Didn't you want me to stay to lunch then?

Donald shrugs.

I see. I'm sorry, Don. I mean, she asked me, didn't she. I didn't want to be rude to your friends. I didn't know *you* didn't want me.

Donald (*after a pause, looking at Les*) Well, you know now, don't you? (*In a mutter.*)

Les turns, goes out of the main door. The front door slams. Joanna enters.

Joanna Has Les gone?

Donald (*gets up*) Um, Les had to go after all, he just remembered he had to do some shopping for his mum, and the shop'll be closed.

Joanna Oh!

Donald He said to say sorry.

Blackout.

SCENE TWO

The Howarths' living room. Evening. The hatch is open, and through it come sounds of Howarth and Donald washing up, and their voices, quite distinct. Joanna is at the piano, picking quietly the melody of 'Danny Boy'.

Howarth Maintenant, tu le prends *ou* vous le –?

Donald Prenez . . .

Howarth Pour le sécher. Et moi, je vais laver cette assiette – donnez-le-moi, mon enfant, s'il vous plaît. Merci – oooops!

Sound of a plate crashing to the floor. Joanna stops playing the piano, looks towards the door.

Well, what do you say now?

Donald Um, je suis desolé.

Howarth laughs. Joanna cocks her head to one side, ironically.

Howarth (*raising his voice*) Darling!

Joanna (*slightly parodying*) Yes, darling?

Howarth (*looking in through hatch*) I'm afraid there's been a little – (*in French*) accident, darling.

Joanna Oh, that's all right, darling. Not to worry.

Howarth It was only one of the plain white ones.

Joanna Oh, that's *good*.

Howarth Sorry, darling.

Joanna begins to play again.

Non, non, laisse-la. Et le café, c'est prêt?

Donald Oui, c'est prêt.

Howarth Bon – ça, c'est pour madame.

Donald wearing an apron, appears at the door, carrying a mug of coffee. He wipes the base of the mug on his apron and puts the coffee on the piano.

Joanna Do you know the words?

Donald Well, um, not properly.

Joanna I bet you do.

Donald Well . . . (*Nods.*)

Joanna And sing them beautifully?

Donald laughs, shakes his head. Joanna smiles, and as he turns to go:

Come here.

Donald comes back apprehensively.

(*Strikes a chord.*) Go on. Please.

Donald Well. (*Shakes his head, laughs.*) I can't.

Joanna Please!

Plays again. Starts to sing the first few words.

Oh, Danny boy . . .

Donald joins in and they sing together.

Joanna and Donald
 . . . the pipes, the pipes are calling . . .

Joanna stops singing and Donald goes on alone.

Donald
From glen to glen, and down the mountain side.
The summer's gone and all the roses falling.

Howarth, from the kitchen, puts a coffee mug on the hatch shelf, moves quietly in to the doorway.

'Tis you, 'tis you must go and I must bide.
But come ye back when summer's in the meadow
Or when the valley's . . .

Howarth appears from the kitchen, wearing an apron and carrying a mug. He stays in the doorway, staring at Donald.

. . . hushed and white with snow,
And I'll be here, in sunshine or in shadow,
Oh Danny boy, oh Danny boy I love you so.

Joanna (*ending the song*) I knew you'd have a beautiful voice.

Howarth All the Irish do. It's because they're so sentimental.

Howarth shuts the door. Donald takes off the apron and leaves it on a chair. Howarth turns to the hatch, brings down the coffee mug there to Donald at the table, puts his own coffee mug on the table. Joanna gets up, picks up her coffee cup and goes over to the sofa. She sits down and looks towards Donald. Donald sits at the table, gets his books and makes as if to begin some work.

Joanna I'm sure you shouldn't, Donald. You've been at it all afternoon.

Donald looks at Howarth.

Howarth (*looking up*) Perhaps you should give it a rest, but you can have a little dictation for a nightcap, if you want.

Joanna So come and talk.

Donald, reluctantly, takes his coffee and sits by Joanna.

May we?

Howarth takes off his apron, sits at the table and begins marking books.

Howarth What? Mmm, go ahead.

Joanna He never minds when he's marking. Tell me more about your Paris adventure.

Donald Well, I'm, um, I don't think I'm going to Paris.

Glances towards Howarth.

Joanna Oh? (*Puzzled.*) Les seemed to think it was all arranged.

Donald Yes, well, I don't think I'll go. (*Clears his throat.*)

Joanna I'm sure you would have enjoyed it. I did at your age – and every age since. Won't Les be very disappointed?

Donald (*shrugs*) Well, he can go on his own.

Joanna Will he?

Howarth looks at them.

Donald (*shrugs again, laughs awkwardly*) I don't know, but I'm not going.

Joanna I see. Wouldn't you enjoy Paris with Les, then?

Donald (*shakes his head*) No.

Joanna Why not?

Howarth Poor old Donald. He's getting quite a grilling.

Joanna looks towards him, shocked, then turns back to Donald. Howarth looks back at his books.

Joanna I'm sorry. (*Silkily.*) Am I grilling you?

Donald No. No, it's all right. (*Laughs.*)

Joanna I may ask you a question or two – by way of conversation?

Howarth lifts his head and looks towards them. Joanna looks at Howarth. Donald glances towards him.

(*Very silkily.*) Well, may I, sir?

Howarth (*laughs*) Darling . . .

Joanna Good. (*Turning back to Donald.*) You were saying you wouldn't enjoy Paris with Les.

Donald I just don't want to be with him – making his scenes and that.

Joanna Scenes? I thought you were friends.

Donald Not any more. He gets on my nerves.

Joanna I see. Poor Les, no wonder he didn't stay for lunch. (*Sips coffee.*)

Howarth He didn't stay for lunch because he'd forgotten the shopping.

Joanna (*looks at Howarth, pause, looks back at Donald*) What does he do that gets on your nerves? (*Little pause. Looks at Howarth.*) May I ask? (*This meant genuinely.*)

Donald (*glances at Howarth*) Well, he's odd.

Joanna looks back at Donald.

There's something wrong with him. He's always depending on me and nagging at me.

Joanna Well, I agree that does sound unpleasant – like a wife. (*Laughs. Looks at Howarth.*)

Donald Yes. (*Nervous laugh.*)

Joanna looks back at Donald. There is a pause as if the conversation is finished. Howarth goes back to his exercise book.

Joanna Why do you think he's like that – with you?

Donald looks across at Howarth for help. Joanna follows his gaze across to Howarth. Howarth looks down at his books.

Donald Well, because, um, his feelings are confused. (*Little pause.*) He's a homo – (*checks himself*) sexual.

Joanna (*after a pause*) Really? (*Pause.*) Has he told you he is?

Donald glances towards Howarth again. Joanna follows his glance. Howarth looks towards them, and pretends to go on correcting.

Donald No, but I can see it now. I really knew it before. I mean, from the way he was always depending on me and making me apologise for things that were his fault. I always knew there was something with him.

Joanna But what *exactly* put you on to him – it must have been very recent. *He* certainly doesn't realise yet that you know.

Donald looks towards Howarth. There is a long, embarrassing pause. Howarth looks at Donald.

Donald Well, um, Richard –

Joanna turns to face Howarth.

– when he saw him and knew who he was from school, he warned me about him.

Howarth I don't think I quite did that, Donald.

Joanna What *did* you say? (*Pleasantly.*) Or is it something private that I oughtn't to know?

Howarth Merely something to the effect that people are what they are, and that we haven't the right to judge them. Donald was slightly worried about Les's tendency to cling. He was finding him a bit oppressive.

Joanna (*to Donald*) Clearly not the person to go to Paris with.

Donald No, that's what Richard said too.

Joanna looks at Howarth.

Howarth Well, again, not quite that, Donald. All I meant – or at least meant to mean – was that if you're going to be forced into someone's company a great deal, then you've got to be sure of the company. I wasn't prescribing, I wouldn't dream of doing so. (*Goes on with his marking.*)

Joanna (*watches him*) But this thing at school – that you knew about. *Is* it private?

Howarth No – well, yes, of course it is. (*Pause.*) It was just the usual schoolboy business. He got a crush on another boy, and there was a little – (*shrugs*) trouble, but it's not for publication – I'm sure Donald knows that.

Joanna (*ironically*) Well, I'll try and guard my tongue too. But I suppose boys grow out of that. I actually wrote anonymous love letters to one of my teachers.

Howarth (*sharply*) The point is that Donald – Les, I mean – hasn't grown out of it – at least from what Donald tells me. Anyway – (*laughs*) it's a bit hard. He just dropped in to be, um, friendly, and we seem to be giving him a bit of a going-over between us. I mean what I said about not judging.

Joanna We are mean, aren't we?

*She looks at Howarth, clearly furious, gets up and
goes out of the room into the kitchen and shuts the
hatch from the other side. There is a silence. Howarth
goes on marking. Donald looks towards him, then
looks down.*

Howarth (*marking, not looking up*) One of the facts of
marriage, Donald, is that ladies, when in an advanced
state of pregnancy, tend to be a trifle, um, dramatic, poor
dears. Still – (*looks at Donald*) you will be careful never
to repeat to anyone – and particularly Les – what I told
you about him.

Donald Oh, no. (*Shakes his head.*) No.

Howarth Anyway, perhaps you'd better get an early
night, eh? In view of tomorrow. (*Turns, smiles at him.*)

Donald (*rising*) I thought we were going to do that last
dictation, you said. I'll be all right for that.

Howarth (*hesitates, then regretfully*) I think we've left it
a bit late really.

Donald Oh. (*Disappointed.*)

Howarth Goodnight.

*Donald takes the dictionary and satchel, makes for
his bedroom door, stops, turns, looks at Howarth.*

Donald If – if I get through my O level, would you help
me then? With my A levels?

Howarth I don't know, Donald.

*Donald looks at him for a moment, then turns, goes
into the bedroom. He turns on the light there, puts
down the satchel, takes off his tie, hesitates, picks up
the dictionary and returns to the living room.*

Donald I just remembered – I mean, I might forget it in the morning. (*Puts it down on the table.*)

Howarth Oh yes, I can't let you have all the luck, can I? Someone else may need it sometime. (*Smiles.*) I've got a lot going on at school at the moment, and next term – when I've finished with that blasted Bishop – I've got to organise the French play, and then I've got the football, the colts, and of course there'll be the baby. (*Smiles.*) But I'm sure we'll manage *something* – for your A levels.

Donald Thank you, Richard.

Howarth Because, you know, you're going to pass tomorrow – and I want you to go on. I intend to take all the credit.

Donald smiles.

Now you go to bed.

Donald turns, goes back to the room. Howarth goes back to his marking. There is a pause. The door opens. Joanna comes in, picks up the cups, etc., then goes out again. Howarth watches her. She comes in again.

Joanna Donald gone to bed?

Howarth Yes. What about you?

Joanna Has he gone to the bathroom yet?

Howarth Um, I don't know. I don't think so.

Joanna sits down.

You going?

Joanna (*coldly*) In a minute.

Howarth looks at her, then turns back to his marking. Donald comes out of the room, in trousers and shirt

413

*with sponge bag. He looks towards Joanna and
Howarth, then hurries out.*

Now then, what the hell were you up to?

Howarth What do you mean?

Joanna Were you trying to put me in my place?

Howarth (*laughs contemptuously*) Of course not.

Joanna Then I assume your odd turns of phrase –
grilling, going over, etc. – were an attempt to cover up
your own indiscretions.

Howarth What indiscretions?

Joanna Your revelations about Les – but then you were
covering a lot of territory – moral and psychological. Do
you do that with all your boys?

Howarth You're being very offensive.

Little pause, they stare at each other.

The occasion doesn't usually arise. He asked me my
advice about Les and I gave it to him. Yes, come to think
of it, I'd do that with any boy – I consider it part of my
job. He simply got hold of the wrong end of the stick,
that's all.

Joanna Well, that's certainly a bad omen for his
examination – if he makes such a hash of understanding
you in English.

Howarth shrugs.

Well?

Howarth Well? (*Little pause. He throws his pen down
on the table.*) What do you want me to do – tell him he's
a bloody little fool for getting it wrong? I've already

414

been extremely tactless with him once today, the last thing I want to do is mess him up again, especially with the examination in the morning. With the chance he's got.

Joanna Richard. (*Pause.*) Richard, look at me, please. (*Politely.*)

Howarth What?

Joanna That's better. You've been dodging your eyes all round me for weeks – except once or twice when you've glared at me. (*Looks away.*) Perhaps I'm not very pleasant to look at.

Howarth What?

Joanna Do you think I don't know? Nine months of just getting fatter and squatter, and going on at you about foetal stages and membranes splitting and shows of water and bottles of urine, not to mention vomiting at the beginning and lying all over the place now. Do you think *I* don't feel it – with *my* tendency to cling?

Howarth Don't be silly.

Joanna And off and on I think, who *would* want to lie beside this swollen sow, *not* flower, and then I think, well, hell, it's just as much your doing, so you can damn well lie beside me and like it. (*She smiles sadly.*) But you don't like it, you haven't liked it for months, and there's nothing I can do about that. Nothing at all. I can't stop you from being disgusted by me, not by law or love.

Howarth Disgusted?

Joanna Don't do that. Not now. If you need time to think, just ask for an intermission. I won't scream.

Howarth gets up, goes over to her, bends down, kisses her on the cheek and sits beside her.

Thank you. But think about it. When did you last kiss me properly? When I was three months gone?

The door opens, Donald comes in.

Donald (*turning, smiling*) Night, Joanna.

Joanna Night, Donald.

Donald Night, Richard.

Howarth Donald.

Donald goes on into his room, puts down his sponge bag and clothes, turns out the light and gets into bed. There is a pause. Howarth attempts to kiss her properly.

Joanna Don't be ridiculous. (*Gently.*) Do you know what I've found out this weekend? I don't like good teachers.

Howarth Don't you?

Joanna They really are self-indulgent. All this business with Donald – moralising, philosophising, gossiping, weeping, advising – it's just self-indulgence. You don't know anything about anything at all, not really.

Howarth (*smiling*) Not really.

Joanna Least of all yourself.

Howarth Least of all myself.

Joanna And you're not, actually, charming me one little bit. (*Gets up.*)

Howarth (*gets up*) Darling . . .

Joanna This isn't a good time to find you out.

Howarth steps back, as if he's been hit. Joanna turns, goes to the door.

Howarth You can't leave it just like that.

Joanna You're busy.

Howarth That can wait, darling! I – (*Gestures to the exercise books.*)

Joanna No, it can't wait. You be as long as you like, Richard. Because I'm bloody tired and want to be asleep.

She opens the door, goes out, closes the door. Howarth stands for a moment, makes a gesture of frustration and anger, then goes to the door, stands there, hesitating, then opens the door and goes into the hall as if to call Joanna. Pause. He goes into the kitchen and comes back munching on a biscuit, looks at Donald's door, then sits down, carrying the biscuit tin and begins marking. There is a slight dimming of light in the lounge to suggest the passing of time.

Donald (*as the lights start to fade, cries out in his sleep*) Please . . . please . . . please . . .

The lights fade out and fade up again. In the living room the centre table lamp on the shelves is on, with just a pool of light round the table where Howarth is still working. In the bedroom, the lights are on and Donald is discovered, moaning and rocking himself to and fro on the chair, still asleep. Howarth hears the sounds, rises and goes to the bedroom door, knocks. No answer.

Howarth Donald, Donald – (*He goes in, leaves the door open.*) Donald! Donald!

He gently puts his hand on Donald's shoulder. Donald wakes with a start, looks up at Howarth.

It's all right, Donald. It's all right.

Donald I'm sorry, Richard, I'm sorry.

*Donald suddenly clasps Howarth round the waist,
burying his face against him. Howarth gently raises
Donald up from the chair. Donald puts his arms
round Howarth.*

Howarth There's nothing for you to be frightened of.
Not here.

Donald starts to cry.

Donald, don't. Don't. (*Puts his arms round him.*) There
there, my Donald, there, my dear old Donald. There, I'm
on your side. I care about you, you know I care about
you. I'll see that nothing can harm you.

*Still embracing Donald, but now with more feeling,
he closes the door, then takes Donald's head in both
his hands and turns his face to his.*
     The lights fade out. As the lights are fading:

Donald, Donald . . .

*After a pause a beam of light comes up in the living
room, focused on the back of the sofa. Joanna, in
dressing gown, is seated there, her head bowed. She
raises her head to face the bedroom door and a beam
of light comes up in the bedroom, focused on the
chair beside the door. Howarth is sitting there, head
raised. Donald is in bed, but the bed and the rest of
the bedroom is in darkness. Howarth looks at
Donald, gets up slowly and leaves the bedroom for
the living room, closing the door. The light fades in
the bedroom and increases in the living room.
Howarth steps into the living room and is going
towards the door when he sees Joanna. They stay
staring at each other for a long time, then Joanna rises
and slowly goes to the door and opens it. Howarth*

*slowly goes past her and out of the room. Joanna
follows and closes the door.*

    *After a pause the morning light slowly builds,
strong sunlight seen through the curtains which are
still shut, and we are into Scene Three.*

SCENE THREE

The Howarths' living room. Morning.

    *Donald wakes, sits up in bed, hunched over for a
minute. He hears a noise from the kitchen and gets
quickly out of bed and starts desperately and hurriedly
to dress, takes off his pyjama jacket and puts on his
shirt, does not stop to put on his tie.*

    *Joanna enters, looks toward the bedroom door, crosses
to the window and opens the curtains by their pulley
cord. Morning light floods the room. She crosses to the
table, pushes the school books downstage on the table
to make way for the tray, slowly goes out again to the
kitchen. After a pause she returns with a tray, having on
it tea, bread and butter and knives and forks, places it on
the upstage side of the table. All this while Donald has
been hurriedly dressing and cramming his possessions
into the carrier bag. Joanna leaves the table and has
reached the door when Donald, dressed and carrying his
bag and satchel starts to open the door. He sees Joanna
and leaps back into the bedroom, begins to close the door.*

Joanna (*still in her dressing gown, sees the door closing*)
Donald!

Donald (*opens the door slowly, carrying the carrier bag
and satchel*) Um, morning, Joanna.

Joanna Good morning, Donald. Your breakfast's ready.
Would you sit down?

*Donald sits at the table. Joanna goes out into the
kitchen. Donald puts his things on the floor beside
him. Joanna returns with a plate of scrambled egg.*

Here you are.

*Sets the plate down in front of him on the tray and
starts to pour him out a cup of tea.*

What time have you got to get to work?

Donald I'm going to the examination hall. It's in the
town hall. Um, at nine o'clock.

Joanna Well, you'd better hurry then, it's already half
past eight. Sugar?

*She passes him the basin from the other side of the
tray. Donald nods, helps himself to sugar. Joanna sits
by the table, watching him. Donald drinks tea, his
hand trembling, and slowly starts to eat the egg,
acutely conscious of her presence. Joanna rises slowly,
takes the biscuit tin from the table up to the hatch,
puts it through and closes the hatch. She continues
watching Donald. Donald takes another sip of tea
and one more forkful of egg to his lips. He can't eat,
looks at Joanna, puts the fork down.*

All right? Nothing else I can give you?

Donald No, thank you. No. That was very nice. Um –
(*Gets up and picks up his things.*)

Joanna (*goes over to the door*) Richard! Donald's just
leaving. (*Goes out to the kitchen.*)

*Donald stares nervously towards the door, his arms
full with bag and satchel.*

Howarth (*enters*) Good morning, Donald. Condemned
man ate a hearty, um –

Gestures towards the table – there is an appalling silence.

My God, your dictionary.

Goes to the table, picks it up, hands it to Donald.

Donald Um, no, it's yours. (*Tries to hand it back.*)

Howarth I know, but – look. I want you to have it, it's a very lucky dictionary, I –

Donald I – I – can't. (*Shakes his head, tries to give it back.*)

Howarth Why not?

Donald Well, it's not – I mean it's too, er . . .

Howarth Nonsense, bloody nonsense, it's not too anything, except wrong of you not to let me give it to you. I – I need you to have it, Donald. Please.

Donald (*takes the dictionary emotionally*) Thank you, Richard. (*Looks down at it.*) You won't be helping me with my A levels, then?

Howarth (*gently*) No, Donald.

Donald nods, suddenly makes a low, sobbing noise.

Donald I don't know what I'm going to do. (*He starts to cry.*)

Howarth (*shuts the door quickly and goes back towards Donald, not close to him*) Donald – what, look, what happened, it was one of those, well, the kind of thing, it could happen to anybody, it caught us, um, me, the thing is to forget what happened, in the end it won't matter, but try to remember me as a teacher. And a friend. I am your friend, Donald.

Donald Yes, Richard.

Howarth It won't matter, nothing will matter except that we, we liked each other, from our different, um, rafts.

Long pause, puts his hand on Donald's shoulder, glances towards the door.

And when you've got your O levels and all the A levels you want, because you will, Donald, and when you're doing, doing – (*moving away*) what you want to do, think of that, eh?

Donald Sir.

Howarth And Donald – if – well, you won't tell anyone about it, will you, ever? Not Les – no one?

Donald (*looks down, whispers*) No, sir. I'm sorry, sir. I'm very sorry.

Pause. Joanna comes in.

Joanna (*entering to between them*) It's getting on.

Howarth Yes, you'd better go.

Joanna sees the dictionary Donald is holding.

Joanna (*tentatively*) Isn't that ours? (*Looks at Howarth.*)

Donald (*holding out the book as if to offer it back*) Well – Richard said –

Joanna Oh, I see.

She goes to Donald and gently pushes the book back into his hands.

Good luck in your examination, Donald.

Donald Thank you, Joanna.

Howarth (*still at other side of sofa*) Yes, Donald, good luck.

Donald Thank you, sir.

*Joanna goes out. Donald follows without looking
back. Pause. Howarth slowly crosses to a chair by the
table, pulls it away from the table and sits. Pause.
Joanna returns, closes the door. She is carrying the
cake box. She crosses down to Howarth, to his left
and holds the box out to him.*

Joanna To say thank you with.

Curtain.

THE CARAMEL CRISIS

The Caramel Crisis was first transmitted by BBC Films on 25 April 1966. The cast included:

Caramel George Cole
Cloon Richard Pearson
Lame John Le Mesurier
McWithers Bryan Pringle
Sir Roy Kynaston Reeves
Mrs Cloon Barbara Miller
Mrs Lame Rosamund Greenwood
Mrs McWithers Edna Petrie
Mrs Portly Winifred Dennis

Director Naomi Capon
Producer Paul Allan
Music Norman Kay

Characters

McWithers

Lame

Cloon

Secretary

Caramel

Switchboard Operator

Mrs Caramel

Mrs Lame

Mrs McWithers

Mrs Cloon

Sir Roy

Mrs Portly

INT. MCWITHERS'S OFFICE. DAY

*The board, McWithers, Lame, Cloon, are watching
someone leave the room. McWithers stares aggressively.
Cloon modestly, with a suggestion of appreciation. Lame
smiles in a superior fashion. The departing person is not
seen. Sound of his footsteps receding. Noise of door
opening and closing. McWithers leaning back, drawing
on his cigarette, and then confidently.*

McWithers Well, what do you think? What do you think?
Cloon?

Cloon Er, yes, he, well, certainly wants the job. Excellent
medical qualifications, experience, and other things.
Seemed, er . . .

Lame smiles in a superior way.

. . . seemed interested and anxious to, anxious to –

Lame Anxious to please. Yes, I wondered if you'd
noticed that. I agree with you there, Cloon. One hundred
per.

*Little pause, while McWithers frowns and Lame
continues with his superior smile. Between Lame and
McWithers there should be a suggestion of rivalry –
McWithers's bluster against Lame's intellectual poise.
In fact, Lame leads, McWithers pretending that the
ideas are his own.*

McWithers Come on then, Lame. (*Laughs.*) Let's have
your version.

Lame There it is. Anxious to please. (*He waits, pretends to be surprised by the confusion around him.*) This, I mean. Everything just a little too right, a little too bright, a little too good, and a little too true about our friend, Reenis.

Cloon Peenels.

Lame (*stammering slightly*) Pen, er, Renels, Pen, er, whatever it is. (*He tries to sound contemptuous, but somehow recoils from the confusion of the name. Then, recovers himself.*) He *wants* too much. Wants the job, I mean. What does McWithers think?

McWithers I've said it before, I'll say it again. It's not smartness we're after. Not cockiness. Not flash, flash, flash. We want a good doctor, yes, and above all a reliable man. You can always tell a reliable man by his look. (*Pause.*) We'll know the one we want. Know him as soon as we clap eyes on him. Because he's reliable. (*Laughs.*) Eh, Cloon? (*But looks sideways at Lame.*)

Cloon (*nods*) Only, er, actually we've seen, er, five. There's only the one left.

Lame (*paying no attention*) We won't pick him, will we? That's the way it goes on a good selection. Meeting, communication, recognition. He'll pick us.

Cloon Yes. But . . .

McWithers Oh yes. (*He settles comfortably and confidently back.*) We'll know, all right. There's always one. Always one.

Lame (*meditatively*) A connection. A correspondence.

McWithers Look out for the reliable man.

Cloon Yes. Only . . .

Lame Osmosis. Osmotic. We'll perceive him osmotically. (*Laughs.*) Is there such a word?

Cloon (*vaguely*) Yes, well, the next one –

He picks up the application form and stares at the photograph on it.

– is the last one, actually.

They look down at the photograph. A buzzer sounds. They look up as the Secretary opens the door.

Secretary Doctor Caramel.

Caramel crosses the room. He is seen as a hazy outline. He sits down.

Lame . . . degree, Doctor Caramel. Distinguished, may I say? (*Looks down at the papers.*) And then, mmm yes, internships, mmm yes, three years – with, mmm yes, mmm, two years, mmm-huh.

McWithers Had experience in large factories, I see. That's important. *We're* a large factory. One of the largest. We're very large indeed. And we've got a good medical staff, good reputation, good equipment, good supplies. You'd be in charge of all that. All of it. At the centre of it.

Lame Your duties will be complex, of course. At first glance simple, in reality complex. This, for example. Three thousand men here, three thousand bodies, which comes to God knows how many limbs, fingers, ears, locks of hair (*laughs*) you'd be responsible for. (*Laughs.*) The work they do is highly unskilled (*laughs again*) and therefore highly dangerous. One hundred per dangerous. This, I mean. Last month in the western block alone two chaps lost their fingers – one each, actually (*laughs again*) in the Sicrex cogs, one chap got his hair caught in the mill-loading nexus, one chap had his (*sudden confusion*) had his, oh, thumb (*with relief*) sliced right off, and –

> *As Lame goes on, camera fixes on Caramel's face, imperturbably nodding.*

– fainted dead away from what Doctor Leak calls monotonous tension, and this, mark you, and this is the western block alone. Apart from the western . . .

> *After a long close-up of Caramel's face during Lame's monologue, camera settles by his face, to suggest a rounded part of it, and concentrates on the board, who go on eagerly talking at him. Lame didactically, with gestures and nervous laughs, McWithers aggressively, with ponderously emphatic movements, and Cloon getting in a worried sentence here and there. But this is all mime.*

Caramel (*voice over*) Westerns're certainly not what they used to be, oh no, all confused now with talking and stuff like that, and no action, violence, stuff you can thrill to, but if I'm lucky there might be a good thriller on with Glenn Ford as a policeman chopping them down with the side of his hand and no conversation except blows and shots and deadly stuff, a bloodbath. (*Pause.*) Will there be a bath at the hotel?

Cloon Oh, bound to be, a big one, yes, really big.

Lame (*simultaneously, voice over*) We're a large factory. One of the largest.

McWithers Very large indeed,

Lame Have you had any experience of Sicrex cogs?

Caramel (*voice over*) Like my mother's . . . Only *she* won't be there screeching at me all the time to come out, and turning off the gas, screech, screech, screech.

Lame (*simultaneously, voice over*) That's all right then, we have rather a lot of trouble with them.

McWithers Have you got any questions, Cloon?

Cloon I must say, your testimonials seem very sound.

Caramel (*voice over*) I can't help it that I like baths, and she has no right to keep me out of them.

Lame (*simultaneously, voice over*) We do have rather a lot of accidents . . . depending, need we say it? On the weather. Odd how accidents rise as the temperature drops. I call it the Healman paradox.

Caramel (*regally*) Yes. Yes. It does make a difference. Naturally it does.

Lame (*nervously, under the impression he is being thought foolish.*) But I don't have to tell *you* that. Of course not. This, I mean . . . This report proves what I've just been saying. (*Fades away, face becoming indistinct.*)

Caramel (*testily*) Chatter, chatter, chatter. Why are they chattering so much? I hope they won't come chattering after me all the time, once I'm comfortably settled, the fat one is nice though, I like him, he looks as if he'd leave people alone.

McWithers (*comes sharply into focus*) . . . a good flat, with lots of room for a family. Of course, you haven't got a family. (*Laughs.*) But if you did have a family, there would be room for it.

Cloon (*anxiously*) As long as it was a very little family, really.

Caramel Does it have a bath?

McWithers A bath?

Lame Exactly. A bath. This is very much to the point. Does it have a bath? Yes, Doctor Caramel – (*glancing slyly at McWithers*) I think you'll find *all* the hygiene facilities in Healman and Co. are adequate. Do I read you right?

Caramel (*again majestically*) I'm glad to hear it.

He proceeds in his dream voice.

(*Voice over.*) Nice, nice, nice, one I can sink into with just my head sticking above the water, but why are they keeping me so long, I won't have time to go to the cinema if they chatter, chatter, chatter unless I go *after* dinner and have my bath when I come back, and perhaps I can say I have an important engagement.

McWithers (*overlapping Caramel's speech, coming into focus*) We'd like you to take up the appointment . . . soon, Doctor Caramel, if we offer you the position. Leak wants to wrap it up by the fifteenth.

Caramel Oh, yes.

Lame Good. Excellent. One hundred per.

Cloon Yes.

McWithers (*jovially*) Well, perhaps you have some questions, Doctor Caramel? Huh?

Caramel No thank you. (*Rises slowly.*) Everything seems quite acceptable.

Cloon (*staring up at him*) Acceptable?

Caramel Yes, thank you.

Lame (*significantly, to Caramel*) Acceptable. Exactly.

Caramel Yes, thank you.

McWithers That's right.

Caramel Goodbye.

The Board Goodbye.

Caramel goes to the door and steps out.

Caramel (*voice is heard from outside*) I might just make it to the nearest cinema if I get a taxi, taxis are warm, deep and warm, so are cinemas, and baths, baths are . . .

Door clicks shut. We see the eager faces of Lame and McWithers, the worried face of Cloon.

Lame (*exuberantly*) Got him. Got him. Got him.

McWithers He's the reliable man. No doubt about that, eh. Lame?

Lame He knows it too. And that's why we want him. Yes, McWithers, *that's* why we want him. Eh, Cloon?

Cloon Yes, er, but only don't you think there was something a little – I mean, that was a funny question about the bath, and he looked, well, half asleep, almost.

McWithers He's not flash, if that's what you mean. No. If it's the flashy man you're after, then Caramel's not the man for you. He's just a solid, reliable man, a stayer. (*Glares humorously at Cloon.*) Myself, I've said it before, I've no use for the flashy man. Nor has Sir Roy. Sir Roy wants men who will last.

Cloon (*fingering his tie*) Yes.

Lame (*tapping his nose in thought*) You see, he'll be out there now, waiting to be told that he's the man we want. Waiting, confidently waiting, to be told. How do I know? Osmosis. (*Laughs.*) Shall we see what he says to our offer, then?

He rises jauntily, followed by McWithers, with Cloon in the rear. Lame opens the door, he and McWithers

437

stare. Cloon can't see, as his view is being blocked, but he stares at their backs.

Cloon Isn't he, er, there then?

McWithers Of course he isn't. (*Wheeling angrily around.*) Why should he hang about? (*Triumphantly, to Lame.*) It was in the bag.

Lame (*rather desperately*) He knew. He knew. And *that* precisely, is why he's gone.

INT. CARAMEL'S FLAT. DAY

The hall and bathroom of the medical flat. Lots of soaps, bath salts, etc., in the bathroom. A telephone in the hall, on a little table. Caramel, enveloped in an enormous towel, pads into the bathroom. He is carrying a book – a sensational paperback (on the cover a girl bound to a chair, gagged, in limited underwear, and a man holding a gun). He is humming a little, and happy. He climbs into the bath, and settles back in the water, after arranging the book on a contraption to support it. Suddenly there is a knocking on the front door. In the conversation that follows the camera is on Caramel.

Lame (*out of shot*) Hello, hello.

Caramel (*not interrupting his reading*) Hello.

Lame (*out of shot*) Well, um – (*At a loss.*) Are you comfortable in there? Having a bath? (*Laughs.*)

Caramel Oh, thank you.

Lame (*out of shot, after a pause*) Well, er – I've just been to see the methodical medico, Leak. He's looking forward to handing over to you and collecting his pension. (*Laughs.*) Seven injuries this week. Seven.

Caramel subsides into the water until his ears are covered, then bobs out.

Caramel Yes, yes. Look, have you got a television set?

Lame (*out of shot*) What? (*Pause.*) A television set? (*Little pause.*) No, no, we never watch television, my wife and I.

Caramel I said *I* haven't got a television set.

Lame (*out of shot, confused*) I see. Haven't got a television set? A goggle box? (*Laughs.*)

Caramel (*pounding the water with his hand, in exasperation*) Yes, I haven't got one. Shouldn't there be one for the flat? I should think they'd put one in. (*He ponders, then craftily:*) For relaxation.

Lame (*out of shot*) I see.

Caramel (*displaying something like impatience*) I said, what about a television set?

Lame (*out of shot*) Yes, I see. (*Pause.*) Are you going to be long in the, er, bath?

Caramel (*now displaying indignation*) I've only just got in.

Pause.

Lame (*out of shot*) I see. Well.

Caramel Goodbye.

Lame Yes, well . . .

Caramel sits listening to Lame's footsteps retreating.

Caramel They'd better get me a set. It's preposterous that I haven't got one.

He settles back with his book. Chuckles at something on the page.

INT. CORRIDOR. DAY

One of the corridors of Healman. During this scene the three of them walking up and down. Lame and McWithers close together. Cloon a little excluded, sometimes being squeezed against the wall.

Lame A trifle odd, perhaps, to come out with it just like that. A trifle odd, and oddly trifling. (*Laughs.*) But one mustn't worry.

McWithers (*heartily*) He knows what he wants, that's all. I like that in a man. You know where you stand with a man if he knows what he wants, and says that he knows . . . (*Sentence gutters out.*) What he . . .

Lame Precisely. I'm with you one hundred per. But we do have this weensy problem of the set.

McWithers If we stand straight with him, he'll stand straight with us. That's always good.

Cloon Should I, er, speak to Sir Roy's secretary about the set?

McWithers So he was, really, actually *in* the bath, you say? At, er, three, was it three you said, in the afternoon?

Lame This I *have* said, already, four times to be precise.

McWithers Yes, well he probably had his reasons. (*Pause.*) Being a doctor and that.

Cloon I could mention it, er, to Sir Roy's secretary? I'm sure he could think of something.

McWithers (*with false joviality*) No, no, no, no, no. No, no. No, man, no. We've got a battery portable at home. Never use it anyway. No need to bother Sir Roy with this. No, no, sounds strange if you don't know the chap.

Cloon (*humbly*) Well, er, I suppose we don't, really. None of us do, do we?

McWithers (*angrily*) Of course we know him. Of course we do. (*Laughs.*) We appointed him.

Camera settles for an instant on Cloon's face, which is very thoughtful. Fades.

INT. CORRIDOR OUTSIDE CARAMEL'S FLAT. DAY

A close-up of the flat door, from behind which are coming mysterious slapping sounds.
  Slap, slap, slap, slap (*pause*), *slap, slap, slap, slap* (*pause*), *slap, slap, slap, slap* (*pause*), *with one variation: slap, slap* (*pause*), *slap, slap* (*pause*), *slap, slap, slap, slap, etc.*
  Then McWithers appears in the corridor. He is whistling unconvincingly. He knocks on the door. No response. He knocks again. Still no response. Stoops, puts his eye to keyhole, then rises and turns away. Suddenly slapping noises begin again. After a while slapping noises become faint.

McWithers Caramel! Caramel! Are you there? It's me, McWithers. McWithers here, Caramel.

INT. CARAMEL'S FLAT. DAY

Quick cut to naked feet, padding down the flat hall then up to Caramel, carrying a portable television set, which he arranges on the hall table – telephone having been put on the floor – so that it can be seen from the bath.

INT. CORRIDOR OUTSIDE CARAMEL'S FLAT. DAY

Cut back to McWithers, looking both angry and bewildered.

McWithers (*hoarsely*) Caramel?

Pause. Then he creeps back and listens – the sound of gunfire punctuating a Western ballad is quite distinct.

INT. CARAMEL'S BATHROOM. DAY

Caramel dabs at his chest with an enormous sponge and stares, wide-eyed, at the television. He is engrossed in it, so that when the telephone rings, its shrillness is discordant. A slight pause, while Caramel adjusts his responses – a frown of irritation, followed by a sudden smile of recollection – to suggest that he was expecting a call. He leans over the side of the bath, picks up a television controller and almost cuts out the sound, leaving a low murmur in the background. The telephone is still ringing, but he keeps his eyes on the screen as he leans over and picks up the receiver. He then has the receiver in one hand, the control in the other.

Caramel (*in a dignified voice*) Dr J. D. Caramel speaking. Thank you for phoning so promptly. About these supplies. (*There is a clicking noise.*) Hello, are you there?

Switchboard Operator (*voice over, telephone*) Hello, Mr Caramel?

Caramel (*a trifle testily*) Now I wanted to change the order, this is very urgent because I'm extremely busy, from *one* box to two boxes. One of . . . (*Another clicking sound, more telephone noises.*) Hello, hello. (*Testily beating his hand against the side of the bath, but still gazing at the television.*)

Switchboard Operator (*voice over, telephone*) Mr Caramel? This is exchange. Mr Caramel. We have a call for you from Whitstable. Are you willing to accept the charges?

Caramel (*jerking upright*) Whitstable. No, no. (*In a panic, then gathering himself together and attempting to resume his dignified voice.*) J. Campbell speaking.

Switchboard Operator (*voice over, telephone, puzzled*) Mr Caramel?

Caramel Campbell. Campbell. This is Henry Campbell.

Mrs Caramel (*voice over, telephone*) Hog, hog, hog –

Caramel Caramel is not known at this number. Goodbye.

He scrambles receiver onto telephone. He is now sitting bolt upright, gazing ahead, his mouth hanging open. The television control is still in his other hand. The room suddenly fills with:

Mrs Caramel (*voice over, telephone, furious*) A hog, I say. Only a hog spends all his time in the bath. Only a hog steals his dead brother's papers. His own dead brother, who slaved and slaved to qualify. Only a hog lives off his widowed mother's pension, and wears his dead brother's clothes, and wears his shoes, only a hog, yes, a hog, hog, hog, would . . .

Caramel recoils, and as he does so presses the button of the controller so that the last 'hogs' are cut off by the sound of gunfire. Caramel blinks, focuses on the screen, and gradually the smile of comfort and pleasure returns to his face. He drops the controller and settles back in his bath.

INT. MCWITHERS'S OFFICE. DAY

Lame is sitting on the desk, legs crossed and slightly hunched. Cloon is standing sideways to the desk, with a sheet of paper in his hand. McWithers is sitting. The office consists of the desk, telephone, and perhaps a photograph of McWithers's wife – a wedding photograph.

Lame How – precisely – much was it?

Cloon Sixty pounds, eleven shillings and ninepence halfpenny.

Lame Well, yes – (*struggling for insouciance*) that's a tidy little sum, in a sloppy sort of way. (*Laughs.*) Yes. Sixty pounds, eleven shillings and ninepence halfpenny. Most of that – (*appears confident and casual, clearly is neither*) on medical supplies, doubtless? Bandages, syringes, forceps, this kind of thing?

Cloon (*impassively reading*) Two boxes of frozen eclairs, six hundred cigarettes, tipped, six hundred cigarettes, untipped, a carton of crisps, and a box of salt. Five bottles of whisky. An electric blanket. An electric razor. A tin of olives. A box of Turkish delight. Two bars of milk chocolate and a carton of fruit gums. No, er, medical supplies here. (*Pause.*) No cash either. (*Pause.*) Ordered by telephone. (*Long pause.*) Perhaps we ought just to mention it to Sir Roy's secretary. Or I could write to Sir Roy himself enclosing the canteen bill. If I wrote a polite note, explaining that I thought he'd be interested in the bill . . . (*pause*) he wouldn't mind. Er, too much. Er, he might even be pleased.

McWithers No, no, no. No, man, no. He won't be pleased. (*Gazes at Cloon, then at Lame.*) Remember that Sir Roy's very sick. A very sick old – er – man.

Cloon Yes.

Lame Extremely sick.

McWithers Look, look, he doesn't start until tomorrow. Officially he doesn't. *Of course!* (*Stands up and slaps the table triumphantly.*) Look, he wants to pay for the canteen stuff out of his salary. Look, this is all right. All he's done is – (*Pause, blankly, then as if inspired.*) He needs a vacation. Needs to rest up, relax, take baths and – and – and watch television. He's going to start on a big responsibility tomorrow. (*Pauses again.*) I *admire* him for relaxing. I think he's all right. It *shows* he's all right. It shows we were right to pick him. He's a solid man, an independent man. We want independent men. We need them. We don't want yes-men in Healman, do we?

He glares at Cloon.

Cloon No.

Lame (*with assumed brightness*) I'm with you one *thousand* per. (*He exits.*)

McWithers Sir Roy doesn't want yes-men in Healman, does he?

Cloon No.

McWithers No. He *does not*.

He leaves the room. Camera settles on Cloon's thoughtful face.

Cloon No. No, he doesn't.

INT. LAME'S SITTING ROOM. NIGHT

A stiff, fashionable, ridiculously uncomfortable armchair in which Lame is sitting. He is reading the New Statesman, *but partially looking over the top. Mrs Lame is seen only partially. She is basket-weaving.*

Lame He starts work tomorrow.

Mrs Lame Will it be all right, do you think?

Lame No.

Mrs Lame Never mind, my little cream pickles.

Lame stares at her yearningly.

You've something on the tip of your nose.

Lame touches his nose.

Lame It's a pimple. (*Then, self-pityingly*) A worry pimple. (*Yearns more insistently.*)

Mrs Lame Well, we'll listen to the Third tonight. There's always something extra special on a Tuesday.

Lame goes back to his New Statesman. *Speaks wheedlingly from behind it.*

Lame I don't want to listen to the Third, my darling. I don't *want* to hear any music.

Mrs Lame What would you like, my little pineapple? (*Her voice is detached.*)

Lame (*after a pause*) I want to be comforted.

He lowers the New Statesman *and stares at her desperately.*

Mrs Lame The Third will comfort you. You know it will.

Pause. Lame strokes the tip of his nose.

446

INT. MCWITHERS'S BEDROOM. NIGHT

Large bed. McWithers's face is illuminated by a pool of light from a bedside lamp. He is smoking a cigar. Mrs McWithers in the darkness, beside him, her hair in rollers. She is making low, sobbing noises.

McWithers He'd better be there tomorrow. (*Small pause.*) I wish you'd stop that. It's what every husband wants. All men want that.

Mrs McWithers moans.

(*Automatically and abstractedly.*) Shut up, shut up, shut up.

Little pause. Mrs McWithers moans.

I know he'll come. He'll show up all right. He'll do his stuff.

Little pause. Mrs McWithers moans.

If you don't stop that I'll pinch you.

Little pause. Mrs McWithers gasps.

That Lame thinks he's smart, does he? I've got my eye on him. I *trust* Caramel. (*Stubs out cigar, then rolls over, towards the shadow of his wife, and shouts:*) You do want me really, don't you? I know you do.

Increased sobs.

Answer me, you'd better answer me or I'll give you you know what.

Little pause. Mrs McWithers gasps.

INT. CLOON'S KITCHEN. NIGHT

A kitchen stool, on which Cloon, with his toes turned in,

is sitting. The hand passing him the coffee is all that is seen of Mrs Cloon, but it should be a very plump hand. While this conversation takes place, her presence is registered by sinister kitchen noises – saucepans being scraped, perhaps, or crust being grated – anyway, something that contrasts grotesquely with the sound of her voice, which is sweet but also menacing.

Mrs Cloon All I can say, Dirk – (*scrape, scrape*) is that I do hope you know what you're doing.

Cloon is fiddling with the spoon, examining it first, then rapping it nervously against the saucer.

Cloon Yes, I hope so, my dear.

Mrs Cloon Be careful with the spoondle, Dirk. (*Scrape.*)

Cloon Spoondle?

Mrs Cloon The spoon. It's called a spoondle. The top-let unscrews for use as an olive skewer. (*Scrape, scrape.*) And if you're wrong, Dirk, they won't want you any more. If you're wrong, and McWithers finds out you've written to Sir Roy, Dirk –

Cloon I know, my dear.

Cloon is fiddling about with the spoon quietly.

Mrs Cloon And I, for one, won't blame them. (*Scrape.*) You know that, don't you, Dirk?

Particularly dreadful scrape, which causes Cloon to twitch nervously.

Cloon Yes, my dear.

He stirs coffee with spoondle.

INT. SIR ROY'S STUDY. NIGHT

A wheelchair, with Sir Roy Healman in it. Small tables around him, with lit candles on them. A table in front of him, on which is Cloon's letter. There is a stick across Sir Roy's knee. He is being fed gruel by a hand holding up a spoon. Mrs Portly's hand should be covered with bracelets, rings, etc. and should jangle when she plies the spoon.

Mrs Portly (*cockney, sweet, flirtatious voice*) You could do it yourself, you know you could. It's just you and your tricks. You're as spry as a monkey in a barrel of peanuts.

Sir Roy (*in a wheezy voice, rapping the letter on the table with the end of the stick*) I'm going to the factory tomorrow, to have a word with Cloon.

Mrs Portly There you are, you see. If you're nimble enough to get up to the factory, you're nimble enough to feed your own mouth.

Sir Roy (*makes a hideous sound that is probably a laugh*) I'll break them, break them to pieces, if they've made a mistake.

Gruel leaks out of his mouth, dribbles down his chin, and is trapped by the spoon – with a jangle of bracelets.

Mrs Portly Oh, you. You'd break everything, if you had your way. (*Pause.*)

INT. MCWITHERS'S OFFICE. DAY

McWithers is sitting at his desk with the telephone. During this conversation Lame is constantly touching the tip of his nose. Cloon is standing behind McWithers.

McWithers *All* the sheds? You've tried all the sheds?

Cloon Yes.

McWithers And he's not in any of them?

Cloon No.

Lame (*meaninglessly*) Mysterious. A man of mystery.

He attempts his usual, nervous laugh, dabs at his nose instead.

McWithers But God, man, it's half past eleven. Half past eleven. (*Pauses, then, his voice brightening.*) Perhaps he's had an accident? Do you think he's had an accident?

Cloon No.

Lame Indestructible man of mystery. (*Laughs again, in the same ghastly way.*) Super-duper one-hundred-per man of mystery. (*Pause.*)

McWithers Well, it's all right. I'm sure it's all right.

Lame (*pulling himself together*) Someone must have heard something from him this morning? Something?

Cloon (*after a little pause, then with a suggestion of relish*) Yes. (*Little pause.*) He phoned down to the shop. (*Pause.*)

McWithers (*carefully, but expecting the worst*) What did he want?

Cloon He wanted another carton of potato crisps.

McWithers Potato crisps? Well. Well. Potato crisps, eh? Potato crisps, eh? (*Stops pacing and with thundering decisiveness:*) That's one thing we can stop.

He looks to Cloon, who now has a funny little smile on his face. At Lame, who is more hunched – one shoulder higher than the other – than before, and trying to whistle.

We can stop that. That's all right. We can put a stop to that sort of thing.

He picks up the receiver, shakes it, then shouts into it.

Switchboard?

Switchboard Operator (*voice over, telephone*) Yes, sir.

McWithers Listen to this. It's McWithers here. Now pay attention to me.

Switchboard Operator (*voice over, telephone*) Yes, sir.

McWithers Now don't accept any calls from the medical flat. Do you understand me? *Under no circumstances* are you to accept *any* calls from the medical flat. We're putting a stop to it. (*Replacing receiver.*) We've put a stop to that, all right.

Lame (*jerking upright*) If he put through a call this morning, *and* nobody's seen him since – *then* he's probably still here.

Cloon (*showing repressed excitement*) Yes.

Lame And he won't answer the phone.

Cloon (*almost shrilly*) No.

McWithers (*staring at Cloon*) Pull yourself together, man. Everything's all right. Everything's quite all right.

Lame So what we can do is – go up and get him. Bring him down. Fire him. Tell everyone he was – was taken ill. Get hold of that other man, Penners –

Cloon Rennis.

Lame (*stroking his nose*) Reenis, yes, yes, get hold of him. Quickly. This we can do. Without worrying Sir Roy in any way.

451

McWithers That's right. That's right. Sir Roy's a very sick man. He mustn't know a thing. Mustn't bother him with this trivial business. Let's go to it.

He goes towards the door, Lame follows, Cloon doesn't. McWithers calls to Cloon.

Come on, man. Come on.

Cloon Yes, yes. I've just got to, er, make a little call.

INT. CARAMEL'S FLAT. DAY

Caramel, humming, is in the bathroom. The bath is full and steamy, but Caramel, fully dressed, is spreading objects out on a table beside it. A thriller. A bottle of salts. A glass of whisky. Three packets of crisps. An apple. He could be shown passing from the hall into the bathroom, and out again, several times, and with the various objects in his hand. Suddenly there is a banging. He stands still, alert. During the first part of this only he is shown. McWithers and Lame are only voices.

McWithers (*out of shot*) Caramel! (*Imperious.*) Caramel!

Lame (*out of shot*) It's us. (*Facetiously*) Time to come out now, Caramel.

McWithers (*out of shot*) Open up, man.

Caramel stands in the hall, the apple in his hand, looking irritated. He takes a bite of the apple and listens.

(*Out of shot*) Caramel.

Caramel (*frowns, scratches cheek with apple, then quietly*) Yes.

McWithers (*out of shot*) We want to see you, Caramel.

Lame (*out of shot*) Caramel.

Caramel takes a bite of apple, looks wistfully towards the bathroom.

McWithers Are you there!

Caramel Yes. Yes. What do you want?

McWithers (*out of shot, shouting*) Want, man? It's nearly twelve o'clock. You were meant to be on duty at eight thirty. (*A little pause, and then, in a conciliatory voice.*) Did you forget? I expect you thought you weren't on until later. We'd better hurry down there, Caramel. There's at least one case of monotonous tension waiting for you.

Long pause, while Caramel does nothing.

Caramel?

Caramel Yes?

McWithers (*out of shot*) Are you coming?

Caramel I'm not very well. I'm feeling a little feeble. I've been off my food.

McWithers (*out of shot*) What's the matter with you, man?

Caramel Measles. I've got measles.

Lame (*out of shot*) Measles?

INT. CORRIDOR OUTSIDE CARAMEL'S FLAT. DAY

McWithers and Lame in low conference.

McWithers Caramel. Caramel. We'd better take a look at you.

453

Caramel (*out of shot*) Why?

Lame You may need help. There may be something we can do.

INT. CARAMEL'S FLAT. DAY

Caramel is sitting on the edge of the bath. He pulls the coffee table forward.

Caramel (*ponders a second, then*) Well, I'm short on entertainment if I'm going to be cooped up here with measles for a long time. Could you get me some books and magazines? I'm very fond of thrillers.

McWithers (*out of shot, beating on door*) Open up. Open the door, do you hear?

Caramel You'd better go away, because I've got to lie down now.

Lame (*out of shot*) No. You must open the door.

Caramel You'll get mumps, if you come in. You don't want mumps do you?

Lame (*out of shot*) I thought you said you had measles?

Caramel Yes.

INT. CORRIDOR OUTSIDE CARAMEL'S FLAT. DAY

McWithers is pressed close to the door, Lame is standing beside him.

McWithers (*in pleasant, supplicating voice*) Listen, Caramel. I appointed you. Lame and me. We liked you at once. We chose you because you're the right man for the job. I said you were a solid man. Do you hear that,

Caramel, a solid man? I said you were just the kind of man Sir Roy likes, Caramel. I said you were a *stayer.*

Caramel (*out of shot*) Oh, don't worry. I'm not going.

Lame lets out a hysterical laugh.

McWithers If Sir Roy finds out, there'll be trouble. (*He taps on door.*) Terrible trouble. He's a very sick old man. He gets upset. (*Taps again.*) But it'll be all right. If you come down now and look after the monotonous tension case, it'll be all right.

Caramel (*out of shot*) Who's Sir Roy? I haven't met any Sir Roy, have I?

Lame (*turning as there is the sound of a door opening at the end of the corridor*) Here's Cloon. Where's he been, anyway?

He has turned right round and is staring aghast. McWithers turns, too, and is also aghast. Cloon is pushing Sir Roy in his wheelchair. Sir Roy has his rug over his knees, and his stick across his rug. His head is hanging down. Cloon's face is solicitously close to his. Sir Roy lifts his head up, and coughs. His face is full of senile venom.

Sir Roy Get me to the door.

McWithers and Lame surge around him, but he waves his stick at them.

No, no. I want Cloon. Cloon to push me.

Cloon pushes him to the door, as Lame and McWithers fall back, behind the chair. Cloon stands beside the chair, close to the door.

McWithers Yes, sir. Everything's fine, sir. We've sorted things out. You're a very sick old man, sir.

Lame's hysterical laugh is heard.

No, I mean Doctor Caramel is a very sick old man. He's been struck down by a – by a – sickness, sir, but he's a good man, sir. Reliable. The man we want.

Sir Roy (*making feeble gesture with stick*) Tell him to open up, Cloon. Tell him I want to see his face. (*Pause.*)

Cloon (*rapping on the door*) You'd better open the door, Caramel. Sir Roy has come. I advise you to open the door at once. Sir Roy intends to speak to you, and he wants to see your face.

He steps aside importantly, leaving Sir Roy alone facing the door.

Caramel (*out of shot*) What does he want to see my face for?

Sir Roy gestures with his stick, and begins to cry out hoarsely, but his voice gathers a manic strength as he goes on, ending in something close to a scream.

Sir Roy Smash it down. Smash it down, Caramel. (*Brandishes the stick feebly.*) Smash it down. Smash you down. Smash you down, Caramel. Smash.

This screamed, as with appalling strength and in a crazed frenzy, he suddenly launches himself out of the chair, the stick held above his head to deliver a blow at the door. He brings the stick down at the precise second the door opens. He falls into the hall.

INT. CARAMEL'S FLAT. DAY

McWithers Quick, man, quick. You're the doctor. Look at him. Is he all right? Quick, man.

As Caramel comes slowly forward:

He might have broken something.

Caramel, eating crisps, comes between Cloon and Lame and stares with curiosity at the broken figure for a time. Then:

Caramel I expect he's broken everything. He's very old, from the look of him. He shouldn't be hurling himself about like that, at his age.

Noises and cries from the floor, as if in agonised reply.

Lame (*hysterical, to Caramel*) What can we do? Oh, God, what can we do?

Caramel Oh well, I should get him to a hospital if I were you. (*Slight pause, then in a dreamy voice.*) Hospitals are very comfortable.

He turns away from them.

McWithers Yes, yes. We'll rush him to a hospital and save him. It'll be all right if we save him. He'll be grateful.

Cloon (*staring down, dully*) Yes. Save him.

Lame The telephone. Phone for an ambulance.

Cloon (*starting into life*) Yes, the telephone.

Goes to pick it up, but is shouldered aside by McWithers, who shouts:

McWithers I'll do it. *I'll* do it. *I'll* save him.

Grabs the phone, glares at Cloon, who shrinks back.

Hello, switchboard. Hello. Listen to this. This is me, do you understand?

Switchboard Operator (*voice over, telephone, brightly and mechanically*) I am sorry, sir. We cannot accept any calls from the medical flat at this time.

McWithers (*kneeling*) Hello. No, no. It's all right. It's perfectly all right. This is urgent.

Switchboard Operator (*voice over, telephone*) I am sorry, sir. We are cutting you off now. (*Click.*)

McWithers (*pounding the telephone bar*) Hello. Hello. Hello. Hello.

Long pause. Cloon places his hand on McWithers's shoulder. McWithers drops the telephone, turns around.

It's no good now. It's all right.

Lame I'll do it from downstairs. From downstairs.

McWithers (*stands up, then dully as if in a trance*) Yes, but it's no good, you see. It's all right. Everything is . . . (*Voice trails off.*)

Cloon Yes.

During this, Caramel has disappeared. He now reappears with a small bag in his hand, and his pockets stuffed with bags of crisps. He slips past them and out of the door.

INT. CORRIDOR OUTSIDE FLAT. DAY

Caramel goes down corridor, past the wheelchair. His dreamy voice floats back.

Caramel (*voice over*) Ridiculous nonsense, never leaving people in peace. Coming crashing up to *my* flat, shouting and dying everywhere, chatter, chatter, chatter, trouble,

458

trouble, trouble, and trouble with *her* too, if I have to go back there. (*Pause.*) But anyway if I take a taxi I could get to a cinema for the first performance, and if it's a Western it'll be worth it, an old-fashioned simple Western with . . .

Voice fades away as he rounds a corner.

INT. CLOON'S KITCHEN. NIGHT

Mrs Cloon is icing a cake. She is out of shot except for her hands. Cloon, on his stool, sits staring blankly down at an olive on the spike of the spoondle.

Mrs Cloon (*out of shot*) Yes, well, Dirk, I warned you. You're finished there now, you know. McWithers and Lame will see to that. They'll force you out, now the old man's gone. *They'll* have all the power now. You know that, don't you, Dirk?

Cloon (*still gazing at the olive on the spoondle*) I know, my dear.

Mrs Cloon (*out of shot*) Well, Dirk, what are you going to do? Can you tell me that? What are you going to do? Nobody will as much as look at you now, Dirk. What will you do?

> *Cloon plucks the olive off the top, looks down at the pointed end of the spoondle as the scraping noise rises and rises, to an almost unbearable pitch. For a second his face goes mad, his eyes fix on where his wife would be; he holds the spoondle up so that it becomes a menacing weapon, then the noise subsides, his face returns to normal, and he pops the olive into his mouth.*

Cloon I don't know, my dear. (*Pause.*)

INT. LAME'S SITTING ROOM. NIGHT

Lame sits in his ridiculous chair, a bowl of soup in a deep, black, ridiculous bowl, a large almost flat spoon, on his lap. His knees are pressed together. Mrs Lame is unseen, but she makes little slurping noises as she talks – soup-drinking noises.

Mrs Lame (*out of shot*) Why are you looking so sad (*slurp*), my little cactus? I thought it all turned out well. You're very sad –

Lame Am I?

Mrs Lame (*out of shot, slurp*) – and I don't know why.

Lame (*staring intensely towards her*) It's been difficult. A shock.

Mrs Lame (*out of shot*) They're doing Stravinsky, 'Rites of Spring'. (*Slurp.*) 'Rites of Spring' will relax you.

Lame (*almost in tears*) I don't *want* Stravinsky. I want *you*. I want *you* to relax me.

Mrs Lame (*out of shot*) The Stravinsky will do you good. He's your favourite modern. (*Slurp. Her voice becomes coldly affectionate.*) And afterwards I'll pop your pimple. It's ready for popping. (*Slurp.*)

Lame strokes his nose and stares at her.

INT. MCWITHERS'S BEDROOM. NIGHT

McWithers's head in the pool of light from the lamp, as before. His face is mad with triumph. Beside him there is the dark bundle of Mrs McWithers.

McWithers It's all right. I knew it would be. (*Chuckles.*) I knew it would be. They'll have a big burial, and then we're in. I'm in. Oh (*chuckles*), there'll be some changes. (*Chuckles.*) Cloon. (*Voice becomes sinister.*) Cloon. (*Little pause.*) Lie still. Why do you always roll away from me? You've got a duty to me. (*Little pause.*) I'll see about Cloon. I'll settle with him all right. I'll settle with Lame too, later on. (*Chuckles.*)

Mrs McWithers has begun to whimper.

Shut up. I haven't done anything yet.

He laughs. Rolls over, props himself up on his elbow, shows a hand, as if to grab her, but there is a click, and the lamp goes off. Mrs McWithers whimpers.

Darkness.

SLEEPING DOG

Sleeping Dog was first transmitted on BBC TV on 11 October 1967. The cast included:

Sir Hubert Marius Goring
Lady Caroline Rachel Kempson
Greatorix Denys Graham
Claud Johnny Sekka
Young Man Nicholas Critchley
Sir Geoffrey Peter Graves
Barmaid Wendy Ascott

Producer Graeme McDonald
Director Warris Hussein

Characters

Sir Hubert

Lady Caroline

Greatorix

Claud

Young Man

Sir Geoffrey

Barmaid

Removal Man

EXT. COLONIAL BUNGALOW IN AFRICA. NIGHT

Long shot. The bungalow is brilliantly lit, curtainless.
Sound of a woman's voice singing to a piano
'Somewhere over the Rainbow', which goes straight into
group singing of 'For He's a Jolly Good Fellow'.
Then a plump man, not properly seen for the
darkness, comes out onto the porch. The music stops.

Sir Hubert Whitey, Whitey. Here, boy. Come on, boy.
Come along.

Other shapes join him.

Voice One (*slightly tipsy*) What's the matter?

Voice Two Whitey's gone.

Sir Hubert Come along, come along. Chocolates, Whitey.
Whitey, chocolates.

Other Voices Whitey, chocolates, here boy, here sir.

The piano starts again, woman's voice singing
'Somewhere over the Rainbow', leaving the plump
man on the porch. Then he too turns, goes in.

Mix: exterior, bungalow. Same shot of the house, now
completely silent. The plump man on the porch.

Sir Hubert Whitey, Whitey, here Whitey.

There is a silence, then sudden rustlings, bird cries.
Close-up of Sir Hubert's face, lips open. Then shot of
the garden, which appears to be full of strange but

human shapes, figures in feathers, tribal kit, but none of these seen properly. Back to Sir Hubert, staring intently.

(*Tentatively.*) Whitey, Whitey?

Silence, then rustlings, wing flappings, parrot voices.

Parrots Whi-ey. Whi-ey. He-ah, Whi-ey, hah, hah, hah.

Sir Hubert stares around, licks his lips, then bellows:

Sir Hubert Whitey.

More flapping sounds from parrots, to shot of running movements in the garden.

Parrots Whi-eee hee hee.

There is a sudden silence. Long shot of the house, the figure on the porch joined by a lady in a long, white dress.

Lady Caroline Did you hear him?

Sir Hubert No. No. Er, just the birds. Whitey, Whitey, sir. Come along.

This is met by complete silence. Then long shot to the sound of muted chucklings and flappings.

Fade.

EXT. COTTAGE. DAY

A large cottage in the country, set in a lawn, with a drive cutting through. It is mid-afternoon. There is a car in the drive, facing the French windows, although some way from them. Lady Caroline is standing by a neat flower bed, sniffing the flowers. There is a faint hum of a bee. She bends over a flower, the humming becomes louder,

she jumps back, a bee erupts, buzzes noisily past her.
Shot of her in close-up, looking startled. She turns, walks
across the lawn, towards the windows.

INT. LIVING ROOM. DAY

The living room, with the French windows that look
over the lawn and the drive. Lady Caroline enters. The
room is empty, except for a chair by the window. No
carpets. Full of sunlight. She walks across the room to
a door on the left, opens it, calls up.

Lady Caroline Hu-bert. Hu-bert.

> *She waits a second, then turns to the door on the*
> *right, opens that, as if experimentally and for the first*
> *time. There is a small passage opposite, with a door*
> *at the end, slightly open, with a large bolt opposite it.*
> *To her right the hall. Lady Caroline looks to the right,*
> *to the left, frowns at the door, then goes back into the*
> *living room, walks to the chair. She opens her handbag,*
> *takes out a small silver flask, raises it to her lips, takes*
> *a swallow, shakes the flask, puts it back into the*
> *handbag, takes out a bag of peppermints, pops a*
> *couple into her mouth. She sighs, looks around the*
> *room, gets up and goes towards the door, right.*

INT. BASEMENT ROOM

The room, windowless, is lit by a naked bulb. On one
wall there is a ring and a bolt. There are a few boxes,
pieces of wood, old tins, to the right; and to the left
there is a heavy door, padded with old felt.
  Sir Hubert and Mr Greatorix are standing under the
light. Sir Hubert has his hat in his hand, Greatorix has a
sheaf of papers, which he looks at.

Greatorix I must say I can't smell anything, Sir Hubert.

Sir Hubert sniffs.

And I can tell the damp straight away, it goes straight to my nostrils like arthritis, I think it is.

Sir Hubert Come, sir, a definite odour. (*Sniffs again.*) It's a dog. I know a dog when I smell one.

Greatorix Now you mention it, Sir Hubert, the Kerneys did have a dog, an Alsatian, yes. Perhaps they gave it the run of the basement.

Sir Hubert points to the ring and the bolt on the wall.

Sir Hubert Not much of a run, I think. Kept the poor brute chained. (*He turns, points to the door.*) And look at that stuff on the door, so they needn't hear it when it's barking out for them. There's a garden, isn't there?

Looks at Greatorix.

Greatorix Oh yes, Sir Hubert, a particularly lovely one, as you commented yourself.

Sir Hubert (*almost to himself*) Can't say I like that. Can't say I like it at all.

Greatorix lowers his voice confidentially.

Greatorix I quite agree, Sir Hubert. Of course, strictly between you and me and these four walls, Mr Kerney . . . (*Raises and lowers the papers to his mouth, in drinking movements.*) But I think I can promise you we can get the smell out, Sir Hubert, if –

Sir Hubert (*shakes his head*) We have an obligation when we take them on. (*Little pause.*) I'd like you to pass that on to these Kerneys, when you see them. Tell them they need freedom.

Greatorix ducks his head in embarrassment.

Greatorix Oh, I will, Sir Hubert, I most certainly will. Of course, Greendene has a lovely smell in the summer, lovely from the garden –

He is interrupted by Lady Caroline pushing the door open. She should be seen to be still sucking on a peppermint.

Lady Caroline Oh, here you are, I must say I've been looking all over for you, upstairs and outside, shouting at the top of my voice, and Hubert, I was nearly stung by a bee.

Sir Hubert (*in alarm*) But you're all right, my dear? (*Goes to her.*)

Lady Caroline Yes, I am, but it gave me a nasty shock, it was a very big one. (*Looks around.*) What a horrid place.

Greatorix Just an old storeroom we think it was, Lady Caroline.

Lady Caroline Ooooh, and what an odour.

Sir Hubert It was a prison, my dear, where these people Kerney kept their dog.

Lady Caroline Well, why don't you come upstairs and talk there, it's quite fresh upstairs.

She makes for the door, followed by Sir Hubert. Greatorix, following Sir Hubert, makes a cynical face to himself.

Greatorix I can see that you're fond of dogs.

INT. LIVING ROOM. DAY

Lady Caroline enters, talking, followed by Sir Hubert and Greatorix.

Lady Caroline . . . dearest little thing, and we still don't know what happened to him. The MacPhersons have written twice to say they haven't found him. And on the last night too. Of course, Whitey was very intelligent, poodles are, they know when there's going to be a change, don't they. Hubert?

Sir Hubert, an expression of pain on his face, nods.

Sir Hubert Almost certain that a snake got him.

Greatorix Well, I think I can assure you there aren't any snakes in Greendene. (*Chuckles, clears his throat.*) Now my own view, for what it's worth, is that the asking price is very reasonable, very. I'm given to understand that if Mr Kerney hadn't passed so unexpectedly, with an estate to be settled in Scotland, more could have been tried for. But that's only my own personal view.

Sir Hubert So this Kerney is dead, is he?

Greatorix Yes, most tragic and unexpected, although not really surprising, as I think I hinted (*to Lady Caroline*) downstairs to Sir Hubert, Mr Kerney had a little problem.

He makes drinking movement. Lady Caroline glares back at him.

Sir Hubert (*sharply*) May I ask how you intend to convey my remarks to him, sir, if this Kerney is dead?

Greatorix (*after a pause of recollection*) Ah, well, I – his relatives would be most interested to hear. *Mrs* Kerney is still with us.

Sir Hubert A lady, sir? They're scarcely remarks to be passed on to a lady.

Greatorix ducks his head.

Now, my dear, what do you think?

Lady Caroline Well, will we be able to get a gardener?
We'll need one with all the grass, and those beds need
a lot of work to keep them nice. You know how much
I love gardening, Hubert –

Hubert nods.

– but even so it's a big house, I couldn't look after it by
myself, could I? (*To Greatorix.*) We've heard the domestic
problem is terrible now. In Kjiarna we shared two
marvellous boys with the MacPhersons for the garden,
and of course I didn't have to lift a finger around the
house, but I still had to think of everything. It's quite
a responsibility, dear, that's what I'm saying, a garden
this size.

Sir Hubert (*going to window*) But ah, my dear, it's an
English garden, and much more orderly by nature. Think
what that means. I can hear the difference.

Lady Caroline (*to Greatorix*) We had wild parrots in
Kjiarna, we think they were parrots, Hubert never really
found out, but even so, Hubert, it's a lot to bite off by
myself.

Greatorix Well now, I agree that's a very important
point, Lady Caroline, but I think I can assure you on
that. The Kerneys had a gardener, and a girl up from the
village for the house. I think you'll find Greendene is the
sort of house that runs itself once everything's arranged.

*While Greatorix is talking, Sir Hubert has been
looking out of the window, smiling. Then he stops
smiling, squints.*

EXT. GARDEN. DAY

Shot of the garden, serene but slightly out of focus.

INT. LIVING ROOM. DAY

On Sir Hubert's face.

Sir Hubert Do you have any Kibbobolas in the neighbourhood?

He turns to Greatorix, stares at him intensely.

Lady Caroline (*laughs*) In Sussex, dear?

Sir Hubert (*blinks, chuckles*) Habit, you know, habit.

He nods, smiles at Greatorix. Turns back to the window, squints at the garden, now seen in normal shot.

Well, dear, if you're satisfied, I'll meet these Kerneys' – Mrs Kerney's price. (*Smiles at Lady Caroline.*) For a special occasion, after all. (*Said very tenderly.*)

Greatorix Well, I'm very happy. I think Mrs Kerney will be very happy indeed that it's passing into such – and if we're all agreed I can promise to expedite the matter very quickly indeed. As far as I'm concerned you can virtually call it your own as soon as the papers are signed. (*Stops, smiles.*) A special occasion, did you say, Sir Hubert?

Sir Hubert (*after a pause*) A wedding present. (*Smiles at Lady Caroline.*)

Greatorix Well, I'm sure your bride will be very happy here. (*He turns, bows to Lady Caroline.*)

Lady Caroline Thank you very much, although really of course it's an anniversary. (*With a laugh.*)

Greatorix (*laughing*) Ah! I thought so. Of course, of course.

Sir Hubert Our first anniversary.

Lady Caroline They said in Kjiarna that he was so busy sentencing Kibbobola he hardly had time to notice English ladies, did you, Hubert? (*Giggling.*)

Sir Hubert (*very gravely*) I noticed *you*, my dear.

A long pause while he gives her a long, possessive smile. She giggles, takes a peppermint out of her bag, pops it into her mouth.

Lady Caroline It took you five years to say so, though.

Greatorix (*coughing*) I expect you've noticed some changes, since coming back. (*Shakes his head sadly.*)

Sir Hubert turns back to look in the garden.

Sir Hubert None at all.

Lady Caroline Oh, but Hubert, think of the clothes. In my day we wouldn't have been allowed on the beaches in those, some of them.

Sir Hubert Fashion, my dear. Fashion passes. But I look into this garden and I see the grass of the country as it always was. The trees are English, as we remember them. And those are English birds, I know their sounds. (*Turns to Greatorix.*) If you had brought me a Sussex hedge robin during a Kjiarna thunder, I would have known it for a hedge robin, and would have attributed it to Sussex, sir, I think.

Greatorix Greendene's particularly fortunate in its birds, Mrs Kerney –

Sir Hubert (*lifting a finger*) But bring to Sussex the son of the first Kibbobola I had dealings with, show me this young Kibbobola in his suit and let me listen to his parrotings, and I could tell you something about change, sir. (*Little pause.*) And his father from the bjunga would back me up. If you could understand him. (*Little pause.*)

I have the father's voice inside me, just as I have the chirping of the hedge robin inside me. I would recognise the father's son, suit or no suit, Oxford accent or no Oxford accent. Do you follow me, sir? I know a Kibbobola when I see one, sir. And he knows me, I think.

Greatorix nods, very solemnly. Sir Hubert looks out of the window again.

EXT. GARDEN. DAY

The garden shifts out of focus. There is an indistinct dark figure in a far corner of the lawn. Close-up of Sir Hubert's face, staring, lips open.

INT. COTTAGE. DAY

Greatorix (*voice breaking in*) . . . can assure you you won't have that sort of problem around here, Sir Hubert.

His voice fades, Sir Hubert blinks.

EXT. GARDEN

Shot of garden, indistinct black figure becomes more prominent, waving feathers, etc., then disappears.

INT. COTTAGE. DAY

Lady Caroline (*out of shot*) . . . miss them, whatever he says. I never heard them myself, just vaguely, but he's got such sharp ears, he says it comes from listening to so many Kibbobola lies. (*Giggles.*)

Greatorix Well, there's a famous old owl in the woods behind Picker's Dip.

Sir Hubert No. (*Shakes his head, turns into the room.*)
I know an owl when I see one, sir.

INT. BAR IN A SOUTH KENSINGTON HOTEL

*Bar is of the kind that specialises in colonial retireds and
well-off old people: seedy but comfortable, although the
bar itself demonstrates a ghastly attempt to capture the
modish. It is off a main hall that leads to the stairs that
go up to the first-floor rooms: the doorway is very large,
so that a section of the stairs and the hallway is visible.
There is a bead curtain, sometimes lifted back, sometimes
hanging, instead of a door. The bar itself consists of a
counter, with a passage, and behind that shelves on which
the bottles are placed, and of course a large mirror. In
front of the bar are several high stools, and then a number
of chairs and tables scattered about. The effect is at once
cramped and garish (by the bar) and cavernous (the
room as a whole) – brightly lit by the bar, gloomy in the
rest of the room.*

    *Open with a shot of Sir Hubert and Lady Caroline at
the entrance, talking, with the bar behind them and
Claud, the barman, indistinctly leaning on the counter,
over a pad. There are one or two people scattered about
in the bar.*

Sir Hubert Now don't you worry your pretty little head
about a thing, dear, I won't take any nonsense from
Greatorix. I'll see to it myself. (*Takes out his watch,
looks at it.*) But I'll have to hurry along, if I'm to catch
Geoffrey at the Colonial Office. What will *you* do, my
dear?

    Lady Caroline glances into the bar, and away.

Lady Caroline Oh, I'll go upstairs and lie down, I've got
my headache on again.

Sir Hubert You give yourself a rest then. I'll see you later.

Lady Caroline Yes, dear. Give my love to Geoffrey and tell him to come and see us as soon as he can.

She turns and goes up the stairs, out of camera shot. Sir Hubert smiles after her, wiggles his fingers in a sort of salute, turns. As he does so, the bar and Claud come into sharp focus. Claud's face given in a sudden close-up. Then a close-up of Sir Hubert, staring as if in shock. He blinks, turns away, looks back again. Claud is still watching, smiling. Then transfer to a shot of Sir Hubert from Claud's point of view, peering into the room. This shot should be both comic and sinister. Then Sir Hubert disappears from sight. Claud makes an expression of wonder, looks down at the pad. He is doing a savage caricature of two old men at one of the bar's tables. Looks up again as Lady Caroline, peering down the hall, comes into view; she stands at the entrance for a second, then turns, comes in, walking very quickly.

Claud Good evening, madame, and how are you this evening? (*Slipping the pad away.*)

Lady Caroline Good evening, Claud, very well thank you, well, I'm not really, I've got a terrible headache, so I thought I'd better get myself something for it. (*Opens her handbag.*)

Claud I'm very sorry to hear that, it's the heat, I expect. Aspirins? (*Slightly sardonically.*)

Lady Caroline I don't know what it is, but I feel exhausted. No, not aspirins, thank you. (*Takes the flask out of her bag, keeps her eyes off Claud, as if in embarrassment.*) But perhaps you'd be kind enough to fill this up, it takes exactly a quarter of a bottle to the rim.

Claud Certainly, madame. (*Little pause.*) With what? (*As Claud takes the flask.*)

Lady Caroline Yes, gin, please. I think that would be best, it always seems to settle my head.

Watches Claud filling the flask, talks more confidently.

Yes. I'm sure you're right, it's the heat.

Pops a peppermint into her mouth, then as Claud comes back to the counter with the flask, holds the bag out.

Peppermint?

Claud No, thank you. No. That'll be, um, twenty-five shillings, please.

Lady Caroline takes the flask. As she does so the shot changes: Claud and Lady Caroline are seen from the entrance, then a close-up of Sir Hubert, his face grim, standing by the curtains. Lady Caroline's voice and Claud's cannot quite be heard, but there is the sound of Claud's laughter. Lady Caroline turns away from the bar. Sir Hubert dodges away, out of sight. Shot of Lady Caroline coming across the bar, to the entrance, stuffing the flask out of sight. She turns up the stairs. Claud watches her go, drops some money into a box, smiles, then takes the pad out, and begins to draw. Sir Hubert reappears at the entrance, stares at Claud, turns away a second before Claud, frowning, looks up towards him.

INT. LADY CAROLINE'S BEDROOM

It is small, with a single bed, a large wardrobe with a mirror inset in its door; a dresser covered with boxes of make-up, lipstick, etc., in disorder. There are sea trunks

*at one end of the room, with the labels still on them, and
hat boxes. The wardrobe juts out from the wall and adds
a few feet to the passage from the bedroom proper. There
is a sink on the other side of the room.*

*Lady Caroline is sitting at the dresser, putting on make-
up. She has the flask, opened, to hand. A drawer in the
dresser, at knee level, is open and full of underclothes.
She stops powdering her cheeks to take a sip from the
flask.*

*There is a knock on the door. Lady Caroline putting
the top on the flask and putting the flask under the
underclothes, popping peppermints into her mouth,
shutting the drawer with her knee – this done to give
an impression of practised speed.*

Lady Caroline Come in. Oh, hello, dear.

*As Sir Hubert comes into view, with only his middle
part visible in the mirror:*

Didn't you go to see Geoffrey, then?

Sir Hubert No, I – no, I thought I'd leave it until
tomorrow, probably too late, I expect I –

Voice falters, puts his hand to his forehead.

Lady Caroline (*swinging around*) Hubert? Are you all
right, my dear?

*Sir Hubert shaking his head as if to clear it, then
smiling.*

Sir Hubert Yes, yes, thank you, petal, quite all right.
I just remembered – Colonial Office bound to be closed.
(*Shakes his head again.*) London is very tiring, one feels
so dirty.

*Gets up, goes across to the sink, washes his hands.
As he does so Lady Caroline breathes on the back of*

her hand, sniffs, then pops several peppermints into
her mouth.

By the way, saw a chap downstairs, bore a striking
resemblance to – ah – (*Washes his hands a little more.*)
Kibbobola, to one of the Kibbobola.

Lady Caroline Oh? Do you mean Colonel Whimpers,
it's funny you should say that, *I* thought he had a touch
of the tar –

Sir Hubert No, no, my dear, not Whimpers, certainly
not. This was a . . . quite different black. (*Turns off the
tap.*) Downstairs.

There should be a shot of him staring in the mirror
above the sink, watching Lady Caroline.

In the bar, I think.

Lady Caroline Oh! Claud, you mean.

Sir Hubert meets his own eyes in the mirror, then
straightens, dries them on a towel, turns nonchalantly.

Sir Hubert Claud, my dear?

Lady Caroline Well, isn't that his name, the one who
works in the bar? I'm sure it is, and now you mention it
I was downstairs getting some aspirins earlier and he
does have a Kibbobola look about him. I mean so very
black, but he comes from the West Indies I expect, or
somewhere like that. They mostly do around here.

Sir Hubert (*coming back*) And is he a pleasant fellow,
do you think?

Lady Caroline Well, really dear, I've hardly noticed, I
mean, as far as I know he is, why?

Sir Hubert Oh. (*Laughs.*) Just wondering, on account of
his astonishing similarity to . . .

Comes over, stands behind her, puts his hands on her shoulders. A close-up of his face, a look of great pain on it. Then a shot of Lady Caroline, from his position.

My dear, you're looking particularly lovely tonight. May I see you in your dress, my dear? You know how much I admire you in it.

Lady Caroline (*stands up*) Thank you, kind sir. (*Does a little curtsy.*)

Sir Hubert Has anyone else noticed it, petal? (*Looks at her in her dress.*) So gay and so short and flirtatious, my dear.

Lady Caroline As long as you notice it, that's all that matters to me. (*Gives him a smile.*)

Sir Hubert Oh come, my dear, how could anyone *not* have said something? Someone's been admiring you, the blushes are still on your cheeks. (*With a chuckle.*) Surely this – even this Kibbobola West Indian Claud barman fellow had a word to say? Your eyes are bright with compliments, petal. They are, I think. I think they are.

Lady Caroline (*sucking on the peppermint*) They're bright with *your* compliments, you silly old judge. (*Touches him on the cheek.*)

Sir Hubert (*after a pause*) I love you very much, petal, I love you with all my love.

Lady Caroline And I love you back, Hubert, I do, I do.

Sir Hubert (*after a long pause*) And would you prove it to me, my dear?

Lady Caroline (*giggles*) Of course I would.

Sir Hubert goes to the cupboard, takes out a long white evening dress.

484

Sir Hubert Would you wear this for me tonight? It served once, for a very important moment in my life, if I'm not mistaken.

Lady Caroline Well, not quite, dear, but one very like it, the only thing is, isn't it a little long, I mean I'll wear it if you really want me to –

Sir Hubert I do, petal, I do. (*Close-up of his face.*) Please.

> *He turns to the window, stares out. Shot of Lady Caroline looking at him, then she begins to unfasten her dress. Cut back to Sir Hubert: concentrate on his face, licking his lips nervously, once or twice touching his forehead, then takes out his key ring, on which are a few small keys, and jangles it. There should be the sounds too, of a dress being taken off, rustles, etc.*

Lady Caroline It means I've got to change my slip and everything, you wicked thing.

Sir Hubert (*strained smile*) I'm sorry, my dear.

> *More rustling sounds. Sir Hubert jangling the keys noisily, begins to hum, suddenly turns around, as if unable to help himself. Shot of his face, then cut to Lady Caroline, who is standing in the dress, touching at her hair.*

Lady Caroline Well, where are you going to take me?

Sir Hubert Well – (*Blinking, then:*) Beautiful, my petal, how beautiful you look. (*Shakes his head.*) I thought we'd – er, we'd celebrate with a little dinner, a private dinner, of our own, celebrate the purchase of a home, my dear, just the two of us, have it brought up . . . (*hesitates*) here.

Lady Caroline Here? (*Looks around her room.*)

Sir Hubert Yes, my dear. (*Calmly.*) So I can keep you to myself, you see. Now I'll just pop next door and change for you.

> *Cut to Lady Caroline, looking disappointed, watching him as he leaves the room, keys jangling.*

INT. STAIRS. NEXT MORNING

Stairs that pass the bar. Sir Hubert comes down, walking jauntily. Stops, stares. Cut to the bar entrance. Claud is coming out in street clothes, whistling, pad under his arm. Goes down the hall. Sir Hubert takes a few more steps, stops again. Cut to Claud coming back, shaking his head to himself, goes into the bar. Sir Hubert passes the bar, turns his head. Cut to Claud, who is standing with his hands on his hips, staring about him. Sir Hubert watches him, then passes by.

EXT. STREET

Sir Hubert walking along, people passing him, among them some Africans, he stares after them, stops once or twice when he sees Nigerians in full kit, etc., occasional shots of his face, his eyes darting about. He hails a taxi, gets in, shot from inside the taxi at various points. Sir Hubert staring out, catching black faces, his expression intent. Then settling back with a sigh. Taxi draws up outside the Colonial Office. Shot of Sir Hubert getting out, paying the taxi driver, pausing to stare after an African, perhaps several together passing him. Then shot of him going up the stairs.

INT. THE COLONIAL OFFICE

Sir Hubert walking along the corridors, being passed by and passing comfortable English figures in dark suits and comfortable middle-aged women secretaries, etc. The walls should be white, there should be a sheen of whiteness about the faces, the walls. Sir Hubert's face becomes calm. He goes into a door, comes out again almost immediately, accompanied by a Young Man in glasses, who conducts him into a room opposite.

INT. WAITING ROOM

Comfortable armchairs spread about, a sofa, a table with magazines, books, etc., on it. The Young Man holds the door open, and Sir Hubert enters. There is another door opposite.

Sir Hubert . . . unexpectedly, but I think Sir Geoffrey will know me, I think he will. After all, he has for forty years. (*He chuckles.*)

Young Man I'll just go and hunt him up then, sir, if you don't mind a short wait.

Sir Hubert goes and sits down. The Young Man closes the door. Sir Hubert picks up magazines, looks at the first one, which is Drum, *and stares at the cover, of three Africans shaking hands or something, puts it down quickly, picks up a newspaper, begins to glance through it, then straightens, reads very intensely. Shot of his face, shaking his head. Puts the newspaper down, stares straight ahead of him. Then the other door opens. Sir Hubert stares at it, gets to his feet. Cut to a vague figure in feathers, a long gown, this very quick and confusing, then to a black smiling face. Cut to Sir Hubert, his eyes wide, a clicking noise. He blinks, looks at the door. It is closed. The door behind him opens. Two Africans come in. Sir Hubert stares at them, transfixed. They are smiling, coming forward with outstretched hands, a voice behind them:*

Sir Geoffrey No introductions necessary. Hubert, you remember Mr Kwane and Mr Tjomuba – Sir Hubert's just left Kjiarna for ever, a sad day for everyone there, particularly the Kibbobola.

This as Sir Hubert's hand is being shaken by the Africans, then Sir Geoffrey takes Sir Hubert's hand, shakes it warmly, looks into Sir Hubert's face.

Hubert, how are you? Very well, I'm sure. (*To the Africans.*) Brought back a new bride, you know. It's wonderful to see you.

Sir Hubert It's – I –

He looks at the two Africans, then concentrates his gaze on Sir Geoffrey. Seems to be pulling himself together.

Very well, thank you. Very well indeed, Geoffrey. I've just come to ask you around for a drink. Thought I'd drop in while I was passing (*chuckles*) the old place. Tomorrow evening, if you can.

He shifts his glance to the two Africans, then quickly away.

Sir Geoffrey I'd love to. I think we can negotiate a truce in our negotiations (*smiles at the two Africans*) for an evening, gentlemen? *Will* you give me leave?

First African (*smiles*) Of course.

Second African And we will consult our expert, while you consult Sir Hubert. (*He bows.*)

Sir Hubert licks his lips, produces a strained smile.

488

Sir Hubert Talking of Kibbobola, Geoffrey, one of them just put his, er, head through the door – (*Gestures to door.*) Gave me quite a surprise, fine looking – didn't recognise him, though.

Sir Geoffrey A Kibbobola. Here?

Sir Hubert (*smiles*) He looked a little lost, poor fellow.

Sir Geoffrey So he should. To my knowledge, the nearest Kibbobola is ten thousand miles away, in Kjiarna.

Sir Hubert (*drawing himself up*) I think I may say I know a Kibbobola when I see one.

> *Shot of Sir Geoffrey staring at him; then of the two Africans, then a shot of Sir Hubert, staring back at them.*

I think I may say that.

EXT. COLONIAL OFFICE

Sir Hubert coming down the stairs of the Colonial Office. He sees a taxi, hails it. It stops. An African, accompanied by a middle-aged white woman gets in. Sir Hubert stops, stares after it, hails another taxi, gets in.

INT. BAR ENTRANCE. LUNCHTIME

Shot from within to the entrance. Sir Hubert passing, mopping his brow, stops, stares in. Puts his handkerchief away, seems to be bracing himself. Cut to his position, shot of bar interior, then of Claud, bending over the sink beneath the shelves, washing glasses, looking up suddenly and seeing Sir Hubert in the mirror, standing silently, watching him. Turns.

Claud (*smiling*) Sir?

Sir Hubert stares at Claud.

(*Wiping his hands on towel.*) Sir? What can I get you, sir?

Sir Hubert (*smiling suddenly*) Good afternoon, Claud.

Claud Good afternoon, sir. (*Slightly puzzled.*) What's your pleasure, sir?

Sir Hubert My pleasure, Claud? (*Laughs.*) What would you advise as my pleasure, Claud?

Claud (*embarrassed, laughs*) Well, sir, that depends on whether you want a long cool one or a short strong one.

Sir Hubert Tell me, Claud. (*Leans forward, smiling.*) What's your favourite pleasure?

Claud (*thinks, shrugs*) Rum and Coke, with a slice of lemon.

Sir Hubert Then it's mine, Claud. Yes, with the lemon cut from the underneath, Claud, with a touch of the flesh still attached, if you please, Claud.

Claud Yes, sir. Right away, sir.

He turns to the bottles. As he makes the drink, Sir Hubert watches him intently. When he cuts the lemon he looks in the mirror, and sees Sir Hubert's eyes fixed on him. He should become noticeably self-conscious.

There we are, sir.

Sir Hubert continues to stare at Claud.

Would you prefer it at a table, perhaps?

Sir Hubert No. I'd prefer it here – (*Places a hand on counter.*) Please, Claud. Thank you.

Claud You're welcome, sir.

He turns back to the glasses, continues to wash them, glancing up occasionally in the mirror to see Sir Hubert watching him.

Sir Hubert Claud.

Claud Yes sir?

Sir Hubert Claud, how much is this rum and cocoa business, Claud?

Claud Four shillings, sir.

Sir Hubert reaches into his wallet, takes out a pound note, puts it on the counter. Claud picks it up, puts the change on a saucer, puts it back on the counter. Sir Hubert takes out all the change – this registered by Claud – then, as Claud goes back to his glasses (with a slightly sardonic smile), puts some coins, one at a time, back into the saucer. Claud watches this in the mirror.

Sir Hubert Claud, these are for you.

Claud (*turning*) Thank you, sir. Thank you very much.

Sir Hubert pushes the saucer across the counter, nods at Claud to take the money. Claud does, puts it in a box under the counter, but is evidently embarrassed. Sir Hubert watches him.

Sir Hubert Tell me, Claud, where do you come from?

Claud (*tensing slightly*) Stepney Green, sir.

Sir Hubert Really, Claud? Didn't you come from somewhere before you came from Stepney Green. I think you did. I think so.

Claud (*coolly*) My family comes from Trinidad, but most of them live in Stepney Green.

Sir Hubert I see. From Trinidad to Stepney Green. And tell me, Claud, have you been anywhere else?

Claud I was in New York for five years.

Sir Hubert Indeed, Trinidad. Stepney Green. New York. Quite the rover, I think, Claud. Quite the rover.

Claud (*drily*) Yes, sir. Here today and gone tomorrow.

Sir Hubert Here today and gone tomorrow. And gone tomorrow.

Sir Hubert nods, stares at Claud, chuckles.

Tell me, Claud, have you served any . . . (*little pause*) beautiful ladies recently?

He smiles at Claud intensely. After a pause, Claud laughs in embarrassment.

Claud No, sir. Not a one, sir.

After a long pause, during which he smiles at Claud, Sir Hubert says:

Sir Hubert Not a one, Claud? Not a single solitary one, Claud?

Claud shakes his head, laughs. Sir Hubert stares at him. Claud stops laughing.

Ah come, Claud, a rover like you, sir, with a roving eye, I think? Must have spotted *one* beautiful lady?

Claud No, sir.

Sharply. They exchange stares, Claud looks uncomfortable, turns, goes down the bar, fiddles with some glasses.

Sir Hubert Claud.

Claud (*stiffening*) Sir?

Sir Hubert (*patting the counter*) Claud.

Claud (*coming back*) Sir?

Sir Hubert (*lowering his voice*) Tell me something, Claud, in the strictest confidence.

Claud nods suspiciously.

Do you like beautiful ladies, Claud? Ummm? (*He raises a finger jovially.*)

Claud (*after a pause, shrugs*) Of course, sir.

Sir Hubert I was sure you did, Claud, I was sure you did. I could tell at once.

Wags his head reprovingly, then chuckles. Claud stares at him, then begins to laugh, half in embarrassment.

And yet you say, I think you do, Claud, that you haven't seen one beautiful lady recently? (*Shakes his head.*) If you did, you'd know what to do, I think? (*Winks.*) You would, wouldn't you now?

Claud Well, I hope so – (*after a little pause*) sir.

Sir Hubert leans over the bar, his face suddenly serious.

Sir Hubert Do you know me, Claud? Do you know me, sir?

Claud shakes his head, stares at him.

Come, sir. (*Sharply.*) You know me. I . . .

He stops, as he sees in the mirror an elderly gentleman standing beside him, and converts his voice into a chuckling one.

. . . I'm the man for a rum and cocoa thing, and I'll have another, Claud, if you please.

He swallows the drink in front of him down. Claud does him another one as Sir Hubert turns, nods to the man beside him, who looks at him blankly, nods back. Then when Claud brings him his new drink stands uncertainly, then goes across the bar to a far table. Sits down. Watches as Claud serves the other man, then as Claud goes to the far end of the bar. Claud looks towards him. Shot of Sir Hubert in the distance, staring at him. Shot of Claud, making a face to himself. Then smiling. Picks up the pad, props his chin in his hand, begins to draw, as if casually. Looks up once towards Sir Hubert, who is still staring at him. Then down at the pad. He has begun a savage caricature of Sir Hubert. Shot of the page, then of Claud looking towards Sir Hubert, as if casually. Sir Hubert smiles at him, raises his glass in a sort of salute. Claud smiles back, bends over his pad, then as he hears footsteps clicking across the room, shuts the pad quickly. Lady Caroline is approaching the counter.

Claud Good evening, madame. Headache all cleared?

Lady Caroline glances quickly towards the entrance, stands so that she has her back to Sir Hubert.

Lady Caroline Yes, Claud, but something much worse has happened. I'm afraid, something really tragic. (*She takes flask out of handbag.*) I spilt it all over a new dress, every last drop of it.

As Claud takes the flask.

And it was completely ruined, it's so dreadful I don't know what I'll do, I can't go around smelling of gin, can I?

Sucks on a peppermint as Claud, with a cynical smile, fills the flask, then glances again towards the entrance, then back to Claud. There is a sudden shot of them from Sir Hubert's position, Lady Caroline leaning over the bar, Claud leaning towards her, as if they were holding hands. Then cut back to Claud handing over the flask.

Claud There we are, madame. Be careful with this one, now.

Lady Caroline puts the flask in her bag, puts the money across the counter. Cut back to Sir Hubert, seeing Claud leaning towards Lady Caroline again. He rises from his chair, eyes fixed, mouth open, as Lady Caroline turns. Close up of Lady Caroline's face as she sees Sir Hubert, momentarily shocked, then she smiles, waves, comes towards him. Back to Sir Hubert, watching Lady Caroline advance, with Claud watching behind. Lady Caroline is closing her bag as she comes. Sir Hubert forces a smile onto his face, holds out a chair for Lady Caroline.

Lady Caroline (*sitting down, laughing nervously*) I wondered where you'd got to, I didn't expect to find you in here. (*Touches her forehead.*) Oh, this head of mine, I've just been getting some more of Claud's aspirins.

Sir Hubert Have you, my dear? (*Smiles at her.*) And he satisfied you, I hope.

Lady Caroline Yes, yes, I feel a little better already, although not much.

Sir Hubert (*after a pause*) He's as bright as a new penny, don't you think? Most unusual fellow. I've been having a chat with him.

Lady Caroline With Claud? (*Pretending carelessness.*) Oh? What about?

Sir Hubert This and that. (*Little pause.*) I find him rather charming.

Looks towards Claud, who is staring towards them from over his pad.

I admit. Don't you?

Lady Caroline Well, Hubert, I suppose so, he seems very nice, yes, for a – although he gets things muddled up, makes mistakes, not that it matters, of course, they're all like that.

Sir Hubert (*stares at her intensely*) So you *do* remember him, this Claud of mine?

Lady Caroline (*laughs*) Of course I do, dear. It's you who didn't know who he was.

Sir Hubert (*leaning across the table*) And do you think he remembers you, my dear?

Lady Caroline looks at him, nervously: opens her bag, takes out two peppermints and pops them into her mouth.

Lady Caroline Well, that's a strange question, Hubert, he may get me confused with other people, or whatever he's been saying, I don't know what nonsense he's been – but I hope I'm not so dull – after all, it's not as if the hotel was crowded with, well, gay young things, is it? (*She touches her head and blinks.*) Oh.

Sir Hubert (*studies her*) You need a drink, I think, my dear? (*Looks towards the counter.*)

Cut to Claud, who is bent over the sketchbook. He looks up. Sir Hubert is signalling him, he goes around the counter, towards the table. Lady Caroline and Sir Hubert watch him come, Lady Caroline apprehensively, Sir Hubert with a fixed smile.

Lady Caroline So you don't know me, Claud? (*Giggles apprehensively.*)

Claud I beg your pardon, madame?

Lady Caroline I should think you do know me, Claud. (*Licks her lips.*) After all those aspirins I've bought from you.

Claud's eyes meet hers, they look at each other. Cut to Sir Hubert watching them closely.

Claud Oh yes, madame, for your headache. And how is it now?

Lady Caroline (*in relieved excitement*) Oh, ever so much better, thank you, Claud, although it never quite goes, it's always just there.

Little pause. Claud stands waiting. Sir Hubert continues to watch them. Lady Caroline turns to Sir Hubert and smiles.

I'd like a – what shall I have?

Sir Hubert Orange squash, my dear? You were always very fond of that in Kjiarna?

Lady Caroline No, no, I don't think – no, something different.

Sir Hubert Why don't you ask Claud for a suggestion, my dear. He's full of helpful suggestions, aren't you, Claud? (*He stares up at Claud.*)

Claud (*with slight irony*) Well, perhaps madame would like to try a gin?

Lady Caroline Yes. That sounds *very* nice.

Sir Hubert There you are. You know all our pleasures, Claud, I think. I think you do. (*Chuckles.*) Eh, my dear?

As Claud goes off, stares at her, a little pause.

My dear – (*Puts his hand on hers.*) Have I said how, how very lovely you're looking this afternoon.

He stares into her face. Close-up of Lady Caroline's face, smiling at him.
   Cut to Claud's sketch pad. His pencil is just putting the finishing touches to a caricature of a spindly, naked Lady Caroline, sitting on a chair, with an arch smile on her face and a bottle of gin raised to her lips. Claud suddenly looks up. Sir Hubert is standing opposite him, Lady Caroline beside him. He shuts the book, gives a desperate smile.

Claud Sir?

Sir Hubert takes out his wallet, extracts a pound note.

Sir Hubert There we are, Claud. And the change is for you.

Claud Thank you, sir. Thank you very much. (*Awkwardly.*) If it's not too much, sir.

Sir Hubert Nonsense, Claud, nonsense. Tell me, though, what do you do exactly in that book of yours?

Claud Book, sir?

Sir Hubert (*dropping his hand on it*) Yes, Claud, this book. (*Wags his head, smiling.*) I've been keeping my eye on you, you see.

Claud (*licks his lips, smiles*) Well, it's just a pad, sir, for writing notes in, doodling, while I'm waiting between orders.

Sir Hubert fondles the book, as if tempted to open it.

Sir Hubert Is it, indeed? Is it? Notes and doodlings, eh? What sort of doodling? Faces, figures, telephone numbers of your conquests. Claud? Hah? (*Laughs, shakes his head.*)

Appointments with your – dentist, Claud, although I can see *you* don't need a dentist.

Claud should be smiling fearfully, teeth on display.

And I expect you keep your important appointments in a more private place, don't you, Claud?

Claud looks at Sir Hubert's hand, toying with the cover of the pad.

Claud Well, sir, it's not – I don't have that many appointments, sir, no sir. (*Shakes his head.*) I wish I did.

Lady Caroline Claud's far too clever to be caught like that, not like you, dear, aren't you, Claud?

Sir Hubert (*in a serious tone, staring at her, his hand still on the book*) Ah, but he wishes he did, my dear. He wishes he did. But, Claud, if wishes were horses, beggars would ride. You'll have to pass some of those notes around –

He picks up the book, as if unable to resist any longer. Claud starts forward.

Let's see what we can find.

Lady Caroline Oh, you're embarrassing the poor boy, dear.

She tries to take the book from him, with Claud grinning helplessly. Sir Hubert resists for a second.

It's not fair to pry into his personal life. I'm sure we've all got our little secrets. (*She gets the book away from Sir Hubert.*) Haven't we, Claud?

She gives him a significant look. Sir Hubert sees it. Claud takes the book gratefully.
 Sir Hubert, who has been staring at him in loathing and fear, changes this to a smile.

Claud (*to Sir Hubert*) Oh there's nothing there but bad drawings, that's my secret, that I'm a bad drawer, sir.

Sir Hubert (*after a pause, chuckles*) But if I know you, sir, and I think I do, you're capable of more badness than that. I think you are, Claud.

> *He moves away from the bar, with Lady Caroline beside him, chuckles.*

I think you are.

Claud (*laughs*) Good afternoon, sir.

> *He takes up the pad, makes an expression of relief to himself.*

EXT. GREENDENE. THE GARDEN

The black Rover parked in the drive. Sir Hubert and Lady Caroline are walking across the lawn to the French windows, which are open.

INT. LIVING ROOM

There are ladders around the wall, rolls of wallpaper, buckets, etc. Lady Caroline and Sir Hubert enter, Sir Hubert is smiling, jingling his key ring, looks peaceful; Lady Caroline is sucking a peppermint.

Lady Caroline . . . see why, I mean if the men are taking the afternoon off, which is very nice for *them*, I must say, it's just depressing to see it all in this state, Hubert, it makes me despair, with so much on my plate as it is.

Sir Hubert But it is so peaceful, petal, after the rush of London. There is always something to disturb – every time one goes out of the door I see something – (*Shakes* *his head.*) I thought it would help your head to spend a quiet afternoon out of that hotel.

Lady Caroline (*sharply*) What do you mean?

Sir Hubert (*turning to her, sadly*) Nothing, my dear, nothing. I just wanted your company – it was selfish of me to drag you here.

Little pause. He looks towards the drive as a small truck appears, then with a smile:

Besides, I have a little surprise for you.

Lady Caroline (*sees the truck*) Oh. Oh Hubert, what is it?

Sir Hubert Ah. (*He lifts his key ring, jangles it jovially.*) Ah, my dear, wait and see.

He waves to the truck, gestures towards the living room, opens the window wider.

EXT.

The truck stops, a man gets out on the side closest to the window; the door on the other side opens; a figure in overalls, not clearly seen, gets out on that side. The two men go to the back, only one visible, open the door. One gets in, the man who is visible waits, a piano is pushed out. He grabs the end, swings it around towards the window, moves slowly, the other man is behind the piano. It is carried towards the windows.

INT. LIVING ROOM

Sir Hubert and Lady Caroline watch it coming towards them, step aside to let it pass.

Lady Caroline (*claps her hands*) Oh Hubert, you darling you.

She gives him a kiss on the cheek. Sir Hubert, beaming, watches the two men deposit the piano in the centre of the room.

Sir Hubert I couldn't have a home, my dear, without your music in it.

The sentence falters, and his expression changes as he watches the Man nearest him, hitherto not seen properly, straightening, and turning.

Man (*momentarily seeming to be West Indian*) Is this all right for you, just here?

His face seen in close-up.

Sir Hubert (*staring*) I – I –

Lady Caroline Oh, further back I think, please, if you wouldn't mind. (*She goes over to the piano.*) It's beautiful – Where are you going, dear?

Sir Hubert walks to the door, right.

Sir Hubert Just remembered something, my dear, downstairs, check up on the smell, won't be a minute.

He looks at the white mover, who is wiping his hands on a handkerchief, nods, smiles, hurries down.

Lady Caroline Oh.

She looks puzzled, then turns to the two men.

Just a few feet, that's all, so that it doesn't take up the whole room.

INT. THE CELLAR

Sir Hubert enters, sits down on an old trunk, closes his eyes (he has left the doors open), rocks slightly. Then opens his eyes and stares straight ahead. Closes his eyes again. Presses his knees together, begins to rattle the keys up and down compulsively, the camera on his face. He opens his eyes, they widen in shock. Cut to the West Indian face at the door, smiling in. Then stepping into the room, rubbing his hands along his trousers.

Man That's done then. All moved.

Sir Hubert Moved, eh. Moved.

He chuckles automatically, stares at the man.

Man The lady seems very pleased.

Sir Hubert Is she? I think she is. I think I can say that. (*He nods and continues to stare.*)

Man We got it all square for her. She wants to get at it straight away from the look on her face.

He throws back his head and laughs. Sir Hubert looks at him, appalled.

Sir Hubert Does she? Does she now? Does she?

Man Yes, well I just thought I'd tell you it was done. (*He turns and makes for the door.*)

Sir Hubert Ah – ah – ah wait. (*He looks at him, then reaches into his pocket, takes out his wallet.*) Here's a little something . . . (*He hands over two pound notes.*) A little something for your trouble.

Man (*grinning*) Thank *you*, sir. No trouble, it was a pleasure, sir.

Sir Hubert stares at him fixedly, somehow cutting him off.

Sir Hubert Goodbye.

Man (*freezing*) Goodbye, sir. And thank you. (*Exits.*)

Sir Hubert stands, staring at the door, sits down again, wipes his hand across his forehead. Then begins to sniff, Makes a face of disgust. Sniffs again. Suddenly the sound of the piano, playing 'Somewhere over the Rainbow'. He stands stock still, listening. The playing is very coarse and brash. Sir Hubert's face becomes calmer, he smiles, nods his head in time to the music, then goes to the door.

INT. LIVING-ROOM

Lady Caroline is standing by the piano, pushing her flask back into her handbag, and taking out a couple of peppermints, as the door, right, opens, and Sir Hubert enters. She pops the peppermints into her mouth, turns, smiles.

Lady Caroline Thank you, Hubert. Thank you so much, dear.

She smiles at him. Sir Hubert walking across to her.

Sir Hubert I heard your tune downstairs. I could tell your touch, my dear, from the grave itself. (*Walks over and stares at her, very seriously.*) It carried me back, for a minute, to Kjiarna. (*Takes her hand and kisses it.*)

Lady Caroline smiles at him, her face slightly averted. Then they walk towards the windows. Sir Hubert stops, stares out.

EXT.

The truck is backing down the drive, out of sight.

INT. COTTAGE

Lady Caroline Sometimes, you know, Hubert, sometimes – I know it's silly of me, but I can't help feeling everything was easier in Kjiarna, I mean I never got these headaches there, did I?

She looks at him.

Sir Hubert No, my dear. No, you didn't.

EXT. THE LAWN

Shot of Lady Caroline and Sir Hubert walking across the lawn, Lady Caroline leaning on Sir Hubert's arm. Then of Lady Caroline sitting beside him.

EXT.

Shot of street from Sir Hubert's bedroom window.

INT. SIR HUBERT'S BEDROOM WITH SHOT OF STREET FROM THE WINDOW

Sir Hubert is sitting on the bed, fiddling with his keys, staring straight ahead. Suddenly he gets up, goes to a trunk, opens it. Takes out a revolver, looks at it, puts it back. Closes the trunk. Walks to the window, opens it, stares out. Ordinary street noises come up to him. He takes great gulps of air, listens to the roar of traffic, honking, voices rising, shuts his eyes. The noises transform into jungle cries, shrill, like the cries of the parrots in the first scene, only confused. Sir Hubert stares out, jerks the window down. Puts his hands to his ears. Removes them, slowly. Silence. Opens window again. Traffic noises which transform again into the same cries and screechings. He slams the window down, walks around the room, sits down on the bed, jangling his keys, gets up, stares at himself in the mirror. Then goes to the window. Draws the curtains, straightens his shoulders, goes to the door.

INT. LADY CAROLINE'S BEDROOM

She is putting the finishing touches to her make-up as there is a knock on the door, and Sir Hubert enters. She gets up, does a little curtsy.

Lady Caroline Where are we taking Geoffrey for this drink? Somewhere glamorous, I hope.

Sir Hubert (*blinks*) Ah – well, I – perhaps we could have a quiet drink up – send down for something and have it –

Lady Caroline No, Hubert, I'm not having that, dear. We're not going to sit in a poky bedroom, if you won't take us out then the least we can do is use the hotel bar.

Sir Hubert The bar?

Lady Caroline Can you imagine Geoffrey's face if we have him in the bedroom? I don't know why I bother to change for you, I really don't, and you know what an old woman he is about some things.

INT. BAR

Claud is drawing in his pad – a thin, elderly face caricatured into corrupt effeminacy, suggestions of eye make-up and lipstick and a blouse and skirt. Switch from the drawing to Sir Geoffrey (the subject of the cartoon) listening very seriously at a far table, Lady Caroline beside him, also listening. Drink in front of them. Sir Hubert not seen, but the first shot includes a glass of rum and Coke with a slice of lemon in it.

Sir Hubert (*out of shot*) I slept like a log all through it. Yes, like a log. (*Chuckles.*) I could hear this Kibbobola cavorting and cursing outside my window all night, but I just fitted my dreams around him, and slept like a log. (*Chuckles again.*)

Sir Geoffrey *That's* the way to rule an empire, *and* it confirms my favourite moral – never give cures to the native, it teaches them the disease.

Lady Caroline They used to call him Lord Justice. (*Giggles.*)

Sir Hubert (*out of shot*) Justice, justice. It's not only the Kibbobola that need justice.

Little pause. Sir Geoffrey looks at him curiously, Lady Caroline sips from her glass and attempts a serious expression.

It's needed everywhere, I think. Yes, everywhere. For instance, this Meadle –

Camera shifts to his face, he is staring intensely.

– in the newspapers the other morning.

Sir Geoffrey (*politely*) Meadle?

Sir Hubert This Meadle . . . (*turns to Lady Caroline,
addresses the rest of this to her*) was a lodger with a
family in Willesden Green, two adults – husband and wife,
naturally, my dear – and a daughter of ten. A daughter
of ten. (*Pause.*) A daughter of ten. (*Pause.*) Meadle
himself was in his early forties, or thereabout, and
reading between the lines I should say he was definitely
black. A West Indian, my dear. (*Long pause.*)

Lady Caroline Hubert – you don't mean – how
disgusting!

Sir Geoffrey (*suavely*) Good heavens.

Sir Hubert (*nodding*) The parents were suspicious, of
course. Asked him to leave. He had the impertinence to
become angry, actually angry, threatened the father,
insulted the mother, grabbed a taxi from under the nose
of – (*Stops, blinks.*) The daughter didn't understand,
you see, how could the poor child understand? Innocent
and ten years old, very gifted musically. (*Pause, smiles
sinisterly.*) But her actions became most mysterious after
this Meadle's departure. They were forced to watch, to
wait and watch. (*Long pause.*) They found the two-way
radio under a floorboard in her bedroom.

Sir Geoffrey (*with real enthusiasm*) Good heavens!

Lady Caroline (*blinking, sipping*) A what, dear?

> *Sir Hubert has been staring over at the counter, where
> Claud is drawing busily.*

Sir Hubert For transmitting messages to, and receiving
messages from (*looking at Lady Caroline*) another
person, my dear, also in possession of a two-way radio.
They found his, this Meadle's, in the wardrobe of his
new lodging room in Kilburn.

Sir Geoffrey How old did you say the girl was?

Sir Hubert Nine.

Lady Caroline I thought you said ten.

Sir Hubert Going on ten, my dear, I think I said. (*Stares over at Claud again.*) You see, my dear, he was quite open about it. (*Swivelling his head back, staring sightlessly.*) He kept it in the wardrobe, and when he went to bed at night he could take it with him, rest it on the pillow, whisper into its ear, he could talk as softly as he liked and say anything out that was moving about in his head. *That* is the point, my dear. He could say it all in whispers, and it would stretch, so to speak, from Willesden to Kilburn. And she, this innocent child, the little lady, would have hers on the pillow beside her, and would listen to the whispers as if they were dreams, or as if they came from inside herself. And who could get hold of it? You can't track it down when it's under the floorboard or carrying itself through the night air, like the parrots at Kjiarna when Whitey vanished.

Stares towards Claud again. Shot of Claud closing his pad as some elderly people advance into the bar.

Unless you watch for it, and wait, can you? Because he could be anywhere, this – this – this Meadle with his two-way set.

Lady Caroline Hanging's too good for people like that. If you give them an inch. (*Nods.*)

Sir Geoffrey (*staring at Sir Hubert hard*) You read this in the newspaper?

Sir Hubert (*blinking*) It was a short item.

Stares towards Claud again, then as Claud goes over to a very distant table, gets to his feet as Sir Geoffrey says:

Sir Geoffrey There's the real danger of the technological –

Stops. Watches Sir Hubert walking quickly to the counter, turns to Lady Caroline, who is also watching Sir Hubert.

Caroline, is everything all right with Hubert?

Lady Caroline Oh yes, I think so, why?

Sir Geoffrey Nothing, nothing, I was sure it was. Thought perhaps he might be a bit on edge – often happens when they come home for good, you know. I was hoping to get him interested in some troublesome Nigerians we've got swinging about the Office, but he didn't seem quite himself when he bumped into them.

Lady Caroline Well, of course we've got so much on our plates at the moment, what with this new house, there's so much to do settling in, I can hardly face the thought of it sometimes. And another thing, I've had a perpetual head—

Cut to Sir Hubert, who is at the bar, with his hand on Claud's pad. Moves his hand as Claud comes back. Smiles.

Sir Hubert Look after those good people first, Claud, I'm in no hurry.

Claud smiles, nods, goes to the shelves, Sir Hubert watches him, his hand close to the pad. Cut back to Lady Caroline and Sir Geoffrey.

Lady Caroline . . . all over the place when he first got back, he even thought he saw one in the garden at Greendene, but it was just a mood, habit he called it, he hardly ever talks about them these days, he's too occupied with what he's found over here, mark you I wish there *were* a few Kibbobola about . . .

Shot of Claud passing with a tray of drinks, from the table; then cut to Sir Hubert rustling through the pad, stopping at a page, close-up of his face, glaring down, then rips the page out and stuffs it into his pocket. Stands there humming, looks towards Claud, who is now coming back, takes out his key ring and begins to jangle it innocently. Cut back to:

Lady Caroline . . . wonderful about the house after they'd been broken in, I often wonder how we'll manage without them, and very reliable. Ah, Hubert . . .

As Sir Hubert comes back to the table, still jangling his key ring:

Why ever did you rush off like that, dear, Geoffrey thought there must be something wrong with you.

Sir Hubert (*calmly sitting down*) Oh, I'm sorry, Geoffrey, just ordering another round. (*There is a little pause. Very calmly.*) That snake, I buried it in the garden, where it could be watched. I had almost forgotten. It was a long time ago. I've often wondered, my dear, whether those parrot things didn't come at first to dig it up. I think they did, you know, I think they did.

Sir Geoffrey Snake, Hubert?

Lady Caroline Dear, what *are* you going on about?

Sir Hubert Wasn't I telling you about this Kibbobola, the one who danced and cursed all night? (*Little pause.*) The one whose hash I settled? (*Chuckles.*)

Sir Geoffrey Oh yes, of *course* you were. The cure-any-disease witch-doctor chappie.

Lady Caroline nods contentedly.

Sir Hubert (*smiling*) But I didn't tell you *how* I settled his hash, did – Ah, and here's our Claud.

As Claud approaches with the tray, and drinks on it:

Geoffrey, let me introduce you properly to our good friend Claud, who is indispensable to us. He comes from Trinidad by way of Stepney Green.

Sir Geoffrey embarrassed, but smiling smoothly.

Sir Geoffrey How do you do, Claud.

Sir Hubert Caroline and Claud are the greatest of friends, aren't you, my dear? He has a special aspirin that clears Caroline's head.

Lady Caroline giggles nervously.

Sir Geoffrey Really? I could do with some of those!

As Claud takes away the empty glass and puts a fresh drink in front of him:

I was in Jamaica last winter, saw the finest cricket game of my life. Bottles over the pitch, transistors, umpire assaulted – now that's what I call sport. Do you play, Claud?

Claud (*serving Lady Caroline*) No, sir. I don't like cricket, sir.

Sir Geoffrey Oh? I thought it was in your bl— part of your tradition?

Claud (*serving Sir Hubert*) No, sir. I was very bad at sports, sir. All of them.

Sir Hubert All of them, Claud? Come now, Claud, there must be some sport you excel at. (*Chuckles.*) Athletic chap like you, eh, Caroline? Wouldn't you think Claud would be a natural athlete?

Claud No, sir.

Sir Geoffrey (*looking at him closely*) I haven't seen you before somewhere, have I?

Claud (*staring at him impassively*) I sometimes go to the Gay Fellow, sir, off Amble Street, in Kensington?

Sir Geoffrey The Gay? (*Embarrassed but smooth.*) The Gay? No, no, I've never been there. I'm sure I haven't.

Lady Caroline Oh, but you have to be careful with Claud, according to Hubert he's got a roving instinct.

> *She giggles, sips at her drink. Shot of Sir Hubert's face, swinging around to stare at Lady Caroline, then swinging back to Claud.*

Sir Hubert Well, how much do I owe you this time, Claud?

Sir Geoffrey Oh, do let me get these.

> *He seems slightly flustered, avoids looking at Claud.*

My round, you know. Old tradition.

> *Claud looks at him, smiles.*

Sir Hubert Oh certainly not. Certainly not. *I* will settle with Claud. Claud?

> *He takes out his wallet, with the sheet of drawing paper folded around it, takes the paper away, ostentatiously but casually, watching Claud's face all the time.*

Eh, Claud?

> *He puts the paper down in front of himself. Claud smiles again at Sir Geoffrey, who is still avoiding him.*

Claud Um, one Scotch, one rum and Coke, one large gin, eleven shillings, please, sir.

Sir Hubert takes a pound out of his wallet, hands it to Claud. When Claud's fingers are around it Sir Hubert hangs on to the note.

Sir Hubert You wouldn't be cheating, would you, Claud?

Claud (*shocked*) Sir?

Lady Caroline and Sir Geoffrey look at him, and then at Sir Hubert. Sir Hubert releases the note. He should seem utterly confident of himself.

Sir Hubert Yourself, Claud, I mean. What about all those aspirins you've been getting from Claud, my dear, did he let you pay for them?

Lady Caroline Of course I paid, Hubert, what an idea!

Sir Hubert Ah, well, that's all right then. That's all right, Claud. You haven't been cheating yourself, you see. I was worried on your account.

He chuckles, nods at Claud, turns back to the table, taps the paper with his fingers casually. Claud takes change out of his pocket, puts it on the tray, holds it out to Sir Hubert, who affects not to see.

Yes, I think the parrots opened the grave. (*To Sir Geoffrey.*) One morning I noticed that the mud had been turned up and the grave was empty. It's just come back to me.

As he says this Claud slips the change on a corner of the table and goes off. Cut to Sir Geoffrey, who glances furtively at Claud's back.

Sir Geoffrey I've never been in Amble Street in my life. Why should that fellow say –

Sir Hubert Claud! (*He gets to his feet.*) Claud!

Claud stops. Close-up of his face, lips tightening in irritation, rolls his eyes, turns, goes back to the table.

I think you've forgotten something, Claud?

He puts his hand on the paper, then shifts his hand to the change.

Claud Sir?

Sir Hubert The change, Claud.

Claud (*after a little pause*) It's there, sir.

Sir Hubert (*chuckles*) Exactly, Claud. And you've forgotten it, I think.

Claud hesitates, looks at Lady Caroline, then at Sir Geoffrey, their eyes meet, Claud gives a little smile, then puts his hand down on the table and scoops the change onto the plate, missing the paper by a fraction of an inch.

Claud Thank you, sir.

He looks again at Sir Geoffrey, with the same knowing smile.

Sir Hubert My pleasure, Claud.

Chuckles after him. As Claud turns away, Lady Caroline reaches over and picks up the paper.

Lady Caroline Hubert, is this something important? (*Begins to unfold it.*)

Sir Hubert No, my dear, a surprise, you're not to –

Sir Hubert reaches over, snatches it from her hand, knocks over her drink, which spills over her lap. Lady Caroline cries out.

Lady Caroline (*pushing the chair back*) Hubert!

Claud turns, hurries back. Sir Hubert is stuffing the paper back into his pocket.

Sir Hubert I'm terribly sorry, my dear, a surprise, I don't want you to see, I'm so – most clumsy –

Lady Caroline I'll just smell of gin. (*Brushes futilely at the splashes.*)

Claud Allow me, madame.

Claud bends down, mops at the hem of her dress, very rapidly and discreetly. Cut to Sir Hubert watching, with eyes staring, then cut back to Claud's hands, which seem to be travelling everywhere, a multiplicity of hands at Lady Caroline's hem, moving under the dress, etc. Cut back to Sir Hubert gaping.

No harm done, madame. (*Straightening.*) No harm done.

He smiles down on Lady Caroline: close-up of his face, teeth, mouth open, in a sudden exaggeration of a smile.

INT. SIR HUBERT'S BEDROOM

Sir Hubert is sitting on his bed, fully clothed, but his head nodding, as if he had dozed off. The drawing of Lady Caroline, naked, is open beside him.

Sir Hubert . . . anything to say, my Claud, why sentence – (*His voice slurs off, his eyes blink open, leaps to his feet.*) Let madness in and justice out?

Looks down at the drawing, rushes to the window, makes to open it, stops himself, looks out fearfully, comes back, goes to the trunk, opens it, takes out the revolver, puts it in his pocket, folds the drawing, puts it in his pocket, sits down on the edge of the bed, buries his face in his hands.

The devil. The devil.

He raises his face, there are tears trickling down it.

INT. THE BAR

Claud is behind the counter, in his shirtsleeves, putting glasses away. He is whistling softly. There is a crashing noise behind him, he looks up, startled, sees Sir Hubert in the mirror, seated on one of the stools. Turns.

Sir Hubert Just clearing up, Claud? Putting it all straight for the morrow, eh?

Claud Yes, sir.

Sir Hubert What about a last drink with me, Claud? (*Smiles ingratiatingly.*)

Claud Well, sir – (*Hesitates.*) The bar's closed, sir, by law. (*Looks at the clock.*)

Sir Hubert By law? In that case, I mustn't incite you to break it. That's a criminal offence. Did you know that, Claud?

Claud (*shakes his head, smiling*) No, sir.

Sir Hubert Of course you didn't. Why should you? It's my job to know about the law, and your job – (*stops smiling*) and your job to help yourself to whatever will help *you*, eh, Claud? And that's what I want to have a short word with you about. How would you like to earn yourself five five-pound notes? To add to those tips of yours?

Claud Twenty-five pounds, sir?

Sir Hubert Mmmm?

*He tilts his head to one side, smiling. His hand in his
jacket pocket.*

Claud Well, that sounds very interesting, sir.

Sir Hubert But I insist on one condition beforehand, and
that is complete discretion, Claud, complete discretion.
You see, I want you to assist me in a little surprise, one
I've been preparing for my lady wife. (*Chuckles.*) You
know my lady wife, I think?

He stares at him. Claud nods, smiling.

Now what I have in – by the way, do you live with your
family, out in that Stepney Green of yours?

Claud No, sir. I've got a room here, 22 in the basement
corridor. It goes with the job.

Sir Hubert Good. Excellent. I'll know where to get hold
of you, 22 in the basement, although we mustn't be seen
together, or the lady in question will know there's
something afoot. Now . . . (*Leans forward.*)

INT. LADY CAROLINE'S BEDROOM

*She is in her nightdress and nightgown. She goes to her
handbag, takes out the flask and peppermints, goes back
to the bed. Lady Caroline puts the flask under her
pillow, the peppermints beside the pillow, gets into bed
with a book. Sighs.*

INT. BAR

*Sir Hubert and Claud are still at the counter, their heads
together. Shot of them from the entrance first, the low
murmur of their voices, intimate-sounding, then close-up.*

Sir Hubert You're the expert, Claud, you're our barman. When can you come and see the room for yourself?

Claud (*shrugs*) Any morning?

Sir Hubert Well, sir, and are you an early riser?

Claud (*shrugs*) When I have to be. (*Smiles.*)

Sir Hubert I thought not. The nights are not for sleeping in, I think, where you're concerned, eh, Claud? Well, I've a little business to attend to tomorrow, a few purchases. (*Gestures.*) Meet me outside the Gloucester Road underground station at eleven sharp? How does that appeal to you?

Claud (*nods*) That's fine, sir.

Sir Hubert (*looks at him, smiles*) Good, Claud, good. Very good. (*Little pause.*) Tell me, Claud, what do you do with all your tips? (*Sir Hubert takes his hand out of his pocket.*) If I'm not being presumptuous, of course?

Claud (*hesitates*) Save them, sir.

Sir Hubert Do you, indeed? And what for, may I ask? Some special luxury, mmm? (*Wags his head, smiling.*)

Claud No, sir. Well – (*hesitates again*) it's to go to New York on.

Sir Hubert (*raising a finger*) There you are, quite the rover, I think I said that as soon as I saw you. (*Wags his finger.*) Here today, gone tomorrow, now we see you, now we don't, eh, Claud? Why New York, Claud?

Claud Well, I've always wanted to go back, I've got a friend, he just went over, so I thought I would too. You know.

Sir Hubert (*chuckling*) He, Claud?

Claud (*suddenly embarrassed, stiffens*) Yes, sir.

Sir Hubert Well, I don't know that it's a worthy cause, Claud, to contribute to your disappearance.

He laughs, begins to shake with laughter, gets off the stool as Claud smiles in embarrassment, touches him on the shoulder.

See you tomorrow then, my dear Claud, see you tomorrow.

Claud I'll be there, sir.

Sir Hubert And God bless, old Claud. God bless.

Touches his shoulder again, goes to the entrance. He turns, waggles his fingers, Claud nods, smiles.

INT. LADY CAROLINE'S ROOM

Lady Caroline is lying in bed, with a breakfast tray on the table beside her, and her teeth in a glass. She is clearly only half awake. There is a gentle knock on the door, she jerks upright, pops the teeth into her mouth, fixes her face in a smile.

Lady Caroline Come in, dear.

Sir Hubert enters, hat in hand, smiling.

(*Shaking her head.*) I don't know how you do it. I really don't.

Sir Hubert stands over her tenderly.

Sir Hubert And I don't know how *you* do it, petal, so beautiful so early. (*He bends, kisses her on the cheek.*) I thought I'd go over to Greendene for the day, put the finishing touches to this and that.

Lady Caroline Oh. (*Wearily.*) Do you want me to come with you, dear?

Sir Hubert No, this is man's work, my work.

Lady Caroline Oh. Well, Hubert, don't overdo it.

Lady Caroline stares up at him. He stands smiling very gently down at her. She blinks, as if almost in tears.

Oh, Hubert, I hope I don't let you down. It was much easier being a wife in Kjiarna, I mean I felt like a bride there, but I don't seem to know what to do in England, my head pounding, even when I wake up. I don't want to let you down, I don't.

Sir Hubert It's not your fault, my petal. I've never thought it was your fault.

He bends, kisses her on the forehead again.

I'll make everything as it was in Kjiarna – I promise you that.

Goes towards the door, turns, smiles, wags his fingers.

Lady Caroline (*emotionally*) Thank you, Hubert. Thank you for everything.

EXT. GREENDENE. THE GARDEN

Sir Hubert and Claud walking across the lawn, from the Rover. Sir Hubert is carrying a large bag in one hand, holding Claud's arm by the other. Stops, to show Claud a flower. Sir Hubert and Claud then move towards the living room, the windows of which are shut. Sir Hubert takes out his key ring, opens the windows, they step inside.

INT. LIVING ROOM

The walls are papered and the floor is carpeted, but the only furniture is the piano. Sir Hubert ushers Claud in most solicitously, is replying to something Claud has just said.

Sir Hubert Ah, that's what I mean by expert, Claud. Expert. (*He smiles in complimentary bewilderment.*) Tell me, do you see yourself in white?

Claud Sir?

Sir Hubert Oh, but not, of course, if you have some other preference. Fancy dress, feathers and wings, as far as I'm concerned.

He chuckles. Throughout this scene Sir Hubert is very animated, talking more quickly than usual.

Claud (*ironically*) Oh, I think white's more usual, sir.

Sir Hubert I suppose it is, yes, I suppose it *is* usual.

Walks towards him, smiling, then veers away to stand beside the piano.

She loves this instrument, Claud. (*Stares at him.*) She might play for us all, that would be a rare treat, I think. And you, of course, will pay her special attention, won't you? She has a generous nature, Claud, and she lets herself be deceived.

Claud smiles and nods in embarrassment.

As you know, yes, I think you do. She suffers from headaches, a perpetual headache, very frail, frailer even than she thinks. She was sad to leave Kjiarna, and so was I. So we must make this a happy occasion. And you'll be here, Claud, and that'll make a difference. (*Little pause, smiles.*) An expert to keep her under control, eh? (*Chuckles now briskly.*) What were your plans again? Did you bring them with you?

Claud Yes. (*Takes a piece of paper out of his pocket.*) If we have a still bar, we could put it alongside, here, or if the trolley bar, we could keep it in one half of the room –

Sir Hubert listening to this, inattentive, eager, smiles, looks past him, to the garden.

Sir Hubert Is that a robin? I think it was. Do *you* see a robin?

Claud puzzled, looks out of the windows.

Claud A robin?

Sir Hubert (*stands beside him*) In Kjiarna, Claud, we had a special kind of bird we were never able to identify. It cried out at night, its wings flapped noisily –

He lowers the big bag he has been carrying to the ground, it clanks slightly.

– but it was never to be seen during the day. Doubtless it slept during the day. It had an odd cry, unforgettable, Claud.

He turns to Claud, his face very close.

Heeee-eeeee, heeee-eeeee.

Claud takes a nervous step back.

Perhaps *you* know it, this parrot of ours?

Claud shakes his head. Sir Hubert takes a step nearer, puts his hand on Claud's arm.

My wife has green fingers you know, Claud. Everything she touches grows. Even in Kjiarna, where the sun baked the soil barren or the rains washed it into a swamp, she managed to raise a flower or two, and a little bed of tomatoes, with the help of the MacPhersons' gardeners, whom we shared, so to speak. She made them water the tomatoes every day, cover them with glass, nursed them up. But here, you see, everything comes up by itself, if you watch it. Especially the weeds. That's the difference, Claud. It's very difficult to understand, at first, and you have to keep some things down. Especially the weeds, Claud, especially the weeds.

Claud Yes, sir. (*Little pause.*) I'm not one for gardening, sir.

Sir Hubert I know. I know. (*Stares at him, chuckles.*) Tell me, Claud, do you like this room?

Claud Yes, sir. (*Little pause.*) Yes, it's a beautiful room.

Sir Hubert (*chuckles*) But not for the likes of you, eh, Claud? (*Stares at him.*) Come, I know you, sir, with your roving instincts, you wouldn't want a room like this. It's not in your blood, it it? Eh?

Claud (*ironically*) Perhaps it's not my tradition, sir, no. Not quite my style.

Sir Hubert No, you're quite right. (*Pause.*) In the summer there will be flowers. She'll put them in vases around the room. She'll choose them herself. And in the evenings she'll play the piano and sing. Her headaches will go, I think I can promise her that. Everything will be in its proper place, you see. Can you imagine what it will look like then, Claud, the civilisation of it?

Claud Yes, sir, I'd like to see it then.

Sir Hubert But you won't be able to, will you? Because you'll be in *your* proper place then, won't you? (*Laughs.*) With God's help, and if there is justice in the world.

Claud looks baffled.

New York, old Claud. New York. (*Whispers it.*)

Claud Oh. Yes, sir. Well, it's kind of you to help me, sir.

Sir Hubert (*raises a finger*) It's my duty. I see it as that. By the way, there's something I have to put right, downstairs. Would you be good enough to wait a moment?

Claud Yes, sir.

Sir Hubert I'll be right back. (*He goes to the door, right.*) Oh, my – bits and pieces, would you be good enough . . .?

Claud picks up the bag, obviously finds it heavier than he expected, carries it to Sir Hubert, who smiles at him.

By the way, Claud, I have a feeling that you're something of a musician yourself. Are you, Claud?

Claud Well, I like to try sometimes, but not a proper one, sir.

Sir Hubert Please. (*Gestures to the piano.*) Please. While I'm gone, if you feel in the mood.

Claud Thank you, sir.

Sir Hubert Because I shan't be here to judge, if the thought of that puts you off.

He smiles, goes out the door, right. Claud makes a silent, whistling noise, rolls his eyes, stares around the room.

INT. CELLAR

Sir Hubert enters, turns on light. Opens the bag, takes out padlocks, one big one for the door, five lengths of chain, a hygiene spray, and his revolver. Walks across to the ring, very quickly, the chains in his hand.

INT. LIVING ROOM

Claud saunters over to the piano, touches a note very softly, frowns, plays a chord. Makes a face.

INT. CELLAR

The chains are padlocked to the ring. Sir Hubert is pulling on them, they have padlocks in the end. He goes to the cellar door, where the large padlock has been fixed. Shuts it. Stands in the centre, raises his hands, cups them around his mouth, draws in a breath. Cut to:

INT. LIVING ROOM

Claud plays a hideous discord, winces, laughs. Plays another, then raises his hands to play another, and cut to:

INT. CELLAR

Sir Hubert, hands still cupped around his mouth.

Sir Hubert Boy. Claud. Claud. Nigger. Blackie Black-ie.

INT. LIVING ROOM

Claud with his hands over his ears as another discord sounds. Then trails his fingers across the keys.

INT. CELLAR

Sir Hubert Black-ie. (*A mighty bellow.*)

INT. LIVING ROOM

Claud engrossed, picking out a tune very softly. Stops once, as if listening to another sound, then goes on playing. The door, right, opens and Sir Hubert enters softly, comes over and stands behind Claud. Claud stops, whirls around.

Sir Hubert I knew you had the gift. I knew you had it. (*Smiles.*) Play a few more bars.

Claud Well. (*Makes to get up.*)

Sir Hubert Please, Claud. (*Smiles.*)

Claud It needs tuning, sir.

Sir Hubert Oh no, Claud, that won't do. (*He shakes his head, raises his finger, smiles.*) It's already passed that test, I think.

Claud Well, sir, you listen to this and you'll know.

He sits down, begins to play, very expertly, so that everything comes out flat. Sir Hubert stands beside him, tapping his foot out of time to the music, and watching Claud as if hypnotised by him. Claud stops, throws his hands up as if in surrender, turns to Sir Hubert.

You see, sir?

Sir Hubert I see that you've got the touch, Claud. That's what I see. (*Long pause, then rubs his hands together.*) I wonder if you could give me a hand with a little something I've rigged up downstairs – another little surprise, but it needs a finishing touch.

Claud gets up.

Thank you.

He leads the way to the door, right. The camera lingers on the room, full of sunlight.

INT. CELLAR

Sir Hubert holds the door open for Claud to enter. Claud stops, sees the chains.

Sir Hubert Why do you sniff, Claud?

Claud No, sir. I wasn't sniffing.

Sir Hubert (*sniffing himself*) I thought you smelt something.

Claud No, sir.

Sir Hubert Really? You don't? I do. (*Picks up the squirt gun, squirts.*) It's below the earth-line, you see. A subterranean smell. It doesn't rise. Of course it depends on the system's development.

Chuckles, squirts again in the general direction of Claud.

That's where the danger of a bad smell is. Now to work. If you could just pick up the ends of those chains there.

Claud looks at him, goes over to pick up the chains, looks at Sir Hubert.

Yes, and give them a pull, as hard as you can. I've been doing it myself, but I'm probably not as powerful as you.

Claud To pull them free, you mean?

Sir Hubert (*nods*) Well, to see if you can.

Claud gives them a tug.

No, no, harder, Claud, all you've got.

Claud strains at the chains.

Now really savage. (*Pantomimes a savage jerk.*) Ah, excellent, you see, deeply embedded and quality chain, you couldn't get them free in a month of Sundays, I think, Claud. Now, if you'd just slip the third one, have you got it, the third one?

Claud extracts the third one, holds it out.

Yes, around your throat, Claud.

Bends down, away from Claud, who stands looking at him with incomprehension, opens the trunk, takes out the revolver, points it at Claud, then barks out.

Around your throat, sir. If you please, sir.

Claud stares at Sir Hubert, makes a noise like a laugh.

Or die instead, Claud. I will honour you for that. (*His finger squeezes.*)

Claud Sir? Sir? (*Makes another noise like a laugh.*) Please? (*Shakes his head.*)

Sir Hubert And I do honour you, Claud. You've chosen the nobler course.

Close-up of the gun, then Claud staring at it. Then Claud tries to wrap the chain around his throat, has to kneel to do so.

Slip the tongue of the padlock (*this said very smoothly*) into the fourteenth link – that will do. Now attend to your ankles please, Claud, with the extreme left and the extreme right chains, Claud, and do them properly as I shall check, you know.

Claud does them.

Excellent. Excellent. Now your right wrist with your left hand, please, Claud, and tight, you know, very tight. There won't be any second chances.

Claud does this. Then he stares up at Sir Hubert, in terror and pleading. Sir Hubert comes across and inspects him from closer to, then, holding the pistol close to Claud's head, bends down and clicks the other chain around Claud's left wrist, and steps away. Claud stares at him. He should be so chained that he is held back, his hands not able to meet, and his legs in a kneeling position. Sir Hubert advances to him, goes through his coat pockets, breathing heavily, takes out some keys, a drawing pencil, a tube of pastilles (half eaten), a comb. Puts these things carefully into his own jacket pocket, plus a wallet. Then steps away, lowering the gun.

Now Claud, there you are, sir, and here am I.

Raises the gun again, and squeezes the trigger. It clicks empty.

And do you think I shoot men down in cold blood, Claud, without giving them a chance of a hearing? Do you think that is my way, sir? Or that I need *this* to deal with you? (*Opens the trunk, drops the gun in.*) I do not, sir, I do not.

Claud (*shaking his head*) I don't understand. I don't understand.

Sir Hubert You know what I want, I think.

Claud No. No, I don't. (*Little pause.*) I haven't any money, I haven't anything.

Sir Hubert (*gazes at him in contempt*) Money! (*Pause.*) It is the *truth*, Claud, that I want from you. The truth, and nothing more, sir.

Claud The truth? About what, sir?

Sir Hubert I think you know, Claud, I think you do.

Claud Please, sir. I don't. I don't.

Sir Hubert reaches into his breast pocket, takes out the folded drawing, unfolds it, shows it to Claud.

(*Staring at it in horror.*) I – I – I – I'm sorry, sir, I didn't mean anything by it. I didn't.

Sir Hubert sitting down on the trunk, holding the drawing out.

Sir Hubert Tell me about it, Claud.

Claud It's what I told you, sir, that's all. Doodlings. I do them all the time, nothing. I've got them all over my room, sir. I put them on the walls.

Sir Hubert Yes?

Claud That's all. That's all, sir.

Sir Hubert All? But what do you do with them in your room? Do you laugh at them? Do you abuse them? Do you make jokes at them and whisper to them?

Claud I – I don't even see them any more.

Sir Hubert You don't see them any more? After you have undressed ladies, and drawn them down on paper, and laughed at them, you don't see them any more, Claud. My wife, sir. My *wife*.

Rises to his feet, stares down at Claud, then turns to the door, opens it, goes out.

Claud (*tugging against the chains*) Hey! Hey, sir! Sir!

The door opens, Sir Hubert comes back in. He is smiling and composed.

What are you going to do with me, sir? (*Little pause.*)
Please.

Sir Hubert Come, Claud, come look at you down on all
fours. Do you call *that* dignity, whining like a dog?

*Turns off light. There is the sound of the door shutting.
Then the sound of the chains rattling.*

Claud Hey.

EXT. THE GARDEN

*Sir Hubert walking back to his car, stops to examine a
flower, then continues jauntily.*

INT. BAR

*Lady Caroline appears at the door, looks around. The
bar is empty. She goes to the counter, takes out the flask,
sits on a stool, puts the flask under her handbag. Puts
a peppermint or two into her mouth, stares towards the
entrance. Then glances impatiently around the bar.*

INT. CLAUD'S ROOM

*The walls are covered with drawings, most of them
cartoons, but above the single bed there is a line of
sentimental sketches of a boy of about twenty-two. There
is a washstand with a toothbrush and shaving kit, a case
under the bed, the end just sticking out, a photograph
of the boy on the bedside table. But first shot should be
of the cartoon of Sir Geoffrey, a hand reaching out,
tearing it off. Then the other cartoons being torn down,
a hand shown. Then a long shot of Sir Hubert ripping
the pictures down. Stops, looks around, sees the case,*

heaves it out, and working very swiftly, begins to dump the drawings in. Cut to:

INT. BAR

Lady Caroline gets off the stool, walks to the end of the counter, peers behind it. Comes back, walks to the bar entrance, stares up and down the hall, comes back. She comes back to the stool, looks very irritable, puts another peppermint into her mouth.

INT. CLAUD'S ROOM

Sir Hubert standing in the middle of Claud's room, the case in his hand, looking around at the bare walls, etc., to make sure he has missed nothing. He has the key of the room in his other hand. There is a knock on the door. He stands stock still, the knock again.

Man's Voice Claud, Claud.

Another knock. Silence. Sir Hubert's mouth is open, he is breathing heavily. Then he goes to the door, opens it, peers out. Steps outside.

INT. BAR

Lady Caroline sitting on the stool, her expression tight with irritation. She has the bag of peppermints open in front of her, her fingers extracting them and popping them compulsively into her mouth. Sudden shot of the bar entrance, several people passing, followed by Sir Hubert, carrying the suitcase. He gazes in, and steps quickly out of sight just as Lady Caroline turns around. She turns back to the counter.

Lady Caroline This is preposterous.

INT. SIR HUBERT'S BEDROOM

Sir Hubert shutting one of the large sea trunks, goes to wash his hands at the sink. Dries them. Brushes at his clothes. Straightens his shoulders, goes towards the door.

INT. BAR

Lady Caroline at the counter, a large gin in front of her. She takes a sip from the gin, then opens her handbag and puts the flask in it. Her face is composed. She swallows down the rest of the gin, crams a few peppermints into her mouth, then gets up and goes to one of the tables. Sits down. Sir Hubert appears at the entrance, walking slowly and blandly towards her. She sees him, smiles, gives a little wave. A girl in a black dress and an apron follows him, goes behind the bar. His eyes follow her, then go back to his wife. He smiles.

Sir Hubert (*kisses her on the cheek, sits down*) How's the head, my dear?

> *Looks at her tenderly, puts his key ring, now covered with keys, on the table.*

Lady Caroline It's no good complaining about it, I'm trying not to think about it, I've had a very trying evening, what with one thing and another, but what have you been up to, Hubert?

Sir Hubert Getting a few things into place, my dear. Putting the finishing touch to a little plan of mine.

Lady Caroline Oh. Well, I ordered some curtains, I told the man I couldn't be expected to put them up myself, could I? And anyway they're coming along next week.

> *As she talks, the girl in the apron comes to the table, stands beside Sir Hubert, who looks up at her in surprise.*

Girl Yes, sir?

Sir Hubert And where's our good friend, Claud?

Girl (*shakes her head*) Not come in. (*Irish accent.*)

Sir Hubert Do you hear that, my dear? (*To the Girl.*) It looks as if our gone-tomorrow Claud's gone today, eh?

Girl He's probably in trouble, Mr Tomkins says. And if he hasn't got an explanation he can clear his room up, and out.

Sir Hubert Ah, but he's a rover, you see. A real rover, if I know my Claud. And I think I do. I think so at least. A gin, my dear?

    Lady Caroline nods.

And nothing for myself, thank you. (*As the Girl goes off.*) What do you think of that, my dear?

Lady Caroline Well, what do you expect, Hubert, they're always like that, even if they do laugh and get on with people, you should know that, I was here for a long time before – if I wanted anything, I'd just have had to sit twiddling my thumbs, for all Claud cared.

Sir Hubert (*intensely*) And Claud doesn't care. Mark my words, dear, Claud never cared. (*Picks up the keys, and begins to jingle them.*) Never cared at all, you see.

EXT. GARDEN

Sir Hubert crossing the garden, carrying a large brown bag. Goes towards the French windows.

INT. CELLAR

Complete darkness. Scuffling and chinking noises, a little, keening hum. Then Claud's face leaps onto the screen. He blinks and sways his head from side to side, then stares up. The figure of Sir Hubert comes into focus. He is smiling. He picks up the squirt gun, squirts towards Claud, then all around the cellar.

Claud I'm so hungry. I'm so hungry.

Sir Hubert Come then, Claud. The truth.

Claud Please, sir.

Sir Hubert The truth, Claud. Confess it.

Claud (*nods*) I confess. I did it. I confess. I confess, sir.

Sir Hubert You did it, did you, Claud? You confess to it, do you?

Claud Yes, sir.

Sir Hubert (*after a pause*) What?

Claud I – I – I did that drawing, sir. It was a wrong thing to do. I'm sorry for it. Very sorry, sir.

Sir Hubert And what else, Claud?

Claud Nothing, sir. Nothing. That's all I've done wrong.

Sir Hubert sits down on the trunk, crosses his legs.

Sir Hubert How else have you imagined my wife, Claud? What else have you done to her, in here?

Taps his forehead. Claud shakes his head.

Never, Claud?

Claud Never, sir, never. I swear. I swear.

Sir Hubert (*smiles*) Tell me, Claud, do you find my wife an unattractive woman?

Claud looks at him, as if trying to read the correct answer on his face. Shakes his head.

No, sir. She is not. On the contrary. She is beautiful. Is she not?

Claud nods.

And when you had your little conversations with her, what were you thinking about?

Claud (*thinks*) About how much I respected her, sir.

Sir Hubert Do you think you can trick me? Those lips of yours, that hair, your skin? (*Laughs.*) I have spent a lifetime watching you, Claud. I have spent a lifetime sniffing at you. Your smell is everywhere, and I have learnt to interpret it. From the day I first set foot amongst you it came up to me, it filled my breathing, it gave me headaches at night, it caused me giddiness at important meetings. But I learnt about it, Claud, and learnt to endure it. And I know what it means, when I catch the faintest whiff of it.

Stands up, looks down at Claud, who is staring up in horror, and speaks whisperingly.

Did you take her at night, when I was asleep? Or did you notice me once staring from the wrong window? Did you laugh at me as I kept my watch? Slithering into the room, slithering. Here.

Touches Claud's forehead.

Here. Where the stink is.

Sir Hubert straightens, turns away, puts his hands behind his back.

Well, there are no windows in this room, Claud, I think.

Claud Please, please let me go. I'm so hungry. So hungry, sir.

> *Sir Hubert turns around, looks down at him, blinks as if recognising something, looks momentarily horrified.*

I – I promise you, sir, I promise you, I never had anything to do with your wife, sir, never looked at her in that way. I didn't do anything, even in my mind I didn't. I never went to that place. I come from Stepney, sir, like I told you. I was brought up in Stepney, my father was a porter and my mother, she worked for some Jew people in Bethnal Green, she had lunch with them at their table, and I'm clean, sir, I have a bath every night.

Sir Hubert Clean, Claud? (*Laughs.*) This cellar is stinking with you.

Claud (*goes on*) I won't do it again, sir, ever, ever, if you let me go, I'll never do another drawing. Oh God, sir, please, I promise you, please.

Sir Hubert Just tell me the truth, Claud.

Claud I never touched her. Ask her, sir, *ask* her.

Sir Hubert (*stares at him in amazement*) Ask my *wife*?

> *Turns, goes out. Claud begins to sob hysterically. The door opens and Sir Hubert reappears, walking slowly. He is carrying a bowl in one hand of meat and in the other of water. He puts them on the floor, in front of Claud, who of course can't reach them. Goes out. Claud strains down at the food. The door opens. Sir Hubert's hand appears, gropes for the light switch, darkness.*

INT. LADY CAROLINE'S BEDROOM

Lady Caroline is in her nightdress and dressing gown, in bed, with her flask in her hand, peppermints beside her, reading. There is a knock on the door, she flicks the top of the flask, shoves it under the pillow, popping some peppermints into her mouth.

Lady Caroline Is that you, dear?

> *Sir Hubert, in his dressing gown and pyjamas, enters, comes down and sits in the chair.*

What is it, Hubert? Are you all right?

Sir Hubert (*stares at her blankly*) I can't seem to sleep tonight. (*Little pause.*) I went off for a minute, and then I had a dream. (*Little pause, makes a mechanical chuckle.*) I thought I would keep you company for a while. (*Little pause.*) Or perhaps try one of those aspirins you get from our . . . (*Voice trails off.*)

Lady Caroline I've used them all, my dear, I'm sorry, but you know what my head has been. Have you tried closing your eyes and humming to yourself, that's what I do.

Sir Hubert But I don't want to sleep if I'm going to have bad dreams. (*Very intently.*) It's better to stay awake, I think. (*Stares at her.*) It was about you, my dear.

Lady Caroline (*interested*) About me? What was it?

Sir Hubert You were in danger. Great danger. And I – I was powerless to help you, I was bound and helpless, watching you being – (*Shakes his head, unable to go on.*)

Lady Caroline (*eagerly*) What?

Sir Hubert I don't know. I woke up and went straight to the window, but there was nothing there. (*Pause.*) Do you ever have such dreams, my dear?

Lady Caroline No. I have funny dreams, they don't mean anything. When I was in Kjiarna I had dreams about being back in Roehampton with Uncle Richie and now we're in London I have dreams about having tea with Geraldine MacPherson, but I certainly don't sleep as well as I used to in Kjiarna, but that's not surprising with all this worry.

Sir Hubert You don't ever feel, my dear – (*hesitates*) as if someone were trying to break in?

Lady Caroline Break in what, dear, to my sleep you mean?

Sir Hubert Yes. Force his way in? You don't feel that, do you, my dear?

Lady Caroline No I don't, I'm sure I'd remember it if I did, what a funny idea, Hubert.

Sir Hubert, after a long pause, gets up, goes over, looks down at her. She stares up at him, smiling.

Sir Hubert I love you so much, my dear. So very much.

Bends down, kisses her, she turns her mouth away so that he kisses her on the cheek. He exits. Lady Caroline watches him, then reaches under the pillow.

INT. CELLAR

Light on. Claud is staring up, the two bowls out of his reach just below him.

Sir Hubert (*off-screen*) There was resistance, of course?

Claud Yes, sir. (*His voice very husky.*) But I was too strong, sir. And she was asleep, sir.

Sir Hubert Every last garment, I think.

Claud nods. Sir Hubert still off-screen, his voice only just in control.

And then, sir?

Claud I forced myself.

Sir Hubert And?

Claud (*whispering*) I did it, sir.

He looks at Sir Hubert beggingly. There is a long pause, then the camera swings to Sir Hubert sitting on the trunk. A pad on his knee, a pen in hand.

Sir Hubert Let us go back to the scene in the bar, Claud, please.

Claud I saw her there, sir, she was standing there, and I was behind it. It's my work, sir. I looked up and there she was.

Sir Hubert What did she want?

Claud A – (*Frowns, shakes his head.*) Was it aspirins, sir?

Sir Hubert And how was she dressed?

Claud In white, sir?

Sir Hubert (*writing*) And she was –

Claud Very beautiful, sir. Oh, very beautiful.

Sir Hubert (*writing*) Which is why –

Claud (*nodding*) This is why I couldn't help myself, sir, because she was so beautiful, sir, there was such kindness and graciousness in her ladyship, sir, what could I do?

Sir Hubert Yes?

Claud I leaned across the bar and I uttered some words, sir.

Sir Hubert The words, Claud?

Claud (*looks at him, slyly*) I can't remember the words, they rose up in me, they came from something bad, but that's gone now, sir, and I can't remember the words, sir.

Sir Hubert The words, Claud, please.

Claud I can't remember, honestly can't remember, please I can't, sir.

> *Sir Hubert snaps the pad shut, puts his pen away, walks to the door.*

Wait, wait, yes, I remember, yes, sir.

> *Sir Hubert comes back, stares at him.*

I was too ashamed to say them to you, sir.

> *Sir Hubert sits down, opens his pad, waits.*

'Hello, baby.'

> *Sir Hubert writes.*

'How do you like this black boy here, baby?'

> *Sir Hubert writes.*

And she was angry with me, sir, I could see she was disgusted with me for it, sir, like I am disgusted now, sir. She went away from me.

Sir Hubert But you brought her back, Claud, I think?

Claud Yes, yes. No. She come back, sir, because she was so kind and gracious she had already forgiven me, and this time I didn't say anything. I had learnt my lesson, I kept my eyes from off of her and brought her the bottle of gin –

Sir Hubert (*sharply*) The bottle of – ?

Claud As-pirin, not gin, I don't know why I say gin, sir. (*Shakes his head, laughs.*) And she took the aspirins, sir, and she went upstairs.

Sir Hubert (*writing*) And how did you get into her room?

Claud She forgot to lock the door, sir?

 Sir Hubert stares at him.

I picked the lock, sir. I'm very good at that.

Sir Hubert (*writing*) And where was I, Claud?

Claud You were in the next room, sir, watching for me from the window, sir.

Sir Hubert (*writes*) And what did you do?

Claud I – I undressed myself, sir.

 Sir Hubert nods, writes.

Then I climbed in, between the white sheets, sir, and I took her in my arms, your lady wife, sir.

Sir Hubert She remained asleep, Claud, I think.

Claud Yes, yes, she was asleep still. (*Little pause.*) And so was I, sir. Yes, I was, it was in a nightmare it happened, everything was asleep, I didn't know what I was doing, the black in me was moving me to everything, because of my lips and hair you explained to me, sir, and suddenly it was happening –

Sir Hubert (*interrupting*) Keep to the facts, please, Claud. My wife was in a nightgown, of course?

Claud Oh yes, sir. Very beautiful in her nightgown, sir, and gracious.

Sir Hubert Describe, it, please.

Claud It was – it was transparent, sir.

543

Sir Hubert (*writing*) Transparent. You could see through it, therefore?

Claud No, sir. I kept my eyes sealed, sir.

Sir Hubert (*very calmly*) And what did you do then, Claud?

Claud desperately thinking, close-up of his face.

Claud I – I – did it, sir.

Sir Hubert shuts his notebook, gets up, turns to the door.

Please, sir, there is more, sir, more.

Sir Hubert Lies, Claud. More lies, sir. My wife has never owned a transparent nightgown, she *would* not own such a thing. I trapped you there, I think, Claud. (*He goes to the door.*)

Claud (*screaming*) Yes, yes, I lie, yes. I wouldn't touch her, the old bag, I wouldn't touch the old bag, your lady wife, she makes me sick, filthy old white gin filth, makes me sick. She drinks.

Sir Hubert walks on, out of the door, close-up of his face, set and deaf. Claud stares at the door, then Sir Hubert comes back in, leaving door open, the keys jangling in his hand.

Sir Hubert You must be calmer, Claud. You make me forget my responsibility to you.

Claud I'm sorry I said that, sir, your wife is so beautiful, so beautiful. (*Little pause.*) But it couldn't be me who did that to her, sir. Not your Claud. (*Little pause.*) I'm very queer, sir.

Sir Hubert takes out his notebook.

Sir Hubert Yes, Claud?

Claud I had a friend, sir, he left me. Ask them, they all know in the Gay Fellow, Amble Street, South Kensington, sir. They'll tell you there. Find Micky, he'll tell you, he loves me, sir, he's in America now. Yes, he'll help me. (*Little pause.*) That cricketing gentlemen, sir, *he* knows. He knows me, I saw him in Amble Street, he knows me.

Sir Hubert puts his pad away with a smile.

Sir Hubert We all know you, Claud. We all know you for what you are. And now you're beginning to know us a little better, sir, I think.

Bends down, unlocks Claud's chain around the neck, pushes the bowls close. Claud looks up at him.

Come now, my Claud, help yourself.

Goes to the trunk, sits down, watches with a smile. Goes out.

> *Time passing indicated – about a week.*

INT. LIVING ROOM

Lady Caroline enters, followed by Greatorix.

Lady Caroline . . . you to say that, and I would have given you more notice, but *I'll* have to do the clearing up, won't I, and frankly, Mr Greatorix, I'm not up to it any more. I'm really not, and nor is Sir Hubert, he's got a great deal on his plate, you know. (*Looking around the room.*) Wherever he is.

Greatorix I think I can assure you, Lady Caroline, that we'll find someone to help you out. Perhaps he's upstairs.

Lady Caroline If I know him, he'll be doing something he shouldn't be, he always takes on more than he can chew.

In on Sir Hubert, smiling, seated on the trunk.

Claud off-screen, and in between gobbling noises.

Claud Into her, sir, you know me, sir, grabbed hold of him and tore off the clothes he was in. White. Oh, she's beautiful, so scrawny white and beautiful, sir, I confess to it, me touch her for you if you wish, you know me, sir, I think, this one for black Claud, that one for sir. I think you know me, sir, I can't help myself.

Sir Hubert There there, Claud, it's all right, sir, it's all right, boy.

INT. LIVING ROOM

Lady Caroline is sitting on the piano stool. Greatorix is standing by the door, left, which is open.

Greatorix There'll be nothing for you to do but unpack your personals and have a nice hot bath. (*Little pause.*) I'd be happy to give you a lift back if you think you might have to wait. Or shall I try the cellar, first?

Lady Caroline No, no, he'll turn up – well, perhaps if you wouldn't mind, the only thing is, Mr Greatorix, is this person you have in mind reliable for the garden and the girl – can she be trusted?

Greatorix (*ducking his head*) I'm sure you'll be satisfied with her, Lady Caroline, she's never been in trouble that I know of.

Lady Caroline Oh dear! I don't know, I really don't. This gardener, now.

INT. CELLAR

In on Claud who is staring up, nodding.

Sir Hubert (*off-screen*) Should bring out the best in a man, if he's a real man. That's what a crisis is for, sir, in a sense. They had to know who they were dealing with. So I strapped it over my handlebars, the tail dangling over the crossbar, the head level with the bell, and pedalled along to the compound. He screeched, of course, and jabbered and capered about, but you could have knocked him over with a tjonker. (*Little pause.*) That night these parrots of ours started up, every tree in the garden, sir –

INT. LIVING ROOM

Greatorix is standing by the window, Lady Caroline with him.

Greatorix . . . again, Lady Caroline, unless you want to change your mind about that lift. Which would be *my* pleasure, of course.

Lady Caroline No, I'll catch Sir Hubert at whatever he's up to – Oh, you were kind enough to offer to peep into the cellar for me, I really can't bear it down there, the smell makes my head spin.

Greatorix Of course.

Ducks his head, goes to the door, right. Opens it, goes on down. Shot of Lady Caroline sitting down again, feeling in her handbag, pauses, takes out two peppermints, which she pops into her mouth.

INT. THE DOOR BEFORE THE CELLAR

Greatorix approaches the door before the cellar, which is slightly open.

Sir Hubert (*off-screen*) Kept an eye open all night, but how could I see any black bodies in all that darkness. That was it you see, devils to track in the dark, you've got to have them somewhere you can leave them without a spot of worry –

> *Greatorix a close-up of his face, frowning, clears his throat slightly.*

INT. LIVING ROOM

Lady Caroline is just stuffing the flask back into her bag. She looks up, looks very embarrassed.

Lady Caroline Oh. (*Laughs.*)

Greatorix Well, he *is* down there, Lady Caroline, but he seemed to be in the middle of a serious talk, so I didn't want to disturb him, I thought I'd just let you know where he was.

Lady Caroline Oh, well thank you, Mr Greatorix, thank you very much. (*Gets up.*) How kind you are, well –

> *As Greatorix goes towards the windows, accompanying him.*

– we'll see you soon with those persons you've got arranged to help me, then?

Greatorix Yes indeed, Lady Caroline. (*With a knowing smile just on display.*) Yes, I'm at your service, whenever you want me.

> *Steps out, into the garden. Lady Caroline turns, makes a worried face, puts peppermints into her mouth, closes her handbag, walks to the door, left. Stands at the door, calls.*

Lady Caroline Hubert! Hubert!

INT. CELLAR

Sir Hubert is standing pumping the hygiene spray around, there is a clinking of chains.

Sir Hubert . . . a wash and brush-up, Claud, and clean out this mess, which is a filthy job, let me tell you that, but it's my responsibility, it's always been my responsibility, and always will be, I think. But I'll keep you clean, Claud, whatever *you* may want . . .

INT. LIVING ROOM

Lady Caroline leaning through the door calling irritably.

Lady Caroline Hu-bert! Hu-bert!

She disappears from view, her voice fading as she descends.

Hubert! Hubert!

INT. LIVING ROOM. EVENING

Open with a close-up of an African face, laughing, as much like Claud's as possible. Then distance away from him, to show him behind a table which has been made into a bar, and taking in the room as a whole. It is fully furnished now, table, chairs, flowers everywhere. The room is full of elderly people, most of them white, in evening suits, formal gowns, etc., with a few Africans. The windows are open. There is conversation and laughter.

Include a shot of Lady Caroline at the bar, talking to the barman animatedly. She has no glass in her hand.

Then cut to two beside the open window, their backs to it, and shift from them to Sir Hubert and Sir Geoffrey, standing directly in front of the open windows but facing into the living room.

Sir Hubert . . . because someone has to tell them, hasn't he, what it's like to live over there, work amongst them and live for them? To show the feeling of the place and people, I think. I know them, you see – ah, there you are, my dear, how's our Fred the barman shaping up? I saw you winding him around your little finger.

He chuckles. Sir Geoffrey smiles.

Lady Caroline Oh, he seems very nice, but Hubert, dear, I thought I heard him a minute ago, howling.

Sir Hubert Sixth sense, my dear, sixth sense. You couldn't have heard him, you must have been listening for him in your mind.

Sir Geoffrey Sounds like a dog?

Sir Hubert (*as he and Lady Caroline smile at each other*) Most like, extremely like, Geoffrey.

Lady Caroline A very hungry one, dear.

Sir Geoffrey Oh, what kind? And what's his name?

Sir Hubert A rather wild one, when I first got hold of him, to tell you the truth, I think he's a mixture of things, but almost exactly the opposite of poor little Whitey.

Lady Caroline We call him Rover. He gets very upset sometimes, if Hubert hasn't been down to keep him calm, or if his meals aren't punctual, he throws himself against his chain and tries to break free, we're afraid he'll do something to his neck. (*Little pause.*) It's for his own good, you know.

Sir Geoffrey Ah, my favourite domestic moral. The dog's the master, the master's the servant.

Sir Hubert (*shaking his head, chuckling.*) Oh, he is a great responsibility, feeding him, keeping him clean and healthy, but you know, once you take one on, Geoffrey – (*Shakes his head*).

Lady Caroline (*winsomely*) Can I go down and give him a snack, dear?

> *They exchange looks. Then Sir Hubert smiles and nods, Lady Caroline goes through the crowds, to the door, right.*

Sir Hubert (*watching her*) He and Caroline didn't get on at first, there was some – (*Smiles.*) You should have seen her face when I brought them together, and his – jealousy, some jealousy about I think, but now she's got used to him, and he's got used to her, they're the greatest of friends, can hardly tear them apart. (*Shakes his head.*) Now where were we?

Sir Geoffrey I know where *I* was. I was in the middle of thinking that you're quite your old self again. (*Little pause.*) You seemed a wee bit on edge when you first got back.

Sir Hubert Was I? Perhaps I was. (*Gets up, turns to the window, looks out.*) Perhaps there was something missing, that I'd left behind and thought I'd never recover. It's peaceful here, after all. Listen to it, if you can hear it above the babel of human voices – the calm of England. It's a real sound, I tell you, Geoffrey, a real sound. I'd forgotten it, you see, how peaceful a home was. But there was the extra feeling, you know, of Kjiarna, that I'd got used to. I missed it. You have to have it sometimes, and to know that you've got it safe, where it can't get at you. Or if it's going to get at you, then to know where it comes from, what it looks like. (*Little pause.*) I found it here all right, in the end. I couldn't miss it, once I'd set myself to watch for it. Now I've got it pinned down, you see, got it straight in my mind and keep it under control. (*Turns, smiles.*) After all, I've kept it under control for thirty-five years. Do you know what I mean?

Sir Geoffrey (*after a pause*) More of you chaps come back mystics – poets, philosophers, saints – I suppose that's what happens to you, if you carry the experience of a whole continent around in you, the bureaucrats at home know what we owe to –

Lady Caroline (*coming between them*) He's asleep. I must have imagined it, dear, after all.

Sir Hubert But it was as well, to look, I think. (*Smiles at Lady Caroline.*) My dear, your hand is empty.

Sir Geoffrey What can I get you, Caroline?

Lady Caroline Nothing, thank you, nothing.

Sir Hubert Well, my dear, in that case, what about a tune?

Sir Geoffrey Oh, yes please.

> *Lady Caroline smiles graciously, and goes off. The two men watch her, then Sir Hubert turns to the window, looks out, smiling calmly.*

INT./EXT.

The camera rests on Sir Hubert's face, then retreats slowly to a long-distance view of the house. There should be, first of all, the laughter and talk of the party, then the sounds of a tranquil English night – a few bird noises, an owl – then unmistakably, although muted, the slightly off-key chords of Lady Caroline at the piano.

Fadeout.